THE FOOD AND WINE GUIDE TO
NAPLES AND CAMPANIA

This is the South, exuberant,
colourful, sybaritic,
Eastern, Byzantine, Greek
Waverley Root, *The Food of Italy*

The Food
and Wine Guide to
Naples
and
Campania

Written and
photographed by
Carla Capalbo

PALLAS ATHENE

THIS ONE'S FOR MY WOMEN FRIENDS
(INCLUDING ISABELLE)

WHO GOT ME THROUGH IT

AND IN MEMORY OF
LUIGI VERONELLI
CRITIC AND CATALYST

WHO GOT SO MUCH OF ITALY'S FOOD AND WINE
WORLD GOING

Contents

*Opposite:
Chef Antonio
Pisaniello's hand-
made cecaluccoli
pasta, a classic
Irpinian recipe*

3 Under the Volcano   From Vesuvio to Pompei   117

4 The Emperors' Islands: Capri, Ischia and Procida   143

5 The Sorrento Peninsula and the Amalfi Coast
From Castellammare to Vietri — via Sorrento, Agerola and Amalfi   171

6 Salerno to Paestum
Buffalo farms, Greek temples and artichoke fields   233

7 South from Paestum
The unsung beauty of the Cilento and Vallo di Diano   273

8 Avellino and Irpinia
Beyond the earthquakes to native grapes and mountain foods   315

9 Benevento and Il Sannio
Vineyards and villages of the interior   397

*Opposite: Despite
summer fires, the
Cilento's macchia
mediterranea always
renews itself*

Preface

by Antonio Bassolino
Governor of the Region of Campania

Modern travellers to Italy are increasingly interested in our country's traditional foods and wines; the search for these distinctive flavours, colours and tastes now forms an important new facet of tourism.

Campania is very fortunate here: the native foods and unique wines of our gastronomy complement the cultural and natural treasures of our best-known tourist sites, as well as the many largely undiscovered areas of the interior.

Agriculture, in the widest modern sense, covers food, the environment, culture, and health. The sector has much to offer – including *agriturismo*, rural and nature tourism, sport and learning activities – and its role in the economic and social development of our country is set to grow even more important as we move towards a more complex food production system, particularly in the context of the European Union.

With this in mind, and in the conviction that support should be given to projects that publicise the territorial and agricultural specialities of Campania, the regional administration has encouraged the publication of *The Food and Wine Guide to Naples and Campania*. This English-language guide book takes the traveller across the entire region to discover – or rediscover – places famous and not, seen through the eyes of an author looking for the images, flavours and rhythms that reflect Campania's culture and traditions.

This is not the usual kind of guide book, but rather the personal diary of a very special traveller. It is rich in information that goes beyond wine and food to speak of local and cultural customs; it features the producers, cooks and sellers that Carla Capalbo felt should be included.

Opposite: The terraced lemon groves on the Costiera Amalfitana near Maiori are within a UNESCO World Heritage site; they are built with dry-stone walls that the Campania Region is protecting

It is our hope that *The Food and Wine Guide to Naples and Campania* will also make foreign travellers aware of the considerable resources of Campania's interior, and thereby play its part in the growth and development of the whole region.

Foreword

by Vincenzo Aita

I was enthusiastic as soon as I was asked to become involved in the production of *The Food and Wine Guide to Naples and Campania*: as the Agriculture *Assessore* for the Campania Region, I was immediately convinced of the importance of Carla Capalbo's project. Agriculture no longer simply means the producing of 'primary resources': it now actively plays a larger part in the economic and social development of our region, from the safeguarding of the landscape and its inhabitants to the conservation of the cultural identity of the thousands of towns and villages that exist in Campania.

Agriculture has recently become a new kind of tourist attraction, with the power to draw large numbers of visitors from within Italy and abroad. They come seeking our traditional foods and native wines, whose character, colours and flavours are given by the specific soils on which they are produced as much as by the centuries-old methods of working them – methods that remain an inspiration even as they are brought up to date.

The Food and Wine Guide to Naples and Campania shares this attitude of celebrating both the new and the traditional. For the first time, it provides these travellers with a compendium of information – well researched and well written – that I feel sure will inspire them to visit the many fascinating areas of tradition and food culture that make up the region of Campania.

Opposite: Silver garfish (pesce bandiera) are local to Campanian waters and delicious

Acknowledgements

This has been a long and complicated project for one foreign woman in southern Italy to do by herself, and I've been particularly lucky in making friends with some exceptional people who have made it easier and more enjoyable. Thank you all, for my life over the last three years in Campania wouldn't have been the same without you.

The first thank you has to go to the great Campanian chef, Alfonso Iaccarino, and to his son, Ernesto, whom I met fortuitously just after the publication of my *Food and Wine Lover's Companion to Tuscany*. Had it not been for their determination to have me write a similar book about Campania, it would never have happened. Thanks too to Livia and Mario Iaccarino, and to the warm and wonderful staff at Don Alfonso restaurant – including Costanzo Cacace, Maurizio Cerio, Fortunato Maresca, Hans Schuller and *le Signore* – which became a home away from home for me on so many occasions.

Through them I met Vincenzo Aita, who was the Agriculture *Assessore* of the Region of Campania, and who was equally enthusiastic and determined about my proposal. He took me under his wing, offering me advice, background information and even travel instructions when I got lost! His commitment to the region and to its small, artisan foodmakers has been an inspiration. Aita introduced me to the Governor of the Campania Region, Antonio Bassolino. He too was inspiring in his vision for the region, and in his belief in its potential. He was always appreciative – and patient – about my endeavours to cover the whole region in depth, not just the better-known areas. Within the Region's offices, many people have offered assistance and encouragement: Mariella Passari, who has been supportive from the very first day, Antonietta D'Urso and Angela Calabrese, as well as Michele Bianco, Maurizio Cinque, Vittorio Ecuba, Michele Manzo, Stanislao Sconamiglio. Special thanks too to Bruno Danise, who read the book in English, and gave important advice. The Region's agricultural development department, ERSAC, has also been very helpful: sincere thanks go to its director, Raffaele Beato, and to Patrizia Magliacane, Dottore Mellucci, and all the other people there whose paths I crossed. I appreciate also the other *Assessori* – Teresa Armato for Tourism, with Roberto Formato, and Gianfranco Alois, for *Attività Produttive* – and their co-workers within the Region and its Provinces who offered support when it was needed. Many thanks to the people of Cetara and Nusco, who have welcomed me so generously into their villages.

Opposite:
A friendly wave
from a goatherd on
the road to Paestum

A special thank you must go to the great Neapolitan songwriter and singer, Pino Daniele, for allowing us to reproduce some of the words of *Napule*, and for unknowingly helping me learn Neapolitan dialect so that I could understand them.

As I moved from area to area while doing the research, I was lucky enough to encounter many people who helped in various ways. A big thank you is due to Antonietta Scovotto, who often put me up, took care of me when I was ill, and has been a support throughout. Erminia Di Meo was always saving my life in one way or another: with her brothers, Generoso and Roberto, her delightful aunts and extensive family (including Palmira), as well as her late mother, Alessandrina, who lives on in the stories and places of her childhood memories, she showed me what Campanian generosity really is: thank you all. Many thanks go also to chef Antonio Pisaniello, his wife, Jenny Auriemma, and their children, 'Bu' and little Filippo, who was conceived and born and had his first birthday during the making of this book. They offered me their hospitality from beds to delicious meals to phone lines, and helped me find a new community to live in at Nusco – I don't know what I would have done without them. The extended Pisaniello family, with all the staff at Il Gastronomo, have also offered invaluable assistance and sustenance – *grazie infinite*.

The way that food and its makers are thought about in Italy – and the rest of the world – have been deeply affected in recent years by Carlo Petrini and the association he founded in 1986, Slow Food. My work has often run parallel to theirs, and I am grateful as always for their solidarity and willingness to share ideas, ideals and information. At Bra, a particular thank you goes not only to Petrini himself, for whom my admiration is unbounded, but also to John Irving, Valter Musso and Paola Nano, and to Giacomo Mojoli, Cinzia Scaffidi and the rest of the core team there. Our thanks must also go to Fiamma Pintacuda Petrilli, for her environmental activism and her gift of a part of the Cilento coastline to FAI in order to save it from being built on illegally. If I have dedicated this book in part to Luigi Veronelli, whose recent death has left the Italian food and wine world much poorer, it is because he was the first person – decades ago – to have encouraged Italian growers and chefs to aspire to individual, territorial identity and excellence in both wine-making and food-cooking; much of the fertile gastronomic environment in which we in Italy now find ourselves is indebted to him.

A large thank you must obviously go here to all the growers, shepherds, fish-wives, winemakers, bakers, food producers, basket-makers, sellers and cooks of Campania, and to all the restaurateurs, chefs, waiters and sommeliers who have shared of their knowledge, foods and wines, and opened their hearts and kitchens, cellars and shops to me – it's been a fantastic, life-enriching experience: *grazie a tutti*.

I am lucky too to have other wine- and food-writing friends who have always been generous with their contacts and expertise: Luciano Pignataro, of Il Mattino, who has written the best book yet on Campanian wines (in Italian); Manuela Piancastelli, a fine wine journalist (who, with Peppe Mancini, often had me as a guest); Nancy Jenkins, who invited me onto the Oldways tour in Salerno, and the people at Oldways for their fascinating visit there; Nicolas Belfrage, for his continuing friendship and for his excellent books on Italian wines; Giampaolo Gravina, a great wine taster and new friend, who let me join some of the Campanian tastings for the Espresso guide and was encouraging about the work-in-progress; Fred Nijhuis, for still being a wonderful tasting teacher and friend; Arthur Schwartz, for his infectious passion for Campania and his great Neapolitan cookbook; Paolo and Luisella Marchi for their support, and for giving me space when I want it in their newspaper; Roberta Corradin, for being a keen translator and fellow writing enthusiast; Rosaria Castaldo, who was a cheerful helper in the final stage; Marco Bolasco, for coming right down to Nusco; Roberto Ricci for his coffee expertise; and Luigi Cremona, who knows more about Italian restaurants than anyone I know, and who saved me in the nick of time. Thanks also to Mary Taylor Simeti, Anna Tasca Lanza, Carol Field, Henrietta Green, Alice Waters and Frederika Randall for setting such wonderful examples. Ursula Thurner and her co-workers were ever-patient when deadlines overlapped. The editorial staff of Decanter (especially Amy Wislocki), Bon Appetit, Departures, and Gourmet were supportive throughout. Thanks too to Marc Millon and Rosemary Barron, and the friends in the Guild of Food Writers and Eatwords for their solidarity.

Thanks to Roberto Rubino for his help and encouragement, and for the inspirational work he does on free-grazing animals, their cheeses and pastures at ANFOSC, where a special thank you goes to Clara Laurita; Gennaro Esposito, Vittoria Aiello and their lovely staff for having me to dinner so often; Vincenzo 'Luminoso' D'Alessandro and his family at Sant'Anastasìa, for taking me into their fold and always picking up the pieces, and to Fiorenzo D'Avino for his great eye; Paul De Bondt and Cecilia Iaccobelli for their fabulous chocolate that kept my brain going; Giorgio Del Sorbo for taking me to all his favourite restaurants; Alberto del Buono for passing on the names of places he loves; Antonio and Caterina Palmieri for being gracious hosts and enlightened dairy owners; Salvatore and Annamaria De Gennaro for keeping in constant touch, sharing so many taste experiences, and for running that shop; Enzo Ercolino and Mirella Capaldo for their commitment to all things Irpinian, and Donato Episcopo and the Marennà staff – with Cynzia Alvino and Paolo De Cristofaro – who helped me when I was working with them; Lella, Luca and Massimo Vignelli, for sharing their style; Heinz Beck for his discerning palate and for being so much fun to work with; Berardino

Lombardo for offering beds and rustic soups. Thanks too to Patrizia and
Sergio Cappelli who first showed me Napoli all those years ago; Riccardo
Dalisi for his projects with Neapolitan children and his collection of
unique coffee pots; Michele Minieri, who helped me discover hidden
parts of Alta Irpinia; Enzo Crivella, of Slow Food in Sapri, who was par-
ticularly generous with his contacts, and became a new friend; Tony May
in New York, for his unflagging enthusiasm about Campania, and to
Piero and Stacy Selvaggio for their encouragement and true hospitality in
Los Angeles; a special thanks to Luigi Scorziello and the Banca di
Aquara, who offered technical assistance at a critical moment; and to
Lucilla Morelli, for her help. Other friends in Slow Food in Campania –
Enzo Luciano, Rita Abagnale, Vito Puglia and others – have also been
helpful.

I appreciate the help too of Antonio Marchetti, Vito Trotta, and Fabio
Guerrini, the pasta mavens; Raffaele Ferraioli and the Tramonti
Comunità Montana; Louise Mc Dermott of Italica Books, for her supply
of out-of-print titles; the D'Ambras of Ischia and the Mastroberardinos of
Irpinia; Luigi Moio, Laura Di Marzio and little Michele; Alessandra,
Lucia and Vito Aita, and Annamaria Ruggia; Giovanni Ascione; Bernardo
Barlotti; Roberto Della Monica; Enzo Falco; Ottavio Fusco; Imma
Gargiulo; Teodoro Naddei; Vincenzo Ricciardi and Antonio Fusco of
AIS; Paolo Conti and Laura Santoni of the Amiata, who have been wait-
ing patiently for this book to be finished; Melanie Young in New York,
who is a big fan of Campania, and Constance D'Agata Wark in Boston,
who is one too; Alberto Biagetti in Milano, who kept my Apple rolling.

The photographs for the book were all taken as 35 mm slides using
Fuji professional film, on good old-fashioned Nikons. So, many thanks
go to the people in the labs and photo shops for their assistance:
ColorDue, Giovenzana, and DPF Photocenter in Milan, (especially Beppe
at DPF who was so supportive when my cameras were stolen), Il Colore
in Rome, and Copyright in Naples.

One of the most important aspects of producing this book is the excellent rapport I have with my publisher, Alexander Fyjis-Walker, of Pallas
Athene in London. It has been a pleasure to work with him again: a true
book-lover, his passion for writing, reading and, now, Campania, has
made that phase of the process stimulating and rewarding – a rare experience in today's publishing world. With him I must thank Simon Coury
who has patiently and painstakingly read and edited the text; Harold
Bartram, who designed the book, and then re-designed it to accommodate the many more photos; and Polly Hudson and the children for
always having me around in the final stages. In Verona, many thanks to
the book's printers, Graphic Studio, whose expertise and attention to
detail clearly show in the final result: Gianfranco Dall'Ora, Francesca
Carrara, Renato Veggiato, Alberto Falsarolo, Lorenzo Romagnoli,

Giorgio Agnoli and Giancarlo Terragnoli. On the American side of the Atlantic, thanks to Paul Feldstein at Trafalgar Square Publishing who has been enthusiastic about the book all along.

Antonio Pisaniello's staff at La Locanda di Bu at Nusco have become part of my extended family: thank you to Daisuke Umehara, Vincenzo Squarciafico, 'chef Antonio' Natale, Pina Gramaglia, Lorenzo Vernacchio, Ore Dagan, Didina (and Costantino), and Cristina...as well as to the foreign visitor, chef Chris Hille, who left Il Gastronomo after a few months to create A 16 in San Francisco. Also at Nusco, thanks to my neighbours downstairs, Anastasia and Aurelio Schiavone, and their affec-tionate children, Sara, Piero and Alessandro, for the constant kindnesses they bestow on me; Signor Luigino, who found me the house with the view; and Alfonso Conte, who printed out chapters at the drop of a hat.

There are several other people who, although not in Campania, helped me to write this book. Thanks to: Luigina and Giulio Aiello, without whom I wouldn't feel safe leaving my house on the lake; my sister Isabelle, who always kept in touch with me; my mother, Pat Lousada, and father, Carmen Capalbo, for their support and help; Marc Capalbo, Sebastian, Sabra, Lily and Raphael Lousada, Joey, Iris and Adam Sodowick, and my extended family in London and America. My sister, Sandra Lousada, a great photographer, urged me to wake up early and take the pictures myself – I'm glad she did.

If my life has a free-form, nomadic shape to it when I'm on the road alone researching the books, the core structure remains in place thanks to friends (far-away) whose love and support are constants: I'm grateful for the true friendship of Nicky Rudge, Lauren Crow, Wallace Heim, Silvia Imparato, Peter Frank, Maddalena Susino, Angelo Di Stefano, Harriet Shapiro, Tracy Tynan, Bridget Belgrave, Dianne Wight, Elizabeth Heyert, Becca Cross, Alessandro Guerriero, Mary Fedden, Sam and Robert Pease, Rosemary George and Christopher Galleymore, Maria Teresa Giannarelli, Chris and Gina Russell, Toney and Maggie Hopp, Carlo Arlotta, Franca De Filippis, Paola de Calò, Eithne Cornish, Marco De Bartoli and his family, Stefania Moroni, Patrizia Felluga; Siri, Claudia, Joanna and Tony Harris; Marielle Hucliez, Antoine and Joni Bootz, Mara Papatheodorou.

I lost several people I was very close to during the writing of this book: John Lowenthal, whose desk looked just like mine, piled high with papers, cuttings and books, and whose single-minded approach to book-writing was a silent bond between us; Brian Richards, my brother-in-law, whose commitment to the architectural (and moving) potential of the future was inspirational; Jocelyn Herbert, my could-be godmother, a remarkable woman, artist and role-model; Sandra Clark, one of my clos-est friends, who was present in so many of the chapters of my life; and FS, who might have been present in more. I miss you all.

VENDITA DIRETT... 'RODOTTI LOCALI

- MOZZARELLA   € 6,20 a kg
- BOCCONCINI   € 6,20 a kg
- CACIOCAVALLO   € 6,20 a kg
- PROVOLA AFFUMICATA € 6,20 a kg
- RICOTTA PECORINA D... ...ONTI € 5,20 a kg
- FORMAGGIO PECO... ...ONTI € 5,20 a kg
- FORMAGGIO PECORI... ...ONTI € 10,00 a kg

ESONERATO   ...   ... SCONTRINO
FISCALE IN QUA...   ... SPECIALE.

How to use this book

Campania is made up of five distinct provinces: Avellino, Benevento, Caserta, Napoli and Salerno. For the sake of this book and to make it easier for travellers, I have divided Campania into nine sections (and chapters). Some correspond to the provincial boundaries (as with Caserta, Avellino and Benevento). Other chapters have been determined by their subject matter rather than official borders: the province of Napoli appears in four chapters (the city of Napoli and the Campi Flegrei; the area of Vesuvio; the islands of Capri, Ischia and Procida; and part of Chapter 5, the Sorrento Peninsula and Amalfi Coast). Salerno, the largest of the provinces, is also split (the other part of Chapter 5; from the port of Salerno down to Paestum; the Cilento and Vallo di Diano).

THE MAPS

Each chapter begins with a map showing the area's key towns. Names printed in bold indicate towns for which an entry appears. These maps are intended to help you organize your visits to restaurants and producers, but I strongly recommend obtaining Touring Club Italiano's Campania 1:200,000 map (with a green cover) to anyone planning to do much driving in rural Campania. It is readily available within Italy and is the only map I have found that shows the smaller roads in enough detail to be useful. Throughout this book I've referred to town names in Italian (Napoli instead of Naples), as that's how they appear in Campania and on Italian maps.

THE ENTRIES AND
THEIR CATEGORIES

Towns and villages containing entries are listed alphabetically within each chapter. Within each town, the entries are grouped by category—by food type (cheese, olive oil, wine) or establishment type (*agriturismo*, restaurant) — and within these categories, the listings are arranged alphabetically by key words: within the same town, *agriturismo* will be listed before restaurant or wine. Some entries have more than one category. Others may suggest additional products within the text: for instance, some wineries also offer rooms for guests.

In addition to the town and category, each entry offers the ADDRESS and TELEPHONE NUMBER of the business, with FAX or INTERNET addresses when available. In Italy, house numbers are written after the street name.

*Opposite: A detail
from Riccardo
Giordano's small
dairy at Tramonti*

OPENING HOURS   In Campania – as throughout the south of Italy – OPENING HOURS are different from other countries': depending on what they sell, most shops open between 8.00 and 9.30, close for lunch at 13.00, 13.30 or even 14.00, to re-open again anywhere between 15.00 to 17.00; the afternoon session ends between 19.00 and 20.00 or later – so don't forget to allow for this mid-day *pausa* – it is sometimes several hours long. If you are making a special trip, always phone to check before setting off. I also recommend phoning to make an appointment before visiting wineries and other private artisan producers; not all are set up to receive drop-in visitors. They are also helpful at indicating the best way to get there. Restaurants, too, should be booked ahead – even if it's only a few hours or a day before. CLOSING DAYS and holidays are given whenever possible, especially for restaurants.

PRICES AND CREDIT CARDS   The PRICE CATEGORY is used only for restaurants, and gives the average cost per person of a three- or four-course meal without wine, beverages, or service and cover charges (prices accurate as of summer 2004). Obviously, meals based on pizzas or fewer courses will cost less.

Here are the ranges used:

€ up to 18 Euros
€€ 18–26 Euros
€€€ 26–38 Euros
€€€€ 38–52 Euros
€€€€€ 52–72 Euros
€€€€€€ 72 Euros and over

These price ranges should be used as a guide only. Meals may cost more, depending on how much fresh fish is in the menu; it is often a good idea to choose the *menu degustazione* – or tasting menu – in which several courses are offered for a fixed price.

I've also indicated, whenever possible, whether restaurants accept CREDIT CARDS or not, but if this is important, phone to check before going. Most farms and estates sell their products directly to the public, but may not be set up to take credit cards.

THE RESTAURANT REVIEWS   I don't give scores or points in my wine or restaurant reviews: this is not an 'objective' book written by a nondescript person posing as a travelling salesman. I'm quite recognizable and quickly became known within Campania, so I couldn't have remained anonymous even if I had wanted to. The idea was to capture the mood, essence, ideas or tastes of each place I ate in, and to get to know the chefs and owners – that's the part I find interesting. I like all kinds of restaurants. This does not mean that I haven't used a critical eye, or palate, when eating in them; the places I really didn't like, I haven't included. What I look for is well-cooked food using fresh, seasonal ingredients, however humble. This is a book about the differences between the areas of Campania, so I've tried to give an idea of what to expect in each place – not a list of what's on the menu. I have reviewed restaurants in all price ranges and styles. Some specialize in pizzas or traditional cuisine, others take a more modern approach. These are necessarily subjective accounts – you can take it from there!

GETTING THERE   Always take a good map with you: I recommend the Touring Club Italiano's Campania 1:200,000 map mentioned above. Ask advice from the producers: most now have websites that can provide detailed maps. In rural Campania few roads have names (and of those, few have street signs). The most important visible indicators when leaving a village or town are the blue-and-white signs pointing to the next town or village. 'In the town centre' means within the *centro storico*, or historic centre. These are easy to find: look for the black-and-white 'target' symbol on road signs near the cities or towns. Most villages have a large map in the main square or on the road entering the town showing its landmarks and streets. For Napoli and other large towns, I suggest buying a map with a street index. They are sold at local newspaper stands or bookstores.

THE FOOD ENTRIES   These entries describe food producers and/or some of their products. I have included information about how the products are made and descriptions of those I was able to taste or liked best. Other products are also often available – mine is not intended to be an exhaustive list.

THE WINE ENTRIES   This book covers a large selection of Campania's quality wine estates. It's a rapidly expanding sector, with exciting new wineries opening all the time – too many to include here. This book gives an overview, with the personal histories of some of the key estates. Rather than focus always on detailed tasting notes, I've adopted a free-form approach to my visits, and written about different aspects of Campanian winemaking in each case. I'm lucky to be able to speak Italian, so I've tried to garner information that other visitors may find useful. It's up to you to decide which wines you prefer. There is no substitute for the experience of tasting a fine wine in the cellars where it was made. Wines may be bought directly from most estates at prices that are the same as or slightly lower than nearby wine shops. At all but the biggest wineries (which may have permanent staff on hand to show you around), it is recommended to phone ahead to arrange a visit. All are hospitable and keen on receiving interested visitors—novices and experts alike—so don't miss out on this wonderful, fascinating opportunity.

In the listings, the wine entries are arranged alphabetically according to the key word in their company titles: Cantine Di Meo is under 'D', as Di Meo is a surname.

Note: The entries vary greatly in length; reduced length does not imply that the products or producers are less interesting – I just didn't have space to write a lot about everyone I visited. Nor does not being included in the book imply that a winery or restaurant is not good: there's a limit to how much one person working alone can accomplish, and I hope to enlarge the list in future editions.

BIBLIOGRAPHY   I have included a selected list of the books I found helpful—and entertaining—in researching the background for the book, or in my travels.

GLOSSARY   Translations of Italian food and wine terms commonly used in Campania and in this book. The glossary also will help in translating menus written in Italian.

INDEX   At the end of the book you will find a comprehensive general index which also lists the entries and their foods by category. For example, you can see where buffalo mozzarella is made within Campania, and thus read about the dairies before deciding which ones to visit.

Opposite: Aniello Corritore, a skilled basket-maker from Tramonti

Introduction

The sfusato lemons of Amalfi make the best granita

Opposite: Costanzo Cacace making la passata di pomodoro San Marzano, the keystone of Campanian cuisine

The Food and Wine Guide to Naples and Campania is the result of three years of my work – and life – in the southern Italian region of Campania. It's the guide I would have liked to have had with me when I started on my journey there in search of the most authentic and flavourful foods, wines and restaurants – but it didn't exist. Some Italian guide books cover selected restaurants, or wineries, but they are usually too impersonal, the piecemeal result of 'too many cooks', or simply too intent on score-giving to be of much interest to me. I wanted to experience the human sides of the stories, to get to know the food producers, shepherds, fishermen, vegetable growers, winemakers and chefs, and to talk to them about their lives and their work.

So I began at the beginning, learning from everyone I met, tasting my way through pizzas and wild greens, *mozzarelle* and olive oils, wines and pastries, to discover which I preferred. I often spent days selecting a road on the map and then driving it, slowly, taking in the geography, the colour of the soils, noting which crops were growing where. Just to get a feel for the complexity of the region, the differences from one area to another. Even the photography had a casualness about it: some days I felt like taking pictures, others I didn't. I hardly knew anyone in Campania when I began, and depended largely on luck in working out where to eat, where to sleep. Fortunately, the Campanians are among the most generous people in the world, and they opened their kitchens and houses to me in a spontaneous and unforgettable way. Early visitors to Campania such as Craufurd Tait Ramage and even Norman Lewis write of areas in which the locals had never before seen an Englishman; I can only say that I have, more than once, found myself in places in Campania in which the people had never before seen an American woman, at least not of the independent, grey-haired variety.

Visiting an artisanal food or wine producer, or a little-known country restaurant run by enthusiastic – and talented – young chefs can be as rewarding a cultural experience as a trip to a famous museum or historic palace. They're just usually harder to find and to negotiate for those who don't speak the language or know where to look. This book is designed to help English-speakers and visitors to Campania discover hundreds of these gems scattered throughout the region in the form of cheese-makers, olive mills, fig-curers, *trattorie* in medieval villages, wineries, farmhouse *agriturismi*... the list is long. They are all aspects of agriculture in the widest sense – indeed they reveal the cultural half of that word – which today forms such an important draw for modern travellers to Italy.

It has been a pleasure to work under the auspices of the Campania Region on this project, as its President, Antonio Bassolino, and former Agriculture *Assessore* (or minister), Vincenzo Aita, as well as the great chef, Alfonso Iaccarino who has become its gastronomic 'ambassador', are passionate about their homeland, and fully committed to safeguarding its countryside and traditional foods and flavours for the future. Their hope is to promote and protect Campania's gastronomic treasures through an appreciation of the uniqueness of their ingredients and recipes, and the viticulture that is based on the wonderful grape varieties that are special to Campania.

This is a time of worldwide concern for and interest in our foods, water supplies and environment. Activists and associations – including Slow Food and the Social Forum – are fighting to raise our awareness of the plight of small producers in Italy and beyond, and to safeguard their livelihoods and lifestyles as well as our health. In sharp contrast to some of the more industrialized countries or regions, Campania offers a wealth of local foods, and a positive role-model for eating well and living a more natural, peaceful life. After all, the Mediterranean diet is based on this country *cucina*, rich in sun-ripened vegetables and fruits, olive oil, grains and fish. In this sense, it's lucky that Campania has not been completely catapulted into the modern world of processed foods and hectic schedules: people stop everything and shut up shop at lunchtime to sit at a table with their families to eat together. Food here still represents a tangible link to specific territories, the seasons – even to ancestors.

Traditions are important, but so is change. In that respect, this is an exciting time to be in Campania. Since I moved to the region to start researching this book, I've witnessed an explosion of talent and interest in Campania's food and wine world. Young chefs are opening new restaurants featuring only delicious local produce; wineries are celebrating the region's indigenous grapes (and winning prizes with them); native ingredients are being appreciated, and protected, for their unique flavours. It's a fine tribute to the handful of pioneer chefs and winemakers – and to the region's growers,

Summer fruit: melons and tomatoes in abundance

artisans and fishermen – who have been battling for decades on behalf of the excellence of Campanian foods and grapes. And to the people – and governors – of Campania, who have often had to overcome prejudice and (foreign) unfamiliarity to reassert what they have always known: that Campania is one of the Mediterranean's key cultural and agricultural centres. From Magna Grecia's wines and ancient Rome's 'vegetable garden', to the Bourbon court's model vineyards and Gragnano's nineteenth-century pasta artisans, food has always played a decisive role in Campania's history.

Campania's wine world is full of promise: its volcanic soils are home to over one hundred autochthonous grape types – more than all of France's, and many only recently rediscovered – that offer a refreshing antidote to too much Chardonnay and Merlot. Today these varieties – like Fiano, Greco, Falanghina, Pallagrello, Casavecchia and Aglianico – are among the most sought-after by those looking for wines of character that reflect specific terroirs. In the past ten years, great new wines being made from these original grapes have been earning accolades and justifying extensive investments.

As for the foods, not only do the region's five provinces offer original culinary traditions – the coast's menus are quite different from those of the interior – but the ingredients themselves are being recognized at European and world levels for their distinctiveness.

The *sfusato* lemons of Amalfi and their *limoncello*, the white figs of the Cilento and the artichokes of Paestum, buffalo mozzarella and Provolone del Monaco, San Marzano tomatoes and Avellino hazelnuts – these are but a few of the unusual and excellent Campanian foods that are now part of the Italian – and international – gastronomic palette.

In the past year, new books in Italian have come out on Campanian olive varieties and wines, *agriturismi* and restaurants, raw-milk cheeses and historic anchovy sauces. UNESCO, the World Wildlife Fund, Slow Food, and the European Union have taken an interest in protecting Campania's parks, animal species and food types. So I'm sure the time is right for a detailed guide book in English that will help foreign travellers discover these wonderful foods and wines, and put them into a cultural and historical context.

To many people – foreigners and Italians alike – southern Italy is still a little-known world. Whether for sociological, geographical or PR reasons, the south – *il sud*, *il Meridione* or *il Mezzogiorno* – has been slower to reveal its treasures than parts of the centre and north like Toscana or the Veneto. The southern regions – Abruzzo, Molise, Campania, Basilicata, Puglia and Calabria – have often been clumped together as being simply 'south of Rome', a grouping

Repairing the fishing nets at Cetara

that left little space for personal differences (Sicilia has always had a higher profile, by definition). Happily, that's starting to change, for each of these regions has its own distinct identity.

For far too long, the foods and cooking of the Italian south have been undervalued – even within Italy. While the industrialized north boasted French-style dishes enriched with cream and butter, the south was seen to have a 'mere *cucina povera*' of vegetables and fish dressed only with olive oil. The tables were turned when the Mediterranean diet became fashionable, and the south's uncluttered country cuisine was proven to be far healthier than the north's cholesterol-heavy dishes. This rustic *cucina* based on sun-ripened, seasonal ingredients has become an international model for healthy living.

Today, we are ever more aware of the problems of globalization, of the risk and cost of losing the traditions and customs of our countrysides. One has only to visit places that sold out these apparent 'details' to see how culturally and socially bereft they have become. I'm glad to report that Campania is healthy and doing fine on that score: its œno-gastronomic roots run deep and are firmly ingrained – indeed, I could easily spend a further three years and hundreds of other pages writing more about them.

If Campania has something of an identity problem among foreigners, who easily confuse the region's name with *campagna* – countryside – it's enough to mention the words 'Naples', 'Capri' and 'Amalfi Coast' for people to know exactly where you mean. They immediately conjure a picture of the fascinating city, and of a dazzling coastline with sun-bleached Mediterranean villages and exotic flowers. Of pizza and pasta, lemon groves and olive trees. Of great food and wine, and warm-hearted people. That is the Campania most people now know or know of. Luckily, we've come a long way since Karl Baedeker's famous guide books recommended that travellers to Campania avoid 'macaroni, cheese and all greasy Italian dishes' in favour of a diet 'confined as much as possible to cocoa, biscuits, oatmeal porridge, lean meat, and rice seasoned with cinnamon'.

This book goes beyond first impressions to the areas that are less familiar, even to Italians: the high cheese-making villages above the Amalfi Coast that are so steep only mules can reach them; the olive groves and unspoiled coast of the Cilento; the Picentini hills above Salerno, where the finest hazelnuts grow; the mountain foods of Irpinia; the wine-valleys of Benevento; the upper Casertano, with its native animal breeds and rare grape varieties; the vineyards of Roccamonfina and of Asprinio with their high, festooning grapes that every traveller to the region wrote about, whatever century they came in; the slopes of Vesuvio, with its mineral-rich fruits; the

pasta towns, like Gragnano, where *maccheroni* are still produced by artisans; the new–old vineyards at Pompei; the island of Ischia, with its unusual rabbits and autochthonous grapes... this book is a compendium of these discoveries.

Whenever possible, I've gone beyond talking just about food and wine to the area's cultural and historical background – after all, you can't appreciate what you'll find in the Casertano without some idea of the Bourbon court, or understand why Irpinia looks the way it does without knowing about the 1980 earthquake there. While researching the book, I became fascinated by the accounts that travellers before me wrote about Campania. Vesuvius, Naples and Paestum were key destinations on the Grand Tour, and writers like Dickens, Dumas, Goethe and Steinbeck have left exceptional records of their impressions; I have included a bibliography, but as far as the travel literature goes, it only scratches the surface.

I'm sure that the hundreds of thousands of desperate people who left Campania in the late 19th- and early 20th-centuries in search of a more prosperous life would be proud to see what modern Campania – and Italy – have become. Their children and grandchildren are now returning here to explore and find their roots. It's a fascinating experience: I myself am the granddaughter of three Italians – two from the south, one from the north – who left dramatically poor homes for America before the First World War. The internet may have brought many things closer to us all, but nothing can substitute befriending the local people, tasting the true flavours of foods and wines, and seeing the countryside of this wonderful region. My hope is that this book will make it easier to do. When I first moved down to Campania after living for twelve years in the north of Italy, I knew only one person, and the prospect of creating this book was both exciting and daunting. An early Campanian friend told me: 'You'll see, Carla, things are different here in Campania... we'll get under your skin and you won't want to leave us again.' They did, and I don't!

Opposite:
Annamaria Cuomo
of La Tradizione
at Seiano with
traditional scamorze
cheeses from
Vico Equense

Campania and its foods

As anyone who spends time in Italy quickly realizes, once you cross the invisible line below Rome into the 'real south', foods take on an intensity of flavour and colour that makes everything above that line pale. The combination of fierce Mediterranean sun and fertile volcanic soils that earned the land around Napoli the term of 'Campania Felix' at the time of the ancient Romans still works its magic.

Take the tomato: in Campania this 'red gold' is a symbol of sensuality and character, the *sine qua non* of much of Campania's culinary identity since it arrived in Europe from the New World, famous on everything from pasta to pizza. The quintessential *pomodoro* – or *pummarola* as Neapolitan dialect has it – is of the San Marzano variety, for its blood-red colour and concentrated sweetness have none of the acidity that northerners usually associate with tomatoes. These really are fruits – closer to peaches than potatoes. The same is true of the deep-violet *melanzane*, and vermilion and yellow peppers that brighten Campania's summer dishes (the indigestible large green peppers we stuff and bake are correctly dismissed as unripe by southern Italian cooks, and left on the plant to mature). This palette of primary flavours is filled out by the bitter-sweet bite of Campania's wild *erbe* – escarole, nettles, artichokes, borage – and accented by spicy basil and mint, aromatic myrtle and fennel seeds, and by hot *peperoncino*.

The white range comprises radiant buffalo mozzarella as juicy as it is solid, frail ricotta, piquant raw-milk cows' cheeses – Caciocavallo Podolico, or Provolone del Monaco – and tangy goat *caprini*. Durum wheat makes slow-dried, golden pasta – *maccheroni* as they call it here – while softer flour yields crisp, puffed pizza crust, and the assorted *pasticceria* – from grainy *pastiera* to rum-soaked *babà* – that are the Campanians' pride. Hazelnuts with creamy centres are specialities of the interior, at their most inviting in honey *torrone* and crumbly cakes. Brown-black is the searing, seductive shot of adrenaline that here goes by the name of *caffè* – to

Opposite: These are beans to shell and eat fresh, or dry for the winter

many, Napoli's is the best in the world.

Geographical differences lead to taste changes: along the coast are landmark dry-stone-walled terraces of pointed lemons to perfume sorbets, *limoncello* and candied peels. As for Vesuvio, its microclimate concentrates the sugars of apricots, persimmons, melons and walnuts, making them unforgettably fragrant. In the mountain valleys are the rustic apples, pears and plums that defy industrialization – they're happily too small, too sour, too tricky, or too much themselves to be mass-produced. Add to this the characterful fish and seafood of the Tyrrhenian Sea, the meats of farmyard and forest animals, and the just-pressed oils of native olives, and you have the elements of a *cucina* that has been in place for well over two millennia.

The political history of Campania is reminiscent of a board-game's speedy succession of take-overs, occupations and resistances: starting with the Greeks in the 8th century BC, this fruitful, beautiful territory was battled for by Samnites, Oscans and Romans, Vandals, Goths and Byzantines, Lombards, Normans and Angevins... and that's only up to the 14th century. Then came the Aragons, and over 200 years of rule by Spanish Viceroys, followed by 130 years under the Bourbons; even after the unification of Italy, in 1861, 'another foreign power' came: the royal House of Savoy with its seat in Piemonte. In this dizzying give-and-take of power and culture (including foods), the only constant seems to have been the character of Napoli's people – ever ingenious, peaceful, enterprising, life-loving and accommodating, they remained uniquely themselves, whichever way the political winds blew.

The city's population too rose and fell, growing to huge proportions – larger than Paris in the 14th century, and twice that of London at the beginning of the 16th – before being often cut back by earthquakes, volcanic eruptions and plagues; today, Campania is the most densely populated part of Italy. It wasn't just the city's size that expanded. Napoli was a key Mediterranean port, with all the intellectual, architectural and artistic development that befitted such a metropolis, as any visitor there will soon attest.

When the Greeks colonized and developed the area as Magna Grecia, they too left an indelible cultural mark: Greek was still spoken in Napoli during Roman times, and Paestum remained a Greek colony until it fell to the Lombards in 640 AD. The Roman emperors used the fields of northern Campania for their food production: it wasn't difficult, as the loose black volcanic soil 'offered its fruits almost without effort. Depending on the product, there were two to four crops per year,' as Waverley Root noted in

Opposite: Rolled pancetta contadina from the Monti Lattari

The Food of Italy. In Roman times, the Mediterranean was almost thick with fish: the emperors who built vacation palaces along its coastline had their pick of seafood. The Greeks had brought grapes when they settled at Cuma and on Ischia, and the vines trained high through poplar and fruit trees were a feature that many writers on the Grand Tour wrote about two thousand years later. Some are still there to be seen; the wines too are their legacy.

If the coastal and volcanic areas were rich in fruits and vegetables, the mountainous interior – in what are now the provinces of Benevento and Avellino – offered a more austere, frugal lifestyle. Indeed, much of the large-scale emigration from Campania to the Americas affected those areas of the *interno*. Today they are being repopulated in a revival based on the healthy agricultural products of the woods, orchards, olive groves and vineyards.

During the Renaissance, in the second half of the 15th century, when it was governed by Alfonso V 'the Magnanimous', King of Aragon and Sicily, Napoli was beautified with palaces, villas and gardens, churches and an important university. He was followed by the Spanish Viceroys under the Holy Roman Emperor, Charles V. Here again, Napoli flourished as a free-thinking capital that traded easily throughout the Mediterranean. The 'new' ingredients from the Americas – including tomatoes, potatoes, peppers, beans, gourds, maize and chocolate – quickly found their way into the Neapolitans' diet. The ruling classes enjoyed these advantages, while the poor suffered from over-population and lack of work. Colourful vendors became a trademark of Napoli's streets, as thousands lived without cooking facilities – or even roofs – and relied on these *venditori ambulanti* for their sustenance. Over the next two hundred years, the chaotic city's inhabitants developed a real passion for street food, sold by those whose costumes and cries were easily distinguishable. I love this description of the snail-vendor, or *maruzzaro*, in Jeanne Caròla Francesconi's epic cookbook, *La Cucina Napoletana*:

> 'The frame upon which the *maruzzaro* carried his wares was unique: Imagine a large, wide, two-handled basket with, on one side, held miraculously upright, a lamp lit by an oil-wick. Inside the basket: a little stove that supported a terracotta cooking-dish; another little pan – this one miniscule – full of fried hot *peperoncini*; and, finally, plates, spoons and ladles. A smaller basket with just one handle contained the *freselle* (crisp baked breads) to dunk into the mollusc broth. This he carried on one arm, while the big one – I imagine – must have been balanced on his head and held in precarious equilibrium with his free hand.

Opposite:
Pomodorini and the
pink-green tomatoes
of Sorrento

'The *maruzzaro*, who by day was just an anonymous street vendor, at night showed himself in all his splendour with the lamp lit and, sometimes, when he was in a particularly good mood, with a crown of little lights made of snails' shells filled with oil and lit, arranged around the edge of the cooking-dish. He positioned himself by the entrance to the *osterie* – those that sold only drinks – a right for which he often had to pay the *osteria*'s host a percentage. Modest but tasty, a portion of snails accompanied by a *fresella* bathed in broth cost two *soldi*.'

In the mid-18th century, the royal court of the Bourbons, with its new palaces, hunting reserves and cultural extravaganzas, brought prestige to the cosmopolitan and increasingly powerful city. As for its sovereign, Ferdinand IV, the King of the Two Sicilies, he was a passionate sportsman, and seems to have spent most of his time eating, drinking, hunting and fishing. The Bourbons were also enthusiastic about wine grapes, and planted an historic fan-shaped vineyard of their favourite varieties (see p. 67). The rich socialites of Napoli enjoyed the sorbets and ices their cooks learned to produce, as well as the intense *caffè* that would later become such an integral part of Neapolitan culture.

By now, the *cucina* of Campania had incorporated the medieval and Renaissance – and surely Roman and Greek – liking for the sweet, sour and spicy as accents to their vegetables, fish and meats. This was in part the legacy of the Arabs who had dominated Sicily in the 10th century – with their raisins and pine nuts, citrus fruits and flower-waters – and the exoticism of Eastern spices that were familiar through the port's trading.

Spooning the syrup over a babà

La cucina napoletana, as it is known pretty much throughout the region, was to stretch to other influences too, beyond those of the Ancient and New Worlds. If Napoli's 19th-century streets were alive with the sights, sounds and smells of popular local foods, the kitchens of the aristocracy now moved in another direction – towards the 'refinement' of French cuisine. Here the key players were the resident cooks of the noble *palazzi*, known as *Monzù* (by the Italianization of 'Monsieur'). The *Monzù* were introduced by the Bourbon Queen Maria Carolina to gentrify this elemental *cucina povera*, and in so doing, they changed the history of Neapolitan cuisine. Here butter, cream and lard reigned above olive oil; potatoes were invariably '*alla duchesse*'; and pâtés and gateaux (or *gattò*) became conversation pieces. Over time, some of these dishes worked their way into the repertoire of even the humblest families, while others exist only in the nostalgic memories of what remains of the nobility.

Wild greens are a traditional part of the Campanian cucina

Immediately after its liberation from the Germans, in 1944, Napoli was once again crippled by hunger. Norman Lewis, in the marvellously written journal he kept about his year there, *Naples '44*, one day comes upon a large group of Neapolitan women and children who had walked for three hours out of the city into the fields near Afragola, to search for edible plants along the roadsides: 'There were about fifteen different kinds of plants which were worth collecting, most of them bitter in flavour,' he explains. The only ones he recognised were dandelions. This *contadino* approach to the land still exists: every season offers 'free' foods to the gatherers, from mushrooms to nuts, pasture greens to wild fruits. These simple ingredients have wonderful flavour: nothing can beat a bowl of *la minestra maritata* – mixed cuts of pork 'married' in a soup to at least seven types of wild *erbe* – or a pizza stuffed with *scarola*, a few olives and local anchovies. As Arthur Schwartz points out in his fine cookbook, *Naples at Table*, these are recipes that pre-date the tomato, when Neapolitans were known as *mangiafoglie* – leaf-eaters – before becoming known as *mangiamaccheroni* – pasta-eaters. Indeed, by the end of the 16th century, dry *maccheroni* (see p. 188) was already on its way to becoming a staple not only of the Campanians but, eventually, of large parts of the world. Even Garibaldi's army of die-hard northerners is said to have arrived in Naples eating risotto and to have left preferring pasta.

In modern Campania you'll find a mix of all these themes. The classic Neapolitan *ragù* – the thick, slow-cooked tomato sauce enriched with occasional chunks of meat – dresses pasta, meat and vegetable dishes. It has become a sacred cow, an intimate institution, as the great thespian Eduardo De Filippo's poem to it, *'O rraù* testifies: no one but his mother knew how to make it.

'For *il ragù*, the meats must be cooked very very slowly,' explains Enzo Ercolino, a wine producer and connoisseur of Campanian foods. 'The tomatoes should almost go brown, becoming *un Nepente*, a mythological figure that is born of nothing and turns into something else – the process is a mystery. But, one wonders: if the tomatoes are to become something else, how can they ever have been the beginning?'

To the Campanians, dishes like these – or the fried, layered and baked vegetable *parmigiana*, or Easter *pastiera* cake – are charged with so much emotion that they go far beyond being simple recipes to become carriers of memory within the public–private culture that food represents here. On a recent re-entry from London to Napoli's airport, I witnessed a heated discussion between the frontier police – all men – about how long the onions for the *genovese* sauce should be cooked. I knew just where I was: I was back.

EATING IN CAMPANIA

RESTAURANTS
AND EATING OUT

Campania offers many options for eating out. A *bar* sells drinks, coffee, and snacks. *Enoteche* are wine bars; many also serve food. *Trattorie* and *osterie* feature rustic home cooking and are often family run. *Pizzerie* serve pizzas: some do little else, while others offer *antipasti* and even pasta or main courses; look for *forno a legna* – wood-burning oven – as these make the best pizzas. *Ristoranti* (restaurants) include world-class establishments and are usually well appointed. I have grouped them all under the category 'restaurant'.

Mealtimes in the south tend to be later than in central or northern Italy. Lunch is normally served from 13.00 to 14.30 or later, and dinner from 19.30 to 21.30 or later. Do not expect restaurants to serve a meal in mid-afternoon, though a *panino* (sandwich) can usually be found in a bar. Some *pizzerie* are open between lunch and dinner, but they are the exception.

In Campania, people often still eat three or four courses at each meal, especially if they are out at a restaurant: *antipasto* (hors d'oeuvres), *primo* (pasta or soup), *secondo* (meat or fish main course with a *contorno* of vegetables), and *dolce* (dessert). These habits are changing somewhat, and it is now usually acceptable to have just two or three courses. Some restaurants may not look favourably on those wanting only a pasta and salad, but others understand that not everyone eats as many courses as the Italians. Most of the grander restaurants expect diners to order a full meal.

Not all restaurants have printed menus; in some the proprietor recites the day's offerings. If you want a full meal, many restaurants offer a *menu degustazione*, or tasting menu. In a good restaurant, this offers a chance to taste dishes in each category at a fixed price.

To avoid disappointment it is always advisable to make a phone reservation: popular restaurants may be fully booked, and country trattorias sometimes close off-season if no customers have reserved.

FOOD MARKETS

Most villages and towns host a weekly market in addition to any permanent market structures they have. These are fun to visit not only for shopping—prices are usually lower than in the super-markets, and the produce is fresher—but also to see what is in season. Vegetables and fruits are priced and sold by weight: either by the kilogram (2.2 lbs) or the *etto* (100 grams, or 3.5 ounces). Any item sold and priced singly will be marked *cadauno* or *cad.* (each).

Opposite: Mixed antipasti of home-grown vegetables at Lo Scoglio

FOOD FESTIVALS

At least once a year, almost every village in Campania holds a food fair, which may be called a *sagra* or *festa* and may be big or small. On summer weekends many villages hold fairs on the same day. *Sagre* are usually dedicated to one particular food or dish: *sagra del fusillo* (*fusillo* pasta festival), *della castagna* (chestnut), and so on. They range from elaborate events with costumes, music and a rich assortment of foods to very local village affairs with a few tables set up in the main square. Whatever their size, they are usually fun to attend and offer an insight into rural life. Usually, local cooks prepare the village's specialities using the seasonal ingredient the fair is dedicated to. Visitors pay a modest fee and sit at large communal tables for their meal, or go from stand to stand trying different dishes. Nowadays many of these festas are also good places to find local speciality foods (*prodotti tipici*) or hand-made baskets or other artisan crafts. The Campanians love musical bands, so the festas are lively, with dancing for all ages. The best way to find out about food fairs is to look for posters which are put up a week or two before the fair, or to buy a local newspaper, which have sections dedicated to upcoming events.

TABLE CRAFTS
AND KITCHEN
SHOPS

For those who collect hand-made ceramics or baskets, some towns are known for their ceramic traditions (see index); however, there are generally fewer artisans now than in the past.

Well-stocked kitchen shops offer good presents to take home: individual espresso makers, olive-wood cutting boards or cheese graters, rolling pins for making some of the local pasta specialities, or any of the modern design objects the Italians are so good at producing. In country villages, the best place to find housewares is

*Opposite: At Vietri,
even the fruit shop
has painted ceramic
decorations*

OLIVE OIL

As in many areas of Italy, modern methods of cultivating olive trees, picking the olives and extracting the oil have guaranteed much higher quality oil-making in recent years in Campania. If the Cilento is still home to some immense, sculptural olive trees more than one hundred years old, current thinking about oil dictates that it is from small or low trees that the best oil can be obtained, as the olives should be hand-picked before they are ripe enough to drop from the trees, and very high trees make this all but impossible. The region of Campania is home to dozens of native olive varieties, usually divided by their geographical zones, and many of these are discussed in more detail in the relevant chapters.

The olive is a fruit. At its purest and best, olive oil is the 'juice' of this fruit—just crush and press the olives and it will drip free. Unfortunately, the process is rarely kept that simple. There is a world of difference between industrial extra virgin olive oil and estate-bottled oil made from home-grown, hand-picked olives. The latter will more than repay itself in quality. An aromatic, fruity oil can turn a good meal into a great one.

It is worth knowing that industrial extra virgin oil is bought as 'crude extra virgin' from many Mediterranean countries, regardless of where the bottler is located. It is always a blend, often including seed oils—though companies are not obliged to declare that on the label. Industrially refined 'virgin olive oils' and 'light' olive oils have been stripped of their natural taste and defects by chemical solvents.

Campania now produces many varieties of high-quality extra-virgin olive oil. As with all natural products, each oil's particular characteristics are determined by plant type, climate, and geography. Sorrento's coastal oils, like Liguria's, are light in colour and sweet in taste; they go well with seafood. Oils from Irpinia's central hills – such as those made with the native Ravece variety – are more decisive in flavour, with a peppery aftertaste and agreeable bitterness; they are best on salads and vegetables or drizzled on grilled bread.

Reputable small producers are attentive to each stage of the (necessarily costly) process. To make the best oil, healthy olives are hand-picked early in the season, before they are ripe enough to fall to the ground. (Falling means bruising, and the likelihood of rotting or fermentation.) They are carried in airy crates to the *frantoio*, or mill, and preferably milled within 36 hours of being picked. There are currently two non-industrial systems for extracting the oil: the traditional stone mill and the modern continuous cycle plant.

Opposite: A very personal way of separating olives from their leaves, above Sorrento

'Until recently, everyone agreed that stone-ground oil was the finest,' explains Marco Chiletti, an organic oil producer. 'It certainly is the most picturesque system—nothing could be more dramatic than to watch the great round stones as they crush the olives, with the air full of a fine mist of aromatic olive oil.'

In this method, the washed olives are ground to a dark brown pulp. This is usually heated very slightly, or it would not release its oil, and then kneaded before being spread onto circular woven mats. The mats are stacked onto a steel pole, sandwiching the paste between them. A hydraulic press squeezes the mats together, forcing the oil out. A final spin in a centrifuge separates the oil from its accompanying vegetal water. The residue of the paste, a hard brown substance that looks a bit like cork, is called *sansa*. It may be burned as a fuel or sold to refineries that extract more oil from it using chemical solvents. This *Olio di Sansa* should be avoided.

'Nowadays, the modern "continuous cycle" system is increasingly popular,' Chiletti adds. 'It has several advantages. It is more hygienic: the olives and pulp are worked entirely in stainless-steel containers, which are easily cleaned and reduce the risk of contamination from one batch of olives to the next. Each client can tailor the machinery to their needs, as it is temperature-controlled at every stage. In some machines, the olives are not crushed but cut with a series of fine blades, enabling the oil to drip away by gravity. This is definitely the way of the future.'

Many fine wine producers also make olive oil: the terrain required to grow olives is similar to that for grapes, and the harvesting seasons are staggered, the grapes being picked in September and October, the olives from late October through December.

There has been a lot of talk about acidity levels and cold pressing in olive oils. Although an oil must have less than 0.1 percent acidity to be considered extra virgin, low acidity levels alone do not guarantee good flavour (industrial oils may be manipulated chemically to 'correct' acidity), and some experts claim that the difference between 0.02 and 0.06 percent acidity cannot even be distinguished by the tongue. Even the word 'cold' is relative: unless the olive paste is at least 15°C/59°F, little oil can be extracted; below 8°C/46°F, the oil freezes. The most important factor for the layperson is the reputation of the producer—all the rest is personal preference.

A bottle of artisan-made, pure extra virgin olive oil may seem expensive, but used sparingly, its wonderful fresh flavour will enhance any meal, lasting much longer than a comparably priced bottle of wine.

HOW TO STORE
YOUR OIL

Pure extra virgin olive oil is a delicate natural product. Keep it away from its principal enemies, heat and light. Oil is also easily contaminated by bad odours, so never refill your oil cruet unless it has been perfectly cleaned and dried. Even a little oxidized residue

Nets in a Cilento olive grove catch any olives that remain after the harvest

is enough to ruin the taste of fresh oil. Unlike wine, oil does not improve with age. Use it within a year of being made.

Several associations are dedicated to the appreciation of fine olive oils, and they organize tastings and publish literature. Contact Corporazione dei Mastri Oleari, www.mastrioleari.org.

For information about extra virgin olive oil in Campania, many associations exist. Here is a selection:

APROL (Associazione Produttori Olivicoli), Via Scaramella, 23/25 Salerno SA; TEL 089 221339

Coordinamento Regionale Città dell'Olio (Association of Oil Cities of Italy), Comune di Sorrento, Piazza Sant'Antonino, 14, Sorrento NA; TEL 081 5335244; Giuseppe Ercolano: 333 3481190; INTERNET sorrentocittadellolio@libero.it

OLEUM (oil-tasters' association), Presso Cantina Sociale di Castel San Lorenzo, Via Donato Riccio, Castel San Lorenzo SA; TEL Pipolo: 347 9924525

WINE

Campania is one of Italy's most up-and-coming wine-producing regions, and its best wines are now gaining recognition world-wide. Campania contains many sub-zones that have been granted a nationally recognized winemaking status: DOC (*Denominazione di Origine Controllata)* or the more recent and more stringent DOCG, which adds *e Garantita* to the DOC. These denominations are similar to France's *appellation* system: wines made within a circumscribed area must comply with set standards in order to be accredited with the DOC or DOCG label. Grape varieties, a maximum grape yield per hectare (2.47 acres), and vinification and ageing specifications are established for each type of wine. Ideally, these specifications are strict enough to keep standards high and discourage fraud while still affording producers some flexibility of interpretation.

Winemakers within a DOC region may make wines outside these regulations, but they may not be classified as DOC or DOCG wines. Indeed, in the last twenty-five years there has been a revolution in Italy's winemaking as progressive estates have created new wines outside the DOC categories. At first, these wines had no official name, so they adopted the simple 'table wine' description given to Italy's humblest wines. In Tuscany, where the trend started, these *vini da tavola* were christened 'super-Tuscans'. They are often powerful, barrique-aged, expensive wines modelled on the great wines of France, and have gained an international following. In Campania, some modern-thinking estates have followed suit.

Recently a new Italian wine denomination has been created, IGT (*Indicazione Geografica Tipica*). A large and increasing number of wines fall into this category, and they range from the simplest table wines to the most intense blockbusters. The IGT can suggest a regional wine style, but is more often used for wines whose grape varieties exclude it from the local DOC or DOCG. It should not in itself be taken as a guarantee of quality.

WHAT IS WINE?

I recently heard a foreign visitor ask a winery owner, 'So what is in this wine, aside from grapes, sugar, and water?' The question was fair, but it clearly surprised the winemaker—he assumed everyone knew that wine was made only from grapes. So, for those new to winemaking, here is a simplified description of the process.

Wine is an alcoholic drink made from fermented grape juice—ideally without water or sugar. Red wine is made from red grapes, getting its deep colour from the skins (the pulp of red grapes has little colour): red grapes are fermented with their skins, white grapes are usually not, although some chilling techniques do allow for this.

Opposite: Aglianico ready to be picked in Irpinia

The stalks and seeds contain bitter tannins, and although red wines need some tannins to help them age and give them character, too many are not good, so the stalks are removed. Where the grapes are picked by hand, a machine that looks like a giant corkscrew presses the pulp, skins, and seeds through, leaving the stalks behind; what comes out is called 'must' – or *mosto*.

The must is pumped into large tanks of stainless steel, vitrified cement, or wood, where it begins to ferment. Yeasts (either naturally present or added) heat the mass as they convert the grapes' natural sugar into alcohol, giving off carbon dioxide. The heat must be controlled and should not exceed 25°C to 32°C (77°F to 89°F). (Winemakers used to cool tanks by hosing them down with cold water, but modern steel tanks have built-in coolers.) As the gas rises to the top of the tank, it pushes the skins up into a thick layer called the 'cap'. This should be pushed back down to the bottom of the tank, usually twice a day, to keep the skins in contact with the fermenting juice. That is now done by pumping juice up from below and over the cap, forcing it back down. This fermentation process 'on the skins' may last from one to several weeks, depending on the style of wine being made. For red wines that are intended to be drunk young, and that do not require excessive tannins, the fermenting juice may be separated from the skins and seeds after just a few days and put into another tank to finish its fermentation.

At this point, a second, 'malolactic' fermentation may occur naturally or be induced – a bit of ambient heat starts the wine fermenting again. *La malolattica*, as it is called in Italy, transforms malic acid (as in apples) into lactic acid (as in milk), and the result is a mellower, softer wine. The wine may then be kept in steel vats until bottling or aged in wooden barrels, large or small. Large casks in Italy (*botti*) were often made of chestnut but are now usually Slavonian oak. Large casks hardly impart any of the wood's character to the wine, as the ratio of wood to liquid is very low. Modern-style wines are usually put in small French oak barrels called barriques. These barrels do affect the wine's flavour and structure, giving it added tannins and a woody, toasted taste.

Wine may be aged for anything from a few months to a hundred years – depending on the grape type and structure – in steel, old or new wood, glass, or a mixture of them all. The ageing process continues in the bottle, which is why many 'big' red wines need prolonged cellaring to give their best.

Dry white wine (which may also be made from red grapes) is made somewhat differently, as contact with the skins (and their tannins) is not usually desirable. Here the grapes are softly pressed to

*The hills of Irpinia
seen from Nusco,
majestic in the
morning mists*

separate the juice from the skins and seeds. The juice is filtered
before being fermented at slightly lower temperatures than red wine
in order to keep its flavours fresh and aromatic, usually for ten to
fourteen days. The wine is then run off the sludge of dead yeasts; it
may or may not undergo the secondary malolactic fermentation.
Some modern-style whites are fermented in barriques to give them
more complex flavours and the ability to age longer than normal
white wines.

Campania can boast over a hundred indigenous – or autochthonous – grape varieties; the Region's Agricultural department has
recently catalogued them and is carrying out experiments in vineyards throughout the region to explore their modern potential.

For information on wine courses or sommeliers, contact:
AIS (Associazione Italiana Sommeliers), INTERNET www.
aiscampania.it. In Napoli: c/o Franco Continisio, Enoteca
Mercadante, Corso Vittorio Emanuele, 643, TEL 081 680964.
In Caserta: c/o Vincenzo Ricciardi, Enoteca La Botte, Via Nazionale
Appia, 166-180, Casagiove; TEL 0823 494040.

Chapter 1

Caserta

Kings, shepherds and wines

*Only in these regions can one understand what vegetation really is
and what led man to invent the art of cultivation. The country
round Caserta is completely flat and the fields are worked on till
they are as smooth and tidy as garden beds. All of them are planted
with poplars on which vines are trained, yet in spite of the shadow
they cast, the soil beneath them produces the most perfect crops.*
J. W. Goethe Italian Journey 16 March 1787

TOURIST INFORMATION
E. P. T. Palazzo Reale
81100 Caserta
TEL 0823 322233
INTERNET
www.casertaturismo.it
E-MAIL
a.raiano@ept.caserta.it

In the province of Caserta lies the area the Romans called
'Campania Felix': fortunate – or blessed, we might say – for its
mild climate and extraordinarily fertile land. Here, as in other
parts of Campania, millennia of volcanic activity left their mark
on the land, giving soils so rich in minerals that crops could be
grown on them two, three, even four times a year without difficulties. The Samnites set up in the hills, the Greeks along the
coast, the Oscans in the plains, and the Romans went to war
with all of them to keep possession of this precious 'market garden'. Indeed, for centuries Campania Felix fed first Rome and
later the Kingdom of Naples. The area is also known as Terra di
Lavoro, 'land of work', though some historians suggest it may
have been so dubbed in the Middle Ages from the Latin *terra
Leboriæ* – i.e. the land of the Leborini peoples who lived there.
The Casertano was the gateway to the Mezzogiorno; it hosted
the revolt of Spartacus, and saw the passage of both Horace and
Virgil along the Via Appia (today sadly ruined visually by commercial construction for a good part of its length). Capua, after
being taken from Hannibal's Carthaginians, became one of the
most important cities in the Roman Empire.

EATING AND DRINKING
If the province of Caserta formed an important stopping place
on the Grand Tour, today it is less known than other parts of
Campania, save for the great palace at Caserta that reminds
many travellers of Versailles. Yet the area offers a cultural – and
gastronomic – range that is impressive. Less than an hour's drive

*Opposite: Vegetables at
Le Campestre, Castel di
Sasso*

from the Bourbon silkworks of San Leucio, or the spectacular formal gardens Vanvitelli designed for the Reggia di Caserta, are rustic stone and tufa villages where goats are milked by hand and cheeses matured in flasks – a method that has its roots in antiquity.

The volcanoes of Roccamonfina and the Campi Flegrei are now considered extinct, but their slopes still give character and intensity to the fruits and vines that grow on them. And the coastal plain still features the unique rows of poplars and high festooning vines that so impressed Goethe.

Today, the Casertano is known for its buffalo mozzarella (different in taste and texture from that made in the Salerno plain). And its fruits, like the native apple, Mela Annurca, which is picked green and allowed to ripen to red on beds of straw, or the chestnuts of Roccamonfina, which grow under the volcano – both have IGP status. The small, crunchy Mastantuono pear with its long stem and round body is now hard to find, but exquisitely juicy and full of flavour. Olive oil is produced from 8,000 hectares of olive groves in the province, and includes the varieties Caiazzana, Cecinella and Tonda. When carefully culti-

Mela Annurca apples vated and milled, these produce excellent oils. *Salumi* include

those made with the well-flavoured Maiale Nero Casertano.

As for the wines, the province's three DOCs (Asprinio d'Aversa, Falerno del Massico, Galluccio) have been joined by equally prestigious IGTs that include the indigenous grapes Casavecchia and Pallagrello – a favourite at the Bourbon court.

Farmers still use the ape to go to the market

Prata Sannita

Miralago

Castello del Matese

Piedimonte Matese

Presenzano

Galluccio

Vairano Patenora

Alife

San Potito Sannitico

Conca di Campania

Pietravairano

San Carlo di Sessa Aurunca

Vairano Scalo

Gioia Sannitica

Roccamonfina

Caianello

Dragoni

Puglianello

Ponte

Teano

Liberi

Telese

Fasani

Sessa Aurunca

San Marco

Castel di Sasso

Cellole

Pontelatone

Castel Campagnano

Francolise

Caiazzo

Nocelleto

Bellona

Dugenta

San Leucio

Mondragone

Capua

Casertavecchia

Sant'Agata
de' Goti

Casagiove

CASERTA

Cancello ed Arnone

Maddaloni

Castel Volturno

Marcianise

Villa Literno

Aversa

Lusciano di Aversa

Acerra

Afragola

NAPOLI

Pozzuoli

Aversa

Wine Shop

Via Belvedere, 50
TEL/FAX 081 5038361
CLOSED Sun p.m., Mon

Enoteca Il Vino

Aversa has given its name to one of the historic wines of the region, Asprinio d'Aversa DOC (see next entry for its main producer), so it's fitting that this Norman city should have a fine wine shop within it – dug into the tufa, not far from the cathedral that contains some of Campania's most important Romanesque remains. You'll find all the best Campanian wines as well as good selections from other regions. On the last Friday evening of every month, wines are accompanied by free tastings of traditional dishes.

Aversa: Lusciano

Aversa is particularly celebrated for a light wine called Asprinio, which is said to be made from vines originally imported into the Neapolitan provinces by Murat from Champagne, in the hope of establishing that exhilarating beverage in his new kingdom.

E. Neville-Rolfe Naples in the Nineties

Wine

Vico De Nicola, 7
TEL 081 8141386
348 5803913
FAX 081 8129507
E-MAIL
info@iborboni.com
Cellar visits by
appointment

I Borboni

Lusciano is a suburb of Aversa (whose cathedral is well worth visiting), and I Borboni's cellar is in a tangle of narrow streets in its city centre. The building has been attractively refurbished around the inner courtyard that characterizes so many 16th-century noble *palazzi*. Carlo Numeroso is at present the only producer left of Asprinio d'Aversa DOC, one of Campania's historic wines. The Asprinio grapes that go into it – and their unique way of growing – have been described for centuries, if not millennia, by visitors to the coastal plains between Caserta and Naples (despite Neville-Rolfe's diverting theory).

The vines are planted 7–8 metres apart, interspersed at regular intervals by poplar (or, occasionally, peach) trees and are trained up into and between the trees. Some reach the amazing height of 13–15 metres – three storeys high. One of the company's oldest vines is almost 700 years old and 40 centimetres in diameter. Protected by the saline marshes and salt winds, the vines resisted the deadly phylloxera attack that killed almost all other vineyards in Europe at the beginning of the 20th century. Watching the Asprinio harvest is a wonderful spectacle as nimble men, young and old, scurry up steep ladders to clip the grapes into traditional pointed baskets (*fescine*), which are then lowered to the ground.

High up on a narrow ladder to pick the Asprinio grapes

'One plant trained *ad alberata* can produce up to three to four quintals of grapes – an unbelievable amount – but the wine made from them never reaches 10° as the yield is too high,' explains Numeroso. 'Now, by pruning the vines down to man-height, we get wines with good structure and an average of 13° alcohol, with each plant giving about six to seven kilos. These lower vineyards were first planted in the 1960s, from cuttings of the big plants on their own roots, so it has been like cloning the indigenous vines of the area.'

In I Borboni's ten hectares of Asprinio, both growing methods are still being used: the *alberata* is best for *spumanti* as it gives more acidity and lower alcohol, while the man-high vines are better for still and dessert wines as they give more structure, higher alcohol gradations, and less acidity.

'In the early 1970s, Asprinio went through a decline – indeed it all but disappeared. When the last big client, a firm making *spumante* and brandy from 300,000 quintals of Asprinio, closed no one wanted it any more. The Campania region even offered incentives to pull the vines down.' In the mid-1970s, Carlo Numeroso's father and brother, with an œnologist from the north, felt that Asprinio still had potential, and began to develop other systems to maintain the grape's unique qualities. Thanks to their persistence, Asprinio di Aversa became a DOC in 1993. Their cellar, dug thirteen metres down in the tufa, is full of soft presses and modern vinification equipment. Working with œnologist Maurizio De Simone, they now produce a range of four wines from Asprinio – a Charmat-method *spumante*; two still wines; a *passito* aged in cherry wood – as well as wines from Coda di Volpe, Aglianico and Casavecchia.

Caiazzo

Pizzeria

Piazza Porta Vetere, 4
TEL 0823 868401
INTERNET
www.pizzeriapepe.8k.com
CLOSED Mon
PRICE €-€€

Opposite: the fescine basket is emptied into harvesting crates

Antica Osteria Pizzeria Pepe
When pizza is good, it is sublime, and I had one of my favourites in this little pizzeria in the tree-shaded central *piazza* of Caiazzo. Like many good things, it didn't happen by accident. My friends Manuela and Peppe, the wine producers from Terre del Principe (see pp. 66-68), raved about it. The *calzone con scarola* was a revelation: a puffed, thin-crusted pizza, browned and fragrant from the wood-burning oven, came stuffed with escarole, capers, and native Caiazzo olives. I could taste the bitter-sweet notes of the olive oil they had used to dress it.

'The secret of this pizza, which is a traditional recipe from our area,' explains Massimiliano Pepe, one of three brothers

Da Pepe's calzone with scarola and olives

who now run the family pizzeria, 'is that we don't boil the *scarola* first. When you enclose the vegetables in the dough and place them in our hot, wood-burning oven, it acts like a pressure cooker and cooks them in just sixty seconds.' But it wasn't only the filling that had seduced me: the crust itself was so soft and light.

'Our father and grandfather were great *pizzaioli*,' says Franco who, like his brothers, has another career but carries on the pizzeria in memory of their father. 'They always kneaded the dough by hand. We have kept this tradition alive even in this mechanized age.'

'We wouldn't know how to make pizza any other way,' adds Nino. 'Father used to say that you had to caress the dough to get it right. How can you do that with a machine?'

The brothers' *'vera pizza napoletana'* is also excellent. Its pastry base is fluffier, topped with fresh *pomodorini* and basil, local mozzarella, and more of that fruity extra-virgin oil. For a crust as good as this, rigid measurements won't work. 'The perfect crust should be soft, high, crisp underneath and cooked through,' explains Franco. They use a 'mother' starter (and sell it too for those who want to make their own). As for the flour, they favour a combination of 'soft' '0' and '00' flours that can be adapted according to the weather and the 'feel' of the day. 'Our dough is not as elastic as that made from the commercial mixes most *pizzerie* now use,' says Massimiliano. 'You can't throw ours in the air. But it is finer in texture. What's important is to know when you have reached the *punto di pasta* – the point at which you must stop kneading or the dough will become over-stretched.'

In addition to the range of pizzas on offer, the Pepe family also cook two or three seasonal dishes from the local repertoire – fried *baccalà* with oven-dried olives, or the decisive *zuppa di soffritto*, a rustic soup of pork organs that was a winter favourite with the *contadini*. In summer, eat outside in the *piazza* as you watch village life unfold.

Pastries

Via Cattabeni, 22
TEL 0823 868707

Pasticceria Michele Sparono

A few steps down from Caiazzo's central square, Michele Sparono specializes in pastries featuring almond paste – *pasta di mandorla* – like his *ricciarelli*, made with almonds ground more finely than those you find in Tuscany. His other speciality is *sospiro d'angelo*, a rich, semi-frozen dome-cake layered with custard, chocolate chips and nuts, and dusted with cocoa powder. No wonder the angels sigh for it.

Restaurant

Via Monte, 1
TEL 0823 610788
FAX 0823 610788
CLOSED Mon
CARDS All
PRICE €€€

Le Volte di Annibale e Bacco

Giovanni Ascione's idea for a restaurant located in the heart of this fertile countryside was to present a *cucina di terra* that could make the most of the local produce. So his menu features the meats, cheeses and many vegetables of the Casertano. The meats include some unusual and well-flavoured choices: buffalo, duck, Podolico beef, Laticauda mountain lamb, and the native Maialino Nero, or black pig (see pp. 82-83).

'This breed went out of fashion for many years as it is fattier than the others, but now it is being rediscovered as it has much more flavour and can only be reared outdoors,' he explains as we sit over lunch on his pretty vine-covered terrace overlooking the valley of the Volturno. 'These were poor areas whose local cuisine used very little meat other than organs and off-cuts. But now we are rediscovering our heritage and rescuing these fine breeds from extinction.' The only fish you'll find here are the *pesci di terra* – salt cod, stockfish and salted anchovies – that are closer in tradition to land than to sea.

Hand-picked field greens

Pastas are hand-made, vegetables are used creatively, and there is an interesting selection of local cheeses like the decisive Provolone del Monaco, or Conciato Romano produced in the hills nearby (see pp. 69-71) to go with the ample menu of Campanian (and other) wines. A perfect place for a relaxed, affordable, and gastronomically stimulating meal.

Cancello ed Arnone

Mozzarella

Via Agnena, km 0,500
TEL 0823 856267

Caseificio Agnena

This dairy produces pasteurized *mozzarella di bufala* from the herds belonging to the three partners in this company who are able to control exactly what the animals eat. Their shop is open daily from 7.30 to 20.00.

Capua

Masseria is the name in southern Italy for a farmhouse; in the outskirts of this town are two farms making fruit and vegetable preserves:
Masseria Giò Sole (Via Giardini, 31; TEL 0823 961108) specializes in fine conserves and *limoncello*. Masseria La Colombaia (Via Grotte di San Lazzaro, 9; TEL 0823 968262) is a certified organic farm that produces fresh vegetables and bottled preserves.

Caserta

The new castle is a palace worthy of a king, a huge quadrilateral building like the Escorial with a number of inner courtyards. Its location is extraordinarily beautiful – upon one of the most fertile plains in the world with a park extending to the feet of the mountains... The gardens are beautifully laid out and in perfect harmony with a region that is itself a garden.'

J. W. Goethe Italian Journey 14 March 1787

PALAZZO REALE
TEL 0823 277430
FAX 0823 354516
INTERNET WWW.
turismoregionecampania.it

Built for Carlo II by the architect Luigi Vanvitelli, *la Reggia di Caserta* was completed in 1774. Its fantastical landscaped garden – with spectacular cascades and endless vistas – is still one of the greatest in Italy. The 1,200-room palace was built at a safe distance from Napoli, which was so often attacked as a strategic port. President Eisenhower, who visited the Reggia when Allied High Command took it for its headquarters in World War II, was less impressed: he described it simply as 'a castle near Naples'. Modern Caserta has been built on a grid around the Reggia – also known as Palazzo Reale.

The main avenue of the grounds [of Caserta's palace] is peopled with an enormous number of second-rate statues, of which the most celebrated group is that of Diana and Actæon which decorates the

The view of Caserta from high ground shows the Reggia's giant park running diagonally in the centre

large basin at the foot of the cascade. This basin… is used as a preserve for trout, which are caught and sent up to the royal dinner table at Rome weekly in Lent, to smooth over the austerity which the court (as in duty bound) exercises at that season. When we look at these beautiful fish swimming in goodly numbers in the foaming water at the foot of the waterfall, we cannot but reflect that to the ordinary mortal it would be no great hardship to make his dinner off one of them, especially if it were dished up by the chef of the Quirinal.

E. Neville-Rolfe Naples in the Nineties

Wine, Speciality Foods

Enoteca La Botte

Via Nazionale Appia, 166–80
Casagiove
TEL 0823 494040
FAX 0823 468130
E-MAIL
info@ enotecalabotte.it
INTERNET
www.enotecalabotte.it
CLOSED Sun

This is one of the great Italian wine shops: you can't miss its wide storefront and enticing window displays – on the main road that leads from the Caserta Nord *autostrada* exit to the Reggia of Caserta. Inside, the choice is overwhelming: more than 20,000 labels of wine, whiskeys, rare rums, grappas, and liqueurs of all types compete for space with pyramids of chocolates, dried fruits, conserves, preserves – just about everything a gourmet could hope for. There are counters of fresh and aged cheeses and *salumi*, and fine selections of olive oils, pastas and other local products that make great presents to take home. You can understand why Vincenzo Ricciardi, its owner, was awarded an 'Oscar' for best *enoteca* in Italy in 1999.

'We also offer a *caveau* service,' says the dynamic Ricciardi. 'We put bottles down for people who don't have the correct cellars to store them in – particularly important in a climate as hot as ours.' There are plans afoot to create a family trattoria (with

CASERTA MOZZARELLA DOP

If Campania is rightly famous for its exceptional *mozzarella di bufala*, it is thanks to two areas of production: the flat plain between Salerno and Paestum (see p. 248-51), and the province of Caserta. In both you will find many dairies along the roads selling their products, often next to a wood-fired bakery making the *pane casereccia* that accompanies it so well. Both areas include what were once coastal swamplands – a type of landscape favoured by the moisture-loving buffaloes. And although the cheeses from these two zones are similar, there are subtle variations in taste and texture that lead people to prefer one over the other.

Buffalo

'One reason for this difference,' explains Salvatore De Gennaro, cheese expert and owner of Campania's best cheese store and delicatessen, La Tradizione at Seiano, near Vico Equense (see pp. 217-19), 'is that in the Casertano there is a tradition of adding a little of the whey from the day before to the milk as it is being made into cheese – rather like a sourdough starter in breadmaking. This *cizza*, as it is known here, adds more acidity to the cheese, giving it a hint of the flavour of yoghurt. For those of us who prefer the Casertano, the Salernitano seems sweeter – easier to like, perhaps, but less complex.'

For a full description of how mozzarella is made, see pp. 248-251. For more information about Mozzarella di Bufala DOP: Consorzio di Tutela della Mozzarella di Bufala Campana, Viale Carlo III, 128/b, S. Nicola La Strada CE, TEL 0823 424780, INTERNET www.mozzarelladop.it.

Plaited mozzarella stars at a buffet lunch

local grandmothers taking turns at doing the cooking) in a large space next door to the shop. So treat yourself to some time in this monument of œnogastronomic culture.

Where to go for lunch (or dinner) in Caserta
Antica Hostaria Massa 1848 (Via Mazzini, 55; TEL 0823 456527; E-MAIL info@ristorantemassa.it) This centrally located, rustic restaurant–pizzeria has been a fixture in Caserta for as long as anyone can remember. Five years ago it was brightened up and given a new lease of life. Now it's a good place for classic trattoria dishes and pizzas in a convivial atmosphere. Another possibility for lunch before or after a visit to the Reggia, also within easy walking distance, is Ristorante Le Colonne (Via Nazionale Appia, 7–13; TEL 0823 467494) The dining room is spacious, with 1970s décor. The menu is a mixture of innovative recipes based on traditional *cucina* (with creative use of buffalo and other local meats), and vegetarian dishes (with some esoteric ingredients). A limited wine list, good desserts, friendly service and owners.

At Mezzano (between Caserta and Casertavecchia), Enoteca Il Torchio (Via Gabriele Fusco, 10; TEL 0823 386264; CLOSED Sun) is a small but very fine *enoteca* – wine shop with tastings and cheeses – that specializes in Campanian wines as well as other Italian favourites.

Casertavecchia

Casertavecchia

On a clear day it's well worth driving up to the high medieval *borgo* of Casertavecchia, the original nucleus of Caserta before the present city was built down below. The views are exceptional: out over the plain of Caserta, past Napoli to Vesuvio, Capri and the sea. The Longobard village is remarkably unspoiled and it's fun to walk its narrow streets and visit the Romanesque cathedral. In summer the cool breezes offer respite from the hotter plains.

Take your pick of two good, age-old pizzerias (they also offer full menus for those wanting more) – they are right next to each other: La Rocca di Sant'Andrea (Via Torre, 8; TEL 0823 371232; CLOSED Mon in winter) and Da Teresa (Via Torre, 6; TEL 0823 371270. CLOSED Wed except in summer). Both are open for lunch and dinner, take credit cards, and offer panoramic dining.

At San Rocco, just outside of Casertavecchia, is Ristorante Gli Scacchi (TEL 0823 371086) for simple traditional food, well prepared.

Castel Campagnano

Wine

Via Chiesa, 35
TEL 0824 972460
FAX 0824 972740
E-MAIL
info@castelloducale.com
INTERNET
www.castelloducale.com

Castello Ducale

Antonio Donato's winery is located in a beautiful castle on the border between the provinces of Caserta and Benevento. Like most defensive castles, it's in a dominant position, with views in all directions over the countryside. It was built over centuries, between the late Byzantine period and the 18th century, when it belonged to the Countess Ferrara, and served as a hunting lodge for Ferdinando IV. The lofty wine cellars are spectacular, carved right out of the tufa mountain. Donato is presently working with œnologist Angelo Pizzi on the wines, whose production is currently 80,000 bottles. Of these, 10,000 are Pallagrello and 5,000 Casavecchia – the two recently 'rediscovered' Bourbon grape varieties. 'I prefer fruity wines that are not dominated by wood,' he says. 'I also cultivate organically, but I don't push that aspect of my wines. It's enough for them to express themselves cleanly.' Good news for castle-lovers: the plan is to convert some of the noble rooms into a luxury hotel.

Wine

Contrada Mascione
TEL 081 8541125
335 878791
E-MAIL
terredelprincipe@libero.it
INTERNET
www.terredelprincipe.com

Terre del Principe

This new winery is an œnological phoenix risen from the ashes of another estate, Vestini Campagnano, that made its name 'rediscovering' two great indigenous grape varieties – Pallagrello and Casavecchia. (The 2003 *Vini d'Italia* wine guide awarded the Casavecchia its highest rating, *Tre Bicchieri*). Sadly, the partnership that created Vestini Campagnano 'divorced' in May 2003. Giuseppe Mancini, who was the primary mover in the winery and responsible for its success, kept the vineyards but lost the name (despite Vestini being his mother's maiden name). His ex-partner, Alberto Barletta, kept the name and the cellar but lost almost all the vineyards.

Manuela Piancastelli

Peppe Mancini and his wife, wine-writer Manuela Piancastelli, moved a few kilometres down the road, set up another *cantina*, and started again. In the split, they were followed not only by their œnologist, Luigi Moio, but also by the *contadini* who had produced grapes (under the supervision of Mancini's agronomist) for Vestini from the beginning, eight years ago. So the name may have changed but the new wines will be the same – or better. They now have eleven hectares of vineyards – three of their own and eight rented. I was curious about these two unusual grape varieties. 'The red Casavecchia is a very old Campanian *uvaggio*,' explains Peppe, 'and it's extremely productive on vines that are in some cases over a hundred years old.'

'Almost nothing is known of it,' adds Manuela. 'But in the 1930s, pre-phylloxera Casavecchia plants were found near remains of a Roman villa. Their DNA shows that it is not related to other grape types. It must be an ancient variety – maybe even the Tribulanum of antique fame.' Casavecchia is traditionally trained onto wires three metres high as it grows from the fourth bud upwards and shouldn't be pruned short; the Mancinis choose instead to train it low (to 1.5 metres) but prune it long. The couple's success with Casavecchia has had interesting consequences for this area as many growers are emulating them, revitalizing existing Casavecchia vineyards, or converting new ones to this previously undervalued grape type.

Pallagrello, another native variety that exists in both red and white versions, was very important in the 18th century. Manuela explains: 'Ferdinando IV, the Bourbon king, planted a fan-shaped vineyard at San Leucio (see p. 80) with the ten grape varieties that were most important for the Kingdom of the Two Sicilies. Pallagrello was the only Campanian variety to be included in this beautiful *vigna del ventaglio*.' At that time, the vines were named Piedimonte Nero and Bianco for the mountainous area they grew in.

Manuela's tomatoes drying in the sun

'From the Piedimonte area in the 16th century, it made its way along the Volturno river to Caiazzo, where it arrived in the 19th century,' continues Peppe. 'In 1750, Pallagrello vineyards were planted to a density of 7–8,000 plants per hectare; the grape's very round berries also earned it the name of *la Pilleolata*.'

When Mancini, a lawyer from Caserta province, bought his country house and land in 1990, his thought was to make wine for the family. The neighbouring *contadini* explained that the prevalent grape variety in this valley near Caiazzo had been Pallagrello. He located a few very old Pallagrello plants and took cuttings. 'I started by planting 400 vines, and made the first wine as my grandfather had. We drank it from *damigiane* – demijohns.' He started reading about making wine. 'Angelo Pizzi, the œnologist then with the Cantina del Taburno (see pp. 415-416) wanted to study this unknown variety in the context of modern vinification. Our first stainless-steel tanks were cooled by wellwater and ice,' laughs Peppe. 'Quite a difference from today's temperature-controlled tanks.' A meeting in 2000 with œnologist Luigi Moio proved decisive: research had begun began on Pallagrello's DNA with the experimental viti-vinicultural institute at San Michele all'Adige, in the north of Italy. Until then, Pallagrello was thought to be related to Coda di Volpe, but tests established it to be a different variety. With Moio, Pallagrello grapes underwent five years of micro-vinification. 'At that time neither Casavecchia nor Pallagrello were in the region's register of vinifiable varieties,' says Peppe. 'But by 2002, thanks to this research, they were admitted and no longer consigned to the *abusivi*, or "unauthorized", category.' The Terre del Volturno IGT followed; DOCs Pallagrello delle Colline Caiatine and Casavecchia di Pontelatone will become operational in 2005.

As for the grapes, both red varieties are late to mature, with harvesting in mid to late October. They undergo long macerations of 15–22 days and, after fermentation in steel, the wines go into new barriques for 12 months, spending 6 more in the bottle. Casavecchia has low acidity and very high anthocyanins, so its colour is intense. It also has very low malic acid and does not require the malo-lactic fermentation. 'It's a bit like Merlot,' says Manuela. 'With its immediate *morbidità*, it could be used to "better" other wines. Pallagrello Nero is also deep in colour; it has higher acidity than Casavecchia but less than Aglianico.'

Mancini and Piancastelli make two whites from Pallagrello Bianco: Fontanavigna is fermented in steel, Le Serole in new barriques. (The barrique grapes are picked eight days later to have a bit more maturity.) The steel comes out in March; the barrique-fermented has a few months in the bottle and comes out in summer. Both reflect Pallagrello's richness, with balanced acidity and good length. As for the new reds, Pallagrello Nero, in a wine called Ambruco, is proclaiming itself to be elegant, long and well-structured, with tannins to carry it into long ageing. Centomoggia, of red Casavecchia, demonstrates this variety's big range of perfumes and intense colour. Like their predecessors, these wines have a clear identity and character.

Terre del Principe's wines are pure: no other grapes are included. (The DOC's regulations, the *Disciplinari*, forbid the addition of other varieties.) New vineyards have been planted at densities of about 5,000 vines per hectare – less than the Bourbons'. Judging from first results, Terre del Principe is bound to be a success; thanks to Mancini's belief in them, Casavecchia and Pallagrello are becoming sought-after varieties. So here's to the launch of a great new winery: *auguri*.

Wine

Via Barraccone, 5
TEL 0823 862770
E-MAIL vestini
campagnano@inwind.it
INTERNET www.
vestinicampagnano.it

Vestini Campagnano

After the directors split (see above) this winery has had to begin again too (though they kept the wines that were being made in the estate's cellars); they have engaged a fine œnologist, Paolo Caciorgna, but their new vineyards are not yet fully in production. So we'll wait and see how things go.

Vineyard below the village of Castel di Sasso

Via Strangolagalli, 4
TEL 0823 878277
340 3567062
E-MAIL
info@lecampestre.it
INTERNET
www.lecampestre.it
OPEN
All year by reservation only

Castel di Sasso

Cheese, Restaurant, Agriturismo, Organic Produce
Agriturismo Le Campestre
Livia Liliana Lombardi's Le Campestre is everything a country *agriturismo*–farm should be: it is located in beautiful, unspoiled countryside with woods, tiny stone villages and great views just twenty kilometres from Caserta; grows very pretty flowers and has productive, organic vegetable and herb gardens; makes hand-made cheeses from its own sheep; has ducks, geese, cats and dogs. And it has a wonderful restaurant with an outdoor terrace, where Livia and her mother cook genuine food that is traditional to their area. In winter a hearthfire provides warmth and a delicious way to grill meats. The three guest rooms are simply but comfortably furnished with antiques and personal touches.

'We want people to feel at home here,' says the welcoming Livia, who has run the farm for twenty years, and opened the *agriturismo* five years ago. Why organic, I asked? (It's still an all-too-rare choice in southern Italy.) 'The area all around us is completely uncontaminated,' she says, as we walk up through her vineyard planted to the local grape, Casavecchia, 'so it seemed a travesty to use chemical fertilizers or pesticides here.'

Livia has become well known for the unusual cheese she produces: Conciato Romano. She explains: 'The Conciato gets its name from an ancient cheese that was found near here, stored

*Livia and the freshly
made cheeses*

*Opposite:
Conciato Romano
cheeses ageing in a
glass flask*

in Roman amphoræ – and we presume that this cheese is similar to that made by the Romans.' Livia makes raw-milk cheese from her herd of sheep and goats all year long, but only from January to May can she produce those that will be aged in flasks. 'These cheeses weigh about 100 grams each – small enough to fit through the neck of large glass flasks. After they are made, I place them out to dry on a cold balcony for several days until firm. They are then "washed" with the water that pasta has been boiled in (for the starch), and placed inside the flasks, with a mix of walnut leaves, wild thyme, extra virgin olive oil, vinegar and hot *peperoncino*. They are shaken in the mixture, and left to age in a cool dark place to keep damp. The cheeses need to "weep" in the aromatic mixture.' The *conciatura* (*conciare* means to cure or pickle) lasts from six to ten months. Then it's ready to eat. Livia likes to serve her Conciato Romano at the end of a meal. 'I always keep enough for my customers here at the restaurant. There is a big demand now that Slow Food has discovered the cheese, and has made a Presidium – a project to assist artisan producers – for it,' she says. 'But there are very few producers of authentic Conciato,' she says modestly. Indeed, she's the only one I have been able to find.

Castello del Matese

Hotel

Miralago
TEL 0823 919315

Hotel Ristorante Miralago
At the time of going to press, this lovely hotel's restaurant was undergoing a change, as its successful chef was leaving... so we'll have to wait and see how the cuisine develops, but the hotel is anyway worth a visit for its beautiful setting and comfortable rooms.

Cellole

Wine, Agriturismo

Strada Statale Domitiana,
18
TEL 0823 932088
FAX 0823 932134
E-MAIL
info@fattoriavillamatilde.
com
INTERNET
www.fattoriavillamatilde.
com

Villa Matilde
I heard of Villa Matilde's wines long before I came to Campania to write this book: indeed, it was one of a handful of new Campanian wineries that in the 1990s successfully projected an image of quality, modernity and terroir outside of the region. Villa Matilde's story began much earlier, in the 1940s, as the result of the hobby horse of a Neapolitan lawyer and scholar: Francesco Avallone wanted to re-create a wine that the Ancient Romans – from Horace to Pliny – had lauded as the greatest of

the south – Falerno. 'My father and his *maestro*, Arangio Ruiz, spent over twenty years trying to solve the question of what that legendary wine had been like,' says Salvatore Avallone who, with his sister Maria Ida, has run the winery since 1984. 'Ultimately, the issue was not so much which grape varieties went into the wine, but which land those grapes were grown on,' he continues. 'For the wine that was considered so excellent by the Romans was a balsamic syrup, diluted with sea water and flavoured with honey and herbs... clearly not anything we would drink as wine today. However, the land it was grown on is the same as it was then.' During the research, Avallone became convinced that Falerno must have been produced from grape varieties brought to Italy by the Greeks 3,500 years ago, for there was no large-scale winemaking before that civilization. 'For the white Falerno, this would have meant an antecedent of Falanghina. As for the red, he excluded Primitivo, as it came from Puglia and had a completely different provenance. That left the Aglianico family and he set about trying to find examples of it in the area.' (For another theory on this, see p. 76.)

Unfortunately, most of Europe's grape vines were devastated by the deadly phylloxera aphid at the end of the 19th century, but Avallone discovered that some plants had survived the attack. From these, the *contadini* had fortunately preserved a few vines for their kitchen gardens, and Avallone was able to take cuttings from twenty plants – fifteen reds and five whites – some of which were well over a hundred years old.

'This led my father to buy land in this area – historically the birthplace of Falerno – and his experimental vineyards soon became a serious venture that needed more than weekend care.' Salvatore and his sister decided to give up their other careers to develop the estate, and adopted a more modern, professional approach. 'We wanted a personal style, but those were difficult times in the south – especially in the wine business.' In 1996 they engaged œnologist Riccardo Cotarella, who had begun working with both Silvia Imparato (pp. 269-71) and Galardi (pp. 79-80). 'He came from central Italy, but was sensitive to the flavours and quality of southern Italian wines, and he was always able to produce full, expressive wines that we admired.' At first Cotarella pushed to plant international varieties rather than the indigenous grapes Avallone had found, but he soon realized the potential of these lesser-known vines.

The relationship has been very successful, and today Villa Matilde is one of Campania's senior estates, with over sixty hectares and a well-rounded list – including both white and red Falernos, and fine Falanghinas. There is even an unusual

Falanghina *passito*, Eleusi, that is elegant and not overly sweet.
The Avallones also run an *agriturismo* and restaurant from the
winery.

Conca della Campania

Agriturismo
Agriturismo La Palombara

Via I Novembre, 149
Cave di Conca della
Campania
TEL 0823 679074
INTERNET
www.lapalombara.com

A beautiful 19th-century *borgo* is the setting for this attractive
agriturismo, complete with livestock.

See also La Caveja (p.76)

Fasani di Sessa Aurunca

Agriturismo
Masseria Pietrachiara

Via Palombi, 24
TEL/FAX 0823 706396
INTERNET
www.pietrachiara.com

Most *agriturismi* in Campania have been opened so recently
that one needs a good imagination to picture how they will look
in ten years' time, once the plants have grown up around the
buildings, and the stone and paintwork have faded just enough
to look artfully aged. So it's a real pleasure to discover a beautiful country house that has been created with style, and a garden
that has had time to grow into itself. Count Giuseppe
Matarazzo di Licosa and his wife Totaia first opened
Pietrachiara as a children's camp many years ago, but recently
they decided to change tacks and refurbished their 19th-century
farmhouse – which they bought as a ruin and completely rebuilt
– as a comfortable luxury hideaway, complete with large private
swimming pool and an in-house restaurant (non-guest
customers are welcome in summer, but must book ahead) that
serves simple but delicious local dishes, using mostly the organic
vegetables grown on the farm. It's the kind of place where you
feel so comfortable you don't want to leave.

*Totaia Matarazzo with
her homemade pizzette*

Francolise

Olive oil
Monte della Torre

Via Appia Km 184.5
TEL/FAX 0823 882073
338 1793523

This olive-producing farm, on the Via Appia between Capua
and the sea, has been in the family of Countess Franca Marinelli
Marulli since the 16th century. Her sons, Alberto and Antonio,
now run the oil-producing business, milling the small farm's
hand-picked olives of the Coratina, Pignarola, Leccino and

Frantoio varieties. They favour the Sinolea system for extracting the oil, a state-of-the-art machine that draws the oil free from the ground-up mass by the use of metal blades, ensuring that only the choicest part of the oil is extracted. The farm produces two lines of oil: Famiglia, which is a good, everyday oil, and Riserva, which is a more costly oil with an intensely vegetal fragrance of artichoke and green tomato, and a pleasant peppery bitterness to the taste. Both are for sale at the farm.

Galluccio

Wine, Restaurant

Telaro

Via Cinque Pietre
TEL 0823 925841
FAX 0823 925021
E-MAIL
info@vinitelaro.it
INTERNET
www.vinitelaro.it

The landscape on and around the extinct volcano, Roccamonfina, is one of my favourites: something of the soil's intensity is communicated in everything that grows there. The large Telaro family has long believed in this terroir, and the five brothers have become the standard-bearers for the local Galluccio DOC wines, working with the native Falanghina, Aglianico and Piedirosso varieties, as well as some Greco and Fiano for their Roccamonfina IGT wines. It's a large estate, with over 40 hectares of vineyards and 450,000 bottles produced. At the winery's headquarters, there is also a restaurant serving the home-cooked local dishes of the area, and rooms for visitors to stay in. Working with the Campania Region's agricultural sector, the Telaros have been participating in a project of experimental vineyards to establish which types of grapes – indigenous or otherwise – do best in the post-volcanic soils.

Marzuli di Sessa Aurunca

Olive Oil

Luigi Campione

Via Piazzetta, 1
TEL 0823 938893,
337 944244
FAX 081 5513240
Visits by appointment

Brothers Luigi and Bruno Campione have recently taken off on an interesting project: they want to relaunch a little-known indigenous olive variety, la Sessana, which was in danger of disappearing completely. Their family's villa, set in attractive countryside with widely spaced olive groves and a spectacular palm-tree avenue, has a large cultivation of these olives trees, but they were falling ill with disuse until the younger generation decided to intervene. 'We have 44 *moggi* of land here, 85 per cent of which is planted to olives,' says Luigi. '*Moggi*? What are they?' I ask. 'It's an old land-measuring term that our *contadini* still use,' he says, laughing. 'One *moggio* is 3.333 square metres, so 3 *moggi* make 1 hectare.' The Sessana, or Ciccinella, tree is low-

The post-volcanic landscape near Sessa Aurunca and the Massico mountain

yielding, and its fruit gives a delicately fruity oil with very low acidity – just right for subtle foods or for deep-frying. The brothers use a modern Pieralisi press at Sessa Aurunca for milling the olives, at temperatures below 25°C. The oil is available in bottles and cans, and can be bought by appointment from the farm.

Mondragone

Wine

Viale Margherita, 6
TEL/FAX 0823 978017
Cellar visits
by appointment

Azienda Vinicola Michele Moio

On one of the central streets of Mondragone, the largest coastal town on the flat shore of northern Campania that runs into Lazio, is an imposing doorway. Behind this protective entrance are the cellars of the Moio winery, built around three sides of a courtyard wide enough to accommodate several horses-and-carts. The Moio family – who live above the winery – have been in the wine trade for over 300 years. The old-fashioned farm buildings, with their cellars full of large barrels and museum-quality presses (now only on show) are witness to that.

So is their *padrone*, Michele Moio, now in his mid seventies. Like Mastroberardino (see pp. 325-326) and D'Ambra (see pp. 162-164), Moio is one of the legendary figures of Campanian wine history. He was the first, in the post-war 1950s, to bottle his family's wine, made from Primitivo grapes grown between Mondragone and the Massico mountain that sits to its north. Up until then the area's large wine production was all sold *sfuso* – unbottled.

'Unlike the land farther down the coast, which has been reclaimed, this area was never swampland,' explains Michele Moio, a dignified, upright man still very much in command of everything that goes on within that courtyard. 'Our Falerno is the wine that Horace, Virgil and Pliny wrote of. And to me, the only grape variety possible for producing Falerno is Primitivo. No other red grape thrives in this hot land of ours – indeed, I challenge anyone to show me good Aglianico growing close to the sea.' The Moios' Primitivo has existed in this area since the replantings of the early 1900s following the phylloxera attack that destroyed almost all the previously existing vineyards. Later growers introduced Aglianico into the area. When the DOC Falerno del Massico was drawn up in 1989, it was created to allow for two separate dominant grape varieties: Primitivo and Aglianico, as Michele Moio would not permit any Aglianico to be added into his wines. 'Up until forty years ago, this whole area was given over to grape cultivation, with 1,000 hectares of Primitivo in the province of Caserta, but now most of those vineyards are "under cement",' says Moio as he shakes his head. Luckily his defence of Falerno has safeguarded the continuation of this historic wine. You can taste it, along with his other affordable classics of pure Primitivo: Moio 57 and Gaurano. All three reflect the warmth, ripe-cherry sweetness, and unmistakable character of Primitivo – especially as expressed in this terroir.

Michele Moio

One of Michele's sons, Bruno, now works with his father at Mondragone. His other son, Luigi Moio (see also p. 353), is a professor of œnology, and consultant for some of Campania's most prestigious wineries. With his father, he has created a new modern-style wine, Maiatico Falerno del Massico, using Primitivo that is fermented and aged in barriques, and so is keeping the family at the cutting edge of Campanian wine-making.

Pietravairano

Restaurant, Hotel, Agriturismo
La Caveja

Via SS Annunziata, 10
TEL 0823 984824
FAX 0823 984342
E-MAIL
albergoristorantecaveja
@virgilio.it
CLOSED Sun eve; Mon
CARDS All
PRICE €€€

Berardino Lombardo's La Caveja is one of Campanian food-lovers' favourite restaurants: it is comfortably rustic, relaxed, moderately priced, convivial and offers the finest *sapori della campagna*: hand-made cheeses, hearty soups and pastas, and meats grilled in a huge open fireplace whose *profumi* remind you of your childhood. Following the seasons, Berardino uses all the wild foods that the woods and fields can provide. The dining rooms have wooden beams, stone floors, and copper pans on the walls, as well as a vast collection of wines to

Wild asparagus frittata

accompany the food. In summer, there's an outdoor terrace under the simple but attractive hotel rooms.

La Caveja is the proof that peasant culture is alive and well: a few kilometres from La Caveja, Berardino's farm, Terra di Conca, has opened as an *agriturismo*. There he raises and butchers his own pigs, which roam free in the woods hunting for acorns; breeds fowl for the table; and grows vegetables. The fields are flanked by a vast orchard with 32 varieties of rare apple, and there are olives in the groves: an idyllic country life.

Pontelatone

Buffalo Meat, Buffalo Cheeses

Via Pontepellegrino
TEL/FAX 0823 659104

Cooperativa La Baronia

There has always been one rather sorry by-product of delicious buffalo mozzarella: the male calves. In the female-dominated world of milk-giving, these little creatures had no chance. Many were just abandoned in the fields at birth or slaughtered for pet food. Recently this enterprising buffalo-milk cooperative has come up with a more dignified solution for this half of the buffalo population: the young calves are being raised for one year for their meat. The members have invested in airy pens for the calves, which are fed on grain and vegetable feeds. Their meat is either sold fresh, to be eaten like beef, or is used in buffalo *salumi* – salami, sausages, *bresaola*. Buffalo meat, when properly hung, is very tender; it is much leaner than beef, has more iron, fewer calories, and less cholesterol. So it's a healthy alternative to more traditional meats. La Baronia also produces buffalo cheeses, and is beginning to improve its wine, too.

Wine

Via Ragazzano, Funari
TEL 0823 301382
E-MAIL
info@trebulanum.com
INTERNET
www.trebulanum.com

Alois

The countryside couldn't be more beautiful and unspoiled around the Alois wine estate, with the Monte Maggiore to one side, and a slow descent towards the Volturno river on the other. 'We're in a natural amphitheatre,' explains Michele Alois, who has long run a successful family business in silk at San Leucio (see pp. 80-81), and is now completing his 'dream' of a winery with his sons: large modern buildings for the cellar and its headquarters, with recently planted vineyards all around. 'Like some of my neighbours, I'm fascinated by our Casertan indigenous grape varieties, Casavecchia and Pallagrello, and have invested most in them,' he says. He has also availed himself of star œnologists: first Angelo Pizzi, and now Riccardo Cotarella. Trebulanum, of Casavecchia aged in barriques, is the top wine so far.

Opposite: hand-made mozzarella

Presenzano

Cheese
Caseificio La Fenice

Via Vado Piano, 5
TEL 0823 989372
FAX 0823 989921

If it's great buffalo mozzarella you're after, this dairy is considered the best in the province of Caserta – which is full of mozzarella makers. Signor Cozzolino 'transforms' only the milk from his own herd of buffalo, so he can control exactly what they eat and, being up at 400 metres, this means that even in high summer the animals maintain a diet of fresh green forage. He makes his cheese from the still-warm milk, and works it at low temperatures, unpasteurized, to retain all its flavours and nutrients. The stables and dairy are of exemplary cleanliness, as is the shop where the mozzarellas, ricotta and other cheeses are on sale. If you're on your way north from Campania, stop in and stock up on cheeses to take to your next destination, in convenient styrofoam boxes – they taste even better the next day.

Puccianiello

Pasta
Il Manicaretto

Via SS Nome di Maria, 2
(5 km from Caserta)

This is a lovely pasta shop making many types of local pasta: *scialatielli*, *fusilli* and *stringozzi*, as well as stuffed *ravioli*.

Roccamonfina

This is the name of the now extinct volcano from which Ferrarelle mineral water – uniquely, naturally, lightly bubbly – comes. Its mineral-rich territory includes a string of pretty villages that circle Roccamonfina (see Conca della Campania, Ponte and San Carlo di Sessa Aurunca) and excellent products that go from wine to oil to cheese – as in the local speciality, Caso Peruto, a raw-milk goat's cheese aged for over one year with olive oil, vinegar and dried wild thyme from the mountain.

San Carlo di Sessa Aurunca

Wine, Olive Oil
Galardi

Strada Provinciale Sessa
Mignano, at Vallemarina
TEL 0823 925003
E-MAIL
galardi@napoli.com
INTERNET
www.terradilavoro.com

Maria Luisa Murena and her cousins, Dora and Francesco Catello, have the good fortune to live on a volcano – one that has been inactive for thousands of years. The volcanic soils of Roccamonfina are fertile, rich in minerals, and yield intensely flavoured fruits – be they grapes or olives. 'About fifteen years ago we of the younger generation of our family decided that we wanted to improve the wine that was being made here,' says Maria Luisa. With her late husband, Baron Roberto Maria Selvaggi, they began, as many do, by making a little wine for their own consumption. The wine was good and, through a friend, they brought it to the attention of œnologist Riccardo Cotarella, who was one of the first non-Campanians to appreciate the great potential of this region. He was immediately enthusiastic, and began a collaboration on the wine, called Terra di Lavoro, that continues today. 'In 1994 we produced a mere 650 bottles from our Aglianico and Piedirosso.' The 2003 vintage will yield 18,000 bottles and that figure will increase to 40,000 in four years' time when the newly planted vineyards come into production, 80% Aglianico and 20% Piedirosso. The wine is full of territorial character, austere yet intriguing, with balanced, fine tannins and impressive length.

'The family farm is big, and comprises chestnut woods as well as orchards,' explains Maria Luisa as we walk through the vineyards with their spectacular views of the valleys and distant coast below. 'Some wine had always been made here as the name of a nearby village, Vigne, testifies but in recent times there was pressure to plant fruit trees instead of grape vines.' The area suffered greatly in the Second World War as the German lines were nearby (another family villa was mined), and was also hit by the 1980 earthquake. 'When you really believe in a place, you'll do anything to defend it: here each little terrace of vines has its own character – in spring they are filled with wild strawberries – how can those qualities not find their way into a wine?'

San Leucio

COMPLESSO MONUMEN-
TALE DEL BELVEDERE
DI SAN LEUCIO
Via Atrio Superiore
TEL 0823 301817
FAX 0823 301706
INTERNET
www.belvederedisan
leucio.it

Close to Caserta is the *borgo* of San Leucio, with the spectacular Bourbon silkworks built in 1789 by Ferdinand IV. Despite being a conservative king, Ferdinand had a utopian vision of a community in which workers and their superiors would live in equal-sized houses, joined by a common goal to produce and manufacture the world's most exquisite silks. The palatial complex has been refurbished enough to make it fascinating to visit, and is now a museum of industrial archaeology. There are even some of the original looms and silk-winding machines, whose invention enabled the work of forty people to be done by one machine. Silk production gave the mulberry tree – the only food the silkworms liked – an important role in Campanian

The royal coat of arms above the gateway into San Leucio

agriculture. When silk ceased being produced in Campania (Chinese silk was cheaper), the mulberry trees were cut down: on the Amalfi Coast, which had once been covered by mulberries, they were replaced by lemons.

Silk

Annamaria Alois

ALTO ARTIGIANATO
TESSILE PER
L'ARREDAMENTO
TESSUTI D'ARTE
PASSAMANERIE
Via Planelli, 9 &
Via Quercione, 42
Briano
TEL 0823 304062
FAX 0823 363938
E-MAIL
annamariaaloisinteriors
@tin.it

Annamaria Alois comes from one of San Leucio's historic silk families: indeed, she represents the fourth generation of high-level silk production. But, until she had the courage to set up business on her own twenty years ago, it was a completely male-dominated field. 'Women were of course working at the looms and as dyers,' says the elegant Annamaria, 'but not at management level. I tried to persuade my father to let me join the firm but he was against it at the beginning.' She started working for free, selling her own designs; then she set up her own personal company which is now firmly established as one of the most exclusive for furnishing and designer silks. Her showroom features sumptuous antique and modern patterns in exquisite colours. As with all silks, these make wonderful table coverings for elegant dinner parties.

For a good meal nearby, Ristorante Leucio (Strada Panoramica; TEL 0823 301241) is worth a visit.

San Potito Sannitico

Farm, Restaurant, Agriturismo, Genetic Research Centre

Azienda Agrituristica Quercete

Via Provinciale per Gioia
TEL 0823 785924
E-MAIL quercete@tin.it
OPEN
Tues–Sat 9.00–13.30,
16.00–19.30;
Sun & hols 11.00–18.30
CLOSED Mon

TRATTORIA:
TEL 0823 911520
OPEN All year
CLOSED Sun eve, Mon
PRICE €€ for full meal.

SHOP:
TEL 330 543562

This enterprising farm is situated within the Parco del Matese, on sixty hectares of open country, gentle slopes that herald the higher, rougher Apennines. In 1979 Osvaldo Palmieri began a project to revive the Laticauda sheep which had been lost completely from this area, and were reduced to very small numbers in the high Beneventano and in Irpinia. 'This breed is particularly suited for the table,' explains Sergio, Osvaldo's son. 'It gets its Latin name from its unusually wide (*latis*) tail (*cauda*), which is used by the sheep as a fat deposit for withstanding the cold (much as a camel uses its hump to store water): they were cross-bred in the Bourbon era with male sheep from North Africa to make the Apennine races more robust.' Another of its characteristics is that, whereas most sheep give birth to one or at most three lambs, the Laticauda ewes often bear four or five. The flavour of the meat is very delicate, as it has lower quantities of volatile acidity. Likewise, the milk is sweeter: the animals give less of it, but it yields more cheese as the fat content is higher than other sheep's.

In 1987–91, the Agrarian University of Naples at Portici became involved and set up a genetic research centre to study the farm's rare animal breeds, and to establish sperm banks to protect them from extinction. At present the farm has about 500 sheep and 200 pigs. This is a lovely farm to visit, especially with children: the countryside is beautiful, and it's fun seeing the sheep and Podolico cows, or watching the Maiale Nero Casertano piglets playing in the mud with their mothers.

Laticauda sheep grazing at Quercete

A black Casertano sow on the farm

'This black – actually, dark grey – pig can't be bred indoors,' explains Osvaldo, as we spot some big males snoozing in the mud in a field. 'The animals don't survive when they are locked up. So on our farm the sow (*scrofa*) and male (*verro*) are given ample outdoor space to dig and grub for worms.' The Casertano has more fat that other pigs, even when it is bred outside. This explains why, for a time, they were less in demand. Now there is a return to well-flavoured foods, and this breed is highly sought-after. 'Our animals eat only natural grains, plus whatever they can scrounge outside: the young ones get to spend a few weeks in our orchard, and they love the windfall fruit.'

One of the products that are special to these pigs is *lardo insaporito di Casertano*: the thick strip of fat that runs down their backs is salt-cured and flavoured with herbs and spices. Eat it sliced very thinly on hot toast.

The farm shop sells fresh meat, home-made *salumi* and cheeses (made entirely with the farm's milk, pasteurized) as well as pasta, vegetable and fruit preserves, and fresh produce. A cheerful, modestly priced restaurant serving *piatti tipici* is open to the public. It's a great way to sample the farm's foods – traditional dishes like *cavatielli* pasta with hearty Laticauda lamb *ragù*, or meats grilled over wood embers. Six apartments are available for holiday rentals.

Vairano Patenora

Restaurant

Via IV Novembre, 60
TEL 0823 643018
FAX 0823 643835
CLOSED
Tues; 2 weeks in July
CARDS All
PRICE €€€-€€€€

Il Vairo del Volturno
The Vairo was a mythological animal – part wolf, part fox – that haunted the valley of the Volturno river. Vairano is a medieval hill town, complete with castle, that provides a good place for a walk. Below it, in the town's recent outskirts, is a restaurant that belongs to the architecturally – but not gastronomically – nondescript. The young chef Renato Martino has transformed his family's unpretentious trattoria into a restaurant serving modern cuisine. At their best, Martino's dishes are imaginative, clear-flavoured, and make good use of local produce. If at times technique falls short, it's hardly surprising: this ambitious chef is self-taught, and like so many young cooks from rural southern Italy, has had to improvise a culinary structure for a cuisine whose strengths are decisive-tasting ingredients and verve. His admittance into the Jeunes Restaurateurs d'Europe association says a lot about his determination.

The menu offers traditional and experimental dishes, with a welcome accent on vegetables – after all, this is Campania Felix. There's a good wine list (lots of Tuscans), including many by the glass.

As for the food, the mid-summer *benvenuto* sets a cheery Mediterranean tone: a yellow *zucca* flower filled with ricotta is placed centre-plate, like a long nose, with cherry tomato 'eyes' and 'mouth', and drops of basil-oil. Hand-chopped tartare of peppered buffalo meat comes with buffalo mozzarella and tomatoes. If the gazpacho is too solid for my taste, the risotto with *zucchine alla scapece* and candied citrus is more refreshing; the courgettes taste pickled beside the orange-zest accents. I like the play on the 'Caprese' trio, with basil in the green, fragrant pasta dough, a lightly cooked tomato sauce, and buffalo mozzarella inside the *tortellone*. Marjoram-scented rabbit stuffed with Gaeta olives is accompanied by a *sformato di cicerchie* – a hot pudding of this legume, somewhere between a bean and a chickpea.

The jazziest dessert is saffron-rice *gelato* with a coulis of *peschiole* – pickled peaches the size of green olives that come from this area. An exotic end to a summer's lunch.

If you get hooked on the crunchy *peschiole* (see above), tiny pickled peaches that offer explosive sweetness and a hint of acidity – and that make a great alternative to olives at *aperitivo* time – you can get them from their producer, Salvatore Parente (Azienda Agricola Verticelli, Vairano; TEL 0823 988716).

Vairano Scalo

Jams, Fruit and Vegetable Preserves
La Credenza

Via Rapoli, 155
TEL/FAX 0823 642025
E-MAIL lacredenza@tin.it
INTERNET
www.lacredenza.it

You can't help being charmed by the young Creta sisters and by their story.

'It all began one night in August,' says Roberta.

'Yes,' continues Maria Concetta. 'It was too hot to sleep and we were lying in bed – we grew up sharing a bed – talking and dreaming of plans for the future.'

'We have always loved making the traditional jams and other preserves that are linked to the abundant fruit orchards in this part of the country, and we decided to try turning this hobby into a business,' says Roberta. They chose the name Credenza, which means both 'sideboard' and 'belief' – of which they were to need a good deal. 'It was very hard: we had no money, and no one here was in the least interested in helping two young

girls get started. Everyone including our parents were against us:
they were all convinced we were crazy.' But they persevered, and
within a short time found buyers for their fine products. The
sisters do all the preparation of their now extensive line themselves, so it really is a cottage industry.

'We have won respect, and the business has grown slowly but
steadily,' says Maria Concetta as she offers me a taste of their
unusual beer jelly, that uses the natural beer made by their
young male counterparts at Saint John's Bier (see p. 413). The
jelly is delicate and memorable, a good accompaniment to
cheese. The product line includes fresh fruit jams and vegetable
pastes – *creme* – that can be used to dress pasta or top *crostini*.
I particularly like the unusual chestnut and *porcini* mushroom
mixture, with its intriguing balance of sweet and smokiness
from the chestnuts and earthiness of the mushrooms.

Chapter 2

Napoli and the Campi Flegrei

Street foods and Greek mythology

Napule è mille culure	*Napoli is a thousand colours*
Napule è mille paure	*Napoli is a thousand fears*
Napule è 'a voce d' creature	*Napoli is the voices of children*
Che saglie chianu chianu	*Rising slowly slowly*
E tu sai ca nun si sulo	*And you know you're not alone*
Napule è nu sole amaro	*Napoli is a bitter sun*
Napule è addore 'e mare	*Napoli is the smell of the sea*
Napule è na carta sporca	*Napoli is a sullied paper*
E nuisciuno se ne importa e	*And no one cares and*
Ognuno aspetta 'a	*They're all waiting for their*
ciorta	*own luck*
Napule è na camminata	*Napoli is taking a walk*
Inte viche miezo	*Through narrow streets*
all'ato	*amongst the people*
Napule è tutto 'nu suonno	*Napoli is all a dream*
E 'a sape tutto 'o munno	*That the whole world knows*
Ma nun sanna 'a verità	*Without knowing the truth*

FOR TOURIST INFORMATION:
Azienda Autonoma di
Soggiorno Cura e
Turismo di Napoli
Piazza Gesù Nuova, 28
TEL 081 2471318
INTERNET
www.turismoregione
campania.it
www.innaples.it

*Opposite: Neapolitans
love raw shellfish: a
street seller offers fresh
mussels at the market*

This beautiful song of Pino Daniele's – written and sung in the dialect that only the Neapolitans can understand – has become Napoli's popular anthem, expressing the contradictions of this great and complex and difficult city. It accompanied me on my travels through the region, so it seems a fitting place to begin talking about Napoli (or Naples), its food and its people.

This chapter incorporates two areas: the city of Napoli, and the Campi Flegrei (Phlegrean Fields) and Pozzuoli to its west. Assuming that Napoli is your base, these are places that can be reached easily in a day if you don't want to spend a night out, as are Caserta, Vesuvio and Pompei (see Chapters 1 and 3).

This area is well served by transportation: if you have a car, the *tangenziale* and *autostrade* link them easily; Napoli's new metro lines are very efficient for inner city travel and go as far as Pozzuoli and Bagnoli, via the Campi Flegrei. The best way to reach Pompei if you don't have a car is by train: the Circumvesuviana line does just what it says – the tour of the volcano's towns – and goes as far as Sorrento.

I Campi Flegrei – the Phlegrean Fields

FOR TOURIST
INFORMATION:
INTERNET
www.icampiflegrei.it

This large area (about 65 square kilometres) to Napoli's northwest was named 'the Fiery Fields' by ancient Greek sailors who were awestruck by the landscape's continually changing morphology: the volcanic subsoil kept altering the lie of the land. Add to that the sulphurous vapours that constantly 'smoked' from its fissures, and the area's many caves and imposing rock formations, and we can easily understand how the Campi Flegrei became the stuff of myths and legends. Virgil spent a lot of time here, and the 'fields' also provided the perfect setting for Homer's tales: thunderous eruptions, with flying stones and incandescent projectiles, were transformed into the boulders tossed into the sea by the Laistrygonians to sink the ship of Odysseus. The eerie Lake of Averno, whose reeking, poisonous fumes prevented even birds from crossing it, was thought to be the gateway into hell. At Cumæ (now Cuma), a deep echoing cavern became the cave of the oracle Sibyl, the woman who spoke the words of Apollo and held the keys to Hades.

Despite theses inconveniences – or perhaps because of them – the Greeks settled at Cuma, and after them the Romans, who turned the port of Puteoli (today's Pozzuoli) into one of the Mediterranean's most important trading centres. As a reward for braving the 'fiery' landscape, the settlers found a perfect climate, highly fertile soils for their cultivations – among which vines played an important part, as they still do today – and a beautiful sea full of fish. At one great banquet to honour Cæsar, 6,000 eels were consumed; indeed, breeding fish and oysters became a lucrative business in the area's salt and fresh waters. The richest Romans and emperors chose the coast for their holiday villas, and frequented the curative thermal baths which were the positive side-effects of this often disquieting landscape.

Over the centuries, after shifts and earthquakes due to the territory's continuing bradyseisms – slow, vertical movements of the ground's surface caused by the underground pressure of deep masses of magma – the sea reclaimed much of what the Romans had created, and today this area is famous for its fascinating archaeological remains – many of which are under water.

Napoli and Vesuvio

Unfortunately, the unscrupulous building crazes of the second half of the 20th century ruined a great deal of the previously unspoiled landscape, but several regional parks have now been formed to protect what is left of this unique area.

Campi Flegrei Wines

Pliny the Elder praised the Falerno Gaurano wine, made along the coast from Pozzuoli to Mondragone, and it remained a favourite of the royal and noble tables of the Neapolitans for centuries. The grape varieties that have withstood the tests of time are Falanghina dei Campi Flegrei, and Piedirosso: Falanghina means 'vine supported by a pole' in Greek; Piedirosso was appreciated in Imperial Rome. In some areas these varieties even survived the deadly attack of phylloxera at the beginning of the 20th century, as the root-parasites could not survive in the volcanic soils; original rootstocks that pre-date the 20th century have been found.

While many *cantine* sprang up around the capital city in recent decades, almost as many produced wines from grapes bought elsewhere – in the provinces of Benevento or Avellino, for example. They were geared to quenching the big city's thirst rather than to offering quality wines that reflected the character-istics of their terroirs. Today, a handful of enterprising wine-makers are bringing dignity back to Napoli's wines, from the Campi Flegrei, Vesuvio (see Chapter 3), and Gragnano (see Chapter 5).

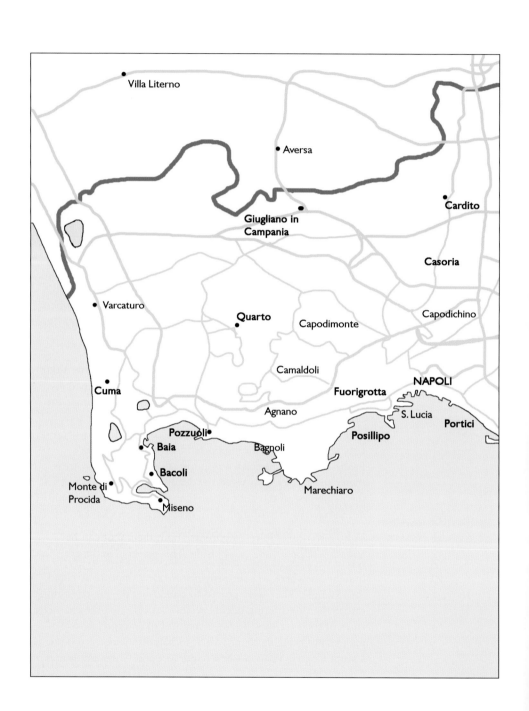

Bacoli

Wine
I Vini della Sibilla

Via Torre di Cappella,
13 and
Via Ottaviano Augusto,
19
TEL/FAX 081 8688778
E-MAIL info@sibillavini.it
INTERNET
www.sibillavini.it

'The Campi Flegrei offer an unusual chance to taste a
Falanghina wine that has been grown on sand,' says winemaker
Maurizio De Simone, who has been working with the younger
generation of the Di Meo family since 1998. 'Here Falanghina is
quite different from the Beneventano variety, as it has had to
adapt to being by the sea, with very hot sun and loose soils. The
result is a thin-skinned grape that is mainly produced on mature
plants that were by-passed by the phylloxera attack of the last
century, and which are still grown with high yields per plant
and low density plantings.' Falanghina is a delicate wine that is
low in alcohol (around 11.5°) and that is characterized by floral
notes and finesse. It is fermented in five-hectolitre French tonneaux, untoasted, to give the wine its soft tannins and natural
stability. The winery makes a *passito* from the Falanghina,
Aureum, and also works with the local red grape, Piedirosso.

Cardito

Cheese
Caseificio Delle Rose

Corso Italia, 23
TEL 081 8317707
INTERNET
www.salvatorecorso.it

Just outside Napoli, in an area between the city and its surrounding countryside, Signor Corso 'transforms' selected buffalo
milk from the province into cheese, and sells it in an attractive
shop that also sells wines, Neapolitan *salumi* and other speciality DOP foods.

Giugliano

Restaurant
Fenesta Verde

Via Licante (Vico Sorbo, 1)
TEL 081 8941239
INTERNET
www.ristoranapoli.it
CLOSED
Sun evening; Mon;
2 weeks in Aug
CARDS All
PRICE €€€

Some restaurants have a rightness about them that can be
sensed as soon as one steps inside. This goes beyond mere décor,
though the eye must play its part. It has more to do with the
creating of a convivial environment, free of pretension or stress,
that is conducive to the art of eating – to what the Italians call
stare bene, or 'feeling good'. That's how I feel about Fenesta
Verde. A provincial trattoria in a nondescript town, it opened in
1948 – and even before that was offering bowls of soup and
plates of pasta to travellers passing through Giugliano on their
way to and from Napoli, told to look out for the 'green windows' near the church – a name that stuck. Fenesta Verde has

always been in the Guarino family; the current generation of cooks are two sisters, Laura and Luisa Iodice. Their husbands, Giacomo D'Alterio and Guido Cante, work in the attractive dining rooms, with their light terracotta floors, tablecloths of soft cream and ivory, and straw-seated wooden chairs painted mustard-yellow and three shades of green. There is a serious selection of Italian wines, a wall full of them; the other walls are given over to temporary exhibits of photographs, like the fascinating black-and-white portraits of Neapolitan street life that I saw. This is a favourite lunch spot for the locals: many have forged friendships at these tables.

Of course it all hinges on the food. I went in summer, and Guido was keen to explain that their winter dishes are some of the most popular, when they work the local pork in rustic soups like the *minestra maritata* (pork with at least seven types of greens), or cook tripe, or *baccalà* or stockfish stewed *in casseruola*. I'll have to go back for those. Meanwhile, I was delighted with my warm-weather *antipasti*: a little 'teaser' of deep-fried shrimp and shelled mussels; a delicate fried *fiore di zucca* filled with a cloud of ricotta and basil; the bright yellow and green flowers again, caught in a slice of golden *frittata*, as light as an omelette; an unusual *parmigiana* of *melanzane* 'in bianco' – without tomato: layers of aubergine/eggplant interspersed with *prosciutto* and smoked cheese. Tiny white beans, *fagioli di Villaricca*, appear on a little toast, stewed with an octopus half the size of my hand and three crushed cherry tomatoes: perfectly Mediterranean flavours in this mix of sea and land. The women's touch was apparent too in two ravioli stuffed with a bechamel tinged pink by the plump shrimp inside; and in a common *pasta e fagioli* made rare by fresh *spolicchini* beans (the kind you shell yourself), a light tomato broth and a hint of spicy celery to set the tone. The cooks offered me one winter dish, a warming *ragù* of tomatoes enriched with melted *lardo* on narrow tubes of pasta. Delicious. *Secondi* were simple: grilled steak or tuna, garnished with pink or green peppercorns and wild *rucola*. That, plus a fine *tortino* of dark chocolate, and a great meal was complete.

The family recommend the mozzarellas from Caseificio Mimi Costanzo (Viale Marconi, 29, Lusciano; TEL 081 8142341).

Opposite: freshly picked fiori di zucca ready to be stuffed

Napoli

*At almost every corner of the main streets, there are pastry-cooks
with their frying pans of sizzling oil, busy, especially on fast days,
preparing pastry and fish on the spot for anyone who wants it.
Their sales are fabulous, for thousands and thousands of people
carry their lunch and supper home, wrapped in a little piece of
paper.*

J. W. *Goethe* Italian Journey 29 May 1787

EATING AND DRINKING

Napoli is a city to experience in the streets, more Orient than
Occident in its ability to express itself out in the open. So it is
not surprising that many people – including my food-writer
friend Luigi Cremona, whom I believe has eaten in practically
every restaurant in Italy – maintain, and I agree, that modern
Napoli is best enjoyed for its street food: fried delicacies of fish
or dough from the *friggitorie* stands; tripe and other offal from
the sellers of *frattaglie*; the baked *taralli* – crisp, miniature
dough rings of flour, suet and pepper – that are sold on many
street corners; *o' per' e o' muss* – pig's trotters and beef jowl –
displayed in pink-neon-lit vans decorated artistically with
wedges of lemon, and sprinkled with salt from shakers made of
polished bull's horns; delicious pastries of every description to
sample at *pasticcerie* or bars; and, of course, pizza in all its
forms and flavours. Some vendors have become quite rare, like
those hawking cupfuls of hot *brodo di polipo* – octopus soup –
in winter, or the woman carrying scales who sells frogs for making broth for babies as a pick-me-up.

Today the appeal of Napoli and, by extension, its food has as
much to do with the grandeur of its *palazzi* as with its vivacious
street life, for they help set the tone in this city of contrasts. In
the late-18th and 19th centuries, Napoli was the capital of the
Mediterranean, seat – with Palermo – of the Kingdom of the
Two Sicilies, with an elaborately structured aristocracy and an
active court life. Their predilection for abundance, for baroque
and rococo showiness filtered into their food too, with its tiered
puddings and elaborately decorated pastries.

In the noble dining rooms that continued to flourish until
after the First World War, it was the Monzù who cooked. These
personal chefs to each noble family were French-trained (Monzù
is the Italianization of 'Monsieur'), and were brought to the
court of Napoli by the Bourbon queen Maria Carolina of
Austria – Marie Antoinette's sister – in an attempt to upgrade

*Opposite: Babas being
soaked in rum syrup*

Seafood stall at the street market in Napoli

Some Neapolitans lower their baskets from high floors to do their shopping

the flavourful but rustic Neapolitan *cucina povera*. Their effect is still to be found in Neapolitan cuisine, with its penchant for *besciamella*, *pâté* and *gattò*. Indeed, the ever-popular fried *crocché* that are sold from street stands and *pizzerie* are direct descendants of French potato croquettes.

As one would expect, there are also legions of trattorias, *cantine* and restaurants in Napoli, covering the whole range from simple, rustic, family-run eating houses to refined hotel dining rooms with romantic views of the volcano Vesuvio. Those in search of creative young chefs or *cucina territoriale* will do better in some of the other areas of Campania – inland or on the coast – as they are usually to be found far from the costly and chaotic city centre. These listings begin with unpretentious street food and pizza, and continue with more elaborate *pizzeria*; *ristorante*; simple *cantine*; Neapolitan *osterie*; and elegant restaurants. Prices, where given, are for three- or four-course meals, without wines. Pizzas cost much less.

If you want to visit a street food market, leave your valuables at home and wander the streets behind the station or in the Vergini quarter (off Piazza Cavour). If it's repro 'Vuitton' and 'Prada' you're after, the street vendors on Vico Belledonne at Chiaia produce perfect look-alikes at much lower prices.

Street-Food Shops

Via G Ninni, 1–3
(Piazza Montesanto)
TEL 081 5528665
OPEN 7.30 to 24.00 daily
except Sun

Friggitoria Fiorenzano

This is an historic shop: it's been frying and roasting as long as anyone can remember. Particularly good is the range of fried *paste cresciute* – raised doughs like *zeppole* and *panzarotti* – often with vegetables or *fiori di zucca* in them.

Via Cimarosa, 44
TEL 081 5783130
OPEN All day

Friggitoria Vomero

Here too, there are many different types of fried foods, from sweet to savoury, including *cannoli*, *polenta* and vegetables, as well as stuffed *pizza fritta* and *scagliuozzi*: *panzarotti* stuffed with ricotta and tomato.

Via Foria, 212
TEL 081 451166
Also on sale from
Via Epomeo, 71
and Via Colonna, 46
TEL 081 416161

Tarallificio Leopoldo

A Neapolitan speciality: Gianni Infante's *taralli* are crisped rings of suet-enriched dough studded with almonds and seasoned with black pepper. If the idea of the fat puts you off, try the fat-free, boiled and baked *taralli* flavoured with fennel seeds. They have been made by this family for three generations – and they're addictive.

Vico della Quercia, 17
TEL 081 5512280
OPEN 10.00–21.00
CLOSED
Sun afternoon

Timpani e Tempura

This is a great place for picnic or snack food to take away, but the choice is so enticing you'll end up making a meal of it (if you're lucky, you'll find space at the counter). In addition to the delicately fried *tempura*, and classics like the *sartù di riso* or *pizza con le scarole*, the Tubelli family make pastry *timballi* (or *timpani*, as in drums) stuffed with various fillings, from vegetables to cheese. There is also a fine assortment of artisan-made raw-milk cheeses and *salumi*, as well as wines to take home.

Via Pignasecca, 14
NO PHONE
OPEN 8.30–20.30
CLOSED Sun

Tripperia Fiorenzano

For over a hundred years, this shop has specialized in *carnacotta*, cooked meats, which in this case mean offal, or *frattaglie*: tripe, *la centopelle* – the stomach with its 'hundred skins', lights, spiced head cheese (*la testina*), etc. These foods are treated with respect in Italy where, in the *contadino* tradition, nothing went (or goes) to waste. They are always nicely arranged, as if to ennoble them visually, with bright fresh lemons around them. Seeing the shop reminded me of Norman Lewis's descriptions of wartime Napoli in 1944, when food was scarce and people queued for scraps.

LA VERA PIZZA

Pizza as a mid-morning snack

Talk to any of the new generation of pizza-makers in Campania, and they'll tell you that the real secret to a great pizza – beyond the use of high quality ingredients – lies in its digestibility. If you think about it, it's true: how many times have you had pizza and then had to get up six times in the night to quench your thirst? Or felt it sitting on your stomach like a ton of bricks? Or sensed that all that yeast was finally rising – inside you?

Once you have eaten a pizza that has been made using a natural yeast starter – *o' criscito* or 'mother' – and '00' flour, and has been allowed to rise and ferment for any-where from 8 to 36 hours, you'll see and feel the difference. For the secret to a great pizza is that it has to be cooked in about one and a half minutes or the dough will harden. So the oven has to be at very, very high heat (about 400°C/ 750°F): there is no time in the cooking phase for the dough to rise much, it has to be ready to go. The *pizzaiolo*'s approach may be instinctive or scientific (there are now Italian websites dedicated to the fine-tuning and chemistry involved, such as www.pizza.it or the Gambero Rosso site, www.gamberosso.it) but the result must be a soft, airy, cooked-through crust, just lightly crisp at the outer edge, that tastes of the fragrance of wheat and yeast and wood-ash.

The *pizzaiolo* will also insist that the movements he makes – *la gestualità* – are also very important as they give the dough texture and elasticity. No rolling pins are used: all the stretching and twirling is done by hand, so as not to compress the dough.

how to spot a perfect crust
After baking, cut through the pizza: in section there should be irregular air bubbles throughout the cooked dough, from the top of the crust all the way down. If there are no air bubbles at all, or the dough has a very evenly spaced, cake-like texture, it has been made with industrial or the wrong kind of yeast, or been compressed, or not been given ample time to rise.

where to get it
One quarter of all Italian restaurants are pizzerias. Not all

*Pizza to go: folded
like a handkerchief*

of them make great pizza, but Napoli has more than its
share of the very best. Some of the top Neapolitan pizzerias
are no-frill places, with bare-bones service, little choice of
drinks, and a list of pizzas that is over before it begins.
Here pizza is king, and connoisseurs are willing to put up
with minimal extras to get it. In some *pizzerie* with windows onto the street, pizza is still sold for eating on the go,
folded in four into a piece of brown paper, *a fazzoletto* –
like a pocket handkerchief.

As with all foods, it is the quality of the ingredients that
make the difference. You may prefer *mozzarella di bufala* to
cow's-milk *fior di latte* (many experts maintain that the latter is preferable, as it has better texture when baked), or
like ripe cherry tomatoes more than puréed plum tomatoes
– but in all cases they must be fresh, flavourful and well
made. If you want to sample the classics, ask for *pizza
Marinara* (tomato, oregano, garlic, olive oil) or *Margherita*
(tomato, mozzarella, basil, olive oil), or *la pizza fritta* (fried
calzone).

PIZZA

Via Fontanelle, 46/47
TEL 081 5446292
CLOSED Weds; Aug

Pizzeria Add' ò Riccio

Tucked away in one of the most popular and least touristic areas of town, the Sanità, this is a Mecca for lovers of the true pizza – if there are photos of Totò and 'la' Loren on the walls, it's because they often ate here. The crust remains paper-thin and light even when stuffed with vegetables before being topped with mozzarella and tomatoes – one of Riccio's specialities. A plateful of freshly fried foods to start the meal and a good beer are all you need to complement these great pizzas.

Via Luigi Palmieri, 13
TEL 081 5520996

Antica Pizzeria del Borgo Orefici

A small pizzeria with a wood-burning oven, a limited menu, and a few tables out in the quiet side street for use in warm weather. Central and authentic.

Via S. Anna di Palazzo, 1–2
TEL 081 416928

Antipasto of scarola, raisins and pine nuts

Brandi – Antica Pizzeria della Regina d'Italia

The story about how *la pizza Margherita* got its name has become part of Napoli's folklore, but it would seem that this pizzeria near the Teatro San Carlo was its birthplace. In 1889, Raffaele Esposito, forefather of the current owner, was called to the royal palace at Capodimonte to prepare pizzas for Queen Margherita. When a letter arrived confirming the queen's approval of the pies, the pizza whose ingredients – tomato, mozzarella, basil – had the most patriotic colours was christened Margherita. Today Brandi is a shrine to Neapolitan extroversion, a celebration of this city's unique ability to create joyous atmospheres and theatrical environments – and, of course, good pizzas.

Via Giulio Cesare, 156
TEL 081 2395281

Pizzeria Cafasso

Ugo Cafasso's pizzeria is one of the purists' favourites, a place to sample the crust as it should be: soft, airy and lightly crispy at the edges.

Via Antonino Pio, 94/A
TEL 081 7672017
CLOSED Sun
E-MAIL
calderopoli@libero.it

Il Calderone

I've become an habitué of this pizzeria in the Fuorigrotta area of the city: I always have lunch here when I come to get my slides developed at Copyright. Che Guevara and Totò look down over checked tablecloths to diners eating pizza or simply cooked soups and pastas. The friendly owners are active in social projects; they even showcase foods from around the world that give their peasant producers a fair deal.

Antica Pizzeria Da Michele

Via Sersale, 1/3
TEL 081 5539204
OPEN 9.00–23.00
CLOSED
Sun; 2 weeks in Aug

Michele Condurro's family has been making pizza for over four generations, since 1870, and they are dedicated to pizza in its quintessence: the choice here is limited to the two classics, Marinara and Margherita, plus the *calzone*. They say you can judge the state of the city's economy by the amount of pizzas that are made each day in this great oven.

Pizzeria Di Matteo

Via dei Tribunali, 94
TEL 081 455262
OPEN 9.30–24.00
CLOSED
Sun; 2 weeks in Aug

Open from early morning to late evening, this pizzeria has been operating since the 1930s. It's tucked away in the narrow *vicoli* of the heart of Napoli, a *quartiere* full of character and characters. Di Matteo's fate changed in 1994, when President Bill Clinton stopped by for a pizza during the G7. It's not hard to imagine the impact the presidential procession of bullet-proof limousines must have made in this popular neighbourhood, where life is lived as much in the street as indoors. 'We made him an Americanized pizza – with onion, hot sausage and French fries on it,' says the pizzeria's owner. 'He ate two.'

Pizzeria del Presidente

Via Tribunali, 120
TEL 081 210903
CLOSED Sun

Maestro pizzaiolo Ernesto Cacialli worked just down the street at Di Matteo until 2000, when he opened his own pizzeria, naming it 'del Presidente' in honour of President Clinton. His pizzas are classics, using slow-risen dough and high quality ingredients, such as the *fior di latte* cheese – like mozzarella – made at Agerola (see p. 175). This is also a good place to sample the *pizza fritta* – a *calzone* stuffed with ricotta, mozzarella, pork crackling and tomatoes, and fried in suet.

Pizzeria Trianon da Ciro

Via Colletta, 46
TEL 081 5539426
OPEN 10.00–15.00
17.00–23.00
CLOSED Sun lunch

Pizza and Vesuvio are Neapolitan fixtures

This pizzeria, which has been going since 1925, is by the Teatro Trianon. Its owners, the Leone family, are part of the Vera Pizza Napoletana association, and the pizzeria, with its white marble tables and huge wood-burning oven, serves over twenty varieties of pizzas and *calzoni*. Try the pizza topped with *friarielli* when they are in season – typically Neapolitan greens.

Cheese morsels wrapped in lemon leaves are ready to be heated for a great antipasto: the leaves add flavour, but are removed before eating

Restaurants

The following restaurants (many of which also double as pizzerias), offer better service, bigger wine lists and more choice in the menu

Via Riviera di Chiaia, 64
TEL 081 668101
OPEN Dinner only
CLOSED Sun
CARDS All
PRICE €€€

La Cantina di Triunfo

In Napoli, the *cantina* is the equivalent of a northern *osteria* – a convivial, informal place to eat unpretentious food with good music, in good company, and at reasonable prices. There are many of these traditional *cantine* in the city, places where the Neapolitans often go as regulars, for they always have very hospitable owners who quickly make you feel at home.

Via Sauro, 23
Lungomare di Santa Lucia
TEL 081 7648684
E-MAIL
la.cantinella@lacantinella.it
CLOSED
Christmas; 12–27 Aug;
Sun except Nov–May
PRICE €€€€-€€€€€

La Cantinella

La Cantinella is located on the seafront in central Napoli. It's something of a landmark of Neapolitan dining and was the first of the city's more elegant restaurants to have won – and lost – a Michelin star. Over the years all the stars from Pavarotti to Antonioni have graced the Rosolino family's tables, in search of a refined, cosmopolitan ambience and a great wine collection.

La Chiacchierata

Piazzetta Matilde Serao, 37
TEL 081 411465
OPEN
Lunch only, except Fri
CLOSED
Dinner, except Fri;
Sat & Sun in June–Sep;
Aug
PRICE €€

Una chiacchierata means a nice long chat, and this one is located across from the back end of the Galleria Umberto I, just off Via Toledo. The small, family-run trattoria excels at the simplest (but best) dishes from the Campanian repertoire. Indeed, my friend Livia Iaccarino, of the great restaurant Don Alfonso (p. 212), describes their *spaghetti al pomodoro* as '*sconcertante*' – disconcerting in its purity and flavour. A woman's touch in the kitchen can be sensed at the table. The limited menu changes with the seasons, but it always presents satisfyingly home-cooked food. Make sure to book ahead as the restaurant is only open at lunchtime (as well as Friday evening) and is well loved by the Neapolitans.

Ristorante Pizzeria Ciro a Santa Brigida

Via Santa Brigida, 73
TEL 081 5524072
FAX 081 5528992
CLOSED
Sun (except in Dec);
7–25 Aug
PRICE €€€

Another centrally located restaurant (between Piazza del Plebiscito and Piazza Municipio), another Neapolitan institution, in period rooms that have been modernized without losing their evocative framed views of Napoli. Antonio Pace is the president of the Vera Pizza Napoletana association, whose aim is to define the characteristics of the 'true' pizza, and keep the standards of the city's pizzas high. So here you'll be treated to well-risen dough that gives soft, fragrant pizzas with quality ingredients to dress them. But the large menu also offers a full range of other dishes, including hand-made pastas, vegetables to reflect the seasons, fresh fish and meats.

Ristorante Pizzeria Da Umberto

Via Alabardieri, 30/31
(Piazza dei Martiri)
TEL 081 418555
INTERNET
www.umberto.it
CLOSED Mon PRICE €€€

Vegetable antipasto

Neapolitan families love to eat out all together, and when they do, they like their food in abundance. Da Umberto has long been a favourite destination: a welcoming, lively restaurant with lots of colour and lots of food. Platters of *antipasti* precede the pizzas – fried *zucchini* flowers, plaited mozzarella, sun-dried tomatoes, stuffed aubergines, purple fried beet balls, *caciotta* cheeses flecked with hot pepper flakes: the list goes on and on. There are pastas for those who want them, but the pizzas are well made and varied. Indeed, there's often a little group of students waiting outside for their pizzas to go. My favourite is the pizza with cherry tomatoes, buffalo mozzarella, fresh basil and extra virgin olive oil, or the large fried pizza with smoked mozzarella, ricotta and herbs in it. 'The *pizza fritta* is a classic,' says owner Massimo Di Porzio as he brings it to the table. 'It even appeared in a film by De Sica, to be paid '*da oggi a otto*' – on credit, eight days from today.'

Locally-caught anchovies are ever-popular

Ferdinando IV was an enthusiastic sportsman. He reserved a portion of the sea at Naples for his own fishing, and built himself a fishing-lodge at Mergellina, which is now known by the name of Palazzo Torlonia. It is said of him that one of his great amusements was to sell his own fish at the water-side of Mergellina, and to banter, chaff, and bargain with his beloved 'lazzaroni'.

E. Neville-Rolfe Naples in the Nineties

Strada Mergellina, 4A
TEL 081 681817
FAX 081 661241
E-MAIL
donsalvatore@virgilio.it
CLOSED Weds
CARDS All
PRICE €€€€
(less for pizza)

Ristorante Pizzeria Don Salvatore a Mergellina

This large, lively, family-run restaurant is by the waterfront, and is another of the Neapolitan classics. It's a perfect place if you're in the mood for pizza or pasta plus. There's always a large buffet of seafood and vegetable *antipasti*, and a display of fresh fish for those who want more. Host Tonino Aversano is a mine of information about the history of Neapolitan cuisine, and often makes authentic dishes from the repertoire, such as the delicate soup of potatoes and *zucca* flowers, or *pasta 'ncaciata* – a recipe from 1850 that was one of the first to incorporate tomatoes and Caciocavallo cheese in a pasta dressing. There is a good range of Campanian and other wines to accompany the food. Save room for desserts, as there are many delectable Neapolitan pastries to enjoy with a glass of local *passito* – such as Villa Matilde's Eleusi, made from semi-dried Falanghina grapes.

Ristorante Pizzeria L'Europeo di Mattozzi

Via Marchese
Campodisola, 4–8
TEL 081 5521323
CLOSED Sat eve and Sun
in July and Aug;
Mon, Tues and Wed eves
in other months;
15–31 Aug
PRICE €€€€
(less for pizza)

This *ristorante* has remained a constant in Napoli for over three generations, through the city's thicks and thins. Today it still retains a feeling of time past with copper pots and painted plates on the walls, and a lively mood once the tables are occupied by the many businessmen (Campania's strictest food critics) who are regulars.

The food is very fresh, from the *antipasti* of assorted seasonal vegetable dishes – that are as one would find them in Neapolitan homes – to sautés of mussels or clams, or salads of octopus. *Primi* are at their best with the simplicity of *la cucina povera*: pasta with potatoes and *provola*, or soups of peas or fava beans. Fish prevail for *secondi*, though there are meats or pizzas for those who want them. The location (not far from the station) is handy, and prices are fair.

Jap-one Sushi Bar

Via S M Cappella
Vecchia, 30
(off Via Morelli near
Piazza dei Martiri and
Via Chiaia, but around
the back)
TEL 081 7646667
INTERNET www.jap-one.it
OPEN Dinner only
CLOSED Sun, Mon; Aug
PRICE €€€€€

You'd never expect to find one of Japan's most talented young sushi chefs working in the centre of Napoli. Yet Yasumi Yamasaki, with his business partner, Roberto Goretti, run what was the first Japanese restaurant south of Rome – and it has been a big hit ever since it opened, over four years ago.

Chef Yasu, as he is known, trained in several of the disciplines of Japanese cooking – grilling, tempura, mountain cooking, as well as seafood – before joining the Nobu organization, where he worked both in Tokyo and in New York – he even cooked for Robert De Niro's birthday. When he wanted a new country to move to and a chance to be his own boss in the kitchen, he looked on the internet for contacts. Meanwhile, Roberto had decided to change his life: his passion for Japanese food was winning over his work as a lawyer. He put an ad on the internet, and Yamasaki, who had never been to Italy, answered it.

The result is a fragrant, individual cuisine that is firmly Japanese-based, with some new influences of Mediterranean ingredients and flavours. Yamasaki's work with the local fish is extraordinary: I spent a day watching him going to the market to select the freshest seafood, piece by piece; cleaning and cutting the fish according to meticulous, time-honoured Japanese traditions; then serving or cooking the fish and its accompanying ingredients with the grace of a painter. If you're a sushi lover, don't miss this opportunity to taste the food of a very talented artist.

Chef Yasu checks a market tuna for freshness

Via Alfonso d'Aragona, 21
TEL 081 5538525
FAX 081 289004
E-MAIL
info@mimiallaferrovia.it
CLOSED Sun; 13–22 Aug
CARDS All
PRICE €€€

Mimì alla Ferrovia

La ferrovia is the railway, and this busy restaurant is located just a stone's throw from the Garibaldi train station. The cuisine is primarily vegetable- and sea-based, with a good selection of *antipasti* that go from stuffed peppers to delicate sheep's ricotta to sautéed shellfish. The most popular dishes are classics from the local repertoire, and include *spaghetti alle vongole* (with small clams), *pasta e ceci* (pasta soup with chickpeas), *polpi in cassuola* (stewed octopus), *fritto misto* (deep-fried mixed fish). There are also some meat dishes to accompany the reds on the extensive wine list. Finish the meal with a good version of the Sicilian *cassata*, or the house *babà* which comes with what they desbribe as '*i creaturi*' – miniature *babàs* to accompany their 'mother'.

Piazza Salvatore Di
Giacomo, 134
TEL 081 5756936
E-MAIL info@alpoeta.com
INTERNET
www.alpoeta.com
CLOSED Mon; 10–25 Aug
PRICE €€€

Al Poeta

When the bustle of Napoli is too much, and you're in the mood for a quiet dinner in a great location, drive up to Posillipo. There the Varriale brothers' restaurant–pizzeria is set in a leafy *piazza* that has full views of the bay. And it's a classic, serving the Neapolitan favourites – from spaghetti with fresh *frutti di mare* to great pizzas, to grilled or baked fish. After fine mixed *antipasti*, move on to hand-made pasta dressed with vegetables or seafood. There's an impressive wine collection and real desserts – all served in a friendly, professional setting.

Vicoletto Sant'Arpino, 21
TEL 081 401578
OPEN Dinner only; lunch
by prior booking
CLOSED Sun and Mon
PRICE €€€€–€€€€€

La Stanza del Gusto

At the top of a little *vicolo* off the busy Via Chiaia, up a staircase that is a street – and vice versa – is a door on the left. Inside are two high vaulted rooms that were once the *cantina* of a noble *palazzo*, but since 1972 have contained a restaurant. 'When I took it over in 2000,' says Mario Avallone, 'it was full of *putti* – little angels.' He simplified the décor, painted the walls soft yellows and greens, added some modern touches like the stoneware and glass dishes, and created an intimate atmosphere. Avallone opened his first Stanza del Gusto – literally, the Taste Room – in 1996, with just one table for six to twelve diners. 'It was a place to cook for friends where I could be free to experiment. This restaurant grew naturally out of that first Stanza.'

The *cucina* is still an eclectic mix of creation and tradition, as in the *gattò di patate* – a popular mashed potato pie served here with a light tangy *pecorino* sauce. The menu changes with the seasons, but there are always hand-made pasta dishes, like the square *quadrotti* of *grano duro* and water served with chunks of swordfish and fennel. *Secondi* include fish, meat and vegetable

Fresh Mediterranean fish at a restaurant

dishes. There is also a vegetarian menu.

Avallone is an expert on Italian cheese and *salumi*, especially those from the southern regions. He is a partner in Taberna Imperiale, a company that selects and distributes artisan products to restaurants and shops throughout Italy. Here he matches them with a fine collection of local wines. Of the desserts, I particularly like the *crostata forte*: a tart with a filling like mincemeat, of bright local citrus, with just a hint of fiery *peperoncino* to it.

Avallone also runs the Officine Gastronomiche Partenopee, where he sells local jams, liqueurs and other products.

Terrazza Calabritto

Piazza Vittoria, 1
Chiaia
TEL 081 2405188
CLOSED
Mon; 2 weeks in Aug
INTERNET
www.
terrazzacalabritto.it

The dining room of this centrally located restaurant is upstairs on the first floor of a *palazzo* that overlooks the busy *piazza*, the boardwalk and, beyond that, the sea. The owners and chef are young, and keenly interested in promoting the region's quality foods and wines, so it's a good place to try pasta topped with seasonal vegetables or fish in an attractive setting.

Castel dell'Ovo is on the Golfo di Napoli

HOTEL DINING

Like all the greatest cities, Napoli has its share of grand hotels, with views of the bay and Vesuvio. Some also have fine restaurants with panoramic terraces. Here are three of the best:

Excelsior Hotel, Ristorante La Terrazza, Via Partenope, 48; TEL 081 7640111; FAX 081 769743; E-MAIL info@excelsior.it

Grand Hotel Parker's, Ristorante George's Corso Vittorio Emanuele, 135; TEL 081 7612474; E-MAIL info@ grandhotelparkers.it

Grand Hotel Vesuvio, Ristorante Caruso, Via Partenope, 45 TEL 081 7640044; FAX 081 7644483; E-MAIL info@vesuvio.it

FOOD SHOPS

Via Toledo, 147
TEL 081 5516219

Gastronomia Pasticceria Augustus

This small, well-preserved, period bar–*pasticceria–gastronomia* is conveniently located on Via Toledo not far from Piazza del Plebiscito. It's a perfect place for a stand-up breakfast or mid-morning snack of coffee with a slice of *babà* topped with fresh fruit and custard, a delicious *sfogliatella*, or any other of the many home-baked pastries. In summer a handful of *gelati* complete the sweet offerings. If you're more of a savoury person, the little counter at the back of the store offers well-made cheeses and *salumi*. Augustus also sells local chestnut honey, jams and the excellent preserves from Vesuvioro (see p. 131).

Pasta cresciuta – fried dough balls

and also:

Baffone (Via Ponte di Tappia, 67; TEL 081 5520596) specializes in fruits and vegetables from all over the world.
Pescheria Luigione (Via Mergellina, 47; TEL 081 681741, 081 680886) is one of Napoli's historic fishmongers.

GELATERIA

Piazza Carità, 4
TEL 081 5520272
OPEN
8.30 to 1.00 am in summer
CLOSED Wed in winter

Gelateria della Scimmia

When this *gelateria* opened, in 1933, a monkey in a cage by the front door diverted passers-by, and the shop was nick-named '*gelateria* of the monkey'. The monkey is long gone, but the name stuck, and its memory also lingers on in the shape of the banana ice-cream on a stick that has remained one of the *gelateria*'s favourites ever since. Another throwback to former times is the *formetta*: two flavours (of your choice) sandwiched between two crisp wafers. This ice-cream sandwich prototype is hard to eat, but amusing to see being made in its square box. The *gelateria* is now run by the third generation of the Monacelli family, and makes all its own *gelati*, using fresh fruit, real espresso coffee, hazelnuts and almonds. It also makes a group of *semifreddi* – cream-based frozen desserts that are between a mousse and an ice-cream.

Two of the Scimmia's ice-cream classics

PASTICCERIE

Via San Pasquale a
Chiaia, 21/22
TEL 081 411348

Pasticceria Moccia dal 1920

A great *babà* should never be gummy or spongy, but well '*bagnato*' – evenly soaked in its rum syrup – and the Romano brothers' *babà* fits the description. Indeed, the whole range of pastries in this shop is enticing, so it might be best to buy a trayful and sample them all. Moccia also produces delicious breads, prepared foods, *gelati*, cakes – and fabulous *caffè*.

Pasticceria Gelateria Scaturchio

Piazza San Domenico
Maggiore, 19
TEL 081 5517031

You may have to fight your way to the cash desk in this tiny *pasticceria*, competing with Neapolitan businessmen and housewives buying *vassoi* (trays) of pastries, or simply a few *Ministeriali* to take home. This 200-year-old shop seems unchanged by time, a point of reference in the gastronomic landscape of the city. I first was taken there fifteen years ago by a Neapolitan designer for whom a visit to the shop was as important as a trip to the Archaeological Museum. Do as the natives do: linger over a slice of *pasteria*, or a juicy *babà*, then down a steaming *caffè* in two or three swift sips.

The *Ministeriale* is a rum and chocolate ganache-filled chocolate that resembles a flat medallion. As legend has it, its creator, a Scaturchio ancestor, spent years doing the rounds of the ministries as he attempted to introduce the sweetmeat onto the royal table at Capodimonte. By the time he achieved this goal, a 'ministerial' name had been coined for the chocolate.

Pasticerria Di Costanzo

Piazza Cavour, 135
TEL 081 450180

Rosaria Castaldo maintains that this *pasticceria* has the best *babà* in Naples – but don't take her word for it: check it out.

Gran Caffè Gambrinus

Via Chiaia, 12
TEL 081 417582

Blessed with a key position (on the corner of Piazza del Plebiscito) this busy *belle-époque* café was the preferred meeting place for Neapolitan society. The cakes and ices are still good, but I find the service leaves a lot to be desired.

OTHER FINE NEAPOLITAN *pasticcerie*
Pasticceria Carraturo Via Casanova 97; TEL 081 5545364
Pasticceria Pintauro Via Toledo, 275; TEL 081 417339
Pasticceria Ranaldi Vico Lungo del Gelso, 97; TEL 081 400773

An Easter pastiera tart

THE WHYS AND WHEREFORES OF NEAPOLITAN PASTRIES

At Napoli the *pasticcerie* are as much an institution as the *pizzerie*, for both carry on a tradition that is centuries-old. As in other parts of the south – especially in Sicily – many of the best (and best-guarded) recipes for cakes and pastries came from the within the walls of the local convents. In the 18th and 19th centuries, these desserts were highly sought-after among aristocratic Neapolitans who were willing to pay handsomely to get them. It was believed that the virginal hands of the nuns who baked them conveyed a special sweetness to the (already sweet) confections. Seen from the inside, the production of these desserts was of the utmost importance to the cloistered nuns. Mary Taylor Simeti, in her fine book, *Sicilian Food* (known in the United States as *Pomp and Sustenance*), explains: 'As a vent for creativity, competitiveness, and ambition, it was one of the few alternatives to madness that the convent could offer.' She goes on to quote a revealing passage from an 1864 account of life in a Neapolitan convent, *Misteri del chiostro napoletano*, by Enrichetta Caracciolo.

But the principal occupation, the summa rerum *of the convent, lies in the preparation of sweets... Each nun is the mistress of the pastry oven for an entire day, which begins at midnight on the preceding day; but since at times this is not sufficient, the nun takes recourse to a second and a third, so that the poor lay sisters are dying for want of sleep and some of them actually fall ill. More than one elderly lay sister, grown hoary in the cloister, has said to me that she had never seen the Holy Week services, not having ever had a free minute during that period in which to enter the choir and look into the church.*

Certainly *la sfogliatella*, the delicate puff-pastry spiral baked with a filling of ricotta, semolina and candied peel that has become a set piece of Neapolitan gastronomy, would seem to have originated from within the convents' walls. Jeanne Caròla Francesconi, author of *La Cucina Napoletana* – a veritable encyclopædia on the subject – confirms this and recounts how, as a girl, she heard that this marvellous pastry had been created in the Neapolitan convent della Croce di Lucca (and not in the convent located on the Amalfi Coast to which the pastry is sometimes

attributed). Whatever its provenance, today it is made both in puff- (*riccia*) and short- (*frolla*) pastry versions; when perfectly executed, the former is superior by far.

There is much ritual surrounding Neapolitan desserts, and certain seasons and festivities are celebrated by specific cakes or pastries. Christmas in Napoli wouldn't be complete without *struffoli*, grape-size dough balls that are deep-fried before being dipped in honey, formed into high piles and decorated with multi-coloured sprinkles. Jeanne Francesconi is of the opinion that this rudimentary sweet-meat may date back to the Greeks who, after all, brought far more complicated traditions with them when they colonized nearby Cuma: she notes a close resemblance between *struffoli* and the Greek *lukumates*.

Easter is celebrated with another unique cake, *la pastiera*. 'How could we not love it,' Francesconi writes, 'we've become used to it over generations and generations... One thing is for sure: during the Easter period this dessert, whose perfume is a harbinger of imminent spring, certainly gets itself talked about.' Indeed, every aspect of *la pastiera* is open to discussion: its height (must it be as high as four fingers?), its aroma (is orange-blossom-water better than rose-water?), the type of grain that goes into the filling (can modern bottled plumped wheat-berries substitute for the traditional home-cooked grain?), the temperature at which it should be served (hot or cold?)... Luckily for those who only visit Napoli occasionally, it is now made all year long, so we no longer need to wait for Easter to eat it.

As for *il babà*, everyone agrees that it was 'invented' in the early 18th century by Stanislas Leszczynski, king of Poland who later became the Duke of Lorraine. It was a Polish cake: whether it was named for its resemblance to the skirts of a *baba* – grandmother – or for its ability to conjure up the exoticisms of Ali Baba – apparently some of the king's favourite reading – is unclear. However, the recipe reached France with him during his period of exile but only became famous a century later.

These and other pastries made the fortunes of Napoli's *pasticcerie*, many of which are still going strong, housed in their handsome, original locations.

Opposite, top to bottom: hazelnut deliziosi; almond delizie; babà. This side, top to bottom, sfogliatelle; custard-filled babàs; pastiera is often sold in the baking tray

Gay-Odin's original paper still wraps their chocolate bar

CHOCOLATE

For anyone suffering choco-withdrawal, here are some of Napoli's best chocolate shops.

FACTORY:
Via Vetreria, 12
TEL 081 417843
OTHER SALES POINTS IN:
Via Toledo
214 e 427
Via Cervantes, 37
Via V. Colonna, 15b
Centro Direzionale E
7–5

Gay-Odin Fabbrica Cioccolato

An historic Neapolitan artisan chocolate producer from the 1920s – begun by Isidoro Odin and his wife, Onorina Gay, both Piedmontese. I'm fonder of the original art-nouveau packaging (and the décor in the oldest shops) than I am of the chocolate itself, but it's worth a visit for fun presents and to get a whiff of the *belle époque* as it was lived in the city.

Antica Cioccolateria

Another very pretty old-fashioned shop, selling chocolate (with some good brands) and fruit pastes, at TEL 081 406127

Dolce Idea

Via S Liborio, 2 (Piazza Carità); TEL 081 4203090
Via Bonito, 2/b; TEL 081 5560563
Via Solitaria, 718; TEL 081 7642832

Perzechella

Some fun shapes of chocolate here, including Pulcinella's mask.
Via Pallonetto a Santa Chiara, 36; TEL 081 5510025

Peyrano

This famous Torino chocolate firm has recently opened a shop in Napoli. Via Morelli, 3; TEL 081 7641755

WINE SHOPS AND WINE BARS

L'Armonia
Via San Carlo, 15; TEL 081 410045; OPEN Always

La Barrique
Piazzetta Ascensione, 9; TEL 081 662721; OPEN Evenings;
CLOSED Monday

L'Ebbrezza di Noè
Vico Vetriera, 9 – next to Delle Palme cinema; TEL 081 400104;
CLOSED Monday; July and August

Euridice Genio Vinicolo
Via Scarlatti, 30; TEL 081 5560398; CLOSED Monday after
20.00; last two weeks of August

Enoteca Partenopea
Viale Augusto, 2; TEL 081 5937982, 081 5935336

Wine

Varchetta

Via Padula, 145
TEL 081 7158906
Cellar visits by
appointment

As has often been the case since I met him, I am grateful to
Luciano Pignataro, wine expert and journalist (see the
Bibliography for his excellent wine guides to Campania in
Italian), for introducing me to Varchetta's wines. The company
began its story in the 19th century, making wine from grapes
bought in from areas around Vesuvio, Benevento and the Campi
Flegrei. With the more recent request for quality wines from
identifiable vineyards, Varchetta decided to invest in the specific
and unique territory of the crater of an ex-volcano, the Parco
degli Astroni, just outside the Neapolitan city limits. Here they
now produce an old-style, characterful Falanghina dei Campi
Flegrei DOC, worked exclusively in steel, with unmistakable
mineral and honey notes, as well as a red Piedirosso dei Campi
Flegrei DOC, drinkable, unpretentious and highly affordable.

Olives in the market

Pozzuoli seen from the Ischia ferry

Pozzuoli

The birthplace of La Loren, Pozzuoli has a famous wholesale fish market, *il mercato ittico*. It's located on the waterfront, by the Temple of Serapide, and was rebuilt in 1998. Another famous reconstruction project is at the Rione Terra, using the excellent lime-based house paint made by Cimmino Calce at Casoria (Via Benedetto Croce, 90; TEL 081 7593256; INTERNET www.cimminocalce.com). Lime, or *calce* as it is in Italian, is a natural product with no synthetic components, and is therefore very eco-friendly for the walls of sleeping rooms and restaurants (as in Pisaniello's La Locanda di Bu, pp. 367-68). The colour range is very beautiful, with many of the shades one sees in the Pompeian murals – shades that have represented Mediterranean ideals of colour ever since.

If it's good fish you're after in Pozzuoli, try Ristorante Alos Club (Via Icaro, 1/3; TEL 081 8665475): it's more authentic than the usual tourist places, and has great coffees and a cigar list. Dolci Qualità (Via Carlo Rosini, 45; TEL 081 526528; E-MAIL dolciqualita@libero.it) sells local honeys and other apicultural products, as well as organic and fair-trade foods.

Restaurant

Vineria del Mare

Vico Torrione, 14/18
Vecchia Darsena
TEL 081 5266656
CLOSED
for lunch; Mon
PRICE €€€

This is a trendy restaurant–wine bar in the centre of Pozzuoli, with eclectic but stylish interior design. Maurizio Piancastelli, brother of the wine-producer and journalist Manuela (see pp. 66-68), has assembled a nice collection of wines, especially Campanian, and good *salumi* and cheeses to go with them. He also cooks: self-taught, his is a *cucina* of uncomplicated dishes with some frills. A good place to spend an evening.

Quarto

Wine

Cantine Grotta del Sole

Via Spinelli, 2
TEL 081 8762566
FAX 081 8769470
E-MAIL
grottadelsole@iol.it
INTERNET
www.grottadelsole.it

The area known as Quarto got its name from the *mansio ad Quartum*, a rest and supply post four miles (*quarto* means 'fourth') from Roman Puteoli. In 1227 Federico II built the Belvedere castle there (today called Monteleone) and boosted the area's agricultural economy. The Martusciello's historic winery still boasts some age-old vines, saved from the phylloxera parasite by the volcanic soils of the area. The family are now in the fourth generation of winemakers, producing 900,000 bottles from vineyards owned or rented. Indeed, the Martusciellos are to be applauded for naming the otherwise anonymous producers whose grapes go into the wines in their packaging, and for having always believed in the drinkable, pleasant wines that were so popular with the Neapolitans, Gragnano and Lettere (both Penisola Sorrentina DOC's). Seek them out for a taste of local wines as they should be – *allegri* and *vivaci* – and don't miss the winery's Falanghina dei Campi Flegrei: it too can boast of authenticity.

Chapter 3

Under the Volcano

From Vesuvio to Pompei

After refreshing our eyes with the view and our throats with wine, we wandered about observing other features of this peak of hell which towers up in the middle of paradise...

A magnificent sunset and evening lent their delight to the return journey. However, I could feel how confusing such a tremendous contrast must be. The Terrible beside the Beautiful, the Beautiful beside the Terrible, cancel one another out and produce a feeling of indifference. The Neapolitan would certainly be a different creature if he did not feel himself wedged between God and the Devil.

J.W. Goethe Italian Journey *20 March 1787*

This chapter is dedicated to Vesuvio, the largest volcano in mainland Europe. It includes the volcano itself – now a national park – as well as the circle of towns at its base, and goes as far as Pompei, whose history is inextricably linked to that of the volcano. Between Vesuvio and the sea, from Portici to Castellammare, is the area that was chosen by the rich and powerful – from Romans to Bourbons – for their holiday villas, some of which still remain. Unfortunately, many of these noble residences have been buried by the destructive flow of modern cement, but a keen observer can still spot the gems.

The volcano's mineral-rich soils are very fertile, so fruits and vegetables grown in them have particularly good flavour. These include grapes: wine appellations with the evocative names of Lacryma Christi Vesuvio DOC and Pompeiano IGT are constantly being improved by modern viticulture. The area is famous for its pastries, and there are a handful of wonderful places to eat where traditional and modern recipes do justice to the produce of the volcano's slopes.

Opposite: Vesuvio seen across Pompei's winter vineyards

If you don't have a car, the best way to reach these towns and Pompei is by train: the Circumvesuviana line links the towns around the volcano's base, and also goes from Napoli to Sorrento.

On Vesuvio

PARCO NAZIONALE
DEL VESUVIO
Piazza Municipio, 8
San Sebastiano al Vesuvio
TEL 081 7710913
INTERNET www.parco
nazionaledelvesuvio.it

*Wild orchids on the
volcano*

*Vesuvio's anti-erosion
programme includes
building natural wood
'brakes' that are covered
with earth and planted
with native bushes*

Vesuvio, the large double-coned volcano east of Napoli, was one
of the most important sites on the Grand Tour, and there is no
way to overstate the magnetism that it still exerts. The volcano
is not technically dormant, so one can't drive by it or see it sil-
houetted on the horizon, or visit Pompei, without wondering if
and when it might become active again – and if it did, what
would happen. One also can't help wondering how so many
people have managed to build houses (often without permission)
up its sides. Recently the volcano's two peaks, Vesuvio and
Monte Somma, have been declared a national park – the smallest in Italy – and a Unesco World Heritage Reserve. The park's
president, Amilcare Troiano, is now fighting a tough battle to
remove some of the hundreds of these outlawed '*abusivo*' con-
structions.

On a more positive note, the volcano is beautiful and fascinating to visit. There are 54 kilometres of tracks and trails within
the Parco – often bound by dry-stone walls made of lava that
were conceived by the Bourbons 300 years ago – and the excep-
tionally fertile black soil is rich in wild flowers (including 21
varieties of orchid), vegetation, and wildlife: there is even a pair
of ravens (*Corvus corax*) nesting on its peak. The area is now
very well cared for, with specialists who monitor both wildlife
and vegetation; scientific studies and anti-erosion projects are
under way and there is an observatory to monitor volcanic and
seismic activity.

Visits to the park and cone (by car, foot, horse or bike) can be
organized, including those for the disabled. For information
contact the Parco Nazionale del Vesuvio at the address given.

*The Gammella family at
the apricot market at
Sant'Anastasìa*

EATING AND DRINKING

The Fruits and Vegetables of Vesuvio

The volcano offers unique growing conditions: its mineral-rich
volcanic soils are colours you rarely see elsewhere – rust-brown,
blood-red, purple-grey, clinker-black. Add to that the height, the
sun, and the sea breezes, and you have a micro-climate that
affects everything that grows here, from wild flowers to apricots. Fruits and vegetables attain higher concentrations of sugars
and flavour as plants are stimulated by the fertile earth but
stunted by winds and lack of water. Many crops are grown on
steep terraces that are hard to reach and even harder to work,
so the true produce of Vesuvio is always a little more expensive
than that of the plains but the extra cost is amply justified by
the exceptional flavour. Recently, the Campania Region has
helped some of these products gain IGP (Indicazione Geografica
Protetta) and DOP (Denominazione di Origine Protetta) status,
and national organizations like Slow Food (www.slowfood.com)
have been working to make them known and to stimulate
younger generations of growers to keep cultivating them. Here
is more information about some of the most important varieties.

Apricot – Albicocca Vesuviana IGP

The terrain on Vesuvio's sides and at its base is dotted with
apricot orchards. This delicious fruit has always thrived here:
4th-century references to its existence in this area have been
found, but in the 16th century it began to be cultivated more

Vesuvian crisommole

Terracotta 'hats' keeps these artichokes tender

Ripe persimmons

Opposite: Gennaro D'Auria with Castellammare artichokes grown at the foot of Vesuvio

systematically. Many varieties of *crisommole* – as the Neapolitans call them – exist, with wonderful names in dialect such as Monaco Bello (the handsome monk), Cafona (the uncouth woman), Palummella (the little dove), Pellecchiella (the one with a lot of skin), Boccuccia Spinosa and Liscia... the list is long, for there are at least thirteen varieties growing on and around the volcano. (In June, I visited a huge wholesale market at Sant'Anastasìa that is open only in the apricot season – one month per year.)

Here again, enlightened local food experts are trying to help create a special economy based on quality for these exceptional fruits, as they are under commercial pressure from the cheap – and often mushy and tasteless – apricots that most Italian supermarkets import.

Artichoke – Carciofo Violetto di Castellammare

The purple-green artichokes of Castellammare di Stabia are grown within the Vesuvian territory, in the flat fields between Pompei and Castellammare. Here a special technique has long been used to ensure that the artichokes remain tender and pale: as the buds begin to grow and ripen, the central '*mamma*' or '*mammolella*', the artichoke flower, are covered by little terracotta 'hats' (*pignatelle*) – hand-made dome-shaped covers that sit on top of each artichoke and prevent them from toughening. This product is in Slow Food's *Presidio* for Campania, and they are trying to ensure that some of the land that was traditionally used to grow these and other crops be returned to this use.

Persimmon – Kaki Napoletano

If you drive through the flat lands at the base of the volcano in winter, you'll notice orchards of large leafless trees that look as if they have been decorated for Christmas with bright orange 'balls'. These are *kaki* or *cachi* – persimmons – and this area is one of the most important for producing this curious fruit. My non-Mediterranean childhood memories of the persimmon are of my mother puckering her lips as she described their astringency. So when I was first offered gifts of *kaki* in Italy, my instinct was to arrange them in a bowl on the table – they are quite beautiful with their hot Indian colour – and keep them as decorations. I was amazed to discover that in Italy the persimmon was a sweet fragrant fruit, a mid-winter's gastronomic treasure. In Campania I finally solved the mystery of how the same fruit could be so different. It doesn't depend solely on ripeness, but on whether the fruit has been fertilized or not during pollination: where fertilization has occurred, the fruit is

sweet and tender, with a much shorter shelf life; otherwise, the fruit remains crisp but sour, and has to be brought to ripeness – naturally or otherwise.

Tomatoes – I Pomodorini a Piénnolo

Throughout the Vesuvio area, in every fruit and vegetable store (and in every barn and larder) you'll see *i pomodorini a piénnolo* hanging like big bunches of bright red grapes. These smallish tomatoes have a pointed tip – or *pizzo* – and are particularly thick-skinned and meaty. They are grown high up on the sides of the volcano, where the sun and mineral soil make them resistant to humidity and rot. They are traditionally picked a whole stem at a time, tied into bunches and hung up. In the right conditions they last till after Christmas and provide fresh, intensely flavourful tomatoes – or *pummarole* – long after the growing season has ended.

A heavy bunch of pomodorini a piénnolo

San Marzano Tomato – Pomodoro San Marzano DOP

The San Marzano is the quintessential plum tomato, a keystone of the Mediterranean diet that is favoured on everything from pizzas to pasta. Story has it that first seeds of San Marzano came to Campania in 1770 as a gift from the kingdom of Peru to the kingdom of Naples, and it was planted extensively in what is now San Marzano. Up until twenty years ago, millions of tons of tomatoes were harvested throughout the region, earning them the nickname of 'the red gold of Campania'. Then, in the 1980s, tomato of all varieties went through a series of crises, including the spread of a disease specific to the tomato, and almost disappeared. Luckily the Campania Region's seed bank still had some original San Marzano seeds (collected from the farmers) under refrigeration and from a handful of them the crop has recently been reproduced.

What's so special about it? 'The San Marzano has an elongated plum shape, firm flesh and very few seeds,' says Vincenzo Aita, the Region's former Agriculture *Assessore*. 'The skin is a deep bright red, and peels off easily. Most importantly, it has rich, intense flavour, is low in acidity (but high in nutrients), and is the absolute best for canning, and for making our Neapolitan tomato *ragù* – a sauce that needs to be simmered for at least six hours.'

The San Marzano is tricky to grow: it needs to be staked carefully, and hand-picked when ripe, which means the farmers have to pass through the fields six to eight times per season. So it's more expensive than other plum tomatoes, but well worth the extra – if you can find it.

Walnuts

Almost every country household in Campania has at least one walnut tree in its garden. The walnuts (*noci*) of the Sorrento hills are famous (they have IGP status), and are usually allowed to mature before being picked, for eating or for use in baking. Vesuvian walnuts (of the Sorrento type) are also considered a delicacy. The other traditional use for walnuts is in *nocino* – or, in Neapolitan dialect, *nucillo* – a spiced, sweet-and-bitter digestive liqueur made when the nuts are still encased in their tender green shells. A couple of fine artisan producers in Campania are now making it to sell: Cantine Di Meo (see pp. 375-77) and Vincenzo D'Alessandro of 'e Curti (see pp. 136-137).

The Wines of Vesuvio

As with other crops grown here, the volcanic soils bring minerality and character to the grapes, which in turn affect their wines' flavour and structure. Until recently, the area was known for the vast quantities of grapes it produced but not for the quality of its wines. That is now changing somewhat, and new attitudes to winemaking are paying off; those willing to reduce yields and take more care in the cellar have been able to improve their wines enormously.

The most successful grape varieties on the volcanic soils, and the essential components of the white Vesuvio DOC and Lacryma Christi, are: Coda di Volpe (at least 80% – it may be accompanied by Verdeca), Falanghina and Greco (up to 20%). They result in drinkable, fruity young wines with characteristic mineral notes: perfect for tasting chilled on a hot summer's day by the sea.

Vesuvian soil is full of clinkers

As for the red Vesuvio DOC and the red Lacryma Christi, Piedirosso – also known as Per' 'e Palummo – is the main grape, with Sciascinoso and Aglianico (up to 20%) playing a smaller part. These unassuming wines are perfumed, medium-bodied and enjoyable. Both reds and whites go well with the *cucina di mare* of the coast.

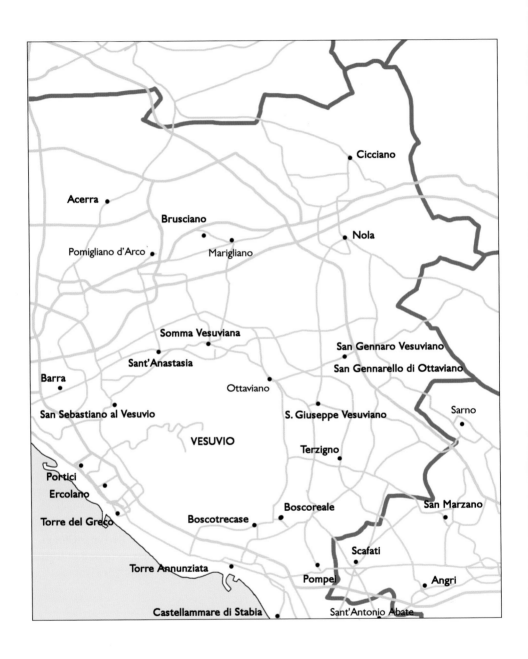

Cicciano

Acerra

Brusciano

Nola

Pomigliano d'Arco

Marigliano

Somma Vesuviana

San Gennaro Vesuviano

Sant'Anastasia

San Gennarello di Ottaviano

Barra

Ottaviano

Sarno

San Sebastiano al Vesuvio

S. Giuseppe Vesuviano

VESUVIO

Terzigno

Portici

Ercolano

Boscoreale

San Marzano

Torre del Greco

Boscotrecase

Scafati

Torre Annunziata

Pompei

Angri

Castellammare di Stabia

Sant'Antonio Abate

Angri

Musical band

Via Risi, 20
TEL 081 949189
FAX 081 5133050

O' Revotapopolo

If you ever need to hire a Neapolitan band for a *festa* (or a film), this is one of the most colourful. The musicians are dressed in Pulcinella costumes, and play an incredible assortment of instruments, including pots, pans and plumber's pipes.

Barra

Honey

Via Villa Bisignano, 13
TEL 081 5721508
333 4039315

Apicoltura La Fattoria

Santina Nocerino keeps her bees within the Parco del Vesuvio. Her delicate acacia honey won first prize in Campania last year. She also makes honeys flavoured with natural products: fragrant rose petals, hazelnuts from Giffoni (see p. 245), and strawberries, as well as royal jelly, propolis and unusual 'shepherds' made from pure beeswax.

Boscoreale

Pasta

Via Brancaccio, 75/a
TEL 081 8594976
INTERNET
www.arteepasta.it

Cooperativa Arte e Pasta

Using bronze dies, this cooperative makes artisanal pasta close to Pompei. They produce many shapes, long and short, including twisted *mafaldine* and ribbed *festonata* lasagna.

Boscotrecase

Wine

Via Rio, 2
TEL/FAX 081 5298492
INTERNET
www.terredisylvamala.com

Terre di Sylva Mala

This is a recent winery that has begun working with the indigenous grape varieties of the volcano: the white Lacryma Christi, of Coda di Volpe grapes, has a nice crispness to it, and reflects the terroir it is produced on, while the red Lacryma Christi shows a herbaceous Piedirosso.

Wine

Via Casciello, 5
TEL 081 8584963
335 6621178

Sorrentino Vini

This is one of the more important Vesuvian wineries: they are converting to organic, and produce the full range of volcanic wines, including several versions of Lacryma Christi and Pompeiano IGT. Working with the œnologist Marco Stefanini, they have modernized their cellars and improved quality in the estate's twelve hectares of vineyards – and the results show. Sorrentino Vini also makes an unusual *distillato* from the Vesuvian apricots.

Brusciano (Pomigliano d'Arco)

Restaurant
Taverna Estìa

Via G. De Ruggiero 68
TEL 081 5199633
OPEN dinner only
CLOSED Mon;
20 Aug–5 Sep
PRICE €€€€

This attractive restaurant offers two dining spaces – inside and out – and it's hard to choose between them. The garden is perfect for warm summer evenings, with tables surrounded by greenery and softly perfumed jasmine. The indoor dining room is equally appealing, with 'stacks' of wines on the walls, a big fireplace at one end, and a large window into the kitchen at the other. The story is unusual in that the owner and chef, Armando Sposito, had a completely different career until very recently. He decided to open a restaurant, and engaged first one, then a second chef – but the results were not what he had in mind. Ultimately he decided to do the cooking himself. After five years, his two grown sons have joined him – one making desserts, and the other in the dining room; his wife Margherita also lends a hand when she finishes her day job. The food reflects the enthusiasm of a keen autodidact: lots of ideas and good-quality ingredients brought together in nicely arranged dishes.

Cicciano

Agriturismo, Bed and Breakfast
Il Cortile

Via Roma, 43
TEL 081 8248897
FAX 081 8264851

Sijtsken Dupon is a Dutch woman who has set up a charming B&B near Nola, furnished with antiques. She is also a great cook, and on January 17 each year she participates in a *festa* to celebrate the slaughtering of the pig, with traditional dishes.

Ercolano

Restaurant, Wine Bar
Vivo Lo Re

Corso Resina, 261
TEL 081 7390207
OPEN lunch and dinner
CLOSED
Sun eve & Mon; Aug
CARDS All
PRICE €€

This wine bar–*osteria* is well located in the centre of what is known as the 'Golden Mile' (*Miglio d'Oro*), a 'strip' of fabulous 18th-century noble villas built along the coast from Portici to Torre del Greco – some visitable, others unfortunately now derelict. The villas, built to emulate the royal palace at Portici, faced both the volcano (whose mini eruptions were considered

FOR TOURIST INFORMA-
TION ON THE VILLAS:
Ente per le Ville Vesuviane
at Villa Campolieto:
TEL 081 7322134
INTERNET
www.villevesuviane.net

Villa Signorini:
INTERNET
www.villasignorini.it

diverting – as long as they remained at a safe distance) on one side, and the sea on the other, and were surrounded by landscaped parks and gardens that have now all but disappeared under an ugly concrete jungle. Of those currently open to the public, Villa Favorita, Villa Campolieto and Villa Signorini are the most beautiful.

Maurizio Focone worked for a while in New York with the Campanian restaurateur Tony May before coming back to open this *simpatica osteria*, which features the simple but delicious dishes of Neapolitan cuisine, and the many fine wines that are now being made in the region.

Pompei and Ercolano – the sites

In a bake-shop was a mill for grinding the grain, and the furnaces for baking the bread: and they say that here, in the same furnaces, the exhumers of Pompeii found nice, well baked loaves which the baker had not found time to remove from the ovens the last time he left his shop, because circumstances compelled him to leave in such a hurry.

Mark Twain The Innocents Abroad

FOR MORE INFORMATION
ON POMPEI, ERCOLANO,
OPLONTIS – VILLA DI
POPPEA AND STABIA:
TEL 081 8575347
INTERNET
www.pompeiisites.org
AND FOR NIGHT VISITS
www.arethusa.net

So much has been written about Pompei and Ercolano, the two cities that were covered by ash and volcanic debris in the great eruption of Vesuvio in 79 AD, that they have become meccas of tourism since they were first uncovered. At present, four million people visit the sites each year. Happily much has changed since I first visited Pompei fifteen years ago: in those days the ill-kept city seemed even more desolate than might have been expected. Recently extraordinary care has been taken to restore the gardens, including vineyards (see below), and to bring back a sense of order and life to the site. Excellent audio guides are available to all sites. Another recent addition to the summer options is to visit Pompei by night, for an unforgettable multimedia evening.

Pompei

Restaurant

Piazza Bartolo Longo, 8
TEL 081 8505566
FAX 081 8633342
E-MAIL info@ilprincipe.com
CLOSED Sun eve & Mon;
1–20 Aug; 23–26 Dec
PRICE €€€€€–€€€€€€

Ristorante Il Principe
This handsome restaurant is in the old centre of the modern city of Pompei, diagonally across the *piazza* from the Sanctuary of Madonna del Rosario. The décor fits the location, with a Pompeian-red ceiling and Pompeian-style murals. Marco and Pina Carli are admirable hosts and, thirteen years ago, their

A MODERN WINE MADE IN ANCIENT POMPEI

Piero Mastroberardino at the launch of his Pompeian wine

'*Il Vesuvio* is a mine of indigenous grape varieties,' says Professor Piero Mastroberardino as we stand within the walls of Roman Pompei, in the experimental vineyard that his family's winery (Mastroberardino at Atripalda, see pp. 325-26) is now running with the Pompei Archæological Authority. 'The Roman emperors were *buongustai* – gourmets are the modern equivalent – and with their large holdings of the best lands, including the volcano Vesuvio, they influenced the cultivation of grapes for their favourite wines.'

This fascinating œnological project began in 1996. The idea was to replant the vineyards within Pompei's city walls with grapes similar to those that had originally been culti-vated there. Clues were provided both by ancient texts, such as Pliny, and by excavations, which uncovered traces of wine in the terracotta amphoræ buried in the ground, and grape seeds whose DNA it was possible to analyse.

'We were able to reconstruct the exact Roman planting densities and training systems for the vines thanks to the "negative" spaces left in the ground by the vineyards' wooden poles after the eruption of 79 AD,' continues Piero Mastroberardino. These holes – spaced 4 Roman feet by 4 Roman feet, or 1.20 metres by 1.20 metres apart – were filled with plaster (just like the 'spaces' created by human bodies in the ash), and they marked the rows and distances of the vines' supports. 'Pompei had many vineyards and gardens interspersed among its villas, and we have been able to replant several, for a total of about one hectare.'

As for the grape varieties, eight cultivars were planted based on research into the types of grapes used at the time:

Vitis Aminea Gemina (Greco)
Vitis Apiano (Fiano)
Vitis Hellenica (Aglianico)
Columbina Purpurea (Piedirosso)
Vitis Oleagina (Sciascinoso, or Olivella)
Cauda Vulpium (Coda di Volpe)
Vitis Alopecis (Capronetta)
Falanghina

The Pompeian vineyards are within the ancient city's walls

'As Pliny the Elder reminds us in his *Naturalis Historia*, these were the grape varieties favoured by the Romans to make the best red and white wines,' continues Mastroberardino. 'Of these, Greco and Aglianico were brought here by the Greeks, in pre-Roman times.'

The initial experiments gave interesting results: of the red grapes, those most suited to the climate and terrains of Vesuvio were the indigenous Piedirosso and Sciascinoso, which now form the basis of the new Pompei wine. Aglianico suffered too much from the heat, and from the lack of temperature change from day to night. The first fruits were fermented, aged and bottled under the name of 'Villa dei Misteri' after one of the most famous of the Pompeian villas. The red wine, from the 2001 vintage, was officially launched in 2003, in 1,721 bottles. For those interested in seeing the Pompeian vineyards, they are mostly located near the amphitheatre.

restaurant became only the second to earn a Michelin star in Campania. 'We have to thank the great chef Alfonso Iaccarino (see p. 212) for the precedent he set, because seeing him get his first Michelin star in 1988 made us believe it might be possible for things to improve in Campania,' says Marco Carli. Carli, who is originally from Tuscany, has long believed in the cultural potential of Pompei, and has been an active promoter of the site; he organizes dinners within it.

Il Principe features several menu choices that include traditional dishes as well as recipes from ancient Rome. 'We have adapted their ideas to the modern palate,' says Marco Carli, 'in order to help visitors understand the type of foods the Romans were fond of.' One ingredient which is particularly interesting is *garum*, the anchovy-based condiment that sparks debate among food historians and writers. 'Some people insist that the Romans' *garum* was made of putrefied fish, and would never appeal to us today. But I can't believe that the Romans didn't also have a 'Chanel Number 5' of *garums*, made with choice ingredients that enhanced rather than masked their dishes,' he says. 'After all, Worcestershire sauce is a *garum* too, copied in the 1890s.'

I enjoyed Il Principe's *lagane al garum*, in which the pasta was served with an oil-based sauce of Sorrento walnuts and anchovies. It was delicate yet a bit richer than a normal walnut sauce – neither pungent nor fishy nor overly salt. Mushrooms are another speciality at Il Principe, as in *Pioppini vesuviani e seppiolini* – delicate, lightly fibrous mushrooms that grow beneath poplar trees – combined with squid, olive oil and parsley.

Dessert offers a perfect chance to taste the Roman dishes – many of Middle Eastern influence – like *gastris*, a hot cake of honey and sesame seeds, or the *cassata* of sheep's and goat's ricotta enriched with walnuts and *canditi*. 'The Romans didn't know oranges and lemons as foods, but kept them for medicinal purposes,' explains Carli. 'But they did have candied citron, or *cedro*.' There is a fine wine list with a wide range of Campanian wines, as well as selected wines from other parts of Italy and beyond.

Speciality Food Store

Melius

Via Lepanto 156/160
TEL 081 8502598
E-MAIL info@melius.net
INTERNET www.melius.net

Melius is a fabulous food store, along the lines of a Dean & De Luca, where you can find everything from rare hand-made raw-milk cheeses to cat food. 'When I took over from my father,' says Sabatino Melius, the dynamic young owner, 'I wanted to upgrade the quality of the products we could sell, but at the same time not lose the local customers who had been coming here all their lives. After all, there are food treasures to save, but not at the cost of our loyal clientele.' The attractive shop has an excellent range of artisan cheeses and *salumi*, freshly butchered meat, as well as ready-to-eat foods, prepared by the family, that are perfect for picnics. In the sweet department, there are prettily packed cookies and nougats that make good presents, as well as serious chocolate for those who prefer their chocolate 'neat'. The shop also sells selected wines and olive oils.

Portici

Fruit and Vegetable Preserves

SALES POINT:
Via Cardano, 30/F
Portici
WORKSHOP:
Via Ferrovia, 188
San Gennaro Vesuviano
TEL 081 7888556
INTERNET
www.vesuvioro.com

Vesuvioro

This artisan company makes some of the most delicious jams and vegetable preserves I've tasted in Campania. The apricot *confettura* is dense, fruit-packed (75%) and made exclusively from apricot varieties special to the volcano: Monaco, Pellecchiella and Vitillo. Vesuvioro also bottles the flavourful small tomatoes '*con il pizzo*' that are otherwise picked in bunches and hung up to dry, and makes a jam from green cherry tomatoes.

ALSO AT PORTICI
Campania Felix (Via Cimarosa, 4; TEL 081 481183) is a speciality food shop selling a wide selection of the best local products: olive oil, fruit and vegetable preserves, honey, candies. And if you are in need of refreshment after all that shopping, stop in at Gelateria Gallo (Corso Garibaldi, 34; TEL 081 475942) and treat yourself to an ice-cream from this classic *gelateria*.

San Gennarello di Ottaviano

Pastries, Gelato

Via Gabriele D'Annunzio, 7
TEL 081 5296831
INTERNET
www.accademia-
maestri.pasticceri.it
OPEN
Tues–Sun 8.00–13.30,
16.00–19.30
CLOSED 3 weeks in Aug

Pasticceria Gelateria Pasquale Marigliano

Pastry-making is undoubtedly one of the greatest expressions of the spirit of Neapolitan cuisine, and Pasquale Marigliano is one of the major exponents of this art – a rising star in the (sweet) Campanian firmament. To visit his elegant pastry shop on a Sunday morning, and see the exceptional display of cakes and tarts being selected by the customers for the *guantiera di dolci* – or tray of desserts – they will take home or to whomever has invited them for lunch, is a spectacular event. In this part of the

region, with chaotic villages strung around the base of the volcano, many of them with severe social problems – the ritual of
the Sunday cakes is sacrosanct. I've often been to lunches at
which not only has the hostess prepared two or three desserts
herself, but each of the guests has appeared with a gigantic
packet wrapped in gold-trimmed, crisp white paper containing
pastries or *gelati* – all of it guilt-free, this being Campania.

The talented Pasquale Marigliano is in his early thirties and
was born in Pompei. He became passionate about pastries at an
early age, training first locally and then in Paris at Fauchon and
Le Nôtre. His cakes have won prizes and awards in all categories. If he is skilled in the technique and artistry of French
patisserie (his wife is French), it is in the range of Campanian
paste that he excels: *la pastiera*, the Easter tart made with
plumped grain and orange-water; *rococò*, ringed meringue-like
biscuits of toasted almonds; *mostaccioli*, biscuits enriched with
cooked grape must; *la sfogliatella*, of ricotta studded with candied fruits; airy *babàs*… the list is wonderfully long, but the use
of only first-rate ingredients and excellent technique is common
to them all. Marigliano also does some catering and makes his
own *gelati*, as well as cakes to order.

San Marzano sul Sarno

Giustizia e Libertà (Via Vittorio Veneto, 5; TEL 081 955483),
Justice and Liberty is the name this fruit- and vegetable-growing
co-operative has chosen for its organic production of San
Marzano tomatoes, apricots, lemons and other native varieties.

San Sebastiano al Vesuvio

Bread

Masseria Monaco Aiello, 1
TEL 098 5741042
081 574 43426

Panificio DOC di Domenico Filosa
This baker makes not only the local bread for which the town is
famous, but also biscuits, *taralli* – peppered savoury dough rings
not unlike pretzels – and pizza, all available from his little shop.

Wine

Via Figliolia
San Sebastiano al Vesuvio
TEL 081 7713755
FAX 081 5745510
E-MAIL info@defalco.it
INTERNET www.defalco.it

De Falco
The De Falco family have long been residents of this town, and
have been making wine, here and in Puglia, since the beginning
of the 20th century. They are particularly interested in the white
Coda di Volpe indigenous grape variety that flourishes on the
steep volcanic slopes of Vesuvio, as their fine Lacryma Christi
whites – especially the special reserve – will attest.

Vini e Dintorni (Piazza Enrico Fermi, 17; TEL 081 5748610) is a
good place to buy wines from the area. Maria Fiore (Via
Panoramica Fellapane, 43; TEL 081 7714392) is a reliable
organic grower of the *pomodorini col pizzo* that are hung in
bunches to dry and last till after Christmas. The farm also
produces other fruits and vegetables.

Sant'Anastasìa

At Sant'Anastasìa every 24th of December, the townspeople re-
enact the Nativity – *il presepe*: the electricity is cut off and the
town lit only by torches and candles, with various scenes from
the nativity recreated in the *portoni*, or doorways, of the old
part of Sant'Anastasìa.

Restaurant

Via Garibaldi, 57
TEL 081 8972821
E-MAIL enzo@e-curti.it
INTERNET www.e-curti.it
CLOSED Sun
CARDS All
PRICE €€

'e Curti

This little, one-room restaurant is quite unique, for many
reasons. Until you memorize the route it can be hard to find,
tucked away in a narrow *vicolo* in the heart of Sant'Anastasìa,
one of the circle of villages around the volcano. But don't worry,
it's never a problem to get there. Once you're in the vicinity, a
quick call to Vincenzo D'Alessandro, the proprietors' son, and
he'll meet and accompany you to the restaurant. I mention this
because it's characteristic of everything this family does: if you
thank him for having helped solve a major problem, Vincenzo
laughs and says: 'Per così poco?' For so little? The mood is
always upbeat, just right to eat enjoyably. Vincenzo's mother and
father, Angela and Carmine, diminutive of stature but giants of
hospitality, are the cook and host at 'e Curti. Even the restaurant's name has a story behind it, for *'e curti* – or 'the short people' (*curti* is Neapolitan for *corti*, or short) – were Signora
D'Alessandro's uncles, perfect midgets who, after spending a lifetime in the circus, retired and opened this restaurant in 1924.

'I still remember them from when I was a boy,' says Vincenzo
as we look at an old photograph of his great-uncles standing
beside the circus fat lady, *elegantissimi* in their miniature tuxe-
dos. 'They were famous for their *bucatini alla carbonara*, and
would stand on a stool at the table to serve the pasta personally.'

If *'e curti* are no longer with us, their traditional recipes and
spirit live on in the form of Signora Angela and her aunt
Assunta (sister to the midgets), who do all the cooking in the
neat kitchen hung with copper pots. 'Sant'Anastasìa used to be
famous for its copper work,' says Angela as she stirs a thick

Vincenzo D'Alessandro

vegetable soup in a shining pan.

'Our dishes are embarrassingly simple!' laughs Vincenzo as his father comes to the table with a platter of little *melanzane* (eggplant or aubergine), rolled and sauced with the special 'hanging' tomatoes from the volcano. Simple maybe, but utterly delicious. Next comes a warming soup of white beans and Pioppini mushrooms. It's late autumn, and the mushrooms are still being found. 'Around here, they pour pasta-cooking water onto the stumps of poplar trees to get them to produce these mushrooms,' says Carmine. 'Our beans hold their shape when cooked thanks to the arid soils they have been grown in.' There's a wealth of culture in this 'simple' food.

La minestra maritata arrives. In this potent peasant soup – which Jeanne Caròla Francesconi calls the Neapolitan national dish *per eccellenza* – seven types of wild and bitter green (including borage and escarole) are 'married' to almost as many poor cuts of pork (including trotter, *prosciutto* bone and blood sausage). 'Our *cucina* is hardly ethereal!' says Vincenzo. 'So you need a big red wine to go with it.' We're not even half-way through this meal of ancient, earthy flavours: still to come are *penne* with cherry tomatoes, meaty mushrooms and flakes of Parmesan; deeply-flavoured mountain lamb chops covered with peas; stuffed *budelli*, where the long intestine is wound like string around its forceful filling; and finally a custard of egg and farmer's ricotta. To finish, I'm offered a tiny glass of *nucillo*, the spiced walnut liqueur that Vincenzo and his sister Sofia make nearby. I'm ready to leave, but not before being invited to join the family for Christmas Eve dinner – I've been adopted.

ALSO AT SANT'ANASTASÌA
Antonio Mollo's Mediterranea Olive (Via Porzio, 53; TEL 081 8982954) is a classic shop selling green olives, stockfish and other local specialties.

Sant'Antonio Abate

Tomatoes, Artichokes

Azienda Sabato Abagnale

Via De Luca, 23
TEL 081 8735300
347 1135440
INTERNET WWW.
miracolosangennaro.it

I'm grateful to Beatrice Ughi of Gustiamo.com for introducing me to Sabatino Abagnale, the young director of this vegetable-growing company. His San Marzano tomatoes – under the brand name of Il Miracolo di San Gennaro – are the most flavourful I've tasted. I asked him why.

'We tried several clones of San Marzano before opting for this one, SMEC-20,' he explains as he offers me a taste of a sun-

*Up the tree, picking
walnuts*

*The walnut-picking
team*

NOCINO OR NUCILLO

'Every Neapolitan family has three secret recipes which are
considered sacred to that family: for *ragù*, *la pastiera*, and
nucillo,' says Vincenzo D'Alessandro, whose parents run 'e
Curti restaurant (see p. 134), and who now produces this
walnut liqueur. The inky brown, after-dinner *digestivo* is
very popular throughout Italy (where it is most commonly
known as *nocino*), as the Italians are fond of spiced –
almost medicinal – sweet-and-bitter *digestivi*, especially during the Christmas season.

'For me, it all started seven years ago,' he says on a hot
day in late June, as we walk through a walnut grove at the
foot of Vesuvio in time to see the fruits being picked. 'I
wanted to preserve the traditional walnut liqueur that has
always been served in our restaurant. It was made from an
1894 recipe given to 'e Curti by a *pasticciere* from Portici –
though its origins are centuries older. Here the family's
recipe is always kept in the 'memory bank' by the women,
and this one was particularly good. Now it's my sister,

Sofia, who is the only one to know the exact proportions of the ingredients.'

Legend has it that the nuts must be picked on San Giovanni Battista's day (June 24), which was celebrated as Midsummer's Day in the pagan calendar and symbolized the victory of good over evil. 'It's like a fable with an underlayer of wisdom, because there are only three or four days before the green outer shell of the walnuts begins to lignify, and they fall exactly at that time of year.'

The green, unshelled walnuts are hand-picked from the trees by men on high ladders, and sacks of the fruit are brought to D'Alessandro's courtyard and processed within six hours of being picked.

First they are cut into quarters, then placed – in precise quantities – into big glass *damigiane* of alcohol. 'Here, outdoors, under big parasols, they will remain to infuse until the end of September. After a week, we add cloves, nutmeg and Madagascar cinnamon sticks, *droghe* still sold in the pharmacies of Napoli.' The infusion, *il fiore*, is strained off the nuts, and added to a sugar syrup before being bottled with the 'e Curti label.

It's perfect after a winter's dinner, or with cookies (*dolci secchi*) that are a specialty of the area. D'Alessandro is also now making a *nucillo* grappa, Assoluto, as well as Espresso Liquoroso, a coffee liqueur made with the coffee company, Illy, that D'Alessandro describes as 'a cup of espresso for eternity'. The bold packaging designs for the bottles are by Fiorenzo D'Avino.

*Each green nut is placed
in the cutting machine
and quartered.
The cut nuts are added
to alcohol by Sofia
D'Alessandro*

Cans of San Marzano and other Campanian tomatoes

Pummarole

dried tomato fillet preserved in oil. Absolutely fantastic! The fruit is almost as concentrated as jam – and very naturally sweet. 'Most of the San Marzano varieties that can be found as seeds are bred for quantity, giving up to 10 kilos per plant, whereas this type only produces $2^{1}/_{2}$ kilos and is vulnerable to all sorts of attacks, but its flavour is infinitely better.' The toma-toes also need to be grown on well-drained volcanic soil to give their best. 'This area was once covered with tomato and artichoke fields,' he continues. It is March, and under the volcano the artichokes are ready for picking. 'But floriculture yields higher incomes faster, so most of the land is now used for intense-growing flowers crops. The problem is that flower-producing strips the land of all its nutrients, so you can't plant vegetables on it again.'

The San Marzano is unique for many reasons. Unlike tomato varieties that are picked green and ripen off the plant, the San Marzano only ripens on the vine, so it needs to be picked and delivered within twenty-four hours, and cannot be worked industrially. The tomatoes have few seeds, and they are visibly separate from their flesh. The skins of the San Marzano are very thin and tender, and when ripe, the tomato takes on an almost Bordeaux-deep red. 'We like to say it's the colour of the blood of the *contadini* who work it,' he says with a smile. Abagnale and his co-workers wash, then boil the tomatoes alone – no acidifiers or preserving agents are used – for about 75 minutes. As a small grower of very high quality vegetables, Abagnale has withdrawn from the powerful San Marzano Consorzio that caters to bigger, industrial producers. 'It's crazy but, by law, the only way to sell San Marzanos in a can is to sell them peeled, or *pelati*. Since we don't peel ours – the skins are so fine there is no need to – we are not allowed to call them San Marzano – yet *ours* are the authentic variety!'

In spring, Abagnale and other local friends grow the Carciofo Violetto di Castellammare (see above p. 120), the artichokes with little terracotta 'caps' placed on each one to keep them tender and pale.

Other good growers nearby are Giosuè Ferrara, Ferdinando Ruocco, Francesco Longobardi, all at Santa Maria La Carità; and Vincenzo Arpaia at Casola di Napoli.

Wine

Via Stabia, 733
TEL/FAX 081 8743029
E-MAIL
info@vinicolalamura.it
INTERNET
www.vinicolalamura.it

Azienda Agricola La Mura, Poggio delle Baccanti
Young Raffaele La Mura is working with his father, Sebastiano, to make wines from the volcanic terrains of Vesuvio. Here again, it is Lacryma Christi which dominates – not only is it the best-known name for Vesuvio's wines, but it offers the producers

the chance to work with indigenous grape varieties like
Piedirosso as well as with the great Campanian red grape type,
Aglianico. Of the whites, Falanghina is the base for the crisp,
mineral wines that work so well here, with the addition of a little known variety, Caprettone.

Somma Vesuviana

Restaurant

Via Costantinopoli
(Rione Trieste)
TEL 081 893 2159
081 893 1486
CLOSED Tues
and 15-20 Aug
PRICE €-€€

Ristorante Lo Smeraldo

Under the volcano might seem an odd place to go for stockfish
(*stoccafisso* or *stocco*), but this town is famous among
Neapolitans for its air-dried and salt-cured cod – imported
directly from Norway. This friendly trattoria's dining room is
large enough to accommodate entire families – when I ate there,
a table of twenty was celebrating an elderly aunt's birthday. The
cooking is simple but flavourful, with traditional dishes taking
centre stage: stockfish served a number of ways – stewed with
Gaeta olives and cherry tomatoes, or as a sauce for *paccheri* –
preceded by a mixed *insalata di mare*, *pasta al forno* (like
lasagne), *polpette con sugo* (jumbo meatballs). There is always a
large home-made *babà* for dessert, served in thick slices.

ALSO AT SOMMA VESUVIANA

Baccalà and stockfish

If you want fresh-roasted coffee beans, Napoli style, the Molaro
brothers at Torrefazione Caffè Picking (Via Fossa dei Leoni, 11;

TEL 081 8996890) are experts at selecting and blending them.

Alimenta 2000 specializes in gluten-free products (Via Marigliano, 40; TEL 081 8932636).

Jolly Fish (Via Tavani, 118; TEL 081 8993420) is the De Mauros' sales point for the imported *baccalà* and stockfish that are so popular in this area.

Il Gocciolatoio (Via Turati, 20; TEL 081 8993262; INTERNET www.ilgocciolatoio.it) is an *enoteca* that offers the volcano's best wines.

At her farm, La Rinascita (S. Maria a Castello, 98; TEL 081 8991617) the young Rosamaria Nocerino is following the family tradition of cultivating rare volcanic fruits and bottling mushrooms – an art she carries on from her grandfather, who learned to cultivate *champignons* as a prisoner of war in France.

Terzigno

Wine, Oil

Villa Dora

Via Boscomauro, 1
TEL 081 5295016
FAX 081 8274905
E-MAIL
info@gruppodorotea.it
INTERNET
www.gruppodorotea.it

This thirteen-hectare estate is working with the talented œnologists, Roberto Cipresso and Maurizio De Simone, who specialize in making wines that express the character of Italy's numerous indigenous grape varieties and terroirs. Here the grapes are Piedirosso and Aglianico, Coda di Volpe and Falanghina for the red and white versions of Lacryma Christi. The reduction of yields in the vineyard and knowing use of wood in the cellar has produced a well-bodied red: Lacryma Christi del Vesuvio Forgiato Rosso – a far cry from the simple, unassuming wine that used to be associated with this name. The company also produces fine extra virgin olive oil under the name of Dorotea.

ALSO AT TERZIGNO

Lello Esposito's Candied Organics (Via Nespole della Monica; TEL 339 3615369; INTERNET www.candiedorganics.it) does just what it says, making candied fruits for use in pastry-making and cooking, or just to eat by themselves.

Torre Annunziata

This was one of Campania's historic pasta-making towns between the 18th and 19th centuries. In part this was thanks to the town's other industry: arms-making. A large arms factory commissioned by the Bourbon king Carlo III in 1785 involved creating an artificial canal to pipe water from the Sarno river

into the town. Along this waterway, mills were built for grinding the flour to go into the pasta. For more on the history and
methods of artisan pasta, see Gragnano (p. 188).

Pastificio Fratelli Setaro

Via Mazzini 47
TEL 081 8611464
E-MAIL info@setaro.it

Begun in 1939, Setaro has become one of the key names in
Campanian artisan-made pasta. Torre Annunziata's first grain
mills were built in the mid-16th century, but it was not until
1850 that its *pastifici* were opened. By 1950 there were more
than 120 mills and pasta factories here, producing what was
known as *pasta di Napoli*.

Today, the family-run Setaro factory is the only one left. The
pasta is excellent, made using hard-wheat durum flour, pure
local water and bronze dies, and the slow-drying process that is
necessary for the best pasta making.

Organic Produce, Wine

Azienda Agricola Casa Barone

Via delle Quattro
Giornate, 35
TEL 081 7711559
348 2539506
FAX 081 5740387
INTERNET
www.casabarone.it

Giovanni Marini's lovely farm is on the black slopes of the volcano. This rich soil produces intensely flavoured fruits and vegetables. Here you can visit the apricot, citrus and walnut groves,
see how tomatoes and other vegetables are grown, and sample
some of the farm's fine jams or preserved vegetables. There is
even a small amount of wine being made from the area's indigenous grape varieties – some still on their original rootstock.

Torre Del Greco

This town is famous for its coral artworks; in the past coral was
believed to ward off evil spirits. The best place to see the
remarkable handiwork of the coral artisans is at the Museum of
Coral (Museo del Corallo, Piazza Palomba, 6; TEL 081
8811360). After that, go for a sweet pick-me-up at Dolce Idea
(Via Roma, 8; TEL 081 8818343).

Trecase

Cantina del Vesuvio (Via Tirone della Guardia, 12; TEL 335
7070738; INTERNET www.cantinadelvesuvio.it) is another of
the area's improving wineries to keep an eye on. Its eleven
hectares are located on the volcano's slopes, commanding views
of the city and gulf of Napoli below. The farm is in the process
of becoming organic, and so far produces rosé, white and red
Lacryma Christi under winemaker Amodio Pesce.

Chapter 4

The Emperor's Islands

Capri, Ischia and Procida

The islands of the Golfo di Napoli (Bay of Naples) are some of the most beautiful in the Mediterranean – or anywhere else, for that matter. Despite their physical proximity to each other, there is a fundamental difference between Ischia and Procida on the one hand, and Capri on the other: the first two are part of the volcanic landscape known as the Campi Flegrei (see p. 88-89), which continued to erupt and change in configuration until relatively recently, whereas Capri is the furthermost point of the limestone mountain range known locally as the Monti Lattari – the 'milky' continuation of the Apennines. This geological diversity is reflected in the islands' geography and agriculture. Capri's rocky cliff structure shows clearly how it 'broke off' the end of Punta Campanella (for more on the other side, see p. 209), and has become famous for its rock formations and grottoes. The black, rust-red – at times, even green – soils of Ischia and Procida are fertile, and have always stimulated the cultivation of vegetables and vines. All three locations are irresistible for their startling natural beauty, picturesque villages and simple but flavourful food; they have long been favourites of the world's most sophisticated people: kings and emperors, cinema stars and artists, travellers and writers.

The islands are easy to reach by ferry or hovercraft from Napoli or Pozzuoli.

Opposite; The Frassitelli vineyard on Ischia: the first Campanian cru

NAPOLI

Pozzuoli

PROCIDA

Procida

Lido di Procida

Ischia Porto

Forio

Fontana

Cuotto

Ischia Ponte

Panza

Buonopane

Barano d'Ischia

S. Angelo

Castellammare di Stabia

ISCHIA

Sorrento

Positano

Massa Lubrense

CAPRI

Marina Grande

Anacapri

Capri

Marina Piccola

CAPRI

AZIENDA AUTONOMA CURA
SOGGIORNO E TURISMO
INFORMATION OFFICES:
Piazza Umberto 1
Capri
TEL 081 8370686
Marina Grande
TEL 081 8370634
Anacapri
TEL 081 8371524

The perfect place to do nothing at all: the Roman emperor Augustus Caesar called Capri *la città del dolce far niente*, and the concept stuck. It's been a chic resort ever since, mecca of the rich and famous in search of beauty, tranquillity – and each other. Who hasn't admired photos of Maria Callas and Sophia Loren, sitting at tables in its cafés, or strolling, bronzed and sandalled, through its cobbled streets? That image of *la dolce vita* remains even now, imbuing a walk through those same streets with added dimensions of memory and excitement. Capri is one of the quintessentially Mediterranean places: exotic with its sun, flowers, Moorish domed houses, hand-painted tiles and stunning sea coasts.

Colonized by the Greeks in the 7th century BC – a century later than Ischia – it was written about during the early years of the Roman Empire; the tyrranical emperor Tiberius chose to spend the last ten years of his life here. Two millennia later, its appeal is still intact. Go in spring, or in early or late summer, to avoid the throngs of July and August. The tourist office is well organized, and can help with maps for walkers and naturelovers, who will enjoy the island's abundance of wild flowers.

Bougainvillea spectabilis

EATING AND DRINKING

In earlier eras, Capri was famous for the quail and rabbits that ran wild all over the island. Today it is better known for *insalata caprese*, the red, white and green salad that has become an icon of the Italian Mediterranean. It seems to have been invented in the early 20th century, and at its best – with sun-ripened tomatoes, fresh buffalo mozzarella from Caserta or Paestum, fruity olive oil, and the aromatic, peppery basil that grows on the salty terraces of the islands – captures the essence of summer. You'll also find Capri's favourite ravioli, of pasta made only with flour and water, filled with cheese, eggs and marjoram, and served with fresh tomato sauce; Elizabeth David first wrote about them in 1954. Seafood is of course a speciality here, so try to sample the fish from local waters. When it comes to dessert, *torta caprese* is another classic. Eat this rich, moist concoction of ground almonds and bitter chocolate in any of Capri's pastry shops and restaurants. The lemons of the Golfo di Napoli are legendary for their fragrance and sweetness, so on hot summer nights round off your dinner with a pretty little glass of chilled *limoncello*, the lemon-yellow liqueur made from the alcohol-infused zest of that fruit. It is traditionally produced

Lantana camara

Capri seen from Punta Campanella

in homes and by artisan companies only on Campania's coast and islands.

Grapes have been grown for winemaking on Capri for almost 3,000 years. Indeed, Tiberius (in Italian, Tiberio) was very partial to the wine, and was nicknamed Biberio by his contemporaries. Fruit and vegetables – like the island's exquisite artichokes – are grown on 900 hectares of Capri's 10.35 square kilometres. Of those, 200 are planted to vines, at heights that go from 30 to 350 metres above sea level. Four-fifths are white grapes: Greco, Biancolella and Falanghina, the rest are red Piedirosso. Total production is 6,000 quintals of grapes. The vineyards are mostly on steep and often inaccesible terraces, and in late summer and autumn, the grapes are transported in the little *ape* (bee) vans that buzz their way around the island's narrow lanes.

Anacapri

Restaurant, Hotel
Ristorante l'Olivo, Capri Palace Hotel

Via Capodimonte, 2
TEL 081 9780111
FAX 081 8373191
E-MAIL
info@capri-palace.com
OPEN
March to Nov
CARDS All
PRICE €€€€€€

The Capri Palace Hotel is fast becoming one of the island's jewels. The Palace was built in 1962 with the first boom of quality tourism, and has recently been renovated and upgraded by Tonino Cacace to five-star luxury category. The investments have included a well-appointed Beauty Farm, immersed in an Italian–Zen garden, as well as redesigning the comfortable rooms – many with panoramic views. The elegant style has also reached the dining room, not only in the form of the white-on-white décor in neo-baroque style, but also in the food. Chef

Ravioli caprese

Oliver Glowig has done a fabulous job in his three years here, earning a first Michelin star in the 2005 Red Guide. With skill and imagination he's created a lightened modernist menu that uses the local produce and many ideas from *la cucina povera*. His *raviolo caprese* is filled with *caciotta secca* cheese and perfumed with the island's best marjoram; it comes dressed with a sauce of local dried tomatoes. A *tortello* of chickpeas accompanies local shrimp and fried bone marrow; a woven turbot patty is served over wilted spinach, and reveals a caviar heart: it is sauced with fresh lemon. 'I use as many local ingredients as possible,' he says, 'as everything else has to be shipped to the island.' As you would expect from a large professional brigade, the breads and pastries are all home-made, and worth an extra lap in the pool. In summer, eat out on the shady terrace, with views of the blue Capri sea.

Wine and Limoncello

Vinicola Tiberio

Via Trieste e Trento, 28
TEL 081 8371261
FAX 081 8382882
INTERNET
www.tiberiocapri.it

To see what a historic winery on Capri is like, you can do no better than visit Vinicola Tiberio, at its turn-of-the-century cellars in the centre of Anacapri. Originally founded in 1909, the *cantina* has over time been modernized by several generations of the Brunetti family, its sole owners for almost a century.

Capri's wines obtained the DOC status in 1977, and the Brunettis produce both whites and a red under the Tiberio, Antico Convento di San Michele, and Capri Blu labels. They also make their own *limoncello* from a separate room within the cellar building. Visits and sales are possible all year, preferably by appointment.

Vinicola Tiberio

From Anacapri, a lovely half-hour walk will take you to Da Gelsomina (Via Migliara, 72; TEL 081 8371499), a restaurant offering well-cooked local dishes and a spectacular terrace with views of Ischia and the Golfo di Napoli. There are also five rooms for those who can't bear to leave.

Capri

A GASTRONOMIC TOUR THROUGH THE TOWN CENTRE OF CAPRI
Capri's Piazzetta Umberto I – which Norman Douglas, travel writer, gastronome, and long-time resident on the island, called 'the small theatre of the world' – is the place to have a morning cappuccino or late-night *limoncello*. Everyone who was – or is – anyone at Capri has sat at Il Gran Caffè or at Bar Tiberio's terrace tables to watch and be watched: Noel Coward, Frank

Opposite: Limoncello

Street in Capri

La Capannina Più shop

Sinatra, Rita Hayworth and Julie Christie are just a few of the best-known Capri-lovers. The Piazzetta is at the heart of the medieval *borgo*, and from there you can set off on a shopping – and gastronomic – tour of its narrow streets.

Via Le Botteghe is a particularly good place to start for foods: Sfizi di Pane (Via Le Botteghe, 4; TEL 081 8370106) has twelve types of flavoured *taralli*, crisped little dough rings that have been boiled then baked: my favourites are those with almonds and pepper, which are great with an *aperitivo*. There are also olive breads, and delicious little rolls (*bacetti*) with cheese or ham. L'Ittica Capri (Via Le Botteghe, 19) is a good place for fresh fish if you have access to a kitchen or just want to take a look at some of the Mediterranean's wonderful sea creatures. When planning a picnic, Gastronomia-Pasticceria Scialapopolo (Via Le Botteghe, 31; TEL 081 8370246) offers everything from ready prepared first and main courses, to *panini*, pastries – don't miss the lemon and orange cakes – and tart lemon *granita*. If you're after wines, *limoncello*, olive oil, or other bottled deli-cacies, stop in at La Capannina Più (Via Le Botteghe, 39/41; TEL 081 8378899). Run by the family that owns the restaurant of the same name (see below), this shop has over 700 wines to choose from, as well as unusual wine paraphernalia and novel food gift ideas. Among those is the Capri Natura range (TEL 081 8375197), many of which are produced on the island – including a fine *limoncello*, and citrus maramalades. Their pret-tier gift bottle of *limoncello* costs a little more than the same *limoncello* in the 'normal' bottle. A rare after-dinner liqueur is Mortella – made by infusing myrtle, which grows wild on the island. (For last-minute presents, Capri Natura also have an outlet shop at Naples airport: Capri Natura Gourmet Shop, Aeroporto di Capodichino, Napoli).

Just a street away, I love the *gelati* at Buonocore (Via Vittorio Emanuele, 35; TEL 081 8377826) especially their sweet-and-sour lemon sorbet, and pastries like Caprilù lemon-zested biscuits or the classic Neapolitan *babà*.

Be on the lookout for some stylish table-top objects: many of these shops cater for the rich and famous.

Perfume
Carthusia

Viale Parco Augusto, 2/c and Via Camerelle, 10
TEL 081 8370368
E-MAIL info@carthusia.com
INTERNET www.carthusia.com

If you can, visit Capri in May. Day and night the island's breezes will seduce you with a million blossoms, of acacia and lemon flower, jasmine and wisteria. If those dates won't work for you, don't despair. Capri is home to Carthusia, one of the best artisanal perfume-makers in Italy, where you can quench your

Carthusia perfumes

desire for exotic – even erotic – fragrances all year long.

Dottore Iovine, a Piedmontese chemist, founded the perfumery in 1948, using secret recipes of the cloistered monks from the island's Carthusian monastery – the spectacular Certosa di San Giacomo is across the street from the perfumery. In the fifties and sixties its perfumes were all the rage, and habitués like Liz Taylor and Jackie Onassis never failed to drop in for bottles of 'Caprissimo' or 'Aria di Capri'. The nineties saw a decline in Carthusia's fortunes, but happily it has recently been given a face-lift. 'The perfumes are still made here on Capri as they were originally – from high quality natural essences,' explains Signor Silvio Ruocco, 'but we've "retouched" their fragrances just enough to make them modern.' The elegant shop also sells soaps and other finely scented products with lovely packaging.

Restaurants

La Capannina

Via Le Botteghe, 12/14
TEL 081 8370732
FAX 081 8376990
E-MAIL
capannina@capri.it,
INTERNET
www.capannina-capri.com
CLOSED Wed;
mid-Nov–mid-March
CARDS All
PRICE €€€€€

This historic restaurant is right in the centre of town, just a few metres from La Piazzetta. Antonio and Aurelia De Angelis have run it for years, and have hosted everybody in its comfortable pink and aqua-green dining rooms lined with photos of the stars. It's particularly popular for dinner, when the chic leave their boats and beaches and head into town. The menu features all the Capri classics, as well as some more northern specialities, like *bresaola* and smoked salmon. The health-conscious will appreciate the *pinzimonio* of fresh raw vegetables that starts the meal, and the good assortment of vegetable *antipasti*, soups and pastas that complement the fish dishes. A fine selection of wines is available also at the Capannina's wine bar next door, and from their shop, La Capannina Più (see above).

Capri Moon

Via Marina Grande, 88
TEL 081 8377953
FAX 081 8373200
CLOSED Jan & Feb
PRICE €€€

Close to the port of Marina Grande, on the road that winds up the mountain, Capri Moon has a garden of lemon trees and pretty external terraces. If you like fried food, you will enjoy the mixed fried *antipasti, fritto misto alla caprese*, including dough balls and ravioli, with their stuffings of ham, mozzarella or mashed potatoes. The pastas are abundant and rustic here, with toppings of fried aubergines and tomatoes, or classic *ravioli caprese* filled with cheese and marjoram. Fish are best simply grilled. Desserts include the famous chocolate-almond *torta caprese*.

Via Madre Serafina, 6
TEL 081 8370461
FAX 081 8378947
CLOSED
Mon except in summer;
10 Jan–20 Feb
CARDS All
PRICE €€€–€€€€

Da Gemma

A haunt of Graham Greene's, Da Gemma is the place in Capri for real pizzas baked in a wood-burning oven: try my favourite, topped with *friarielli* (Neapolitan broccoli rabe) and sausage. Or have one of the traditional fish dishes, like *linguine a modo mio* – with shellfish, tomatoes and *rughetta* – or fish baked in the wonderful old bread oven. There's an outdoor veranda with a fabulous view, and comforting desserts to end the meal.

Via dell'Arco Naturale, 13
TEL 081 8375719
FAX 081 8389234
OPEN Easter–end Oct
CLOSED Thurs except
July–Sep
CARDS All
PRICE €€€–€€€€

Le Grottelle

A delightful twenty-minute walk east from Capri: you set out along Via Matermània, lined with private villas and gardens, and arrive at the coast, with spectacular views over the high, natural rock arch formation, l'Arco Naturale. In warm weather eat out on the panoramic terrace. Le Grottelle is so-named for the grotto that forms part of the restaurant's décor and this rusticity is reaffirmed in the home-cooked traditional dishes on offer: hand-made pastas, like *ravioli* and *scialatielli*, served with *gamberi* and fresh, piquant *rughetta* (wild rocket), or *polipetti* (baby octopus), followed by *fritto misto* or *gallinella all'acqua pazza* – gurnard cooked in a 'crazy water' coloured by tomatoes. Save room for Rosa Distefano's *torta caprese* – it's delicious.

Hotel and Restaurant

Via Camerelle, 2
TEL 081 8370788
E-MAIL info@quisi.com
OPEN March–Oct
LA COLOMBAIA CLOSED
eves April, May & Oct
QUISI CLOSED
lunch; Sun June–Sep
CARDS All
PRICE
LA COLOMBAIA €€€€
QUISI €€€€€€

Hotel Quisisana

Capri's historic Hotel Quisisana, opened in 1845, offers two distinctive restaurants: La Colombaia, which is set beside the pool in the lovely gardens, and serves buffet lunches and pizzas; and Quisi Gourmet Restaurant, for more refined dining with excellent service in a beautiful candle-lit setting. Young chef Mirko Rocca has prepared an elegant menu with a modern, at times experimental, flavour to it that will satisfy those with a taste for *alta cucina*.

Marina Grande

Wine

Via Marina Grande, 203/A
TEL 081 8376835
FAX 081 8377124
E-MAIL lacaprense@libero.it
Wines available through
Capri Vini
INTERNET www.caprivini.it

La Caprense

La Caprense is a wine-producing co-operative that was bought in 2001 by Angelo Di Nardo and Giovanni Colavecchia. They continue to work with the co-operative's members – more than twenty – who are now growing their grapes under the guidance of œnologist Maurizio De Simone, a partner in Roberto Cipresso's winemaking group. The aim is to improve the quality

Lemon granita stall

of the wines, starting with the grapes. De Simone is working with vineyards that were abandoned in the seventies and eighties, but are now being brought back under control.

One of the winery's most interesting new wines is Ventroso Capri Rosso DOC, of pure Piedirosso. 'It's hard to get good Piedirosso, as it matures very late,' De Simone explains. 'Growers are often afraid it won't ripen in time, so they pick it too early. If it is left to ripen unattended, the birds eat it, so we have to use scarecrows and other means to keep birds at bay.'

La Caprense's Piedirosso is allowed time to mature, and is picked late, at the end of October or in the first week of November. Vinified on its own, and aged for one-and-a-half years – half in steel, half in second-passage barriques – it produces a rounded, very fruity wine, with nice *profumi* of cherry and pomegranate. 'It also has a bit of salinity,' he continues, 'and I think it's the only red wine of the south that can be used successfully chilled and served with fish.'

For the present, Ventroso is 100% Piedirosso, but in the future it may have a bit of Aglianico or some other red grape added to give it a bit more structure. Other La Caprense wines include the whites, Punta Vivara and Il Bordo, and red Solaro – all Capri DOC wines.

ISCHIA

AZIENDA AUTONOMA CURA
SOGGIORNO E TURISMO
INFORMATION OFFICES
ISCHIA:
TEL 081 5074231
FAX 081 5074230
PROCIDA:
TEL 081 8101968
E-MAIL aacs@metis.it
INTERNET
www.ischiaonline.it/tourism

Ischia is the biggest of the Campanian islands, with an area of 47 square kilometers. It rose out of the sea during the Tertiary era at the time of one of the Golfo di Napoli's many volcanic eruptions, and has long been famous for its volcanic hot springs and mineral-rich muds – its thermal baths were popular with the ancient Romans, and are still flocked to for their curative powers today. Ischia was also well known for its wines. In the 8th century BC, the Greeks discovered the island and established their first colony on Italian soil (called Pithekoussai for the large ceramic pots that were found there). They planted vines that one would like to imagine are linked to those found there today. At the beginning of the last century, 55 per cent of the island was planted to vines, often in steep terraces bounded by green tufa dry-stone walls. When Elizabeth David went to Capri in 1952, to research *Italian Food*, she had this to say about the viticultural status of the two islands:

As for the celebrated white Capri wine, it belongs, I fancy, to history. With the exception of wine produced for their own consumption by one or two private growers there is not, to the best of my knowledge, a drop of drinkable Capri wine to be had in the whole of the Enchanted Isle. If any is made it is exported, and vast quantities of wine from Ischia, which, although originally quite good, does not appear to travel at all successfully, are imported by the Capresi and sold to innocent tourists as Capri Bianco.

Private vineyard on Ischia

The island of Ischia thrived on its wine commerce but – I hasten to add – a great deal has changed in terms of quality, and the island now produces some very fine wines. The most important name in the wine business now as then is Casa D'Ambra (see pp. 162-64).

Unlike its glamorous neighbour Capri, Ischia did not inspire vast numbers of intellectuals and stars of the arts until the mid 1960s, when tourism began to be developed on the island by Angelo Rizzoli. Among the exceptions were the playwright Henrik Ibsen, who sojourned on Ischia in 1867 (though he soon fled back to the mainland after being caught in the dust storm of a volcanic eruption), and the film director Luchino Visconti (who had a personal impact on Ischian viticulture). Despite its white sandy beaches and charming little villages, Ischia's appeal re-mained more agricultural than social until the late 1960s and '70s.

Ischia has recently become the archaeological front-runner of the islands, as witnessed by the exceptional finds – such as

Coast near Sant'Angelo

Nestor's cup – on view at the Villa Arbusto museum at Lacco Ameno – and by its visible cultural eclecticism: the imposing Castello Aragonese has Byzantine origins. The folk history of Ischia is also full of mythological creatures, like the nymphs and sirens who were held in thrall by Mount Epomeo. There is even a theory that Homer's Odysseus may have landed at Ischia, or Scheria, as he described it. Modern-day garden lovers must not miss the beautiful gardens of La Mortella, designed by Russell Page for Sir William Walton, at Zaro di Forìo (TEL 081 986220; INTERNET www.ischia.it/mortella). If you don't have a car, the best way to get around the island is by micro-taxi, the modern replacement for the horse and carriage.

Home-made babà

EATING AND DRINKING

There are wonderfully flavoured vegetables and fruits of all kinds grown on the fertile terraces worked by the *contadini*, including some rare native varieties, such as the Zambognari beans.

The 'land' cooking of the inner island, with its vegetables and rabbits (see p. 156), has nothing to do with the coastal seafood cuisine. Indeed, the *contadini* practised a 'cala-cala' barter with their seagoing counterparts: the farmers would lower a basket filled with vegetables and fruits down into the boats, and raise it filled with the equivalent value of fish. As is the case all over the Neapolitan area, pastries are great here: sample a *babà*, or any of the other freshly baked specialties from the pastry shops or bars – they make the best breakfasts.

A DRIVE AROUND ISCHIA IN SPRING

Allium neapolitanum

Wisteria;
below, scilla peruviana

Delicate wild garlic flowers like white bluebells (*Allium neapolitanum*) line the roadsides, big bunches of white or yellow marguerites, orange marigolds and sharp yellow gorse, ivory orange blossom nearer the town, large purple bulbs with a crown of tiny flowers like stars that I've never come across before (*Scilla peruviana*). Exotic perfumes hang in the air, of wisteria, *zagara* (citrus blossom), jasmine.

Ischia is still largely agricultural, with tiny *appezzamenti* (each plot less than one hectare) on slopes steep and gentle, given over to vineyards and fruit and vegetable cultivation. The vines are mostly terraced, quite high, on every available inch of ground, with fava beans and peas growing in thick rows beneath them. Each *contadino* produces a little wine for the family.

It's a very old world here: the *vecchietto* I passed in his storefront as small as a cell, with two mirrors, a piece of soap and a shaving brush inside. Had he once been the local barber? Narrow roads wind through these painted villages. You see whitish-yellow *tufo*, but also the grey-black, green-grey volcanic rock all the road walls are made with, as are some of the older houses, like on Pantelleria. Here too is the influence of the Moors, in houses with rounded roofs like breasts. At high noon, the Neapolitan-yellow church of Serrara with its spherical cupola struck the hours, its walls heavy with lilac *glicine* (wisteria).

SAGRE AT ISCHIA
SAGRE AT ISCHIA
If you find yourself on Ischia on Christmas Eve, don't miss
Ischia Porto's Sagra del Baccalà e della Pizza di Scarola – the
salt cod and escarole tart festival. In June, Barano hosts La
Festa della Ginestra, a summer roundup of local food and arti-
san products.

Barano d'Ischia

Restaurant

Via Cretajo al Crocefisso, 3 — Trattoria il Focolare
TEL/FAX 081 902944
E-MAIL
info@trattoriailfocolare.it
INTERNET
www.trattoriailfocolare.it
OPEN All year
CLOSED
Weds except in summer
CARDS
PRICE €€€

Wind your way up above the island's terraced vegetable plots
and vineyards, and you come to woods of chestnut trees that
flourish in the cooler mountain air. Here even the scents change,
rich with mushrooms and leaf mould. Il Focolare restaurant –
positioned high up on the hill – celebrates these 'land' perfumes
and flavours in dishes that reflect the island's true *contadino* –
peasant – identity. 'Financial prosperity has paradoxically
brought an impoverishment of our local food culture,' explains
Riccardo D'Ambra, as he offers me a glass of his home-made
Biancolella wine. One of the three cousins who inherited the
D'Ambra wine estate from their uncle Mario (see pp. 162-164),
Riccardo and his family switched from making wines to running
a restaurant some years ago.

Coniglio all'Ischitana

　　We are sitting in a large cavern behind the dining room that
was dug from the pale grey rock of pumice and clay that forms
this part of the mountain. 'These cellars were perfect storage
places for the wines and home-butchered pork products the
families once made here,' he continues. 'Sadly a lot of these
practices are now being lost. But I am trying to revive at least
one of them, the *coniglio da fossa*.' Breeding rabbits for the
table has been a tradition on Ischia since the 16th century, as
rabbits have always proliferated on the island. Indeed, they con-
stitute one of the farmers' biggest problems as, left to their own
devices, they will eat their way through any cultivation of vegetables, grapes and fruits. So an ingenious, humane way was
developed to breed the rabbits as naturally as possible, without
risk of damage to the crops. Two-to-three-metre pits are dug
down into the soft *tufo* rock, and the rabbits are placed in them,
with a net over the top to prevent them from escaping. The rabbits are free to dig their warrens in this large 'cage' and breed
happily in its tunnels. They are fed on freshly cut wild grasses
by their female keepers, with only the water that is clinging to
the leaves, and lifted out after three to four months, when needed for the table. The *coniglio all'Ischitana* as cooked by the

D'Ambras comes in a large pot, with sections of rabbit stewed in white wine and flavoured with one whole unpeeled garlic head, a few *pomodorini* (this is still technically '*in bianco*' — a 'white' rather than a 'red' sauce), and wild thyme. It is served with bitter, mustardy *friarielli* greens – and with a crisp Biancolella, its traditional partner at table.

The family is a large, cheerful one, and they prepare many other authentic dishes from the Ischian mountain repertoire. I loved the green *pecorara* pasta tubes the women make from the wild leaves called *tunz'* and *paparastiella* that are gathered in the high pastures. The pasta has a leafy intensity, and is dressed with Pecorino Romano cheese. There are many rustic dishes of indigenous beans and home-grown vegetables to complement the pork and rabbit, served in the restaurant's convivial dining room. Save room for dessert: there are always delicious tarts and cakes to round off an enjoyable meal here.

Restaurant

Ristorante I Ghiottoni

Via Migliaccio, 104
TEL/FAX 081 904401
E-MAIL info@
ristoranteighiottoni.com
INTERNET WWW.
ristoranteighiottoni.com
CLOSED
Tues (except Aug); Nov;
lunch in July & Aug by
prior booking only
PRICE €€€

If you don't have a car with you on the island, it's an easy bus ride from Ischia Porto to this sympathetic restaurant run by two young brothers, Rosario and Filippo Sgambati, with a little help from various members of their family. You can't miss the restaurant: it's all alone on the road that goes from Barano to Serrara Fontana, in open country of cliffs and greenery – and the bus stops right outside the front door.

Unlike most other Ischian restaurants, this one is land-based in its menu, and was opened with the local residents – rather than the summer tourists – in mind. 'Of course, visitors are very welcome here, but we wanted to build up our clientele from people who live on the island full time,' explains Filippo, who runs the dining room. 'So we decided to develop a menu of traditional dishes as well as historical recipes from the Bourbon era and the Kingdom of the Two Sicilies,' adds Rosario, the chef. 'We use the well-flavoured Mediterranean ingredients that come from here and that form the basis of southern Italian cuisine.'

The two have researched their dishes well, drawing ideas and recipes from classic texts such as Cavalcanti's *Cuoco Galante* and Il Maestro Leonardi's *L'Apicio alla Moderna* – six volumes published in 1850. For example, a Sicilian mixture of Bronte pistachios and *pecorino* that was used for stuffing meat in the 19th century, here becomes a light and flavourful dressing for pasta.

Ristorante I Ghiottoni

Rosario and Filippo
Sgambati

The young men, who both gained experience working in hotels and restaurants on the island before deciding to open their own five years ago, have created a cheerful dining room that has not lost touch with its rustic, trattoria origins. The *antipasti* change every day, as the mixed plate depends on fresh seasonal vegetables and cheeses. In early summer, mine included lightly sautéed *friggiarelli* (known in other parts of Campania as *friarielli*) – slim green and orange peppers; buffalo ricotta baked with a poppy seed crust; and Rosario's version of the harvester's *caponata*: cherry tomatoes, dried bread, olive oil and oregano – a healthy modern starter. Green spinach *gnocchi* are lifted by the fresh crispness of Webb lettuce spines, wilted by their hot cheese sauce. Main courses include the Ischian stewed rabbit, as well as hare '*alla reale*', grilled Irish and Italian steaks, and duck. 'We didn't want our menu to read like a carbon-copy of so many of the others,' says Rosario. Indeed, the excellent dessert was unique: *il migliaccio di carnevale* is a traditional Neapolitan pudding made of semolina, buffalo ricotta, sugar, eggs and lemon, and usually enriched with candied fruits. Here the fruit has been left out, to allow for a delicious sauce made using Casa D'Ambra's red Tintore wine.

I Ghiottoni's wine list offers good value: a nice selection of southern Italian wines that go beyond Campania to accompany the menu in flavour and prices.

ALSO AT BARANO D'ISCHIA
For great local breads: Panificio Di Costanzo; Via Ritola, 4, at Buonopane; TEL 081 905520.

Forìo d'Ischia

Restaurant

Il Melograno

Via Mazzella, 110
TEL 081 998450
FAX 081 5071984
E-MAIL
ilmelograno@inwind.it
CLOSED
7 Jan–15 Mar; Mon &
Tues in Nov & Dec
CARDS All
PRICE
Menu degustazione €€€€

Take a short drive south from Forìo on the coastal road, turn up into a narrow lane and you'll find Il Melograno – the pomegranate – an intimate, comfortable restaurant set in lovely gardens, with a shady pergola for eating under in summer.

This is a great place to sample the best of the local catch, for Libera Iovine and her husband Giovanni pay great attention to quality and detail – they were rewarded with a Michelin star in 2002. 'I come from the island of Procida,' explains Libera, the restaurant's talented chef, 'and for us it's inconceivable to live far from the sea. *Il mare* has influenced so many things about me, including my palate and my cooking.' Procida's culinary traditions are more sea-based than Ischia's, and Libera likes to combine her seafood with many of the family of *agrumi*, citrus fruits, that are also part of Procida's heritage. She is a self-taught cook, with a natural, spontaneous sense of what goes with what, and what tastes – and looks – good.

My autumn dinner in the creamy yellow dining room with its wooden beams begins with two raw local shrimp, *mazzancolle*, served on a bed of thinly sliced raw artichokes, and dressed with 'raw' oil from the Cilento. A subtle hint of citrus adds zing to the earthy, Procida artichokes. Shrimp appear again – cooked this time – with a crisp light green salad of fennel and Webb lettuce, garnished with orange slices as in the famous Sicilian combination. It's refreshing and summery. *Vongole veraci* are small, fine-shelled clams, and Libera serves them in a Japanese-style bowl with Mediterranean simplicity: sautéed with garlic, parsley and good olive oil. The next fish dish is also deceptively spare: a juicy slice of *ricciola* (amberjack) is topped with a cloud of soft green Neapolitan aubergine that has been roasted then peeled. And it's delicious. I have always loved the singular way women in the kitchen have of turning just a couple of ingredients into seductive dishes. This is seasonal food, and early artichokes feature again in Libera's version of the classic *parmigiana*: here the layers of vegetables and cheese are bound in a lightly set egg custard, enhanced by a bright tomato sauce and peppery basil.

After this abundant sampler of *antipasti*, my pasta is welcome: *mezze maniche* – these 'half-sleeves' are short tubes – tossed with capers, olives and *ricciola* in a pumpkin sauce. I'm curious about the *guazzetto*, or sauce, of tomato and orange she serves with some of her fish. 'While waiting for their husbands

*Santa Maria della Neve
at Forìo*

Orange tree

Opposite: Painted wall tiles from Santa Maria della Neve

to return, the fishermen's wives used to prepare a tomato base with garlic, herbs and a little orange peel to cook the fish in. If they arrived empty handed, the women served this sauce alone on pasta, calling it *pesce fiutt* or *pesce fuggito* – the fish that got away. There are always a couple of meat dishes on the menu too, and Libera will prepare the island's rabbit speciality, *coniglio all'Ischitana*, if you order it ahead of time. Desserts are home-made too, like my fine soufflé of ricotta and dates with its sauce of white peaches. 'It's important to be able to explain why you have used a particular ingredient,' she says. 'Every dish has a story to tell.'

Restaurant

Umberto A Mare 1936

Via Soccorso, 2
TEL 081 997171
E-MAIL
info@umbertoamare.it
INTERNET
www.umbertoamare.it
CLOSED
6 Jan–14 Mar
CARDS All
PRICE
Menus from €€€€

An airy terrace perched right over the sea is surely one of the most heavenly places to eat, always popular with travellers seeking a true experience of the Mediterranean. Located beside and below the striking white church of Santa Maria della Neve – with its beautiful majolica tiles and touching ex-votos – this fish restaurant offers sea views and flavours with elegant simplicity from its white stucco rooms and tiled terrace. On warm summer nights it's even more romantic, with candlelit tables and the sound of the water lapping against the rocks below.

The food reflects this fancy, *ma non troppo* approach: a warm octopus salad is stacked into a tower, the chunks of firm flesh punctuated by cherry tomatoes, celery and basil. It's dressed

Ristorante Umberto A Mare on a terrace below Santa Maria della Neve

with the extra virgin olive oil from the Nuovo Cilento co-operative (see p. 304). There's a commitment here to quality ingredients: the menu informs us that vegetables and fruits are organic whenever possible, and pasta is artisan-made from Gragnano (see p. 188). In November, my pasta was narrow tubes dressed with a pumpkin purée and olives. I added a little fresh *peperoncino* from the glass of them on the table. Large chunks of roasted *ricciola* (the local amberjack from these waters) came with stewed green leaves of escarole, and tiny whole beige Spello beans.

Desserts include a lightened version of the traditional aubergine and chocolate concoction that is also found on the Sorrento Peninsula. Wine lovers will appreciate Mario and Umberto Regine's serious wine list (grandsons of the original Umberto): it's a nice collection of some of the region's best wines, enriched with a good supplement of other classics – you'll even find several vintages of the Tuscan greats. If you don't want to drive after dinner, Umberto's has ten rooms with sea views under the dining room.

Wine

Casa D'Ambra

Via Mario D'Ambra, 16
Panza
TEL 081 907246
FAX 081 908190
E-MAIL
info@dambravini.com
INTERNET
www.dambravini.com
The winery is open for
tastings and sales
Mon–Sat 9.00–19.00
Cellar visits by
appointment

It's a windy, rainy November day, and I'm huddled for shelter in a tiny stone house perched high up on the slopes of Monte Epomeo, surrounded by one of Ischia's loftiest vineyards, Frassitelli. Even in this wild grey weather the position is spectacular, with breathtaking views through the clouds, past narrow-terraced vines and steep green slopes, to the sea. In summer it is idyllic to sit here, at outdoor tables of solid tufa shaded by pergolas, and to drink the characterful white Biancolella wine that is made from these vines.

'Whenever I come up here,' says Andrea D'Ambra, who inherited the vineyard when he took over the family winery, Casa D'Ambra, 'I think of the term "heroic viticulture". For that's about the only way to describe the work that for centuries the *contadini* have done on slopes as steep and inaccessible as these.' Until recently, there were more mules than people on Ischia, and the women still carried baskets of grapes on their heads. Building the dry-stone walls that support the vine and fruit terraces all over the island was a Herculean feat accomplished over time by thousands of nameless 'heroes'. 'Someone has calculated that if you laid all of Ischia's dry-stone walls on these *parracine* terraces end to end, they would be longer than the Great Wall of China!'

If Ischia was known at the beginning of the 20th century for

The Frassitelli vineyard

Stone tables with the mountain top behind at Frassitelli

being a wine-producing island, it was largely thanks to Andrea's forefathers: the D'Ambra family has always played a central role in the island's winemaking history. In those days the wine was sold in bulk, *sfuso*, unbottled, and Andrea's grandfather, Don Ciccio D'Ambra, pushed sales of the island's whites beyond Napoli, to Prague and other important cities. The wine travelled by boat in large barrels; the island survived economically thanks to its wine commerce, as tourism did not begin on Ischia until the 1960s.

In the 1950s, Don Ciccio's three sons took over the estate, and by 1960 the company, led by Mario D'Ambra, started bottling their wines. In 1966, this work was acknowledged when Ischia was awarded the second Italian DOC, Vini d'Ischia. Over the next twenty years, Mario D'Ambra became one of the key personalities in Italy's wine world, a visionary who saw the island's potential and who dedicated himself to rescuing Ischia's winemaking traditions when they were threatened by a ruinous Swiss takeover bid. 'My uncle was passionate about Ischia's wines, and he made friends with figures like film director Luchino Visconti and wine critic Luigi Veronelli, each of whom suggested ways of improving our family's wines and their image,' says Andrea. When Mario died in 1988, the company was about to celebrate its centennial. He left the winery to his three nephews, Andrea, Corrado (see p. 166) and his brother Riccardo (see p. 156). Corrado and Andrea ran it together until 1999, when Andrea took over as single proprietor.

'In winemaking terms,' explains Andrea, 'Ischia is special for the autocthonous grape varieties that grow here, including the whites Biancolella and Forastera, and the reds Guarnaccia and Per' 'e Palummo [the dialect term for "pigeon's feet", or Piedirosso, named for the grapes' stems' resemblance to a pigeon's red talons].' Today, Casa D'Ambra produces twelve wines, and has focused in particular on these Ischian grape types. It is the island's largest winery, buying grapes from over 200 small producers in addition to producing grapes on five hectares of its own property. The D'Ambras have even set up a little monorail train to transport the grapes from the highest terraces.

Andrea D'Ambra, who is also the winery's œnologist, is a self-proclaimed *bianchista*, favouring the making of white wines over reds. The spacious cellars at Panza are equipped with state-of-the-art soft presses for the delicate white grapes. The must is chilled and allowed to decant naturally for two days before fermentation. 'This rids the wine of any unwanted trace elements, and gives us a very pure must from which to make the wines. It's also the best way to retain the wines' *profumi*.' Indeed Casa D'Ambra's whites are characterized by a clear, clean style that allows each variety to express itself. The whites are kept in steel vats, and are not matured in wood. An intriguing recent wine is Kime, made from two grape varieties that Andrea discovered in Greece, and that he feels are connected to the vines the Greeks brought to Ischia in 700 BC. It's a well-structured wine to match with cheese, a rich, unusual white with almond and mineral notes that has been winning high marks in the country's wine guides. As for the reds, Dedicato a Mario D'Ambra is the Ischia Rosso DOC that Andrea and Corrado produced for the first time in 1998, as a tribute to their uncle. 'Of Guarnaccia and Per' 'e Palummo grapes aged in wood,' says Andrea, 'it's not overpoweringly forceful, but well balanced and very drinkable – just what you want from an island wine.'

Andrea D'Ambra eating outside at Frassitelli with a visiting Sicilian wine-maker, Giada De Bartoli

Via Provinciale Panza, 267
TEL 081 908206
FAX 081 908949
E-MAIL
info@pietratorcia.it
INTERNET
www.pietratorcia.it

Wine
Pietratorcia

The *pietra torcia* is the large pierced rock that was used as the counterweight for the rudimentary Ischian wine press. Although the system has long since been supplanted by more sophisticated techniques, the rocks remain as evidence of earlier winemakers' ingenuity. This winery, which opened about ten years ago, chose the *pietra torcia* as its symbol, and visitors to the *cantina* can see one in situ in front of the 18th-century green *tufo* building that houses what remains of the press.

It was the grandparents of the present owners – the Iovine,

*An original counter-
weight stone at
Pietratorcia*

*Winter vineyard at
Pietratorcia*

Verde and Regine families are united under the same label –
who worked the terraces of local vines: Biancolella, Guarnaccia,
Piedirosso, Forastera. Their grandchildren didn't want to lose
this patrimony of experience and labour, so they opened a winery to maintain their families' vineyards.

'From each *vigna*, or vineyard, we make a cru by vinifying its
grapes separately,' explains Ambrogio Iacono, the estate's young
œnologist. 'That way the territory and its microclimates can
express themselves in more individual ways. For instance, Il
Cuotto is in a cool location with soft inclines, whereas Chignole
is up on an extremely steep hillside: each wine has a different
character.' There are now seven hectares of vineyards, located
throughout the commune of Forìo, at altitudes that go from just
above sea level to 400 metres. The estate produces eight wines,
including one *passito*, that range from the young and pleasantly
drinkable Tifeo Rosso to the well structured red Scheria, of
Aglianico, Syrah, Guarnaccia and Piedirosso. It spends over
twelve months in wood and ten more in the bottle before being
sold. Of the whites, look out for the Vigne di Chignole Ischia
Bianco Superiore. Of Biancolella, Forastera with a little Fiano,
this complex, well-bodied wine goes well with the decisive
Mediterranean flavours of Ischia's cuisine. Meditandum is a
late-harvest dessert wine of Viognier and Malvasia di Candia
Aromatica grapes that are left to dry on the vines until the end
of October. These raisins are picked and macerated in a base of
fermenting must, in steel vats. The wine is then transferred to
small oak barrels and usually bottled one year after the harvest.
I found it not overly sweet and pleasantly spicy, with a nose of
white pepper, nutmeg, cinnamon and dried figs. Unmistakably
an island wine, it would go well with the exoticism of a rich
pastiera napoletana.

Pietratorcia has a pretty outdoor courtyard for holding tastings and for wine sales: OPEN April–June mornings and afternoons; July–September afternoons only, but open till late.
Dinner available by reservation only.

ALSO AT FORÌO

Gelateria-Bar Elio (Via Statale, 270; TEL 081 997668) makes the
area's best *gelati*, especially the fruit flavours. For great pastries,
try Pasticceria Fratelli Calise (Via Baiola, 87; TEL 081 997283).
Agriturismo La Pergola (Via San Giuseppe, 8; TEL/FAX 081
909483; E-MAIL agriturismolapergola@libero.it; INTERNET
www.agriturismolapergola.it) is run by the Colella family. As
well as sea-view rooms, it offers wines, home made jams and
other preserves, and well-cooked meals using the farm's pro-

duce. The other feature that is not to be missed is the family's matriarch, 'Nonna Sisina', and the traditional corn dollies and hats she makes. Sisina, a lovely energetic woman, is now the only person to carry on this type of work on the island. 'When I was younger,' she says, 'these Ischian hats were exported all over the world. Now I am the last to do it. It's a shame.' She energetically teaches the work – which involves weaving the threaded corn stalks into all sorts of shapes and forms – in the island's schools and on the farm, so let's hope some enterprising youngsters pick up where she leaves off.

Ischia Porto

Wine, Wine Bar, Restaurant

Il Giardino Mediterraneo Corrado D'Ambra
MOBILE 337 676793
E-MAIL campania@ movimentoturismovino.it

Enoteca Pane e Vino
Via Porto, 24, 80070
Ischia Porto
TEL 081 991046

Corrado D'Ambra: Il Giardino Mediterraneo and Pane e Vino
'It was love at first sight – in fact, I think this property bought me!' exclaims Corrado D'Ambra as we chug slowly to the top of the vineyard he has owned since 2001. We're on a tiny monorail train, and it's so steep I'm afraid to look down. But the views truly are exceptional out past Ischia Porto to the Campi Flegrei. One of the three D'Ambra cousins who, in 1988, inherited the island's most famous winery from their uncle Mario, Corrado is no stranger to winemaking ventures. After years of running Casa D'Ambra with his cousin Andrea (see p. 162), the two parted ways in 1999, and Corrado began his search for a winery of his own.

With this one-hectare vineyard, in which Corrado is experimenting with six types of grape, came a handsome stone cellar, built in 1805. 'It was completely abandoned, but I'm bringing it back to life,' he continues enthusiastically. Inside, you can see the large vats (*palmenti*) where once the grapes were crushed by foot. Now the cellar hosts acacia barrels and state-of-the-art vinification tanks for the new wines. 'Ischia is a little continent unto itself,' he explains as we tour the buildings. 'It is one of only five sites in Italy that have been selected for experimentation because of its myriad micro-climates and soil varieties.'

The *cantina* will be called 'Il Giardino Mediterraneo' – the Mediterranean Garden. 'In Magna Grecia – of which Ischia and Campania were part – the ancient Greeks set up large *colonie* outside of the cities to fulfil their agricultural requirements. Whereas the *giardino mediterraneo* was the first concept of a private house with its own garden; a house surrounded by a fruit orchard and vegetable plot, with dry-stone walls all around it. An organic, self-contained entity.'

Corrado D'Ambra

The harbour at Ischia Porto

Up on the higher level, in the midst of the vines with those panoramic views, Corrado D'Ambra has built a small dining room on a pergola-covered terrace. It's open in summer, by reservation only, and can hold up to twenty, so book ahead.

Back down in town, on the harbour front at Ischia Porto, is Corrado's wine bar, Enoteca Pane e Vino. It's a key meeting place for locals and visitors, and from its forecourt tables you can sit watching the people and boats pass by with a great glass of wine from Corrado's fine collection, and a plate of selected *salumi* or cheeses to go with it. That and a genial host – what could be nicer?

Pizza

Pizzeria Cecilia

Via Edgardo Cortese, 17/21
TEL 081 991850
CLOSED
Tues in winter;
30 Jan–15 Mar
CARDS All

If you are in the mood for pizza, Cecilia Esposito is a member of La Vera Pizza Napoletana – the *real* Neapolitan pizza associ-ation. Her prize-winning pizzeria isn't glamorous, but it's relaxed and lively – and it's always full. The pizzas are great: high quality ingredients, extra virgin olive oil, real cheese, with crusts that are soft but not mushy, thin but not crispy, and with a naturally smoky flavour from the wood-burning oven. Start your meal, as so many locals like to, with a mixed plate of deep-fried rice balls – *arancini* – and croquettes. Then choose one of the forty types of pizza, including the stuffed fried pizza enclosing a filling of ham and mozzarella. Or have a plate of pasta or local fish.

Bar

Via Antonio Sogliuzzo
(between Ischia Porto
and Ischia Ponte)
TEL 081 991270

Calise

For breakfast or dessert or *gelato*, or an *aperitivo* or after-dinner cocktail, the place to go is Calise. With outdoor tables in its night-lit gardens, and a huge display of cakes and pastries to eat at the bar or take away in trays (*vassoio*), Calise is always one of the island's most popular spots. And in summer it's open round the clock. You can even catch a last-minute coffee or *bigné* pastry before boarding the ferry at Calise's other branch, on the waterfront at the port at Ischia.

The streets in Ischia Porto are full of food shops, and good places to find edible presents to take home. At Sapori Antichi (Antica Macelleria, Via delle Terme, 4; TEL 081 9810111) Francesco Esposito is the seventh generation of butchers in his family, originally from Napoli. Try his home-cured pork *guanciale* and *pancetta*. He also sells a selection of Ischian products.
  O Sole Mio (Spiaggia dei Pescatori, 28, Ischia Ponte; TEL 081 981986). If you want to eat with ringside views of the Castello Aragonese, this popular pizzeria–restaurant is right on the beach between Ischia Porto and Ponte. Fine for an *antipasto* and a pizza. Also at Ischia Ponte, Panetteria Boccia is a good bakery for sampling local breads (Via San Giovanni da Procida; TEL 081 982387). A short boat ride from Ischia Ponte is Cocò Mare, run by Di Meglio, who has Da Cocò at Ischia Porto (Piazzale Aragonese; TEL 081 981823): it's where the Ischitani hang out in summer when they want to get away from the tourists. At Pizzeria Gaetano (Via M. Mazzella, 74; TEL 081 991807) Gaetano Fazio is a master *pizzaiolo*, famous for his naturally leavened crust. And for a traditional fish restaurant, try Damiano Ristorante (Superstrada SS 270; TEL 081 983032), located just above Ischia Porto: it has a spacious, airy terrace for summer meals.

PROCIDA

The smallest of the islands and the closest to the mainland, Procida has remained miraculously free of mass-tourist exploitation. Until the 19th century, Procida was a favourite hunting ground for Napoli's rulers. Now it is better known for its lemons: of a distinct type, they are a bit larger and paler in colour than the other varieties found on Campania's coasts, and have a thicker layer of pith, but their flavour is wonderful. Try

Procida seen from Ischia

them in Procida's *insalata di limoni*: ripe Procida lemons are carefully peeled and sliced, then dressed with fresh mint, garlic, *peperoncino* and fruity olive oil. A delightful summer thirst-quencher.

Film lovers will be interested to know that recently the island's picturesque port and landscapes have been used as locations for two important Italian films: *Il Postino*, and Lina Wertmuller's cinematic version of *Francesca e Nunziata*, from the novel of that name by Maria Orsini Natale – a love story within a pasta-producing family.

Bar Pasticceria Dal Cavaliere (Via Roma, 42; TEL 081 8101074; OPEN 7.00 a.m. till 1.00 a.m. or later in summer). Many agree: this is the best bar on the island, and the most pleasurable place to sit – it's right on the *piazza* of Marina Grande, overlooking the sea. Delicious pastries, including the island's specialties, *lingue di bue* – long 'cow's tongues' of pastry with lemon cream. Or get hooked on the *granita di limone* made from Procida's superlative lemons. If you are after a bigger meal, try Caracalè (Marina Corricella, 62; TEL 081 8969192).

Chapter 5

The Sorrento Peninsula and the Amalfi Coast

From Castellammare to Vietri – via Sorrento, Agerola and Amalfi

The coast of Campania, taken singly by itself! So blest with natural beauties and opulence, that it is evident that when nature formed it she took a delight in accumulating all her blessings in a single spot – how am I to do justice to it?

Pliny the Elder Naturalis Historia

FOR TOURIST
INFORMATION:
www.aziendaturismo.sa.it
www.innaples.it
www.turismoregione
campania.it

You have to get in the groove to drive it well. Swing in and out of the curves with one eye on the road and the other on the view. That's how the natives do it, with the zigzag rhythm of a skier. Italy's most spectacular road – seventy kilometres along the Amalfi Coast – snakes horizontally through the steep and jagged mountains, following their every bend above the sea. The gulfs of Napoli and Salerno's legendary towns – Sorrento, Positano, Amalfi, Ravello – are poised between jet-set sophistication and Mediterranean simplicity. But the coasts also host other worlds, just minutes from the tourist crowds. Step off that dividing line, and the perspectives change completely. Ten minutes' drive up into the hills are hamlets so steep only mules can reach them, where the women still carry bundles on their heads and make home-made cheeses in their kitchens. Down below are villages still living from their fishing, where the men spend afternoons mending their nets.

Every occupying civilization – from the Greeks and Romans to the Byzantines, Arabs and Spaniards – has left its mark on this unique piece of natural beauty. In the Middle Ages, Amalfi was one of Italy's three Maritime Republics (the others being Genova and Venezia) and a centre of commerce with the Orient

Opposite: The fishing port of Cetara

and Constantinople. Sorrento was a key destination on the Grand Tour itinerary; Positano has always attracted intellectuals and artists. The *Costiera* contains some of the world's finest hotels, as well as modest accommodation for those who can only dream of the palaces but want to share the same sea, sun and spectacular scenery.

EATING AND DRINKING

The limestone hills that form the Penisola Sorrentina, the Monti Lattari – or 'milky mountains' – are direct continuations of the Apennine Mountain range. They owe their name to the abundance of fine milk and cheeses that, over the centuries, have been produced from its high pastures, where the myriad grasses and wild herbs enrich the flavours of everything that feeds on them. The Campania Region, through its Communità Montane, is supporting projects to improve the technical aspects of its small dairies without compromising the quality of the raw-milk cheeses that are being produced – from the *pecorini* of Tramonti (see pp. 224-26) to the cow's-milk cheeses of Agerola.

Cows graze freely in the woods above Amalfi

The Region is also active in protecting the dry-stone walls that form the extraordinary terraces (*macerine*) of lemon groves that are unique to these hills. In the 10th and 11th centuries, Maiori, Minori and Cetara were the first towns on the *Costiera* to create lemon plantations on steep terraces, and they still exist today. These lemon groves contributed to the Amalfi Coast being admitted in 1997 as a UNESCO World Heritage Site, thanks to the centuries of work of the coast's men and women who still today do the bulk of the work, carrying the lemons in baskets on their heads. The varieties of lemon then included the giant *ponsiri*, at times 'larger than the largest pumpkin'; and the *sfusato* lemons, which are *profumati*, have thick porous skins and a sweetness due to the mild climate that enables them to be eaten by themselves in salads or desserts. These unusually fragrant lemons have gained territorial status: Limone di Sorrento IGP, and Limone Costa d'Amalfi IGP. They form the basis of that ever-popular liqueur, *limoncello*, but here *liquori* are also made from other mountain plants, from wild herbs like *finocchio* and *alloro*, to blueberries and wild strawberries.

Olive groves flank the lemons, and give rise to fruity extra virgin oils – including those of the Penisola Sorrentina DOP – made of native Ogliarola, Minucciola and Rotondella olives. The other traditional companion to the olive, the vine, is present too, in steep terraced vineyards where only a 'heroic' viticulture would ever dare to venture. The winemaking areas of Gragnano

*Bottling anchovies
by hand at Cetara*

and Costa d'Amalfi (Furore and Tramonti) have earned their
DOC status and currently produce some very fine wines from
indigenous – and often pre-phylloxera – varieties.

The towns of Gragnano and Minori were also the historic
homes of pasta – indeed, the small artisan factories of Gragnano
still produce some of Italy's finest pasta. Fish and fish products
are also native to the coasts, though the sea has become more of
a tourist site than a food-giver. Some fishermen still go out at
night with their *lampare*, lighted boats that attract the fish into
their nets, and at Cetara an antique anchovy sauce has recently
attained cult status – *la colatura di alici* (see pp. 182-83). There
are ever fewer fish products, but one can still see anchovies
being stripped of their skeletons in one swift movement by
women who then arrange them in glass jars or pack them whole
in barrels or terracotta urns under coarse sea salt. Practically no
fished tuna come into these shores any more, as they all end up
in Japan, so the custom of home-canning tuna has somewhat
abated. But there are wonderful sea-creatures of all descriptions
living in these clean waters, to be discovered in the many fine
restaurants this strip of coast can boast.

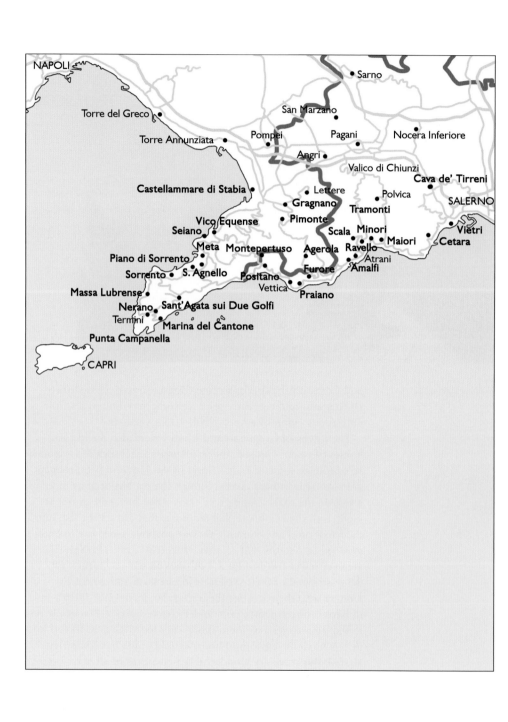

Agerola

Cheese

Via Locoli, 42
Santa Maria
TEL 081 8791339

Caseificio dei Monti Lattari – Fior d'Agerola

Agerola sits high above the coasts, astride the 'Milky' Mountains (Monti Lattari) that rise above Positano and Furore on one side, and Vico Equense on the other. There is a natural dip here, almost a plateau, where cattle graze – or grazed – in natural pastures that have yielded some of Campania's finest cheese. If in the past the cows were necessarily kept outdoors in spring and summer, if not in winter, unfortunately now more are stabled throughout the year, here as in so many parts of Europe. Luckily some small farms still respect the old rhythms, for there is no doubt that the finest cheeses are made from the milk of animals given free choice over what they eat in meadows full of different grasses. Agerola is particularly known for two distinct cheeses: Provolone del Monaco, and *fior di latte agerolese*.

Provolone del Monaco has been made since 1700 in Campania; when well made and well aged, it is one of southern Italy's most noble cheeses. At its best, it is made from the unpasteurized milk of cows – especially of the endangered Agerolese breed, of which currently only fifty remain. The *provolone* is a stretched-curd cheese that is formed into large ovoid balls weighing three to six kilos, tied with four strings and hung up to mature for at least four months – though it only improves with age and is best after twelve to eighteen months. The resulting cheese is grey-brown outside and pale straw-yellow inside, compact and firm to the touch, and rich in the flavours of milk and hay. The cheese is now produced at Agerola and on the Sorrento Peninsula above Vico Equense. To taste it, visit the excellent local cheese shop, La Tradizione (pp. 217-19) at Seiano. (For producers see also p.219.)

Salvatore De Gennaro of Seiano with a Provolone del Monaco that he has aged

The cheese made at Agerola undergoes an unusual process: in order to become stringy (*filare*) when mixed with hot water, cheese needs to have a fairly high acidity level (pH of around 5). This can either be achieved speedily using added acidifiers (as in industrial cheeses) or naturally, allowing the milk to ferment gradually. In the case of the Agerola *fior di latte*, this slow acidifying process takes at least twelve hours: the initial cheese (curdled milk) is made in the morning and is allowed to undergo a natural fermentation until, by night time, the necessary acidity level has been attained. For this reason, the *fior di latte* at Agerola is worked around midnight, as in this dairy.

See also Vico Equense for other cheeses from the same area.

Salumi

Via Roma, 1
TEL 081 8791930

Salumificio Cardone

For those seeking pork *salame* and other *salumi* – including some that are lightly smoked – the Imperati family have been making them for generations. The specialities include stuffed *zampone* and *lardo 'cardoncello'*.

Amalfi

FOR TOURIST
INFORMATION
Corso Roma, 19
TEL 089 871107

The small state of Amalfi was already active in the 6th century: its fortified port played an important commercial role in the Byzantine Empire. By the middle of the 9th century Amalfi had become an autonomous Marine Republic, the oldest in the Mediterranean. Remaining independent for centuries, Amalfi was allied with the Arabs for trade between the 9th and 12th centuries, and took part in the first Crusades in the 11th to the 13th centuries. It was the Arabs who first brought citrus fruits and their culture to the Campanian coast, spreading the word about the lemon's flavours and health-giving properties; a document cites the lemons on the coast as early as 998 AD. Between the 15th and 18th centuries, in an age of great sea voyages, the lemon became indispensable for preventing scurvy, and was a highly prized commodity. The lemon's name – now *limone* – went from *citro* to *limunczello* as a result of the Arab influences. The Amalfi lemons are called '*sfusato*' due to their elongated, pointed shape. Their thick, flavourful skins are full of essential oils, and their juice contains more vitamin C than other varieties of lemon. For more information contact the Consorzio di Tutela Limone Costa d'Amalfi IGP (Via Papa Leone X, 9; E-MAIL cata@starnet.it).

The Duomo in Amalfi

Bar, Pastries and Candied Fruit

Piazza Duomo, 40
TEL 081 871065

Pasticceria Andrea Panza 1830

You can't walk by this elegant bar–*pasticceria* without being tempted to buy a pastry, *granita* or sweetmeat: the window displays with their beautifully arranged candied citrus fruits in soft greens, yellows and oranges are as seductive to the eye as to the palate. Panza is at the heart of Amalfi, right under the stairway that leads up to the Duomo, and has been a fixture in the *piazza* since 1830. In summer there are tables outside; in winter sit in the little *sala* next to the bar. The *frutti canditi* – of lemon, orange and citron – make great presents: to eat on their own or to use, chopped up, in home-made cakes or ice creams.

Panza's candied citrus

Restaurant

Via Matteo Camera, 12
TEL 089 871029
FAX 089 871029
E-MAIL
info@ristorantelacaravella.it
INTERNET
www.ristorantelacaravella.it
CLOSED Tues;
10 Nov–25 Dec
PRICE €€€€€

La Caravella

La Caravella is situated in part of what was once the Duke of Amalfi's private house, on the main coastal road in the town centre facing the sea. This was the first restaurant in Campania ever to win a Michelin star, back in the 1960s, and it has it still – a fine tribute to the consistency of both food and service. La Caravella has always been a keen promoter of the region's viticultural talents, and the Campanian section of the extensive wine list has greatly improved in the decades since the restaurant opened.

The *cucina*, as one would expect, is mainly sea-based, as befits a former sea power, complemented by fresh ingredients native to the coastal mountains and fields. *Antipasti* vary with the seasons, but the *alici* are always fresh and abundant: in winter they are good served fried with *provola* cheese and a sauce of *colatura* from nearby Cetara (see pp. 182-83). I also like the mussels stuffed with mozzarella, olives, *gamberi*, and the *pomodorini* that are dried hanging from the rafters – a dish of wonderfully Mediterranean flavours. After a thick purée of *cicerchie* – a legume that is like cross between a bean and a chickpea – served with *frutti di mare*, we moved onto the pastas: home-made *trenette* with saffron and broccoli flowers, large *ziti* stuffed with *baccalà* and capers, *linguine* with *colatura di alici*, Sorrento walnuts, olives and lemon. A fillet of *pezzogna* – local blue-spotted bream – is strongly accented by a very lemony sauce. Cheeses, too, are well selected and local. For dessert, a spoon of lemon marmalade with lemon sorbet set the tone for a fried *raviolo* stuffed with bitter cherries – *amarene*.

The owner, Antonio Di Pino, told me that his father had once had Andy Warhol as a customer in the restaurant: the artist had

Santa Caterina's panoramic dining room

tried to exchange a picture for his dinner, but the restaurateur failed to take him up on the offer.

Wine Bar

Salita Marino Sebaste, 8
TEL 089 8304549
CLOSED Tues;
mid-Jan–mid-Feb

Cantina San Nicola

In one of the narrow stepped *vicoli* leading off the central street through Amalfi, you'll find this active wine bar. There are simple traditional dishes at fair prices to accompany a large list of wines; the Cantina also organizes tastings and special wine and food events. If you want to try some fine local wines of the Costa d'Amalfi DOC, ask for producers such as Marisa Cuomo, Apicella, Reale or Sammarco.

Hotel, Restaurant

S.S. Amalfitana, 9
TEL 089 871012
FAX 089 871351
E-MAIL
info@hotelsantacaterina.it

Santa Caterina Hotel

Just beyond the town of Amalfi, this marvellous hotel started at the beginning of the 20th century as a series of little cottages: 'People came, and came back every year, wanting the same waiter, the same rock by the sea,' says Beatrice, granddaughter of the original owner, Crescenzo Gambardella. Over the next century the family-run hotel became one of the *Costiera*'s most elegant. There are two restaurants: one down at the beach in summertime, and the other up in the lovely dining room in the main hotel, with its panoramic views of the sea. The food is firmly based on regional, traditional specialties, but is not without a touch of modernity. Many ingredients are grown directly by the hotel's gardeners on the narrow terraces that go down to the sea.

ALSO AT AMALFI

Amalfi was a historic paper-making area, with its valley of

paper mills and export possibilities by sea. Today there is a museum of paper here, as well as the works of one of the historic paper-making families, Cartiera Amatruda (Via delle Cartiere, 100; TEL 089 871315) who still make beautiful things.

Castellammare di Stabia

Pasta

Via Plinio, 40
TEL 081 8723644
INTERNET
www.gerardodinola1.aol.com

Gerardo Di Nola

Giovanni Assante is as well known in Campania as his pasta: indefatigable promoter of *la vera pasta napoletana*, he is constantly in and out of the country's finest restaurant kitchens and speciality food stores with cartons of Gerardo Di Nola hardwheat pasta, made for him at Castellammare di Stabia.

Pastries

Viale Europa, 105
TEL 081 8715561
INTERNET
www.biscottificio-riccardi.it

A. Riccardi Premiata Fabbrica di Biscotti

This classic biscuit factory is one of the few remaining at Castellammare: at one time the town was as famous for its sweetmeats as it was for its thermal – and purgative – waters. If, when it began 150 years ago, it was customary for departing sailors to stock up on Riccardi's dry, rusk-like biscuits before a long sea voyage, today it's more likely you'll eat them on the beach or on an adventurous car trip.

Wine Shop

Via F Petrarca, 31
TEL 081 3941263

Enoteca Perbacco

Giuseppina De Simone's wine shop has a good range of wines as well as a hand-picked assortment of local *prodotti tipici*.

Hotel

S.S. Sorrentina, Km 11
TEL 081 3946700
FAX 081 3946770
INTERNET
www.crowneplaza.com

Crowne Plaza Hotel

This hotel offers a good idea of what industrial renewal can do. A huge eyesore of a cement factory had been abandoned for years, but was recently completely gutted and refurbished, and is now a very comfortable luxury seaside hotel, well placed for visits to Pompei, Napoli and the *Costiera* (see pp. 231).

Cava de' Tirreni

Restaurant, Wine Bar

Corso Umberto I, 38/40
TEL 089 443173
CLOSED Mon;
20 July–20 Aug
CARDS All PRICE €€€

Taverna Scacciaventi

I'm really fond of this cosy restaurant–wine bar, whose name means 'to chase away the winds'. Firstly because it is tucked away, safe from wind and rain, under the portico of a beautiful old street in central Cava; then there is the display case of excellent cheeses and *salumi* – including six-year-old Spanish ham (for those of us who can feast on *prosciutto crudo* any day) that one has to pass to get inside, and that always stimulates both appetite and curiosity; the great wine selection that is cared for by people who really know what's behind the labels and under the corks; and the large open fireplace in the last room at which steaks and other meats are grilled as you watch, eating rustic soups, *polenta* and pastas to accompany a fine glass of *vino* and a stimulating conversation.

Organic food

Orto Biologico

Traversa Vittorio Veneto, 314
TEL 089 344241

Organic stores are still few and far between in Italy – this one offers a good range of both fresh produce and dry goods.

Cetara

FOR INFORMATION ABOUT CETARA AND ITS ACTIVITIES
Vivere Il Mare
Comune di Cetara
Corso Umberto I
TEL 089 261068
INTERNET
www.vivereilmare.it.
FOR INFORMATION ABOUT THE TUNA SAGRA WEEK:
INTERNET
www.atuttotonno.it

I lived for five winter months in this steep, tiny fishing village while I was researching this book. It was a fascinating experience, made difficult at times by the fact that I don't speak Cetara dialect, and many of my Cetarese neighbours didn't speak Italian.

Cetara is one of the only remaining villages on the Campanian coast that still lives from its fishing; indeed there is a large tuna fleet here in addition to the smaller boats that daily come into the harbour with anchovies, octopus and other small Mediterranean delights. Gastronomically, the town is famous for its salted anchovy *colatura*, a sauce that is close to the ancient Roman *garum* (see below). It also lives from its bottled salted anchovies and some tuna canning. Every summer, between July and August, the town hosts a week-long tuna *sagra* to celebrate the homecoming of the fleet. There are few hotels in town, but several good restaurants, easy enough to reach from Vietri which is only five kilometres away.

Above: a religious procession at Cetara

Opposite: freshly caught octopus at Cetara's port

BUYING FISH

If it's fresh fish you're after at Cetara, you can either go down to the port and buy it directly from the fishermen when their boats come in, or from the fishmonger, Pescheria Cetarese (Piazza Ungherese, 2; TEL 089 261795).

For the *colatura di alici* and other salted anchovy products, both Giordano's Nettuno Cetara (Via Umberto I, 64; TEL 089 261147) and Delfino Battista (Corso Garibaldi, 44; TEL 089 261069; INTERNET www.delfinobattistarl.it) make a good range.

LA COLATURA DI ALICI – SALTED ANCHOVY 'SAUCE'

The Mediterranean Sea has always produced an abundance of anchovies and these highly flavoured, small 'blue' fish are eaten both fresh and preserved in salt to be used as a condiment in cooking. Italian has two words for them: *acciuga* and *alice*. The Adriatic Sea is less salt than the Tyrrhenian; the anchovies in Adriatic waters feed on green plankton, grow larger, and are usually eaten fresh. On the western coast of Italy, especially in Campania, the anchovies are smaller and saltier – they adapt to the salinity of the waters they live in. Salt was also available here, traded from Sicily and other salt-producing areas, so it's not surprising that salting anchovies became a prosperous business for the fishing villages along the Campanian coast.

The traditional barrel for making la colatura is weighted down by a rock

When anchovies are packed with salt and pressed, a liquid runs off that is part salt, part fish juices. Salt preserves the fish, but it doesn't completely stop the fermentation or decomposition processes: the 'dripping' (*colare* means 'to strain') has a very concentrated flavour of fish and salt and adds an intense accent to whatever food it is served with. The Romans highly prized *garum*, their name for this type of salty fish sauce; it seems likely they made *garum* in many versions, from the poorest (using rotten or discarded fish and entrails) to the most refined, in which the fish and salt could express themselves more nobly.

If Pisciotta in the Cilento (see pp. 295-97) is famous for salted anchovies that are still being fished with a style of net favoured by the Greeks – *la Menaica* – Cetara is known for its *colatura di alici*. 'Until recently, every household in this village made its own *colatura*,' says Francesco Liguri, the town's mayor and a keen fisherman. 'They kept them in small wooden barrels, pressed down with a rock, and would exchange tiny phials of the precious amber-pink liquid with their neighbours for Christmas as a sign of friendship.' The best *colatura* was made from anchovies fished in May, when they were put under salt; the barrels were drained in December.

Today the *colatura* has been 'rediscovered' by cultural and food associations – indeed, Slow Food established a

Anchovies being salted in large terracotta jars

Presidio to help save it from extinction. This created interest and demand for *la colatura*; initially it did not, however, prevent its being produced in bulk by fish-preserving companies in the Cetara area. Recently a group of anchovy admirers (www.amicidellealici.org) has taken action. 'We managed to find one of the very few artisans still alive who could make the original wooden barrels,' says Secondo Squizzato, president of the association, 'and we salted the fish according to traditional methods. In December 2004 we'll have the first results – about twelve litres of the precious liquid.' Good news for *colatura* cravers.

Cetara's four restaurateurs have banded together (very unusual in the south of Italy) and formed an association – la Confraternita del Pesce Azzurro – in order to guarantee good quality fish and fish products in their restaurants, at fair prices. Here you'll find *la colatura* served to enhance all manner of dishes – from *antipasti* to *secondi* – served by the drop from tiny glass bottles using a twig of dried oregano.

Restaurant

Acquapazza

Walk down to the port on Cetara's central descending street (it runs under the main coastal road) and you'll pass right by the town's restaurants. This one is very near the bottom, just as the street begins to open out into the esplanade. It's on the right, under a portico, a tiny dining room that spills outdoors with a few extra tables in summer, so be sure to book ahead.

Acquapazza is run by the two Gennaros – one serving and the other cooking. Theirs is a simple cuisine of good strong sea flavours (often including an over-presence of salt): chickpeas with *totani* (flying squid) and fennel seeds; small *fagioli* beans with cuttlefish (*seppie*) and *colatura*; butterflied fresh *alici* with parsley, raisins, and pine nuts. Pastas too are accompanied by this range of local fish, followed by cod with potatoes and *bottarga* (salt-cured roe), or tuna *ventresca* with tomatoes and basil. Just right for sea-side dining.

My local greengrocer

Restaurant

Ristorante Pizzeria Al Convento

Pasquale is the amiable host of this spacious, relaxed restaurant that has been created inside the former cloister of the convent at the top of the tree-lined *piazza*, on the right just below the main road as you descend to the sea. In summer he also has shady tables outside overlooking the square. Here you'll find pizzas as well as a good range of *antipasti* of both seafood and vegetables to start the meal, including the well-balanced sweet–salt combination of cured *lardo* with salted anchovies and herbs. Pastas are abundant, from the *paccheri* with their coral sauce of *zucca*, shrimp and *rucola*, to the rare '*conventuale*' recipe of home-made *gnocchi* of stale bread, served with walnuts, white beans, salted *alici* and *peperoncino* – it's not always available, but is delicious. Anchovies are served every which way – fresh and salted – as are other local fish. Desserts are care of the talented local *pasticciere* Salvatore De Riso (see pp. 196-97); wines are well selected, and the service is friendly and casual.

Pasquale and his son with local cheeses

Restaurant

Ristorante San Pietro

At the top of the same central *piazza* (you can reach it by a staircase down from the main *Costiera* road) is another charming restaurant, the San Pietro. The position is luminous, at leaf-level with the trees, and in summer you can enjoy a meal outdoors on the terrace. Franco (with his marvellous Neapolitan profile) is a welcoming host and passionate cook, especially when dealing with the wealth of produce from the sea and hills

Cetara's bar shows the village painted on a Vietri mural

that surround Cetara. He has developed a cuisine of local flavours that suits the context: after a succession of *antipasti di mare*, thick *farro* (spelt wheat) soup is enriched with *pesce azzurro* and *colatura*, and with aromatic dried oregano from the coast; *cicerchie* – a local legume – are served with *totani* (flying squid) and garlic toasts topped with pink peppercorns; stockfish and onions are married in a soft mousse to accompany Venetian *polenta*; pasta is cooked with potatoes and mussels in a southern classic; *provola* cheese is melted between lemon leaves and salted with *alici*; *baccalà* is accented with black olives and a green sauce of fresh *scarola*… lots of good ideas for every season to accompany a range of fine Campanian wines.

Hotel, Restaurant
Hotel Cetus

Strada Statale, 163
TEL 089 261388
FAX 089261388
E-MAIL
info@hotelcetus.it

This is the only good hotel at Cetara; it's beautifully positioned right on the sea (with breathtaking views from the bedrooms over the water), yet is less known and less costly than many of the *Costiera*'s more famous hotels. I also love the location: Cetara is just ten minutes from Vietri and Salerno – so it's easy to get on a highway from there to Paestum, Avellino or even Naples – yet you are in the heart of the landscape and culture of the *Costiera*. There is a lovely restaurant too.

Furore

Restaurant, Hotel

Via Lama, 9
TEL 089 830360
FAX 089 830352
E-MAIL info@baccofurore.it
CLOSED
Fri in low season;
8–14 Nov
PRICE €€€

Hostaria di Bacco

Raffaele Ferraioli has long been one of the major movers in the battle to gain help and recognition for the humble villages up above the Amalfi Coast. He has been mayor of Furore, is still head of the local Comunità Montana, and is active in Slow Food and other associations concerned with saving the mountains' *contadino* culture. He is involved in a project to improve and defend the area's artisan cheeses (see pp. 224-26) and, with his family, also runs Furore's best-known restaurant and hotel, Bacco, which has for years promoted local recipes and products.

'Furore is a straggle of houses without a real nucleus,' he says, 'so the only way to give it an identity was through its culture, œno-gastronomic and otherwise.' Indeed, the village is decorated with murals that have been painted by artists invited each September to participate. The hotel restaurant has a simple modern style, but the food is based on local recipes.

'Why must we go on selling imported wines and cheeses from the north of Italy when we have our own, as well as great desserts made from our own lemons, which were for too long underrated?' he asks. In late summer I tasted *ferrazzuoli alla Nannarella*, an unusual dish of short pasta in the shape of a double tube, dressed with smoked swordfish, *pomodorini*, *rucola*, sweet green grapes and *pinoli* in a tomato-based sauce. *Totani* – flying squid – are served with their traditional partners, potatoes. A *zuppetta* of mussels and clams with cherry tomatoes is wholesome and delicious, and is well paired with his cousin Marisa Cuomo's wines (see below). Raffaele also had me taste a series of unusual sweetmeats, including raisins and candied fruits baked together in little packages of lemon leaves (called *follovielli*, from the Latin: to wrap in leaves). The dining room is on an airy terrace with fabulous views of the mountains and sea.

Follovielli: sticky dried-fruit desserts baked in lemon leaves

Wine

Via GB Lama, 14
TEL 089 830348
FAX 089 04014
E-MAIL
info@granfuror.it
INTERNET
www.granfuror.it
Visits and tastings by
appointment

Marisa Cuomo: Gran Furor Divina Costiera

'We're finally making the new cellar, come and see.' I've visited a lot of cellars being built, but it's rare to find one being dug straight out of the back of a room high on a mountainside overlooking the sea. Marisa Cuomo and Andrea Ferraioli's winery has expanded so much in recent years that there was nowhere else to go but into the *tufo*. The couple's Gran Furor winery has become synonymous with the rise in quality of – and interest in – the Costa d'Amalfi DOC wines.

'Making wines up on these very steep terraces is not an easy

*Panoramic vineyard
above Furore*

proposition,' says Andrea, as we climb to see some of the small plots of vineyards interspersed with vegetable patches and wild fig trees that he oversees. Despite the trellising, these vines are their own masters, growing out from under stone walls, or horizontally along the ground. 'Each *contadino* has a tiny amount of this land, and to make a decent quantity of wine I have grouped over twenty small producers together, and pay handsomely for their grapes.'

'We started twenty years ago, almost from scratch,' says Marisa, whose grandparents used to make wine up at Furore, but never bottled it. 'In 1995 we decided to improve the quality, and that meant controlling vinification methods, and ageing and bottling the wines – we had to get serious.'

They also decided to stick with the many indigenous grape varieties that are well adapted to these unusual growing conditions – a smart move given the wine market's recent swing away from 'international' varieties. 'We are lucky to have quite a number of these rare varieties: whites Ginestra, Fenile, Ripoli, Biancolella (or 'Bianca Tenera') and Falanghina ('Bianca Zita'); and reds Piedirosso – or 'Per' 'e Palummo' as it is called in dialect – and Aglianico,' continues Andrea. The average age of the vines is 70–80 years, ungrafted (or, as they say in Italian, *su piede franco*), and pre-phylloxera. 'Our friend in the Cilento, Luigi Maffini, has flat vineyards and an air-conditioned tractor,' laughs Andrea. 'Ours are so steep we can't even use a mule. Here there are 5,000 stairs and gravity to battle with just to bring in the grapes. As you can see, our viticulture defies all logic.'

*Native grape varieties
abound on the coast*

The collaboration with Campanian œnologist Luigi Moio has been a successful one: his considerable technical experience imposed some discipline on these often anarchic vineyards. They now produce 50,000 bottles here – a remarkable feat under these working conditions. From the delicately fruity Furore Bianco to the substantial barrique-aged Furore Rosso Riserva, the couple produce a range of six wines, many of which have won acclaim and awards. Quite an accomplishment for a winery that a husband named for his new bride over twenty years ago.

ALSO AT FURORE

Agriturismo Sant'Alfonso (Via Sant'Alfonso, 7; TEL 089 830515; INTERNET www.agriturismosantalfonso.it) is located in a recently restructured ex-monastery from the 16th century, formerly of the Ligurini monks. Good vegetable cuisine.

Agriturismo Serafina (Via Picola, 3; TEL 089 830347) is a more rustic *agriturismo*, an authentic farm with cows, lemon groves and vines.

Gragnano

Gragnano has long been one of Italy's key pasta-producing towns; making dried pasta of durum flour and water has been one of Campania's primary gastronomic and industrial concerns for over 400 years – if not longer. To appreciate the importance of the artisanal production of dried pasta one has only to consider how much has changed since Waverley Root wrote this diverting account in *The Food of Italy* of domestically made pasta in Napoli in the 1920s:

On my first visit there, in 1929, I acquired a distaste for macaroni, at least in Naples, for its insalubrious courtyards were jungles of it. Limp strands hung over clotheslines to dry, dirt swirled through the air, flies settled to rest on the exposed pasta, pigeons bombed it from overhead, children invented games to play with it, and the large dog population, finding itself short of lampposts, put up with what it could find. But have no fear today: macaroni and spaghetti are now made indoors in spick-and-span automated factories.

Those spick and span pasta factories (*pastifici*) made the towns of Gragnano and Torre Annunziata famous. In 1860 there were 80 *pasticifi* at Gragnano, and 90 at Torre Annunziata, with another 200 scattered around the area. By 1950 there were still 19 *pastifici* at Gragnano; today only a handful remain, some of which still make the pasta following the artisanal precepts that produce the best pasta. It is possible to visit them simply to buy the pasta, but it is best to call ahead if you want to see how it is made.

Pasta

Pastai Gragnanesi

Via G. Della Rocca, 20
TEL 081 8012975
FAX 081 8013062
E-MAIL
pastai@uniserv.uniplan.it
INTERNET
www.pastaigragnanesi.it

In this *cooperativa*'s office, there's a framed portrait of Antonio Gramsci on the wall. Below it are stacks of papers, tins of tomato, strings of garlic, pots and pans, books and files... Pastai Gragnanesi have been in this 1840 building since 1980; the factory's original owners didn't want to continue making pasta, so the co-op of nine members took it over. It's a large building on four floors: on the first floor are the presses where short and cut pasta are made; on the second are the ovens for slow-drying the pasta at 50°C; the third is used for packing. In the 19th century there were no automatic lifts, and the workers had to carry the flour and pasta up and down the stairs they called *l'inferno* – hell.

'In the old days, the workers had the right to one kilo of

PASTA: THE WHYS AND WHEREFORES

Antonio Marchetti is a pastaholic – he eats pasta with olive oil and lemon juice for breakfast – and runs Gragnano's principal pasta-making co-operative, Pastai Gragnanese. He is an expert on pasta history and on Gragnano – and he helped me compile this brief guide to pasta.

The Origins

Gragnano pasta

There is an ongoing debate about where pasta originated, but it may be more constructive to note that throughout history, civilizations in every part of the globe had some sort of pasta, made of maize, rice, wheat or other farinaceous ingredients. The reason is simple: it's easier and safer to store pasta than it is to keep raw grain, which is vulnerable to temperature, humidity, infection and pests. So every culture found some way to grind and preserve flour by mixing it with water and drying it. In Italy, there are depictions of pasta by the Etruscans as early as 450 BC: at Tarquinia there is an image of a plate of *pici* (a type of hand-made pasta still found in Tuscany), while on a tomb at Cerveteri are portrayed the pasta-maker's tools, rolling pin included.

By 1300 pasta was being produced artisanally by hand, but the industrial breakthrough came in the 16th century with the invention of the press, or *torchio*. This allowed pasta to be formed by being extruded through metal dies, so large volumes of consistently perfect pasta could be made with much less effort, ready to be dried and shipped all over the world. In 1861, 67 pasta companies (*fabbriche di maccheroni*) were operating at Gragnano, and 22 mills; in 1950, 43 *pastifici* and 12 mills; today 11 *pastifici* exist (both artisanal and industrial) and no mills. Today, 300 different shapes of pasta are still being produced at Gragnano.

What's in it?

The ingredients of Gragnano's pasta are *grano duro* (durum wheat), water – and air. These three elements are indispensable for the successful making of pasta, and at Gragnano they co-existed naturally.

Grain

Millennia ago, Vesuvio was probably encircled by the sea, for all around it now is a flat plain, a wide 'valley' of fertile

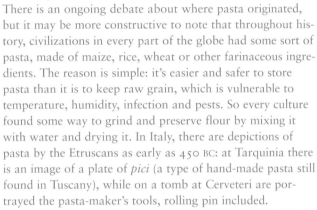

tufo, or compacted volcanic ash. During the Roman era (and undoubtedly before), this large area was planted with the wheat that supplied Roma and Napoli with grain. Indeed, in Roman times Gragnano was called *Prædium Granium*, i.e. a large piece of land cultivated to cereals. If, between Gragnano and Vesuvio, the land is mainly *tufo*, in the other direction, towards the Amalfi Coast, the ground is white limestone, part of the mountain range that makes the Monti Lattari.

Water

Gragnano's water comes from the Monti Lattari chain of mountains which form the backbone of the Sorrento Peninsula, then drop off into the sea to re-emerge in their furthest point – Capri. The river valley below Gragnano is known locally as *la Valle dei Mulini* for the many water-powered flour mills that were built along it, often with origins in the Middle Ages. They began to die out at the end of the 19th century when taxes were introduced on each turn of the mill-stone (as ever, in industry's favour). Until fifty years ago, some were still being used, but today these beautiful stone buildings are unfortunately all in crumbling ruins.

A dish of paccheri: they are tubes when uncooked but flatten after boiling

Air

It seems that Gragnano began as a pasta centre in the 17th century. Its main street, Via Roma, was designed in 1820 for drying pasta. It was purpose-built along the sun's axis so that the racks of pasta the factories put out to dry in the street could receive the sun from morning to evening. It took two to three days to dry the pasta. There was a continual current of air to help this drying process, formed in the channel between the mountain and the sea, and the wind picked up speed at Gragnano, which is why its micro-climate is unique.

With the advent of industrialization, drying ovens were designed to speed up the process and make it more hygienic. Slow-drying the pasta at low temperatures maintains the grain's flavours and nutritional benefits: Gragnano artisan pasta is dried for 32 hours at 50°C; modern industrial pasta is dried in two to three hours in temperatures from 79° to 100°C.

Opposite: Artisan-made pasta from Gragnano comes in many shapes and sizes

pasta per day,' says Antonio Marchetti, the co-operative's director. 'Pasta was their family's staple food. Our pasta is completely different from industrial: it's more fragrant with the flavour of wheat, has higher levels of proteins, and is more easily digestible.'

The Pastai produce 46 shapes of pasta, pushed through the two-inch-thick bronze dies of their 1950s press that is still going strong. Their pastas' names are descriptive of their shapes: *calamari*, *conchiglioni* (big shells), *tortiglioni* (spirals), *lumacconi* (big snails), *mezzi bombardoni* (half bombardons), *mille righe* (thousand lines), etc. The co-op has also revived a shape that is a particular favourite of the Neapolitans, *vermicello bucato*. 'This is like a *spaghetto* with a hole through its centre,' explains Marchetti. After cooking, there is a slight difference of chewability between the inside (slightly less cooked) and the outside. 'It remains *saporito* – flavourful – for longer and, unlike *bucatini*, it won't dirty men's ties with spots of sauce. Eat it with *aglio*, *olio e peperoncino* (garlic, oil and chilli) – it's like spaghetti with an added dimension. By the way, the golden rule when cooking all long pasta is to put it horizontally into the boiling water, which means using a wide or oval pan. This is the only way it will be cooked evenly throughout.' By previous appointment, Marchetti conducts tours of the factory for interested visitors.

Pasta

Piazza San Leone
TEL 081 8012985

Pastificio Faella

This is the other Gragnano factory, over a hundred years old, in the town centre. The elderly Don Gaetano, who declares himself to 'have been born in pasta', still oversees the workings and the shop inside the factory that supplies the local populace. I particularly like Faella's whirligig shape (*elicoidali* or *tortiglioni*), sold in cheerful white, red and blue bags.

Restaurant

Via Sanzano, 18
TEL 081 8795709
CLOSED
Mon except by prior
booking

L'Hostaria Mirenca

This small, family-run trattoria is tucked away at the end of an alley in the upper part of Gragnano, but it's worth seeking out. A garden terrace in summer gives the possibility of eating outside, and for cooler weather the dining rooms have been nicely redecorated to be simple but comfortable. The two women in the family do the cooking, and prepare Gragnano's pastas and other local dishes well (ask to taste the slow-simmered tomato *ragù* that cooks for more than two days). There are local *salumi* and *sott'oli* (vegetables put under oil by the women) and main courses drawn from the household repertoire.

Pastries

Pasticceria Zampino

Here they make, among other delicious pastries, *le cicale*: ground-almond biscuits flavoured with prickly-pear liqueur. I first tasted them at Ristorante Bacco, at Furore (see p. 186).

GRAGNANO'S WINE

The average Neapolitan would as a rule choose neither Falerno nor Lacryma Christi, prestigious though their names may be, but Gragnano. This is the wine Neapolitans have taken to their bosoms. In their Punch and Judy shows, Punch never asks for wine; he calls for Gragnano.

Waverley Root The Food of Italy

Gragnano may have been the name on every food-writer's lips in the mid-20th century, but it slipped into the same sort of backwater as Chianti later in the century. Fortunately the wind has changed again and, with the ever-increasing interest in native grape varieties – such as Sciascinoso, Piedirosso and Biancolella – this ancient winemaking area is now undergoing a re-birth. The wine named Gragnano can contain up to seven types of indigenous grape varieties. Here as in other high terraces that are difficult to reach and work, tiny vineyard plots belong to myriad owners which makes producing large quantities of wine a problem. Some vineyards are still planted with aged vines that survived the phylloxera attack of the late 19th and early 20th centuries, and as such are very interesting to study. The Penisola Sorrentina DOC – including Gragnano, Sorrento and Lettere – wines tend to be light, fruity, and possibly lightly *frizzante*; they are pleasant to drink with pizza, summer pasta dishes and the fried foods that the Neapolitans so adore. Listed here are the principal producers of this DOC.

Balestrieri (Via Quarantola, 13/A, Gragnano; TEL 081 8733016). This family has been making wine at Gragnano for forty years.

Cantine Borgo Sant'Anna (Corso Vittorio Emanuele, 99, Lettere; TEL/FAX 081 8021148). The Sorrentino family has gone from making barrels to making wine, here and on Vesuvio.

Iovine (Via Nazionale, 23, Pimonte; TEL 081 8792123; FAX 081 8749043; E-MAIL iovinevini@tin.it). Pimonte is located in the hills above Gragnano. The Iovines were also coopers by trade; today they cultivate vines that survived the phylloxera attack at the beginning of the last century.

Cantine Grotta del Sole (Via Spinelli, 2, Quarto; TEL 081

8762566; FAX 081 8769470; E-MAIL grottadelsole@iol.it; INTER-
NET www.grottadelsole.it). See p. 115 for more on this important Neapolitan *cantina*.

De Angelis (Via Marziale, 14, Sorrento; TEL 081 8781648).
Sorrento's oldest *cantina*.

Maiori

Maiori was one of the first places on the *Costiera* to plant
lemon groves, some say as early as the 11th century. At the
beginning of the 20th century, Maiori lemons were even quoted
on the New York Stock Exchange. 'At that time, the lemons
were sold singly,' says Vincenzo Aita, the region's former agriculture Assessore – or minister. 'They were treated as precious
commodities and handled by manicured women wearing cotton
gloves. Then, more than 900,000 crates per year were exported
throughout the world – esteemed as much for their delicious fragrance and essential oils as for their high vitamin C content.'

Restaurant

Via D Taiani, 48
TEL 089 877022
E-MAIL info@capodorso.org
INTERNET
www.capodorso.org

Il Faro di Capo d'Orso
This elegant restaurant is located on the tip of rock that juts out
over the sea at Capo d'Orso – a perfect place for a panoramic
lunch.

Marina del Cantone see Nerano

Massa Lubrense

The *comune* of Massa Lubrense contains some of the most
unspoiled and beautiful landscape of the Penisola Sorrentina.
So it's a perfect place to go for *limoncello* (see also Sant'Agata
sui Due Golfi, pp. 212-14), honeys, jams and other fruit preserves. Several fine producers are situated in the town and its
surroundings:

Il Convento (Via San Francesco, 12; TEL 081 8789380). For
three generations the Pollio family have run a farm here, beside
a 14th-century monastery, with olives, lemons and orchards as
well as animals. Today there is also an *agriturismo* to stay in,
and excellent *limoncello*, oil, jams and vegetable preserves to
taste and buy. L'Eden, at Pastena (Via Regina Margherita,
49/51; TEL 081 5330636; INTERNET www.leden.it) has chosen its
name well, as its fruit and herb liqueurs present the essential
flavours of this heavenly area. The Gods are in mind too at

*Many people still drink
natural spring water
from the mountain*

Nettare degli Dei (Via Massa Turro, 84; TEL 081 8789042; INTERNET www.cosedisorrento.com): the nectar here is honey, made from the exquisitely scented *zagara* – lemon blossom – and other flowering trees in these unspoiled hilltops. You'll also find jars of local Sorrento walnuts and Campania's fine hazelnuts preserved in honey.

For authentic breads and savoury snacks baked in a wood-burning oven, seek out Pasquale Gargiulo's Antico Panificio (Via Rivo a Casa, 8–10; TEL 081 8789084) in the historic centre of Massa, near the 17th-century Jesuit monastery that here is called a *convento*.

Meta di Sorrento

Olive Oil

Alma Mater Bio

Via Astarita, 32,
San Cataldo
TEL 081 8088954
INTERNET
www.almamaterbio.com

Alessandra Balduccini produces fine, fruity olive oils from her olive groves overlooking the sea between Vico Equense and Sorrento. As she cultivates her trees organically, she carefully hand-picks the olives, discarding any that show signs of blemishes or of *la mosca*, the olive-fly that attacks all olive trees growing at low altitudes near the water. She mills her olives at Imma Gargiulo's *frantoio* nearby (see p. 216).

Minori

TOURIST INFORMATION:
Pro Loco Minori
Piazza Cantilena, 18
TEL/FAX 089 877087
E-MAIL
prolocominori@
amalficoast.it
INTERNET
www.amalficoast.it/
prolocominori

The remains of an important Imperial Roman villa from the 1st century discovered in the 1930s have given the *Costiera* between Salerno and Sant'Agata sui Due Golfi its most important archaeological site. It is open for visits from 9.00 a.m. to dusk.

Minori was also appreciated by the Romans and later travellers for its pasta: by the beginning of the 18th century the whole village was draped on sunny days with pasta drying from cane racks, and some historians claim that Minori preceded Gragnano as the area's most important pasta town. The necessary conditions of water – from the river Reginna Minor or Reginuolo – and drying air, which came down from the mountains and gorges, made it a successful habitat for this popular Campanian food.

Minori is still famous for its 'ndunderi, ancient Roman precursors of *gnocchi* made then with *farro* flour thickened with milk that had been clotted with *lattice di fico* – the sticky white, rubbery sap of the fig tree. 'The mixture was rolled into small balls, and boiled in water,' explains Ezio Falcone, a local food historian. 'It was originally dressed with *moretum*, a paste of *pecorino* cheese, wild aromatic herbs, oil, wine and walnuts, and served in the *triclinium*, the Roman dining area where one ate in a reclining position.' Today, potato *gnocchi* have taken their place.

Pastries, Gelato

Piazza Cantilena, 1
TEL 089 853618
E-MAIL info@deriso.it
INTERNET www.deriso.it

Salvatore De Riso

Minori has now been put on the gastronomic map by a young *pasticciere*, Salvatore De Riso, whose bar–*gelateria*– pastry shop – with cheerful umbrellas out in the *piazza* on the seafront – has become a haven for those with a discerning sweet tooth.

Minori lemons

'For sixty years, my father ran a tiny bar-*tabacchi* just down the street from here,' says De Riso. 'I loved that shop. We sold a little of everything: cigarettes, candles for the cemetery, string for tying salami ends, spices and salt, home-made sorbets, and my father's famous *granita al limone*. People would come from miles around for it.' Salvatore trained in several of the *Costiera*'s best hotels, but came back in 2000 to set up an ample *pasticceria* with his family, just a few metres from the small *emporio*. He now makes forty cakes, pies and tarts from high quality ingredients, many of which are sold by the slice or in mini-versions. The most famous is *la delizia al limone* – a creamy, pale yellow cake shaped like a rounded breast and perfumed by the aromatic *sfusato* lemons that grow along the *Costiera*. It is based on a traditional recipe. De Riso has also created a modern version of the classic *pastiera napoletana*: his *soffiato di pastiera* is an airy ricotta mousse with candied fruits and plumped wheat on a shortcrust base.

There are also ice-creams, *granite*, and two cakes De Riso has developed for travellers. *Dolce d'Amalfi* is a moist dome of almonds and lemon, and *torta Villa Romana* – inspired by Minori's 1st-century Roman villa – uses local ingredients favoured by the ancient Romans: hazelnuts, honey, dried figs and raisins. These cakes are boxed and can last up to three months, without added preservatives. De Riso also runs a catering business, and sells his cakes to many restaurants in the area – but watch out for imitations.

Restaurant

Via S.G. a Mare, 20
TEL 089 851418
CLOSED Thurs Oct-May

L'Arsenale

Close to the sea, under a high portico, you'll find this seafood restaurant and a family of sons who cook and serve. Massimo Proto is one of the two young chefs. Like all truly passionate cooks, he started off cooking the traditional dishes of the area,

Opposite: De Riso with his delizie al limone

*Gar-fish (pesce bandiera)
at the local fishmonger's*

like pasta with hearty shellfish and tomato sauces, or grilled
fish. These are still available, but gradually he began to be more
selective in both his choice of prime ingredients and in the ways
of cooking them. I particularly like his play on the humble fisherman's classic, *totani e patate* – squid and potatoes. In one dish
I was given: three tiny *moscardini* (curled octopus the size of
one's thumb-joint) filled with a rosemary-scented *soffritto* and a
loose potato sauce; one tender *calamaretto* stuffed with potato;
a larger *totano* (flying squid) sliced into rings and served with
stewed potato. A subtle, interesting combination. Pastas come in
all manner of ways, depending on the daily catch – *scialatielli*
are fine dressed with a sauce of sea urchin, crustaceans and
fresh tomato. A dessert using the intense Domori chocolate
(from Liguria) rounded off the summer's lunch. The brothers
have assembled a fine wine list of Campanian and Italian wines
(including a lot of big Tuscans), with an emphasis on the whites
that accompany seafood so well. I look forward to tasting more
by this charming young man.

A Walk around Minori

Walking around Minori, I spotted some old photos of pasta
being dried out in the street on racks, just like at Gragnano, and
a street called Largo Solaio dei Pastai – the pasta-makers' sunny
street. At Ristorante La Botte (Via Santa Maria Vetrano, 15; TEL
089 877893; CLOSED Mon and Aug) the *'ndunderi* are delicious:
large potato *gnocchi* enriched with ricotta and served with a
hearty tomato and sausage-meat sauce. This modestly priced,
rustic trattoria with some outdoor tables serves traditional dishes, fresh fish, pizzas and very good desserts. If you are somewhere with a kitchen, buy hand-made pasta to cook at home
from Antonio Ruocco's Il Pastaio (Via Largo Solaio dei Pastai;
TEL 089 853706). Traditional *salumi* or fresh meats can be
found at Macelleria Mammato (Via Garofalo, 24; TEL 089
877415) which is just down the street from a fine fishmonger.
For good wines, try Enoteca Sirah (Piazzetta di Santa
Trofimena; TEL 089 853895). Costieragrumi (Via Pioppi; TEL
089 877788; E-MAIL costieragrumi@tiscali.it) is a co-operative
of workers of the steep lemon terraces, some of which were
among the first to be planted on the *Costiera*. They make
limoncello and sell the lemons, which are still brought down
812 steps from the mountain-high lemon groves by men and
women carrying baskets weighing 60 kilos – on their heads.

*A woman carries a heavy
load of lemons down
from the mountain
terraces*

*Opposite: Butcher
Mammato and his
home-made salumi*

Positano

Montepertuso (above Positano)

Restaurant

Via Montepertuso 77
TEL 089 875453
E-MAIL
donnarosaristorante
@libero.it
CLOSED
Tues; from 8 Jan to 3
weeks before Easter;
for lunch in Aug
PRICE €€€€

Donna Rosa

Montepertuso is what they call a 'fraction' of Positano; it's located high above the town, a small village with fabulous views and cooling breezes, and is easily reachable by public bus from the centre of Positano if you don't feel like taking the car. The ticket costs one euro.

Ristorante Donna Rosa is located in the central square; it has a white façade, a shaded terrace out back, and tables in front in summer. The restaurant is family-run: pastas are home-made and good; fresh vegetables flavourful and simply cooked; fish and meats grilled... uncomplicated classic Mediterranean dishes presented nicely in attractive surroundings. There's a well chosen list with selected Campanian wines, including some less-common – as in the organic Solopaca from Antica Masseria Venditti, from the province of Benevento; the younger generation here are keen to expand their knowledge of wines. Save room for dessert: I had an unusual bitter-orange tart with fresh almonds in it – as ever, Positano reveals itself a pastry-lover's haven.

Restaurant

Montepertuso, 77
TEL 089 87545
CLOSED Weds
except in summer
PRICE €€€

Il Ritrovo

This trattoria is on the other side of the *piazza*, and serves the unpretentious, flavourful foods of the Campanian countryside, with home-grown vegetables taking first place in *antipasti* and *primi*, and good wines to go with them. Desserts, too, are home-made. Salvatore in the kitchen and Teresa in the dining room have created a family atmosphere for their cuisine.

Nerano and Marina del Cantone

You can't reach Marina del Cantone (the beach and tiny port) by road without driving down through Nerano; there are three fine restaurants between the two.

Restaurant

Via Vespucci 13/n,
Nerano
TEL 081 8082800
FAX 081 8081271
E-MAIL ristorantequattro
passi@inwind.it
CLOSED Tues eve;
Weds Oct–Mar;
4 Nov–26 Dec
CARDS All
PRICE €€€€€€

I Quattro Passi

This is one of the most highly thought-of restaurants of the *Costiera* – a favourite too of the Anglo-Saxons and other foreigners seeking refined cuisine, great service and a lovely setting: the summer terrace is a shaded arbour overgrown with vines and flowers. In winter you eat inside, in rooms sponged yellow, with clean lines of wood, at tables bedecked with shells, baubles and statuettes, and silver teapots for vases. In spring, chef Tonino Mellino's *benvenuto* comes in a music box (too much for my tastes): an anchovy fillet wrapped around olives, secured with a ribbon of leek, with lightly curried oil. Breads are home-made: a lemon and ricotta roll like a hedgehog is moist and flavourful. For *antipasti*, raw shellfish and salad are served on a blue glass plate with a lot of fresh lemon juice in the vinaigrette; shrimp and *provola affumicata* sit in an artichoke 'bowl' whose flavours are dominated by the smoky cheese. Tuna comes as the centre of a fried 'spring roll' of julienned vegetables with winter melon froth (*spuma*). I preferred the large tubes of Di Nola pasta sauced with *cernia e coccio*, two local fish, and sprinkled with a tasty 'flour' of *melanzana* – a traditional dish with good integrity. There's meat as well as fish on this menu – sliced lamb, for example, served with a piquant *mostarda* of orange with pumpkin sauce – so there's ample possibility to taste both great red and white wines. Desserts are perfectly executed, as in the frozen lemon and chocolate mousses rolled inside a large white-chocolate flake. If you want to sleep over or go to the beach, three rooms are available.

Restaurant

Lo Scoglio

Piazza delle Sirene, 15
Marina del Cantone
TEL 081 8081026
FAX 081 8082870
CLOSED Never
CARDS All
PRICE €€€€€
Reservation recommended
in summer and at
weekends.
A few rooms available

'It's easier to be a doctor than a good judge of oysters. That's what my father used to say.' Peppe De Simone is standing on the open wooden deck built out over the sea that in summer constitutes Lo Scoglio's dining room. He's selecting shellfish from a large pool that is constantly fed with cold running water. 'I learned to tell the difference between *frutti di mare* from the Adriatic and Tyrrhenian seas when I was just a boy – and the Tyrrhenian are better,' he says. 'My father opened this restaurant because he liked to eat, and he married my mother because she knew how to cook.' Mother Antonietta is sitting nearby, intent on peeling an unusual citrus fruit they have grown that resembles a lemon but tastes like bergamot. She might have been painted by Toulouse-Lautrec, with her ruffled apron and top-knot of hair.

Signora Antonietta

Lo Scoglio – the rock – opened in 1959 to serve the fish from this unpolluted stretch of water ('still just as Ulysses saw it') and the vegetables that Peppe's family grows in terraces up the hillside above the restaurant. With his wife, Santina, they prepare an apparently simple *cucina* using whatever the fields, woods and seas have offered that day – dishes that may be uncomplicated technically, but that are rich in the flavours and customs of the country. Vegetable lovers will adore Lo Scoglio for its array of greens – wild and cultivated: *scarola* sautéed with wide raisins and pine nuts or stuffed with olives and capers; *rape novantini* (90-day-old broccoli-tops) tossed with garlic and *peperoncino*; baby *melanzane* rolled around mozzarella and tomatoes, or cooked with *pomodorini* and herbs... to eat with bread scented with wild fennel. 'Ingredients as good as these are fast disappearing,' says Peppe. The sea side of this menu is no

Little-known but flavourful local fish all'acqua pazza and vegetable antipasti are specialities at Lo Scoglio

less enticing: fish and shellfish are served as you like them, raw or sautéed, alone or stuffed, or as sauces for home-made pastas. There are fine wines to accompany them – just right for the sophisticated clientele that have always made a summer jaunt to Lo Scoglio – by land or by sea.

Restaurant, Hotel

La Taverna del Capitano

Piazza delle Sirene, 10/11
TEL 081 8081028
FAX 081 8081892
E-MAIL
tavdelcap@inwind.it
CLOSED
Mon; Tues lunch except in summer; 7 Jan–27 Feb
CARDS All
PRICE €€€€–€€€€€€;
12 rooms, 2 suites

Collectors of curious wine cellars should not miss a visit to Marina del Cantone: La Taverna del Capitano have 'ship-wrecked' theirs into a temperature-controlled shop front. Luckily the 12,000 bottles of wine like it there, and form an important mainstay for the creative cookery going on at the restaurant. The young chef, Alfonso Caputo, is surrounded by the whole family – some in the kitchen, some in the stylized dining room. This room, with its large draped windows right over the beach, is decorated with sober natural woods; there are wooden sculptures on the tables (I never understand the need) and a formal atmosphere.

The food is a mix of unusual juxtapositions with some technical virtuosity, and more traditional dishes – personally, I prefer the chef when he's trying less hard, and the spontaneity of the fine ingredients he uses is able to come through. A fillet of *gallinella* (gurnard) – *cuoccio* in dialect – served with its liver is balanced by the tomato in a fresh-tasting take on *acqua pazza*. Shrimp rolled and cooked in crisp pastry are served with baby clams in a garlic-dominated broth. The abundant fish soup is a meal in itself, and will satisfy any seafood cravings. Breads are home-made: I found the crisp lacy bread strips better than the overly airy rolls. The *piccola pasticceria* is very good, perfect miniatures in the French style. They accompany well-assorted desserts, like the variations on *pastiera* (the Neapolitan Easter cake): frozen, solid and drinkable. The Caputos also have several rooms upstairs, with lovely views of the sea.

Piano di Sorrento

Kitchen Supplies

ICIS

Corso Italia, 222
TEL 081 5341152

If, as I do, you love browsing in local kitchen supply shops for unusual equipment, you'll enjoy this small store that caters to the public as well as to some of the area's top chefs (including Alfonso Iaccarino, see p.212). Among the many items on sale, I spotted *babà* moulds, *espresso* coffee pots, metal spring-rings for frying *cannoli*, tomato crushers and sieves, pasta machines.

Fruit Preserves

Via Cavoniello 10
TEL 081 532 1577
Sales point open only
when preserves are
being made

Deia

Deia produces fruit preserves from local citrus and other fruit trees in the area, including dried figs, and sinfully rich prunes in orange sauce with candied orange peel – delicious over yoghurt, or just spooned right from the jar. Some of their products are available through Don Alfonso (see p. 212).

Pimonte

Restaurant

Via Nuova Tralia, 72
TEL 081 5321577
PRICE €€–€€€

Ristorante Da Silvia

A friendly, uncomplicated restaurant with a veranda that over-looks the whole Golfo di Napoli. Host Vincenzo Aiello is a keen pasta fan, so this is a good place to go for *antipasti* – like cubed pumpkin in oil and garlic – and one of at least ten pasta dishes that are always on the menu.

Positano

POSITANO TOURIST
INFORMATION:
Via del Saracino, 4
TEL 089 875067
INTERNET WWW.
aziendaturismopositano.it

Who can resist Positano's colours: the pale ochre, creamy yellows, whites and peaches of its houses; the dark grey of its volcanic beach; the hot pinks and purples of petunias and bougainvillea; the yellows and blues of painted tiles, with their scenes of sea or garlanded still lifes; the bright white Arab domes and Norman arches; the vivid greens of vines and terraced fruits. That exotic descent under a pergola of jasmine, with *zagara* and honeysuckle adding to the scents; the graphic tones of Mimmo Paladino's mosaics and sculptures in Piazza Flavio Gioia: this is the quintessential Mediterranean sea-town.

Restaurant

Via Colombo, 30
TEL 089 875066
E-MAIL info@sirenuse.it

Hotel Le Sirenuse

For me, it all started at Hotel Le Sirenuse. My first visit to the *Costiera*, many years ago, was to write an article about the food at this extraordinary hotel. I never got over it. The Sersale family are part of Positano's history, and their grace and hospitality are unforgettable: the luxurious rooms, stacked one above the other; the beauty of that terrace, with its undulating wall of exotic hibiscus; the lemon pasta on a lemon plate, and carved gourds for the party dinners... the experience left its mark – and left me wanting to see – and write – more. I have the Sersales to thank for setting my love of Campania in motion.

Lemon pasta at Le Sirenuse

Hibiscus at Le Sirenuse

Via C. Colombo, 157
TEL 089 875392
CARDS No
PRICE €€

Piazza Vespucci, 4
TEL 089 812051
PRICE €€€€–€€€€€

Via del Brigantino, 19/21
TEL 089 875036
PRICE €€€–€€€€

Via del Brigantino, 35/37
[via Rampa Teglia]
TEL 089 811687

Via dei Mulini, 22
TEL 089 875056
INTERNET
www.ristorantemax.it
PRICE €€€€

Restaurants and Hotels

Positano is so full of hotels and restaurants that it's hard to keep track. Here is a rundown of some of the best (and my favourites):

Bruno Ristorante This welcoming, family-run trattoria is up near the high coastal road, and offers one of Positano's most beautiful views – a perfect place for a leisurely summer dinner. Mario, who cooks, started work as a life-guard on his father's beach, but soon adopted his mother's passion for cooking. The menu features fresh fish and vegetables and presents them simply – and affordably. Save room for Ornella's home-made desserts.

La Cambusa I've always liked the *antipasti* here, lots of fresh vegetables (including roasted artichokes in spring) and fish dishes, to be eaten before a pasta or grilled fish.

Chez Black Salvatore Russo is at the heart of the Positano scene. His large, busy, seafront brasserie is always a fun place to be – eating, drinking and watching the world pass by. 'Black' (pronounced Bleck by the Italians) is a true restaurant pro: gracious host, attentive manager, charming character.

Conwinum Chef Alfonso Iaccarino – from Sant'Agata sui Due Golfi – and his sons have recently opened this wine bar–art gallery with a night-club feel: it's colourful, lively, and offers great wines and food in a casual, artsy setting. There is live music on Friday nights, and internet access all week.

Max Ristorante More than just a restaurant, Max doubles as a wine bar. There are pretty tables out in a small garden in summer. The menu goes from the usual suspects – *prosciutto e melone*, grilled vegetables, mozzarella and tomatoes – to other dishes that will please an international clientele.

Next To Tanina Vanacore's new restaurant offers something different: traditional dishes given a face-lift in 1970s décor, with live jazz-lounge music twice weekly. The food is great, and so is the mood.

Via Pasitea, 242
TEL 089 8123516
OPEN March–Oct
CARDS All PRICE €€€–€€€€

Pasticceria La Zagara You literally can't miss this pastry shop and bar: it's well placed half-way up or down the main pedestrian street through the town. *La zagara* is the exquisitely scented lemon blossom that colours the *Costiera*'s air in May, and the shop, with its lemon garden, is a perfect place to sample lemon *granita*, or the *crostata di limone* – as well as the many other desserts and breakfast treats the bakery produces.

Via dei Mulini, 6–8
TEL 089 875964

(For other restaurants very nearby, see also Montepertuso.)

Covo dei Saraceni Hotel If you want to be at the heart of things in Positano, the location of this elegant hotel couldn't be better: it's right over the beach, on a series of panoramic terraces that include a restaurant.

Via Regina Giovanna, 5
TEL 089 875400;
INTERNET
www.covodeisaraceni.it

Palazzo Murat Hotel One of Positano's most intriguing palaces, whose walled garden is glimpsed through an intricate gate one passes going down towards the beach; the elegant restaurant has tables outdoors in summer.

Via dei Mulini, 23
TEL 089 875177
INTERNET
www.starnet.it/murat

Pasitea Hotel Francesco Talamo's friendly – and reasonably priced – family-run hotel has the advantage of being right on the road that winds down into Positano, so there are no stairs to deal with getting there. It has recently been modernized.

Via Pasitea, 207
TEL 089 875500

Poseidon Hotel A 1950s hotel with spectacular views of the sea, and a great pool. In summer, the Poseidon bar is as 'in' as London's Groucho Club, a meeting place for Positano's jet set.

Via Pasitea, 148
TEL 089 811111
INTERNET WWW.
hotelposeidonpositano.it

Savoia Hotel A more modest choice, but no less sympathetic: family-run, with very pretty detailing in the ceramic-tiled bathrooms and a perfectly central position. There are attractive balconies in every room.

Via C Colombo, 73
TEL 089 875003
INTERNET
www.savoiapositano.it

Villa Franca Hotel Mario Russo is the brother of 'Black' (see above), and the family resemblance is apparent in the graciousness of their personalities. The lovely hotel, placed high on the winding road down to Positano, has some of the best views – including at least one bathtub with a view of nothing but sea – and a pretty restaurant, 'Li Galli'. The pastry chef here is excellent, so save room for dessert.

Viale Pasitea, 318
TEL 089 875655
INTERNET
www.villafrancahotel.it

POSITANO: LIFE BEFORE TOURISM

A conversation with Positano's mayor, Pietro Ottavio Fusco.

'Water has always been a rare commodity at Positano, so our agriculture was based on plants that needed little water to survive: olives rather than lemons, and under the olives, beans. The beans were planted on the first Friday of March, and put out to dry for a week on the domed roofs, *sui tetti*, in June. At Praiano, potatoes were more popular.

'It was also difficult to make or keep wine here. We didn't have cellars, and the barrels dried out when empty. In the old days they soaked the barrels with thyme- or fennel-flavoured water before putting in the new season's wine, but of course this changed the character of the wine completely.

'For breakfast there was *pane cott*': the *contadini* boiled water with salt, *peperoncino* and garlic, put stale bread into it and ate it with a spoon. In our culture, the land was the only way to survive. For the families, even a drop of oil was important, it could mean life. Now many young people are cultivating the land to maintain their links with their grand-parents' generation, and in order to experience the true *sapori* of our territory.

A humble way to sample olive oil is on pane biscottato: dried bread soaked in water

'At Positano, the fishermen made up only fifteen percent of the population, four or five families. The rest all worked the land, growing vegetables and making cheese, etcetera, and it was like that all along the coast. Up until the 1950s, 2,000 animals were kept in stables throughout Positano, even right down to the beach. In the high pastures, no more than three goats per hectare were allowed, as they ate the bushes and trees that hold the land in place. Sheep were permitted, but it was very steep for them. The men would climb up to get grass, sometimes using ropes, to feed the cows in captivity.

'Now it has all changed, especially here: the people used to be very poor, now they are all rich, thanks to tourism. Many famous people come to Positano: we all know who they are, but we play it down. And we don't put up com-memorative plaques here or the town would just be plas-tered in them.'

Restaurant and Hotel

Via Laurito, 2
TEL 089 875455
FAX 089 811449
E-MAIL
reservations@ilsanpietro.it
INTERNET
www.ilsanpietro.it
OPEN Easter–end Oct

Hotel Il San Pietro

Last but not least: Virginia Attanasio Cinque and her sons run what is undoubtedly one of the world's greatest small hotels. Perched like an eagle's nest on the cliff about a mile east of Positano, with private beach, pool and everything else one could ever wish for, the San Pietro is the embodiment of the perfect get-away, with its discreet luxury, friendly professionalism, and overall class. The legendary terrace, with its exquisite painted tiled banquettes, scented blossoms and romantic sea views, leads into the dining rooms and their shaded terraces. Recently the food has been taken up a notch, with young chef Alois Van Langenaeker directing the kitchen. The dishes have acquired an elegant style that fits well in the surroundings, and there is a concerted effort to feature the local ingredients – from noble seafood to humble beans – which so characterize Campania's flavours. The restaurant is open too for non-guests, so treat yourself to a heavenly meal.

Il San Pietro's terrace

Praiano

Fruit Preserves

Via Capriglione, 24
TEL 089 813048
FAX 089 813098

Il Gusto della Costa

For Valentino Esposito, 'the flavour of the Coast' is just one: lemon. His company makes everything you could think of from the fragrant local *limoni*: lemon candies, lemon marmalade, lemon honey, *limoncello*… even lemon-liqueur-filled chocolates.

To get to Ristorante La Gavitella (Vettica di Praiano; TEL 089 8131319) you either have to come by boat, or down 400 steps on the mountain. This lovely restaurant is idyllically positioned on a tiny beach with breathtaking views and serves only fresh fish, cooked traditionally but well. Call for information on ferry service from Positano or La Praia; OPEN Easter to end of October; PRICE €€€. Down by the beach under Praiano, at La Praia, near the discotheque carved out of the cliff that was so popular in the sixties with the VIPs, L'Africano, is Ristorante Armandino (TEL 089 874087). The food is deliciously simple, made of the real flavours of fresh vegetables, pasta and fish plucked right out of the sea. The kind of relaxed, unpretentious place you could eat in every night.

Punta Campanella

RISERVA NATURALE
MARINA DI PUNTA
CAMPANELLA
Via Filangieri, 40
Massa Lubrense
TEL 081 8089877
FAX 081 8789663
E-MAIL
info@puntacampanella.org
INTERNET
www.puntacampanella.org

'Punta Campanella, this long finger of rock pointing away into the sea, was the site of a Temple of Minerva,' explains Livia Iaccarino of the great Don Alfonso restaurant at Sant'Agata (see p. 212) as we walk along narrow rows of tomatoes and *zucchine* growing on the sheer mountainside, with nothing but the sea between us and Capri. She and her family run an improbable organic vegetable farm for the restaurant on this heavenly point of land. 'The Greeks and Etruscans came here to heal their lung diseases, to take iodine and the rich air of Sant'Agata. There are also lots of little churches and towers in amazing locations. For us what counts is that the soil and sun yield inimitable flavour in everything that grows here. But working the land here is incredibly difficult – only an act of love makes it possible.'

Punta Campanella is now a Natural Reserve that should protect both the land and surrounding sea from exploitation. Its waters are home to may rare varieties of sea-life, including a small pink shrimp – the *parapandalo* (*Plesionika narval*), or *gamberetto di nassa* as it is more commonly called. The *nassa* is a hand-woven basket trap made from myrtle and Sardinian rush from which the shrimp cannot escape, and this sustainable antique method of fishing has been singled out by Slow Food for one of its Presidia. The shrimp like 'grazing' in the dark

Alfonso Iaccarino's vegetable garden at Punta Campanella

underwater currents near the grottoes, and meet in small groups of ten that look like vibrating pink clouds. Their unusually sweet meat is best eaten raw, including the head, which contains the most flavourful juices. Cooperativa Ulixes (Via Parsano 6/b, Sorrento; TEL 081 8774778/ 333 2218813) will take visitors by boat around Punta Campanella to see the waters and fish alongside them – you can even eat with them on the boat.

Ravello

Ravello is unique among a series of exceptional towns on the Amalfi Coast. Its exoticism – in the form of luxuriant gardens and secluded villas – is intimate and seductive, as is the town's position, high above the curving chaos of the sea road. Its summer concert series, set in the outdoor auditorium of Villa Rufolo, is dedicated to Richard Wagner, who found inspiration for *Parsifal* there, and is always at world-class level. In the hills around the town are the terraced groves of lemons, vines and vegetables that make the *Costiera* so compelling. There are also a few artisan cheese-makers, at Scala and in other villages nearby (for more information on this, see Tramonti, pp. 224-26).

Market day at Ravello

Any excuse is good to visit Ravello, one of Campania's most beautiful towns, and market day (Tuesday) is no exception. The sellers' vans set up in and around the communal car park under the main *piazza*. The colourful mix of food, clothes, and kitchen and home paraphernalia is always entertaining – and can provide some unusual presents to take home.

Restaurant, Hotel

Hotel Palazzo Sasso
Via San Giovanni del Toro, 28
TEL 089 818181
FAX 089 858900
E-MAIL
info@palazzosasso.com
INTERNET
www.palazzosasso.com
OPEN for dinner only, Mar–Oct
PRICE €€€€€€

Rossellinis

The setting for this elegant restaurant is one of the most beautiful hotels in Italy – if not the world. To eat out on the candle-lit terrace on a summer evening, with the moon full, breezes softly scented by night blossom, and spectacular views down to the sea below, seems like a fairy tale, but it is one of the true treats of being on the *Costiera*. Add to this a fine restaurant, with friendly professional service (all in English for those who can't manage the Italian), wonderful wines and food, and the picture is complete. Palazzo Sasso is justly famous: an historic villa with antique furniture in perfect taste, terraced gardens, heated pool... The indoor dining rooms too are sophisticated yet comfortable.

Rossellinis' young chef, Pino Lavarra, maintains this balance of tradition and modernity in the varied menu. His dishes are visually striking, bold with Mediterranean colours, squid-black,

Ravello seen from Scala

pepper-red, basil-green, shrimp-pink. For *antipasto,* a roasted *calamaro* is stood on its base like a cup, filled with buffalo ricotta and summer vegetables and crisped with *zucchine* chips. Long pasta tubes are stuffed too, with soft goat's cheese, and served with hearty *ragù* of rabbit and its liver. Main courses include lamb, with fish and lobster for those who prefer a sea motif. I love the multi-textured chocolate dessert that includes an airy *latte di zenzero* cappuccino look-alike of chocolate and ginger. These are conversation-points to explore and enjoy – the perfect focus for a romantic tête-à-tête. The hotel's second restaurant, Caffè dell'Arte, is for less formal dining. Both are open to non-residents.

Wine

Via Civita, 9
TEL/FAX 089 872774
E-MAIL
info@ettoresammarco.it
INTERNET
www.ettoresammarco.it

Casa Vinicola Ettore Sammarco

Ettore Sammarco started his winery in 1962 – one of the first producers on the Amalfi Coast. He and his family work only the indigenous local grapes – including whites Biancolella, Ginestrella and Bianca Tenera, and reds Piedirosso and Aglianico – planted in terraces around Ravello.

Sant'Agata sui Due Golfi

Agriturismo, Farm Products, Olive Oil

Via Pontone, 43
TEL 081 8080637
E-MAIL
letore.@iol.it
INTERNET
www.letore.com

Le Tore

Le Tore is an organic farm perched high up on the hillside above Sant'Agata, and it's all that an *agriturismo* could ever hope to be: a lovely converted house for the guests – in very good taste – surrounded by vegetable gardens, olive groves and animals. Last time I visited, the courtyard looked like a scene from *101*

Dalmatians, with a huge family of puppies playing in it. The farm's owner, Vittoria Brancaccio, makes prize-winning oil – this year she took first prize at the Sirena d'Oro at Sorrento – as well as delicious jams and many other fruit and vegetable preserves. There is great food to be had too – all in all, a gem.

Restaurant, Olive Oil

Corso Sant'Agata, 11/13
TEL 081 8780026
081 5330558 (office)
FAX 081 5330226
INTERNET
www.donalfonso1890.com

Don Alfonso 1890

I have a special relationship with this great restaurant: not only was Alfonso Iaccarino the first person to believe in the idea for this book, but he and his family took me under their wing when I came to Campania and offered me the friendship and hospitality that is such a special feature in southern Italy. For this I have much to thank them; my respect for the Iaccarino family and their co-workers is enormous. It's worth retracing some of Alfonso and Livia Iaccarino's story in order fully to understand the importance and impact these two exceptional people have had on the recent explosion of enthusiasm for and improvement in Campania's foods and wines. For it was not always so.

In the Italy of the 1970s and '80s, the cuisine of the north, rich in French influences, in butter and cream, was all-powerful. If you asked most northern Italians' or foreigners' opinion, the great wines and restaurants were all to be found north of Rome – they didn't bother to look any further. Seen from the outside, Campania in particular lacked an identity for its cuisine. Even pizza came from Napoli, a city often disembodied from its surrounding provinces.

Luckily some people in the south, and in Campania, had another viewpoint, and couldn't buy this version of northern supremacy because their daily experience contradicted it. Alfonso and Livia grew up in hard-working families in the Sorrento area: his was in the hotel business, hers had successful dress shops.

'We had travelled to France, and eaten in restaurants in northern Italy,' says Alfonso. 'They were exciting to us for their elegance, great service and fine technique. But each time we came home and tasted again our exceptional olive oil, and the fruits and vegetables full of character that grew here ripened by the sun, we felt certain that our culture, too, had something to say.'

'Yes,' Livia agrees. 'And the long history of *la cucina napoletana*, that for centuries had its own identity – both peasant and aristocratic – in those dishes we found the roots for a newer, lighter cuisine.'

Alfonso started by cooking in the family's hotel kitchens after work. By 1983 the couple took the plunge, left the hotel

Alfonso Iaccarino and Tommy

Peaches at Punta Campanella

Opposite: Alfonso Iaccarino on his horse at Punta Campanella

Seared ricciola (amber-jack) makes an elegant antipasto

business and set up their restaurant, Don Alfonso 1890, in hon-our of Alfonso's grandfather. 'Our parents thought we were crazy,' says Livia. 'It took a lot of courage in those days to give up a secure family business on a gamble like ours.' Little by lit-tle, a new repertoire of elegant dishes was created to reflect the spontaneity and flavour of the natural ingredients, including artisan-made foods special to Campania: pastas, cheeses, *salumi* and wines.

'The grand restaurants up north all cooked with imported smoked salmon, cream and caviar,' says Alfonso. 'But what rele-vance could they have here, when our dishes are based on indigenous legumes, fresh fish and vegetables?' After years of swimming against the current, the Iaccarinos' credo of light, flavourful foods paid off: in 1997 Don Alfonso became the first restaurant south of Rome to earn three Michelin stars. Alfonso and Livia had broken all the rules and proved that a great, world-class restaurant could exist – and flourish – in the south.

Some years later, they bought an abandoned stretch of land at Punta Campanella, about four kilometres from the restaurant, in what has since become a protected nature reserve. Here they started another trend by creating an organic vegetable garden just for the restaurant, when organic farming was still a rarity in Italy. This unique farm is situated on the breathtaking terraces of the Sorrento Peninsula. It overlooks open sea and the island of Capri. Here artichokes and fava beans thrive in dark volcanic soil beneath olive and fruit trees. A vast lemon grove is entirely

Livia Iaccarino

*Don Alfonso's restaurant
terrace*

surrounded by chestnut-pole screens, following the local traditions. Chickens, geese, pigs and one goat – Giuseppina – graze
freely.

As the restaurant's range and fame has grown, so too has its
wine collection, stored under the restaurant in a deep cellar
whose origins are Etruscan. The Iaccarinos were the first to
showcase Campanian wines: alongside great northern-Italian
and French labels, they listed Mastroberardino and Casa
D'Ambra, as well as the stream of wineries that followed them,
stimulated by Campania's improved status.

Today, as before, the restaurant offers a wonderful mix of
grandeur and simplicity: the gardens full of flowering plants; the
elegant, luminous dining rooms; the excellent service from what
seems more like a large family than a restaurant staff. All of this
serves as a natural setting for the Iaccarinos and their food.

The couple's sons, Ernesto and Mario, now both work alongside their parents: Mario is as gracious a host in the dining
room as his mother; Ernesto is gradually taking over the running of the kitchen – he decided to become a chef after starting
another career. He has brought new influences and techniques
into the kitchen, taking the food a step away from its traditional
roots. The menu also offers Alfonso's unforgettable classics –
like the *ravioli di caciotta* with tomatoes and basil, or the
extraordinary aubergine dessert, *pasticcio di melanzane*, with
chocolate sauce (based on an antique Neapolitan recipe) and
there are lots of other good reasons to keep coming back.

A final note: the restaurant has several lovely rooms for those
who don't want to travel after dinner; there is also a shop
beyond the library selling hand-selected Campanian foods,
including Alfonso's excellent lemon liqueur and olive oil from
Punta Campanella – some of Campania's finest.

ALSO AT SANT'AGATA

If you're walking around the lovely village, stop in at any of the
bars or *pasticcerie*, they all make very good pastries, including
la sfogliatella vuota – an airy pastry delight.

*The coolness of Sant'Agata is due not so much to its height above
sea-level or to its exposure to the refreshing mistral as to the fact
that it lies in an ocean of fruit-trees and leafy walnuts and hazels.*
                             Norman Douglas Siren Land

Sant'Agnello di Sorrento

Olive Oil, Lemons

Solagri Cooperativa

Via San Martino, 8
TEL 081 8772901
FAX 081 8772776
E-MAIL info@solagri.it

Like the organic farm Le Tore (see pp 211-12) this co-operative also produces prize-winning extra virgin olive oil in the Sorrento Peninsula DOP. The story of how this co-operative came to be is exemplary.

'Ten of us got together and decided to pool our resources,' says Mariano Vinaccia, one of the co-op's members. 'We each put in just 26 euros and, without any help from public money; within a few years our number had increased to the current 320 members, mostly small farmers with lemon or olive groves in these hills.' The plots vary in size and altitude, ranging from sea level to 600 metres. The co-op has six full-time inspectors who help the farmers decide about pruning and caring for their trees. At harvest time, the olives are worked in several mills under the co-op's control, using modern stainless steel equipment and low temperatures – with strict testing for quality in the ensuing oils. The co-operative also produces fresh local IGP lemons and good marmalades. 'From nothing we have achieved so much – including sales to Marks & Spencers in the UK and the Smithsonian in the US. I like to think of our organization as being a perfect mix of Italian passion and American entrepreneurship,' he says as he offers me a beautiful lemon to take home.

Olive Oil

Sorrentolio

Via Nastro d'Argento, 9
TEL 081 8072300
E-MAIL
info@sorrentolio.com
INTERNET
www.sorrentolio.com

Imma Gargiulo

You can't miss – or fail to be charmed by – Imma Gargiulo. And you would never guess that this beautiful young woman, with her uniquely artistic look, was at the head of the large olive-oil mill where she works alongside her father. Imma is passionate about food and, in southern Italy, food starts with olive oil: 'My great-grandfather founded this business in 1849,' she says as we tour the *frantoio*, with its various presses, both modern and old-style. 'Today we mill the oil from our own 2,000 trees, as well as olives we buy from the local *contadini*; we also work for *terzi*, other producers needing a mill for their home-produced oil. The ground pulp never exceeds 29°C, and in this area, healthy olives remain at low acidity levels below 1%.'

Gargiulo produces several oils within the Penisola Sorrentina DOP, including Syrenum, from the single cultivar Minucciola – an indigenous olive that well illustrates the lightly bitter and *piccante* characteristics of these oils. Syrrentum is what Imma describes as 'a traditional oil from here', and it is one of her favourites.

Nets catch the olives in the oldest of the Gargiulo olive groves

Among the other fine estates that the Gargiulos process is Alessandra Balduccini's organic company (see p. 195). These and other oils are available from the Gargiulo mill's sales point.

Scala see Tramonti

Seiano

Cheese, Meats and Speciality Foods

La Tradizione

Via R Bosco, 969
TEL 081 8028869
FAX 081 8029914
E-MAIL
info@latradizione.com
INTERNET
www.latradizione.com

You would be forgiven for driving by this exceptional store and not seeing it – it's on a 90° bend in the main road between Seiano and Meta di Sorrento. But that would be a shame, because you would be missing the best food shop in Campania. Salvatore De Gennaro and his wife, Annamaria Cuomo (whose family run Gelateria Gabriele at Vico, see p. 227-28), have created a unique collection of the most flavourful Campanian and southern-Italian artisan foods. Their shop has been going for twelve years in what was once the sales point for Salvatore's family's farm, where they sold home-made *salumi* and fresh beef and pork. The couple still sell fresh meat and produce some pork products, but their expertise also includes hand-made cheeses. Their selection is more than commercial, it's personal: Salvatore has visited every farm and dairy and hand-picked each

Opposite: one of a pair
of raw-milk Caciocavallo
Podolico cheeses

cheese to age in his personal cellars. Here you'll find *caprini*
from Potenza with their creamy mineral character, firm buffalo
cheeses from Il Moro (see p. 431) and milky *mozzarelle* from La
Fenice (p. 79), aged Caciocavallo Podolico, as well as flavourful
Provolone del Monaco and smoked *provole* from the hills above
the shop. You can't leave without being given a tasting of
cheeses cut just for you. Here's a tip: Annamaria says *salumi* and
cheeses should never be pre-sliced or they'll lose their aromas.

To accompany these delicacies are puffed savoury brioches
enriched with pork crackling (*ciccioli*), and vegetable tarts, local
breads and rolls, jams and honeys, wines and liqueurs, oils and
vinegars, fruits and vegetables, beans and pasta, biscuits and
chocolates: the best of everything you could ask for.

Up the hill above La Tradizione, Salvatore's brother, Paolo,
has opened a charming Bed & Breakfast: E-MAIL info@tenutaro-
mualdo.it. Nearby is the family's farm where artisans will soon
be installed in workshops made from converted stables, producing inlaid wood, fabrics and other local crafts.

Salvatore De Gennaro hand-picks his cheeses from a series of
small producers in villages in the hills above his shop, including:
Caseificio Luigi Parlato (TEL 081 8024063). In his small stone
dairy at Arola, at an altitude of 600 metres, Parlato 'transforms'
local milk into *fior di latte* and fine Provolone del Monaco.
Visits by appointment.
Caseificio Russo (Alberi; TEL 081 8787055). Among the
cheeses this dairy makes is the Toma Sorrentina, a stretched-
curd eating cheese that is pressed into a mould, *fior di latte*, and
the delicate *provola affumicata* that is smoked over straw.
Caseificio La Verde Fattoria del Monte Comune (Via Sala, 24,
Moiano; TEL 081 8023095; FAX 081 8023729). A large dairy
with a sales point, making *fior di latte* and *provole* in various
forms, including smoked, and stuffed with olives.

Restaurant

La Torre del Saracino

Via Torretta, 9
Marina di Seiano
TEL/FAX 081 8028555
CLOSED
Sun eve in winter;
Mon; end of Jan–
beginning of Feb
CARDS All
PRICE €€€€€

I often eat in restaurants, but all too rarely do I find food that
fully attains the elusive balance of flavour and integrity, simplicity and complexity that, to me, makes a great dish. It may just
be a question of personal taste, but it seems surprisingly difficult
to arrive at recipes that are at once true to their ingredients and
origins, yet creative and – most importantly – unforced, natural.
This goes beyond knowing how to cook – after all, many chefs
are skilled in technique. It's a question of aesthetics and of taste,
of knowing by instinct when an ingredient should be left alone,

uncluttered. This pared-down cuisine doesn't mean minimalism or small portions; nor is it lacking in excitement – on the contrary, it couldn't be more sensual. Unlike the current need to heap too much together in the rush to wow or startle, this is food that convinces.

Gennaro Esposito cooks like this. From his immense frame he works with enviable delicacy once he's at the stove. In early spring he'll put one large scallop, seared on volcanic stone to maintain its fragility, over a slice of raw artichoke, and serve it with wilted borage leaves and drops of acute orange sauce – sweet and bitter and good. In a recipe some would consider downright risky, he places pan-flashed red mullet and intense sea urchins into a reassuring warm ricotta soup – and comes away with harmony. His delicious play on the Neapolitan favourite, *la parmigiana*, is anything but classic – he layers garfish (*pesce bandiera*) with mozzarella on a fresh tomato sauce, and leaves the fried *melanzana* as an accent.

Fiori di zucca and mussel antipasto

'Each ingredient needs a cooking method that is right for its character, that will bring it to the table shouting as loudly as possible,' he explains. 'We are surrounded by extraordinarily flavourful foods here, between the *contadini* in the hills and the little fishermen who bring me their day's catch. My job is to maintain their fragrance in dishes that accentuate their personality.'

Parmigiana of gar-fish

Gennaro's partner, Vittoria Aiello, applies the same logic to her fabulous desserts: a large hand-beaten *babà* as light as air, soaked in elegantly aged rum; or the *finissimo ricotta-citrus tortino*, sweetly balanced by a sharp sauce of berry fruits.

If the restaurant has until now (though changes are afoot) maintained the look of its late-eighties décor (Gennaro and Vittoria rent the premises) their location above Seiano's beach couldn't be nicer. In summer you eat outside against a backdrop of laughing children playing in the waves, secure in the personable service, innumerable wines and great cuisine of this most amiable of giants.

Restaurant

Via Torretta, 14
Marina di Seiano
TEL 081 8028559
OPEN
Daily in summer;
weekends Nov–Mar.

'O Saracino Ristorante Pizzeria

This cheerful, popular restaurant overlooking the beach is a favourite for family pizzas and large platters of home-cooked pasta or fish. It is run by Vittoria Aiello's family (see above) and is conveniently placed just a few yards from the more elegant restaurant. When La Torre del Saracino is closed, you'll often find Gennaro, Vittoria and the rest of the staff relaxing over a sizzling pizza here, baked to order in the wood-burning oven.

Gennaro Esposito and Vittoria Aiello

Gennaro Esposito has recently opened a new venue: On (Via Marina d'Aequa, 18; TEL 081 8029186; OPEN May–Oct, 8.00 p.m.–2.00 a.m.; daily July and Aug, Tues–Sun in the other months) is located on a panoramic sea-front terrace at the other end of the beach from La Torre del Saracino, at Hotel Le Axidie. It's the in place to go for a glass of wine, a dessert, a plate of pasta, a late dinner… to the sound of live music.

Sorrento

This elegant seaside town was one of the favoured ports of call on the Grand Tour in the 17th and 18th centuries, particularly in winter. The British loved it, as did the Tsars of Russia, for its perfect mix of humble fishermen on the beaches and noble villas in the hills, with their perfumed citrus gardens and picturesque views that seemed just made to be painted. Above the terraced lemon groves are olive groves, and the walnut woods that produce the famed Noce di Sorrento, granted IGP status by the European Community.

AROUND AND ABOUT IN SORRENTO

Premiata Pasticceria Pollio (Corso Italia, 172; TEL 081 8772889, 081 8782190). This little bar–*pasticceria* makes its own *gelati* in summer and *spremute* (freshly squeezed orange juice) in winter. But its specialities are the dozens of great pastries it bakes: big

Sorrento walnuts

and small doughnuts called *ciambelle*, including an unusual oval doughnut of sweet pastry outside and ricotta and ham inside; real *bigné al caffè*; brioches with various fillings, from jam to *crema* to Nutella... so it's the perfect place to buy the Sunday morning *vassoio* – a trayful of pastries to take to whomever has invited you to lunch. It's across the street from Libreria La Capsa (Corso Italia, 259/D; TEL 081 8771020). Pasquale Ruocco's is one of my favourite small bookstores, the kind one always hopes to find, with genuinely interested staff (who hand-pick and read the books they sell) and a good selection of books relating to Sorrento, Napoli and the coasts, including some in English. If you're looking to taste and buy wines, Bollicine Wine Bar (Via dell'Accademia, 9; TEL 081 8784616) is a fixture in Sorrento and has a great selection.

Restaurant

Il Rampe Marina Piccola, 5 (Piazza S Antonino)
TEL 081 8782354
E-MAIL ilbuco@paginebluonline.it
CLOSED Weds; Jan
CARDS All
PRICE €€€€€

Il Buco

Il Buco is hidden away in one of Sorrento's central piazzas, below the stepped street that is taken over by tables in summer. A few stairs down, and you're in the attractive vaulted dining room that was once the cellar of a monastery (it's been cleverly designed so you're not aware of being underground). I like the food here: it expresses the character of the quintessentially Mediterranean ingredients, the vegetables, fish and cheeses of the surrounding hills and waters. Dishes are created with an attentive eye and served carefully under the knowing supervision of Giuseppe Aversa, who is also an expert on oil and wine – as Il Buco's well-selected wine list shows.

This is is good place to try lightly fried fresh *alici* (anchovies) served in summer with aromatic fried basil leaves. *Totani*, flying squid, are stuffed with breadcrumbs and olives, sliced into rings and accompanied by grilled summer vegetables and basil sauce. A *timballo* of *scampi* and *scamorza* cheese is contained within *zucchine* slices, topped with crisp grated potato, and served on a ripe tomato *concassé*. The chef is fond of combining ingredients by layering, wrapping or stuffing, so local langoustine is rolled in Speck before being presented in a satisfying soup of *farro* wheat and white beans. *Paccheri*, wide pasta rings that flatten when boiled, are dressed in a sweet and spicy sauce of dried pumpkin with chunks of *scorfano*, grouper, and a hint of *peperoncino*. *Coccio* or *gallinella* (gurnard) in *acqua pazza* is poached in a tomato broth flavoured with capers. Desserts are well choreographed, as in the light soufflé of *pastiera* – the fragrant Neapolitan Easter cake – served with a narrow glass of orange sauce.

Restaurant, Museum

Via S Antonio, 12
(Piazza Tasso)
TEL 081 8073156
FAX 081 8072899
INTERNET www.ristorante
museocaruso.com
CLOSED Mon in winter
CARDS All
PRICE €€€€€

Ristorante Caruso

The great tenor singer, Enrico Caruso, was an habitué of Sorrento, and he remains a cult figure in the town. Indeed, this long-established, professional restaurant has not only taken his name, but decorated every available inch of the walls with photos, paintings and documents relating to the *maestro* – an unusual setting for a museum. One can, of course, also go for the food, which can be good: it too is rooted in tradition, though always with an eye to the tourists who form the main part of its clientele.

Hotel

Piazza Tasso, 34
TEL 081 8071044
FAX 081 8072500
E-MAIL
luca.fiorentino@exvitt.it
INTERNET
www.exvitt.it

Grande Albergo Excelsior Vittoria

If you're on the Caruso trail, it's worth knowing that the great *divo* always slept at the Grande Albergo Excelsior Vittoria: his room has been kept intact, and can be visited by appointment. It's hardly surprising that the singer chose the Vittoria: it's right in the centre of town, yet hidden away in an oasis of exotic gardens with beautiful terraces right on the water. Anyone who has read my Tuscan guide, *The Food and Wine Lover's Companion to Tuscany*, may remember the story of Giampaolo Motta, the genial young Neapolitan who went off to Tuscany to find his fortune (and to make wine)… and who is now one of Italy's top wine stars with his Fattoria La Massa in Chianti Classico. Well, the owners of the hotel are his family. Small world.

Of the other important hotels at Sorrento, I must mention
Hilton Sorrento Palace (TEL 081 8784141) with its imposing
modern restaurant; and the Bellevue Syrene (TEL 081 8781024)
with its views of Napoli and Vesuvio, and restaurant Don
Giovanni – one of Sorrento's classic grand hotels.

Tramonti and Scala

*Roberto Rubino and
Gregorio Avitabile with
raw-milk cheeses*

FOR FURTHER
INFORMATION CONTACT:
Comunità Montana
Costiera Amalfitana
TEL 089 876354
or
ANFOSC (Associazione
Nazionale Formaggi
Sotto il Cielo)
TEL 0971 54661
INTERNET
www.anfosc.com

*Opposite: Gregorio
Avitabile with his goats
and sheep high above
the sea*

Tramonti is a group of small villages that straddle two river valleys in the open countryside above the *Costiera*, behind Maiori
and Ravello.

It's an amazing area: tiny stone houses with breathtaking
views are built in clusters so steep only mules can reach them.
This is an area that until recently was a cultural backwater, with
houses and land abandoned in favour of the more lucrative
cities. (One thousand years ago, the high village of Scala, the
Costiera's oldest *comune*, had 36,000 inhabitants; today it has
barely 1,000.) The verdant hills produce grapes, lemons,
orchard fruits and dairy products. Many households have little
herds of sheep and goats that are free to graze in the variegated
pastures of this unspoiled landscape; some make pure raw-milk
cheeses that reflect this range of grasses. Cheese was one of the
few sources of protein available to the *contadini* when only the
padrone could afford the luxury of a pig or cow.

Recently the Comunità Montana Penisola Amalfitana has
embarked on a project with Roberto Rubino – winner of the
Slow Food Prize for Bio-Diversity, and creator of ANFOSC, an
institute researching raw-milk cheeses from animals out at pasture – to help these families make more hygienic, better cheeses
from the high-quality milk they obtain from their herds.

'It's all on such a small scale that it's not easy to get people
interested in this type of project,' says Raffaele Ferraioli, the
head of the Comunità Montana, who comes from nearby
Furore (p. 186). 'Yet this is a mountain whose grasses are rich
in iodine and whose *profumi* are exceptional,' explains Roberto
Rubino. 'By helping these isolated people make better cheeses,
they can earn more for them and help bring positive interest
back into the community.'

'These mountains, Monti Lattari, were named for their milk
products, which in the days of the Dukes of Amalfi were highly
esteemed,' continues Rubino. 'These people are courageous and
used to a difficult life; we are helping them regain dignity for
their work and their products, and with that, hope for a better
future.'

*Carmelina Avitabile
making ricotta*

Here are several of the cheese-makers involved in the project: Rachele and Gregorio Avitabile (Tovere di Amalfi; TEL 089 831419) makes cheeses from a mixed herd of goats and sheep. Riccardo and Maria Giordano (Tramonti; TEL 089 855332) produce fresh and aged *pecorini*, as well as a soft *pasta molla* cheese. Carlo Ruocco and Carmela Del Pizzo (Sambuco di Ravello; TEL 089 857629) make a range of sheep's-milk cheeses. Rita Cioffi (Scala; tel 089 872841) produces hand-made cheeses from her own flock. Giovanni Ferrara Agriturismo La Querce, Tramonti (Valico di Chiunzi); TEL 089 876339. A large friendly family run a real working farm with cows, pigs and other barnyard animals; spectacular views, simple rooms.

ALSO AT TRAMONTI

Tramonti is famous because many *pizzaioli* have been born in the *comune* and have left to carry the *vera pizza* message around the world. When you visit Tramonti, don't miss the beautiful ruins of the *cappella rupestre* (chapel carved out of the rock) of San Michele Arcangelo at Gete; this rare early Christian monument dates from betwen the 6th and 12th centuries and is currently being restored. The monks, followers of San Basilio, who lived in the area cultivated the land; they were allowed to eat each day only whatever food they could hold in the palm of one hand: vegetables, fruit, bread, meat, with little or no oil, and a little wine.

At nearby Gete, Andrea Reale (Via Cardamone, 75; TEL 089 856144; OPEN Thurs–Tues for dinner only, also lunch at weekends; E-MAIL aziendagricolareale@libero.it) makes some fine wines with the help of Bruno De Conciliis (see p. 299) and runs a lovely *osteria* serving flavourful home cooking using local produce; there are even a few rooms for those wanting to stay on this very attractive estate.

Nearby, in the Apicellas' village of Capitignano (see below), Umberto Giordano bakes rustic bread and *pane biscottato* – twice-baked brown bread that is soaked in water before use – in his wood-fired oven. At Pietre, Agriturismo Costiera Amalfitana (Via Falcone, 21; TEL 089 856192; INTERNET www.Costiera Amalfitana.it) offers farm holidays with horses. The imposing Convent of San Francesco at Polvica (TEL 089 876019) runs the Pensione Amici di San Francesco, a tranquil place to stay in what is still in part an active monastery.

Wine

Via Castello Santa
Maria, 1
Capitignano
TEL 089 876075
FAX 089 876075
E-MAIL
api.fio@libero.it

Giuseppe Apicella

'My father, Giuseppe, was ahead of his time,' says Prisco
Apicella, the young œnologist at this winery. 'Twenty-seven
years ago he decided to invest in wine tourism, in an area where
grapes were grown by every *contadino* for rustic wines for the
table, but no one bottled them seriously.'

'Yes,' says his sister Fiorina, who is studying to be a sommelier. 'He began bottling his wines in 1997, when well-made wines
from here were practically unheard of.'

We are tasting a Costa d'Amalfi DOC *cru*, a' Scippata, from
the vineyard of the same name planted high on the mountain-
sides by Giuseppe's grandfather in 1933. 'This is a rare example
of vines grown on their original rootstock (*a piede franco*) and
planted in the old system of 3 x 3 metres, up the slope of the
mountain.' The grapes for this powerful red are three indigenous varieties: 55% Tintore di Tramonti (Aglianico), 40%
Piedirosso and 5% Sciascinoso. It is vinified in steel, then spends
twelve months in large oak barrels, and a further two to three
months in French *tonneaux*. With notes of pepper, cranberries
and leather, this is an authentic, territorial wine whose fruit is
not overpowered by wood.

*Fiorina and Prisco
Apicella at the winery*

The Apicellas have seven hectares of vineyards around their
cellar, on steep terraces in the open countryside; the grapes are
carried by hand at harvest time, not by mules. It's nice to see the
younger generation so keen to work alongside their father, as
this intractable territory all too often scares away potential
young winemakers.

Vico Equense (see also Seiano)

Ice-Cream, Cheese

Corso Umberto I, 5
TEL 081 8016234
081 8798744 (shop)
FAX 081 8016363
E-MAIL
gabriele@gabrieleitalia.com
INTERNET
www.gabrieleitalia.com
CLOSED
Tues except in summer;
15–30 Jan

Gelateria Latteria Gabriele

You can't miss Gabriele if you have a good eye for design: it has
miraculously kept its original 1967 décor, both in the shop's
façade and inside, with stainless steel counters that could go
right into a book on the period. It's hard to categorize this bar-
cum-*gelateria*-cum-food shop: it sells everything from fine
cheeses to hand-made ice-creams, pastries and prepared foods.
'Even back then, the authorities couldn't decide which license to
give us – *pasticceria* or *salumeria*,' says Liberato, who now runs
the family business with his siblings. 'There has long been a tradition of *cremerie* in the Neapolitan area that worked all kinds
of dairy products.'

Certainly the *gelati* are a favourite here, served in cones or on top of delicious butter-rich brioches, as is the custom of the south. 'When our father started out, *gelati* were traditionally only eaten in summer, but he believed they could be sold all year, and he was the first to do that.' The *gelati* are wonderfully fresh, made only from seasonal fruits and whole eggs and milk. I love the *granite* of *gelsi* (black mulberries) or *limone* – lighter than ice-creams and more refreshing.

Other home-made pastries include a fine rum-soaked *babà*, mousse of wild strawberries (*fragoline*), lemon cake, and decorated cakes to take away. With a sister and brother-in-law such as Annamaria and Salvatore De Gennaro (see p. 217-19), the shop could hardly fail to have maintained its interest in cheeses, too, and sells a wide range. There are also nice packages of local candies and other speciality foods.

Pizzeria, Restaurant

Via Nicotera, 10
TEL 081 8798426
081 8798309
OPEN Always

Da Gigino Università della Pizza – Pizza a Metro

It's a lot of fun to visit this vast, spectacular pizzeria with its period 1960s décor (don't miss the light fixtures), which has played its part in the official history of pizza – and is still going strong. Here everything is on a big scale: the restaurant can seat 2,000, the waiters are legion, and the pizzas made in huge wood-burning ovens are sold by the metre – Luigi Dell'Amura's revolutionary invention in the mid-20th century. *Antipasti* and desserts are paraded on huge trolleys, to eat before and after the main attraction – pizza. They are available in myriad flavours and, as the sign says: One metre of pizza is enough for five people.

Vietri sul Mare

Food lovers are very often also plate lovers, so a visit to this ceramics village – where everything from the fruit store to the town hall is decorated with painted tiles – is bound to be a pleasure. It's also a good place to buy presents – for yourself or others.

Ceramics

Via Madonna degli
Angeli, 7
TEL 089 210243
E-MAIL
solimene@amalficoast.it

Opposite: Solimene plates

Ceramica Artistica Solimene

The most fascinating ceramics shop, Solimene, is housed in a unique piece of architecture from 1950, a colourful folly of almost Gaudian proportions that has miraculously resisted being modernized or torn down. Solimene can also be credited with designing the line of 'Campania' plates that were exported

The Solimene factory: above, exterior; below, main hall

all around the world in the 1980s and '90s, becoming a Mediterranean icon.

The landmark building – with more than 20,000 hand-thrown pots imbedded in its façade – was designed by Paolo Soleri, a student of the great American architect, Frank Lloyd Wright. Soleri is now in his eighties and lives in Arizona, but as a young man he met Vincenzo Solimene, owner of three ceramics workshops. One of Vincenzo's ten children, Giovanna, now runs the pottery with her siblings; she explains how the project came to be built.

'Soleri did a pencil drawing and, with a piece of clay, showed him how the columns would be; then he did a watercolour,' she says. The terrain on which the factory would be built was sheer rock, with a row of Maritime pines above – indeed, the undulating form of the façade was inspired by the trees' shapes. 'My father liked it a lot. But it was very difficult to get the project approved and the site was blocked several times. The locals saw is as futuristic – even shocking.' Luckily the building and its interior are still intact, and well worth a visit.

Limoncello

Corso Umberto I, 35a
TEL 089 761717
FAX 089 763719
E-MAIL
shaker@microsys.it
INTERNET
www.microsys.it/shaker

Shaker

Limoncello is a *digestivo* that has always been made by families along the Amalfi coast to make use of the exceptional lemons that grow here. In the 1980s it suddenly became trendy, and many producers have sprung up that sell it in attractive bottles for an after-dinner summer treat. Indeed, it is now being made all over Italy using lemon flavourings that are never as good. Shaker works the local lemons, and produces 40,000 bottles of *limoncello* and other liqueurs, including one made from artichokes. The company also runs a high-level *agriturismo* with five suites.

Restaurant

Via E De Marinis, 18
(SS 18 towards Molina
di Vietri)
TEL 089 761300
CLOSED Wed
except in summer

Pizzeria I Due Fratelli

This pizzeria–trattoria has been going for over 150 years, run by successive generations of the same family. Its position is convenient, 100 metres from the *autostrada*, with views over Vietri and Salerno.

As far as the pizzas go, the speciality of the house is the *parruozzo*, a double-baked filled pizza 'sandwich', but there is an extensive list to choose from. If you're not in the mood for a pizza, the menu covers other *primi* and *secondi*.

At Marina di Vietri, down by the sea, there are two choices: Sapore di Mare (Via Pellegrino, 104; TEL 089 210041; CLOSED Sun evening and Thurs) serves very fresh fish in a family-run restaurant. La Ciurma is small, romantic, overlooks the water, and serves the simple but great sea favourites, including *spaghetti con le vongole*. It's on a beach, or *stabilimento*, only open in the summer.

Another great factory on the Amalfi coast: the cement works at Castellammare di Stabia, now the luxury Crowne Plaza hotel

Chapter 6

Salerno to Paestum

Buffalo farms, Greek temples and artichoke fields

Very early next morning, we drove by rough and often muddy roads towards some beautifully shaped mountains. We crossed brooks and flooded places where we looked into the blood-red savage eyes of buffaloes. They looked like hippopotamuses.

The country grew more and more flat and desolate, the houses rarer, the cultivation sparser. In the distance appeared some huge quadrilateral masses, and when we finally reached them, we were at first uncertain whether we were driving through rocks or ruins. Then we recognized what they were, the remains of temples, monuments to a once glorious city.

J. W. Goethe Italian Journey 23 March 1787

FOR TOURIST INFORMATION ON THE PROVINCE OF SALERNO
www.aziendaturismo.sa.it
www.salernocity.it
www.medivia.it
E-MAIL
info@aziendaturismo.sa.it
promozione
@aziendaturismo.sa.it
OR SEE P. 264

This chapter covers the northern half of the province of Salerno, Campania's largest – the southern is in the next chapter. The whole area was colonized by the Greeks and formed an important part of Magna Grecia. This chapter includes the capital city of Salerno (the extensive port that sits at the eastern end of the Amalfi Coast); the hilly area directly to its north; the Picentini hills and the north-eastern part of the province of Salerno; the towns of Eboli and Battipaglia; and then heads down, through the alluvial valleys of the rivers Sele and Calore, to the Greek temples of Paestum, one of Italy's most impressive archaeological sites. Most visitors to Paestum follow this route, and this chapter offers them some of the gastronomic highlights to look out for in this richly agricultural area.

Until after the Second World War, the flat lands south of Battipaglia were still mainly uninhabited swamps. Indeed, in the book of extraordinary photographs by Angelo Pesce of the American landings on the beaches between Salerno and Paestum

Opposite: Paestum artichokes ready to be sold

in September, 1943 – in what was a decisive move to defeat the German army's occupation of Italy – one is struck by the almost total lack of buildings. The temples stand unencumbered.

After the swamps were drained, or *bonificate*, unrelenting construction began along the coast that soon made up for lost time: today this area is a mix of vegetable fields, buffalo farms, modern hotels and summer accommodation for the many tourists that visit the temples and beaches. One has to go up into the hills to find the ancient villages where, for centuries, the local populace took refuge from malarial mosquitoes and invading marauders – villages many of which, in 1980, suffered the terrible earthquake that damaged so much of Campania.

EATING AND DRINKING

If until recently the river valleys close to the coast (or their mosquitoes) proved detrimental to humans, they suited the water buffalo very well. There's an ongoing debate about how the buffalo got there – did they walk from India or swim from Africa? Or get dropped off a shipwrecked boat? Or come from Asia in the 6th century? However picturesque the folklore (or fakelore, as some of my food-writing friends would call it), they found a perfect habitat in this humid, warm plain. They were free to roam until after the First World War. Waverley Root, who first visited Campania in 1929, wrote of the land around Paestum: 'The country is extremely barren and reminded me of the extensive heath of Scotland. There were numerous herds of buffaloes scattered over it.'

Nowadays the buffalo are mainly kept in muddy fields or large enclosures; their milk gives the exquisite *mozzarella di bufala* that really is worth making a detour for – authentic mozzarella doesn't travel far or well. For more about how it is made, and for producers, see pp. 248-51.

The reclaimed flatlands are now intensively farmed fields for the growing of fruits and vegetables: Paestum is especially known for its artichokes. On the hillsides, chestnut woods and olive groves alternate with vineyards. This is not a traditional winemaking area, but there is great potential here: some of its modern wines are among Italy's most sought-after. As one might expect, there are many restaurants in the vicinity of Paestum, of all price ranges and qualities.

Opposite: Castelcivita, a hill town of the interior

Acerno

*Acerno's chestnuts on
sale from a truck*

Acerno is situated in a dip between the highest points of the
Monti Picentini range before they descend into the province of
Avellino towards Montella (for more on that area, see p. 318).
The little town is surrounded by woods of the chestnuts that
have always been a staple of the local diet of these mountainous
areas. There is a beautiful road up through Acerno: you see how
well the chestnut trees are kept, and come across groups of
cows and pigs that are free to graze along the roadsides and in
the small fields that surround whatever stone houses survived
the 1980 earthquake. The woods offer mushrooms and wild
strawberries and oregano, and in the past these were all harvested by the local villagers to help increase their incomes. This
medieval forest economy lasted until forty years ago, when the
children could still pay with chestnuts or *fragoline* when they
went to the cinema.

After being removed from their outer spiky shells, the chestnuts here are soaked in water for 24 to 48 hours to kill any
insects, draw out some of their tannins, and soften their brown
inner skins. They are then spread out to dry for a few days, so
they don't become mouldy. The biggest are selected and sold to
be eaten roasted or to be used in cakes or other confectionery.

Bar Massimo (Via Duomo 16) is a good place to sample the
local speciality, *la fragolata*. You'll find it in all of Acerno's bars,
a slushy frozen mixture to eat with a spoon made from the naturally perfumed wild strawberries and a 'secret' ingredient – it's
very good. This bar also makes its own *gelati*: the hazelnut, *nocciola*, is particularly clean-flavoured. At Pasticceria Lucia try the
Christmas dessert of chestnuts and chocolate, *la pasticcella*. If
you're in the mood for a rustic plate of pasta, Trattoria la
Pergola (Via Parisi, 25; TEL 0898 69060) is an informal little
restaurant in the town centre. In winter, you might ask for *la
sfrionzola*, a local *cucina povera* dish of potatoes, peppers and
all the leftover pieces of pork from around the bone.

Albanella

Some of the best bottled organic tomatoes I've tasted have come
from Franco Russo's farm (Via Fontana di Jacopo, 29; TEL 0828
780956). If you are interested in an original carved stone fireplace or sink, Serafino (Viale Libertà; TEL 0828 781257, 338
4988766) has a showroom here.

Battipaglia

Pizza

Piazza Repubblica
TEL 0828 302587
OPEN for dinner only
CLOSED
Weds; 15 July–end Aug

Pizzeria Victoria

You could easily miss this pizzeria: it's on a nondescript side street just behind Battipaglia's central square, Piazza Repubblica. But that would be a shame: I had one of my all-time favourite pizzas here. Thin crust, excellent ingredients: real buffalo mozzarella, ripe cherry tomatoes, aromatic basil and decidedly fruity olive oil. Plus a decent Campanian wine.

It's a modern setting, black and white with a coloured inlay-marble panel over the big wood-burning oven spelling out the name Victoria (but reminding me more of a Del Pero painting). Cosimo Mogavero is a real mover in the pizza world. He's in the *Guinness Book of Records* as having made more than two million pizzas. Quantity does not normally guarantee quality, but this is an exception. If you live in the area and are thinking of throwing a party, he'll bring a movable wood-burning oven and make your pizzas. Mogavero also organizes the annual Festa della Pizza in Salerno at the beginning of September.

Just outside Battipaglia, on a country road south-west of the town going towards Santa Lucia (signposted from the SS 18 by the Capiello furniture showroom), Tavernola (Via G Noschese, 26; TEL 0828 631065) is a *locanda di campagna* – a country inn – that serves good local dishes in attractive dining rooms. Cooperativa Allevatori Bufaline Salernitani (Via Belvedere; TEL 0828 671033), between Pontecagnano and Battipaglia, is a dairy that transforms the buffalo milk of its members, and distributes the cheeses throughout Italy.

Experimental Farm

SS 18 Tirrenia Inferiore,
Km 79.8
TEL 0828 347176

Improsta

Azienda Agricola Improsta

This handsome former buffalo farm now houses one of the Campania Region's most interesting and valuable agricultural projects: a collection of rare indigenous fruit trees and plants, and an experimental cheese-making facility. 'The idea is to bring together, study and reproduce old varieties of Campanian fruits and vegetables that are either in disuse or in danger of becoming extinct,' explains Vincenzo Aita, the Region's expert on agriculture and former *Assessore*, as we tour the large farm. We visit a nursery for the fruit trees, walk past experimental fields where different types of tomato are being cultivated, and look in on buffalo mozzarella being made in the dairy. The property includes a marvellous round building that once housed buffalo, and that now is used for tastings, seminars and meetings.

Campagna

FOR MORE INFORMATION:
Campagna Tourist
Association
Corso Umberto I
TEL 0828 46795
INTERNET WWW.
crmpa.it/EPT/campagna

This handsome town is located in a wildlife sanctuary, and is tucked away in a steep gorge: driving up, you don't see it until you're practically inside. This meant it was a strong position, easily defended. Campagna is of Roman origin, and more recently was the seat of a bishopric, which explains the grandeur of its *palazzi* and churches. Once a year, for three days in August, Campagna hosts a lovely *festa* called Portoni Ghiottoni – which roughly translates as 'delicious doorways'. Campagna's many noble *palazzi* and convents often have large inner courtyards or entranceways. During the *festa*, several of these *portoni*, or important doorways, are set up as eating points. The local women cook traditional Campagnan dishes, and offer one dish from each of six or seven *portoni* along a walking tour of the town. The streets are full of people listening to the bands, walking to the next 'destination', and stopping to greet friends along the way. By the time the warm summer evening is over, you have had a simple but delicious dinner, and seen the sights of Campagna – a great idea. Dishes – written in local dialect – include *prusutt'e cas'cavallo* (*prosciutto* and *caciocavallo* cheese), *matass'e fasule* (pasta with beans), *n'zalata all'ortolana* (garden salad), *prucnoc'cu vino* (wine-enriched biscuits).

Capaccio see Paestum

Castelcivita see Eboli

Castel San Lorenzo

Wine, Olive Oil

Via Donato Riccio, 30
TEL 0828 944035
FAX 0828 944034
E-MAIL
valcalore@hotmail.com

Cantina Sociale Val Calore

This large co-operative wine cellar is easy to reach from Capaccio–Paestum: following the road to Roccadaspide, you climb up and up to the small village of Castel San Lorenzo, where the Cantina Sociale is one of the most imposing buildings. Like so many others, this village was very badly hit by the 1980 earthquake, and the co-operative has invested heavily in this modern facility to house the vinification and oil-making activities of its 1,300 members – many of whom have tiny plots of vines and olives. The co-operative cellars have played a very important role in Italian agriculture since the 1960s as they offered a way for thousands of small land-owners and peasants

THE OIL OF THE COLLINE SALERNITANE

Campagna is also part of a prestigious oil-producing area: these gentle hills, many facing the sea, have been known for their olive groves since the time of the Greeks, when this part of Campania was within Magna Grecia – indeed, some very ancient trees are still to be found here. The Colline Salernitane DOP extends from the Picentini Hills to the Alburni Mountains, and takes in the upper Sele valley, Tanagro Hills and part of the Vallo di Diano. The most common olive varieties here are Rotondella, Frantoio, Carpellese or Nostrale, with smaller proportions of Ogliarola and Leccino. I like these oils, as they are well balanced: neither too aggressive nor too delicate and at their best offer that wonderful green, grassy freshness that enhances everything the oil is used on.

Many fine oil producers exist in this area: these were the finalists in the Colline Salernitane DOP category at the Sirena D'Oro Prize 2004, held at Sorrento.

WINNER: Coop La Torretta (Battipaglia; TEL 0828 672615)
La Petrolla (Campagna; TEL 0828 49079, 06 3219608)
Oleificio di Giacomo Lorenzo (Contrada Serradarce, Campagna; TEL 0828 974747)
Oleificio Oro del Sele (Contrada Serradarce, Campagna; TEL 0828 49705)
Fattoria Naimoli (Campagna; TEL 0828 49041)
Coop La Comunità (Contrada Serradarce, Campagna; tel 0828 49740)
Coop Promolio Qualità (Campagna; TEL 0828 240091)
Il Nido di Alfani (Montevetrano, San Cipriano Picentino; TEL 089 882343)
Mastropietro (Controne; TEL 0828 772066)
Olivicola Angelo Maglio (TEL 0828 46071)
Sabato Petrosino (TEL 0828 651006)
Bioitalia Distribuzione (TEL 0828 957434)
Settimia Falcone (TEL 0828 796800)
SOLeC (Contrada Cannito, Capaccio; TEL 0828 880171)
Agrioil (Roccadaspide; TEL 0828 963086)
Val Calore (Castel San Lorenzo; TEL 0828 944035, see p. 239)

Nets are spread to catch any falling olives at harvest time

to join forces and find a place on the market for their produce, enabling them to keep working their land.

The Cantina's large range of wines is very reasonably priced, and includes reds and whites within the Castel San Lorenzo DOC and Paestum IGT denominations. Red grapes are mainly Barbera and Sangiovese, while the whites are Trebbiano and Malvasia – a clear indication of the age of many of the vineyards, for these varieties were popular in the 1960s, '70s and '80s.

The Cantina's fine extra virgin olive oil comes within the Colline Salernitane DOP: indeed, it was one of the first to be awarded that denomination. In recent years, the Cantina has really perfected its oil-making activities, and the results show. The modern mill, with its Sinolea oil-extractor (one of the least aggressive, best machines) produces oil from local varieties Rotondella, Carpellese and Nostrale, as well as the ubiquitous Frantoio. The resulting oil is a *fruttato medio*, with fresh green notes of cut grass and artichoke.

The Cantina has a tasting room and sales point within the cellar, as well as on the main road that runs parallel to the sea, the SS18, at Km 90.700, Capaccio, within the ACI Paestum office (TEL 0828 730039).

Controne

FOR MORE INFORMATION:
Controne Pro Loco,
TEL 339 5254183

The name of this village under the Alburni mountains has become synonymous with one of Campania's indigenous bean varieties, *il fagiolo di Controne*. This medium-size creamy white bean has a tender skin and is traditionally dried in the sun after being picked. It is at its best slowly cooked beside the fire in a terracotta jug with two adjacent handles that is turned often. Unfortunately the authentic bean is hard to find and impostors abound. Nonetheless, attending the annual Sagra del Fagiolo at Controne is fun. Beans are served every which way: with sausages, *scarola*, pasta and so on. The year I visited the *sagra*, a big bonfire had been lit in the centre of the town square to take the chill off the autumn evening, and a colourful street band that seemed to have stepped right out of a Fellini movie kept the crowd entertained with lively Neapolitan music, complete with pots and pans for drums (see p. 125). Everyone ate steaming platefuls of beans and went home happy.

The Sagra del Fagiolo is usually held at the end of November.

Beans drying in the open air

Eboli

Cheese
Casa Madaio

Via Serracapilli
TEL 0828 364815
FAX 0828 333096
E-MAIL
info@casamadaio.it
INTERNET
www.casamadaio.it

Antonio Madaio has been a cheese selector and *affinatore* for many years: he and his wife ran a *gastronomia* in Eboli for fifteen years before setting up their current cheese shop and ageing cellars.

'I've always enjoyed going to the producers to choose my cheeses, and now that I have purpose-built cellars for ageing them the results are really positive,' explains Madaio as we take the stairs down under his shop. The stylish cellars are spectacular: rows of cheeses sit on wooden shelves or hang from strings – including Caciocavallo Podolico and giant *provolone* – in a series of small rooms, each with its own humidity content and temperature around 14°C. The cellar's natural moisture comes from water that runs freely through the loose-pebbled floor. 'This cellar re-creates the rustic cellars of old, but now we can control it by computers.' Madaio was born in the dramatically steep hill town of Castelcivita, about an hour from Eboli. He has recently set up ageing-grottoes there too, as the pure mountain air is beneficial to cheeses needing long ageing.

Smoked mozzarella cheeses at Madaio

The Madaios' business, which they run with their son, comprises preparing and selling cheeses to the public, and to restaurants and *enoteche* in Italy and abroad. For Antonio Madaio, an integral part of this work involves educating his customers about quality cheeses, especially raw-milk – or unpasteurized – cheeses, and in this he has often collaborated with the southern-Italian cheese 'theorist' and researcher, Roberto Rubino (see also pp. 224-26). Other projects include developing a line of soft, spreadable cheeses from goat's and cow's milk – easy to find in northern Italy, but until now absent from the south's palette of cheeses. 'Podolico isn't for babies,' he exclaims as we taste his, named Vetus. Admiring the taste of this firm, decisive, complex cheese, I have to agree with him. 'I want to be able to produce a well-made, healthy alternative to industrial cream-cheeses.' He has also made a 'real' version of the commercial sliced cheese often used in sandwich-making.

Madaio also offers: excellent local mozzarella; cheeses from all four kinds of animal-milks; *pasta filata* cheeses he smokes himself with local straw or coats in ash (*Cinerino*); selected dried local *legumi* – like the diminutive chickpeas from Castelcivita; good local oils; as well as some hand-made *salumi* from 'his' province, as he proudly likes to call it.

Selling wild asparagus

Corso Garibaldi, 112
TEL 0828 330689
CLOSED
Sun eve; Mon; Aug
PRICE €€€

Restaurant

Il Papavero

Good restaurants sometimes appear in unexpected places. Here, in a nondescript square in the centre of Eboli (a commercial, non-tourist town not normally known for its gastronomy) the fresh, young, modernist Papavero – or poppy – has taken root. It opened in late spring of 2003, the dream-child of heart surgeon Maurizio Somma and the young architect, Sabrina Masala. Together they have created an architectonic, clean-lined white space that is broken only by splashes of vivid colour from the over-sized fruit paintings (a little *déjà-vu*). The well-lit rooms are inhabited by an eclectic mix of furniture: blocky steel and wood chairs designed by Ms Masala; stacking (Starckish) cream chairs that go nicely with the steel and glass tables.

As for the food, the cook Domenico Vicinanza may be unknown, but his mentor certainly is not: Gennaro Esposito, of the renowned Torre del Saracino restaurant at Vico Equense (see pp. 219-20) has had a guiding hand in creating the menu and some of the recipes for Il Papavero. And his expertise shows: the food, too, is clean-lined and up to date. The pure, flavourful dishes include a spare, subtle broth of *zucchetta*, *paccheri* with octopus sauce, savoury ricotta mousse, and perfectly cooked slices of line-caught *branzino*, dressed only with a sprinkling of coarse sea-salt. A good start for a courageous restaurant.

Giffoni Valle Piana

FOR MORE INFORMATION
Associazione Produttori
Nocciole Tonda di Giffoni
Via Russomando, 9
TEL 089 866490
FAX 089 9828159
E-MAIL
asstondagiffoni@tin.it

This town, located in the Picentini hills to the west of Salerno, is famous for its film festival, held in mid-July. It is also home to one of Italy's best hazelnuts – Nocciola di Giffoni IGP – which earned its IGP (Indicazione Geografica Protetta) status as early as 1997. The hazelnut, which grows well in the Irno and Picentini valleys, has excellent flavour, and is used in desserts and confectionery throughout Italy. This area alone produces 10 per cent of Italy's hazelnuts. La Tonda di Giffoni, as it is called, is round – as the name suggests. It has a medium-thick shell, and an inner skin that comes away easily. The nuts, which ripen in the last weeks of August, are a good way to make the hillsides profitable.

Locanda del Cardinale (Via De Rossi, 5 [off Corso Garibaldi]; TEL 089 866032) is a double-fronted restaurant, with a rustic trattoria serving home-made food on one side, and a pizzeria on the other.

Lancusi

Via del Centenario, 110
TEL 089 957396

A selection of Matteo's frozen fruits

Ice-cream

Gelateria Matteo

One of the Campanians' favourite desserts for dinner parties or *feste* are the fruit ices of Gelateria Matteo: people come from all around the region to buy them. What makes them special is that

each fruit *gelato* is stuffed into a real fruit of the same flavour – big and small – before being frozen, so you can pick the ones you like best. I love the walnut ice that comes in the hard walnut shell, and the bright *albicocca* inside the scooped-out apricot. The *gelateria* also makes lots of other flavours for cones or cups.

Montecorvino Rovella

Cheese and artisan foods

Corso Umberto I, 157
TEL/FAX 089 980530
E-MAIL zaimar@tiscali.it

Michele Amato – Zaimar

Michele Amato is an expert on cheeses and *salumi*. He runs a personal distribution business supplying restaurants, wine bars and some private clients with hand-selected artisan food products. Although he has no sales point as such, he sends out his list to prospective clients, who order directly. He has just opened a cheese grotto at Montecorvino in which to taste some of his fine products: it can be visited by appointment.

Nocera Superiore

Restaurant

Piazza Materdomini, 24
TEL 081 933562
CLOSED Tues; 2 weeks in
Aug; New Year's week
CARDS All
PRICE €€€€
Live Neapolitan songs
on Friday nights

Osteria Terra Santa

This 'Holy Land' is the ground in front of and beneath the large Santuario di Materdomini church which, since 1997, has been converted into a lovely *osteria*. 'When the church agreed to let me fix up these disused spaces,' says Raffaele Vitale, 'we were excited: the church has always been a central meeting place for the communities of small Italian towns, so what better place was there to launch a *cucina* of wholesome dishes in a convivial atmosphere?' Raffaele and his wife, Antonietta Villani, who also does some of the cooking, have created a lively interior: the high vaulted rooms are decorated with artisan baskets and pots. Strings of peppers and garlic adorn walls and rafters. Local musicians are invited to perform: I was privy to the performance of an animated Neapolitan singer whose spicy, satirical lyrics were much appreciated by those who understood the dialect.

As for the food, Vitale has recently engaged a talented young chef to give the cooking a new direction. Giuseppe Stanzione worked in good restaurants in Roma before joining the Vitales. The result is a mix of rustic foods – like the thistle-bitter tiny artichokes that are served from copper saucepans with chunks of country bread – and more imaginative creations, such as the *millefoglie di pomodoro*. Here warm slices of the green-and-pink local tomatoes are interspersed with mozzarella, basil, and bread in an unusual variation on the Caprese salad. *Farro mantecato* is similar to the consistency of a risotto with spelt wheat cooked with *melanzane*, Provolone del Monaco cheese and an explosive sauce of fresh parsley. Desserts, too, are expertly made. I tasted several, and was impressed by the chef's *zabaglione gelato* dotted with a mirepoix of carrots and celery, and served with caramelized, wafer-thin slices of bread – a new twist on a cookie. A thoughtful wine list completes this atmospheric restaurant: well worth visiting.

Paestum–Capaccio

One straight road – the SS 118 – runs south from Battipaglia to the Greek temples of Paestum. I've nicknamed it 'the Strip'. Buffalo mozzarella producers line it in quick succession, interspersed with drive-in hardware stores, popular eateries and flat fields growing vegetables – in and out of huge greenhouses. It is peopled by farmers selling their produce along the roadsides, and by migrant workers from north Africa and beyond. You spot them easily along the road's borders, doing something the Italians rarely do much of – walking – in a parallel world to that of the fast cars and summer vacationers that use the highway to reach the sea.

THE GREEK CITY OF PAESTUM

Mozzarella shops along 'the Strip'

Built in the 6th century BC, in the part of Magna Grecia that was called Posedonia, the walled city of Paestum, with its three immense temples, was expanded in 273 AD by the Romans, who

MAKING RAW-MILK MOZZARELLA

Mozzarella should be made with the freshest possible milk. At Vannulo (see below), the buffalo are milked twice a day: at 4 a.m. and 3 p.m. (the evening's milk is mixed with the morning's). This milk is not pasteurized, but is heated to 36°C and a tiny amount of natural calves' rennet (*caglio*, from *cagliare*, to curdle) is added: 8 ml to each 100 litres of milk. Milk that has had rennet added to it is called '*la cagliata*'.

After 20 minutes, the milk has coagulated. The *cagliata* is now broken up to begin separating the curds from the whey, or *siero*. (The 'top' or fattiest part of the whey is kept aside for making *ricotta* later – a little fresh, whole milk will be added to it to make the *ricotta* creamier.)

After 4¹⁄₂ hours of fermentation, the fresh cheese is cut into '*spicchi*', like wedges of a cake. These big wedges are left to drain further, before a '*prova di filatura*' – or test of stringiness – is carried out. The cheese is sliced into thinner shreds: it is by now full of small bubbles. For the *prova*, water at 100°C is added to a small amount of the cheese, to see if it will begin to form 'strings' – *filare*. This depends on the level of acidity in the cheese, which must be at about 5 pH (often some whey from the preceding day, *il siero innesto* or *'a 'cizza* – with a high acidity of 2.0 pH– is added to the milk after the rennet to help bring up the acidity level). The *filatura* stage is reached at a temperature of 97°C.

When the acidity level is right, the bulk of the cheese is shredded into little pieces, and placed in a large cauldron. Scalding water (at 96° or 97°C) is added to it in a ratio of 3 parts of water to 5 of cheese. The *casaro* (cheesemaker or dairyman) starts stirring in a circular motion with a wooden stick (wooden utensils help keep the heat in) as the cheese first forms natural 'strings' and then a stringy whole, and separates from the water-and-whey. He stirs until it's all one big mass: pure white, sleek and shiny. (From the separated 'water' Vannulo makes butter.) Quickly, the *casaro* starts to pull big fistfuls of the hot cheese from the mass. Working as a team, he and his

companions begin to '*mozzare*' – to pull the cheese into smaller balls, dropping them into a vat of cool liquid. The men settle immediately into a rhythm: they form little ones first, one person (usually the main *casaro*) pulling them off from the larger balls, the other two or three preparing the balls for him and pulling against him. They always present the *casaro* with the smooth side of the cheese, ('*fare la faccia*' is to keep it warm and moving while they pull off from it), re-forming it into a ball after he has pulled off a piece. They told me it's much harder to cut the cheese than to pull it as they do.

As the mass cools they go from *ovoli* (bite-size) to *mozzarelle* (150 grams) to *aversane* (500 grams) or bigger. The last piece from the *mozzatura* is a bit harder than the rest, and is used to form a smooth *treccia*, or plait. It is stretched into a long rope and then woven into a compact braid.

The temperature of the cheese during the *mozzatura* is about 70°C – very hot – but the men work it bare-handed: they say that the high fat content of the buffalo milk makes a patina that protects their hands from being scalded – nevertheless, they always look bright red and swollen.

The large bath they drop the *mozzarelle* into is filled with cool liquid that 'sets' the hot cheeses as it brings their temperature down. What looks like water is in fact a by-product of the cheese-making: the 'second' whey that remains after the cheese forms the stringy mass. This is carefully set aside. The fattiest part is skimmed off the top, and is used the following day to make butter. The lower part of this skimmed whey is sterilized by pasteurization, and salted, with 2% salt for every 100 litres of *liquido*: this becomes

Making mozzarella
1. *Cutting the fresh cheese into wedges*
2. *Adding the scalding water*
3. *Strands beginning to form*
4. *Stirring the cheese into a sleek mass*
5. *Pulling the cheese into balls*
6. *Pulling the cheese into a long rope*
7. *Forming a plait*
8. *The finished treccia*

the whitish, watery brine the cheeses cool in (*acqua di governo*). It is also spooned into the bags the *mozzarelle* are sold in, as it provides the perfect environment for them to be carried and stored in.

 '*La mozzarella, più è grande, più è buona.*' Mozzarella: the bigger, the better. But as the size increases, so too does the time it needs to stay in the salted whey (*salamoia* or *acqua di governo* as it is called in Campania). Ideally the little bite-size *bocconcini* should stay in the *salamoia* for 3 to 4 hours; the classic *mozzarella* for 8 to 10 hours; and the larger *aversana* for 24 hours. 'Our *mozzarelle* change flavour every hour,' says the *casaro*.

The Other Way: Pasteurized Mozzarella

When making mozzarella (or other cheeses) from pasteurized milk, milk enzymes must be added to the now-sterile milk in order to make it ferment. Unfortunately, pasteurizing causes the milk to lose most of its fragrance (and many of its nutrients), so more salt is added to give it more flavour. When the cheese is worked and stretched by machine, it increases the speed at which it is made, but changes its texture, making it less elastic.

Some larger cheeses are also made

Buffalo Milk versus Cow's Milk

Cow's milk has 3.8–4% fat, and 3.01 grams of protein per 100 g. Vannulo's buffalo milk has 8% fat, and 4.60 grams of protein per 100 g (other farms force the animals to increase their production by feeding them more dried compounds, and this pushes the fat content up to 9%). From 100 kg of milk, they make 27 kg of mozzarella and 5 kg of ricotta.

How to Keep Your Mozzarella

This may come as a surprise, but real mozzarella should never be kept in the refrigerator: in cold environments the cheese seizes up

Buffalo wallowing in mud at Vannulo

and hardens, so you lose the wonderful soft elasticity that good mozzarella has. When you buy it from a dairy in Campania it comes lukewarm, freshly made, and is sold in a plastic bag of slightly cloudy liquid. This *liquido* or *acqua di governo* is in fact the run-off from the mozzarella-making. It has been pasteurized and salted, and provides the perfect sterile environment for the *mozzarelle* to be kept in. Cut the bag and pour the contents – cheese and liquid – into a large bowl, so that the mozzarella is just submerged. Keep the bowl covered with a plate, at room temperature. Raw-milk mozzarella will last five to six days – its flavour will develop and change daily – but is most delicious eaten within the first two or three. The larger the mozzarella, the more flavour it will have, but this is a matter of personal preference, and many people like the small, bite-size *ovoli*, *ciliegine*, or *bocconcini* best.

How to Eat it

When in Campania, do as the Campanians do. If you have really fresh mozzarella, the best thing to do with it is nothing at all: don't smother it in herbs, salt and pepper, oil, vinegar or other dressings. Just eat is as it is, with a simple piece of good country bread. That's when it's at its purest, and you will really enjoy its squeaky, silky texture and rich, sweet flavour.

A Greek temple at Paestum

added thermal baths, a forum and an amphitheatre. After being sacked in the Middle Ages, Paestum was abandoned – malaria had become rampant, and the city was too difficult to defend. It was not until the mid-18th century that Bourbon architects rediscovered it; Paestum soon became famous, a necessary stopping point on the Grand Tour.

The swamplands of Paestum were only finally drained (*bonificato*) in the mid-20th century. Paestum's geographical position, close to the hills and to the sea, also protected it from its biggest threat: earthquakes. Over the centuries, the temples withstood major damage due to the layer of sand they were built on.

The temples are open daily from 9 a.m. to one hour before dusk.

Agriturismo, Mozzarella

La Tenuta Seliano

Via Seliano
TEL 0828 723634
FAX 0828 724544
E-MAIL seliano@
agriturismoseliano.it
INTERNET
www.agriturismoseliano.it

Baronessa Cecilia Bellelli Baratta's *agriturismo* is located in lovely 18th-century buildings surrounded by gardens, with a buffalo farm and vegetable fields nearby; the rooms are furnished with taste. She runs a spacious restaurant that is open all year, but you must reserve ahead of time. Cecilia Baratta has become well known in the States thanks to her cooking-lesson collaboration with food-writer and broadcaster Arthur Schwartz, author of *Naples at Table* – the best cookbook in English on Neapolitan cuisine.

Agriturismo, Mozzarella
La Tenuta Vannulo

Via G Galilei
Contrada Vannulo
TEL 0828 724765
FAX 0828 725245
E-MAIL
a.palmieri@vannulo.it
INTERNET www.vannulo.it

There are many buffalo dairies in Campania – divided between the areas of Paestum and Caserta – but I've chosen to write in detail about this one, as a model for what the others are or might become.

Antonio and Caterina Palmieri's farm, Tenuta Vannulo, is a stone's thrown from the Greek temples of Paestum, at Capaccio, on the road that goes due south to the Cilento from Battipaglia. This farm is unique for many reasons: Vannulo produces organic, raw-milk cheeses from its own herd of buffaloes; it grows the organic fodder for the animals, who are cured with homeopathic treatments as necessary. As well as mozzarella and ricotta, the dairy also makes delicious buffalo-milk yoghurt and ice-creams, using all natural organic ingredients. There are two attractive shops on the farm: one sells the cheeses, the other has tables and a bar at which to buy the yoghurts, ice-cream, desserts and baked goods (try the brioches made with buffalo butter) the farm produces. There are plans for *relais*-level accommodation on the farm, and for buffalo leather crafts.

Beyond all this, what has always struck me about Vannulo is the level of culture that the Palmieris have woven into the fabric of this business: the farm is beautiful, with manicured gardens (including a metaphysical olive-hedge avenue), a museum of tools and objects of country life, a lovely villa that is the centrepiece of the Tenuta and – last but not least – a high sunlit room in the dairy in which the mozzarella is made. This clean, white-tiled room is at ground level, with a large picture window: from outside visitors can watch during the morning as the cheese-making process is carried out. It's addictive. I love to watch as a 'cake' of white cheese full of holes is transformed, as if by magic, into smooth, silky mozzarella. The dairymen, dressed in their whites, enact a series of movements that have undoubtedly been the same for generations, if not centuries. And despite the fact that now it's all in a modern, sanitized environment, this compelling ritual has remained manual and skilled.

'My grandfather bought this land in 1907, when it was still malarial swampland,' says Tonino Palmieri. 'He bought a few fields and eight buffalo. That's how it started.' The herd now numbers 470, with 80 hectares of fields. Tonino and his wife, Caterina, opened their business in 1988. He had a degree in agriculture, and had worked as president of a local bank and of the Consorzio di Bonifico, a consortium responsible for draining the marshland around Paestum. Recently he gave it all up to run the farm.

'I decided that if I was going to run a dairy, I wanted it to be as good as possible,' he says, as we tour the state-of-the-art milking rooms for the buffalo, which were the first to be constructed in the area. The search for perfection runs through everything at Vannulo: when the Palmieris decided to start making chocolate puddings from the buffalo milk, they called in Italy's greatest chocolate expert, Paul de Bondt from Pisa, to work on the recipes for them.

'Success is a sum of little things,' says Tonino, elegant in crisp linens on a hot summer's day. 'But it requires high-level people.' We are watching a herd of the buffalo take their afternoon showers. Everything has been thought of on this farm: in order to maintain the high levels of cleanliness that an organic, raw-milk dairy requires, the buffalo have to be kept very clean so as not to contaminate the milk. But buffalo love moisture – left to their own devices, they will spend whole afternoons up to their necks in mud.

'The solution here was two-fold,' explains Palmieri. 'The cows who are within three months of giving birth are allowed free run of the muddy fields, as they are not giving milk in that period, whereas the milk-givers are treated to showers (which they love) to keep them wet and clean.'

As no chemicals can be used on the farm, flies are controlled with predator insects. Francesco Marino, the farm's charming young manager, told me that buffaloes are creatures of habit, and despite their threatening appearance are both docile and highly inquisitive. 'They like to have a rest in the afternoon, just like us,' he says. 'When we introduced rubber mats for them to lie on they were doubtful at first, but soon learned to enjoy them. When we decided to try out a few thicker, softer mats, they quickly figured out that these were superior and would form queues to take their turn on them.'

One of the main policies of the farm is to use only their own milk for their products (about 1,200 litres per day). This way they can be absolutely sure of the quality – crucial for unpasteurized cheese-making – as well as the quantities of milk they will get each day. The buffalo are fed primarily fresh green organic *avena* (the grass whose seeds are oats), and are under no pressure to over-produce: each buffalo eats about 50 kilos of food (between fresh grasses and organic dried feed) and produces an average of just seven litres of milk per day.

'People tell me I should expand the operations here, as by midday the *mozzarelle* often run out,' says Palmieri. 'But I prefer to stay small. We don't ship our cheeses anywhere. You have to come here to buy them, and most people appreciate that

Buffalo ricotta is served with many condiments – from honey to spices

this too is a guarantee of quality.'

Vannulo's products are truly delicious. To eat the glistening, bright-white mozzarella still warm from the making is an incredible experience and will banish supermarket look-alikes forever. Not overly salty, the sweet yet complex flavour of the unpasteurized milk shines through, yet is saved from being cloying by the finish, which has a slight nuttiness to it. The texture of these Paestum *mozzarelle* is juicier, or milkier, than their Casertano counterparts, which are often more compact, a little drier and saltier.

'We look for simplicity in our products, but it's not easy,' says Palmieri. 'To be technologically avant-garde while making mozzarella the way it was made fifty years ago is a challenge.'

As for the hand-made ricotta, it's like a cloud of sweet milkiness, delicious by itself, or served – as the Palmieris do – surrounded by a choice of condiments: honey, cinnamon, nutmeg, cocoa powder, kumquat jelly. These cheeses will enhance any dish but they are unbeatable alone. Pure and simple.

Tonino Palmieri was also the first to produce buffalo-milk yoghurt and ice-creams, and to create a '*Yogurteria*' to sell them from. The yoghurts are made from pasteurized buffalo milk with the addition of organic fruit purées. The ice-creams use whole buffalo milk which is so rich there's no need to add

PAESTUM'S ARTICHOKE:
IL CARCIOFO DI PAESTUM IGP

*Paestum artichoke;
opposite, the
Artichoke King and
his wife*

Artichokes are part of the thistle family; the artichokes of
Paestum are a local variety, *Cynara scolymus*. They have
been grown in this area since at least the early 19th century,
but began to be farmed systematically only after the marshes were drained in the 1920s. In these medium-clay soils,
they acquire higher sugar levels than normal. This variety,
also known as the Tondo di Paestum, is so called for its
rounded shape; this artichoke has no thorns or spines on its
stem. Sometimes it acquires a pinkish hue. As the winters
along the coast are very mild, these artichokes remain tender; they don't require frost protection, and often ripen well
before those grown further north. The season is from
February to May. They are high in minerals – calcium,
potassium phosphorus and iron – and aid in the lowering of
cholesterol.

Every year, towards the end of April, Paestum hosts La
Festa del Carciofo where you can feast on them fried, roast-
ed, baked, on pasta and pizza, or in *la parmigiana*, *frittatas*,
as a stuffing for ravioli… the possibilities are endless.
   For further information:
   TEL 0828 811651;
   E-MAIL info@festacarciofopaestum.com
   INTERNET www.festacarciofopaestum.com

THE ARTICHOKE KING
'I was born *in mezzo i carciofi* – in amongst the artichokes,'
says Tonino Cavallaro (TEL 0828 811400), a fourth-generation artichoke grower in the Paestum area. 'For my family,
artichokes are a great passion. Now it's been passed on to
my son. As a matter of fact, even our dog loves eating
artichokes.' The Cavallaros own fourteen hectares of
artichoke fields within a stone's throw of the temples.
'When I see weeds, I see the devil,' he says, as he bends to
pull out grass from under an artichoke bush. 'You need to
keep the fields clean and tidy. That's the best way,' he says.
After fifty-three years of growing artichokes, he should
know. During the months of the season, Tonino takes fresh
artichokes to market each morning. His wife is a fine cook:
her speciality – artichokes.

Young male buffalo

cream. They are flavoured with fresh local hazelnuts or fruit: *fichi d'India* (prickly pear), *melograno* (pomegranate) or *fichi* (figs). These *gelati* are at their most sinful piled onto airy yellow brioches, sweet from the buffalo butter they are enriched with.

A new Vannulo project will make use of the meat of the male buffalo calves, which is leaner than beef and very good when cooked well. Until recently male buffalo calves were slaughtered at birth throughout Campania as there was no market for their meat, but Palmieri is keen to change that too.

OTHER FINE MOZARELLA PRODUCERS IN THE AREA:
La Perla Mediterranea, Pontebarizzo; TEL 0828 871097
Caseificio Rivabianca, S.S.18, Km 93, Capaccio; TEL 0828 724030
Caseificio Torricelle, Via Ponte Marmoreo; TEL 0828 811318

Restaurant

Da Nonna Sceppa

Contrada Laura, 53
TEL 0828 851064
E-MAIL
nsceppa@paestum.it
INTERNET
www.nonnasceppa.com
CLOSED
Thurs except in
summer; Oct
PRICE €€€€

This is the most interesting restaurant in the area, though I sometimes wish it were smaller, as undoubtedly the cooks would benefit from being able to concentrate on fewer customers at a time. It's a family affair, with the brothers Raffaele and Luigi Chiumento serving in the dining rooms, indoors and out; their sisters do the cooking, having taken over from their mother some years ago. There is a large wine list, and a lot of care is taken in the choice of fresh, local ingredients and cheeses.

The food is authentically rooted in the area: here *fiori di zucca* are stuffed with fragrant local mozzarella before being deep-fried. *Antipasti* always include some of the varied seasonal vegetables that thrive in the flat Sele valley: *scarola*, artichokes, wild field greens. The pastas are abundant and appetizing: I love thick spaghetti tossed with tomatoes, anchovies and the small green peppers they call *friarielli* (not to be confused with the broccoli-tops of the same name). *Lagane* are also a local speciality: short noodles of water and flour, traditionally paired with Cilento chickpeas, and here enriched with *baccalà*. Indeed, many of these dishes were considered a meal-in-one in their humble birthplaces. So either come to Nonna Sceppa when you are very hungry, or order a little at a time.

The *cucina* also takes in the nearby coast: *cicala magnosa* (*Scyllarides latus*) is a mottled, prehistoric-looking beast in the lobster family, but sweeter in taste than normal lobsters – it's quite delicious served in a light tomato sauce over pasta.

Zucchine alla scapece is a refreshing summery combination accented with mint; here it's used to stuff *totani* – flying squid – with very good results. In winter come for the pork dishes that go so well with great red wines. I'm sure the desserts are also good, but I have never got that far.

Restaurant

Mandetta Ristorante-Hotel

Via Torre di Mare, 2
TEL 0828 811118
FAX 0828 721328
E-MAIL
info@mandetta.it
INTERNET
www.mandetta.it
CLOSED Mon
CARDS All
PRICE €€€€€

On the ground floor of this family-run three-star hotel facing the beach in the little village of Paestum by the sea is a large, pleasant restaurant. The Mandettas all take part: a son and daughter run the dining room, overseen by their father, the seafood expert and purveyor of the restaurant's produce. The central character is out of sight in the kitchen: Signora Mandetta does wonders with the local catch. Her abundant succession of *antipasti di mare* is made to order with a sensitive, light hand. When she's cooking, the food is some of my favourite in Campania: fresh anchovies, delicately fried; little squid stuffed with *fiori di zucca* and *farro*; home-canned Calabrian tuna; sautéed shellfish with *calamari* and their cooking juices... the list is endless (and often constitutes the whole meal). But the pastas are equally fine, as in *linguine alla vedova* – the 'widow's black' here squid ink topped with scampi and tomato. Fresh fish are always available to grill, poach or cook with tomato broth '*all'acqua pazza*'. Save room for the home-made desserts – the trolley will tempt even the most determined abstainers.

Nearby, Mandetta's sister Angela is a baker and produces breads and dried *biscotti di pane* for making *pane bagnato* – soaked breads for use in salads and soups: Antica Forneria (Via Ponte Marmoreo).

Tuna

Restaurant

Nettuno Ristorante

Zona Archeologica
TEL 0828 811028
FAX 0828 811028
E-MAIL
ristnettuno@tiscalinet.it
OPEN lunch only except
Fri & Sat in summer
CLOSED Mon in winter;
12–26 Nov; 7 Jan–7 Feb
CARDS All
PRICE €€€–€€€€

You can't miss this restaurant: it is in the only 19th-century villa standing next to the temples of Paestum, and overlooks the archaeological site. In the remarkable photographs of the allied landings at Paestum's beaches in 1943 (assembled into a wonderful book by Angelo Pesce), this is one of the very few buildings that existed in the area, which was malarial swampland until the 1930s. Indeed, the restaurant was created in 1929. In those days there were few controls over the site, and the main dining room was constructed from huge stones taken from the city's fallen walls.

Today the restaurant is divided into two areas: a large, casual dining area for groups, and the slightly more formal rooms inside the villa for individual customers, with better service, nice linens and a more attractive décor. The food is reasonably priced, well cooked and well suited to its mainly tourist clientele. The Pisani family has always run the business – indeed the elderly Signora Pisani still makes some of the fine desserts by hand.

Restaurant, Wine Bar
Osteria La Pergola di Alfonso Longo

Via Magna Grecia, 1
TEL 0828 723377
CLOSED
Mon except in Aug
CARDS All
PRICE €€€

If you're in central Capaccio – just a couple of kilometres from the temples – and feel like eating outside, this *osteria* is fine for a light, informal meal. It specializes in adding new twists to traditional dishes – with mixed success. I prefer to stick here to the conventional, as in rustic soups and pastas, or simply grilled meats. There is usually a nice selection of local cheeses to accompany a good wine list.

Restaurant, Wine Bar
Ristorante–Enoteca Tavernelle

Via Tavernelle, 14
TEL 0828 722440
OPEN All week
CARDS All
PRICE €€€-€€€€

Guido Tabano's wine bar and restaurant is divided into two distinct spaces, with the kitchen sandwiched in the middle. The oldest part of the 19th-century *taverna* has attractive modern paintings and an intimate feel – a good place to meet friends, choose from the fine wines that line the walls, and sit over a bottle of wine, a light meal or a full dinner. You can also buy bottles to take away. Beyond the kitchen is a high, airy room, clean-lined and relaxed, that in summer spills out into the garden. The food is *cucina di territorio* – local recipes with some flights of fancy, and an insistence on the fresh and seasonal. Cheeses are well selected, both from within Italy and beyond, and there are always a few tempting desserts to be accompanied by a glass of golden *passito*.

In the immediate vicinity of the temples you will also find: Enoteca Il Calice (Via Magna Grecia, 831; TEL 0828 722114). Those longing for a decent glass of wine need look no further: Il Calice has a fine selection, and serves artisan cheeses, *salumi* and other light meals to accompany them. There are even a few tables outside in summer. Ristorante Il Granaio (Via Porta Marina, 86; TEL 0828 721014; FAX 0828 721977). This *granaio*, or barn, has been elegantly rebuilt with a comfortable small hotel upstairs and an attractive restaurant below – all surrounded by a pretty garden, just three minutes' walk from the temples.

Opposite: Elderly artisans show off their work at the Anzianinsieme festa (see Roccadaspide)

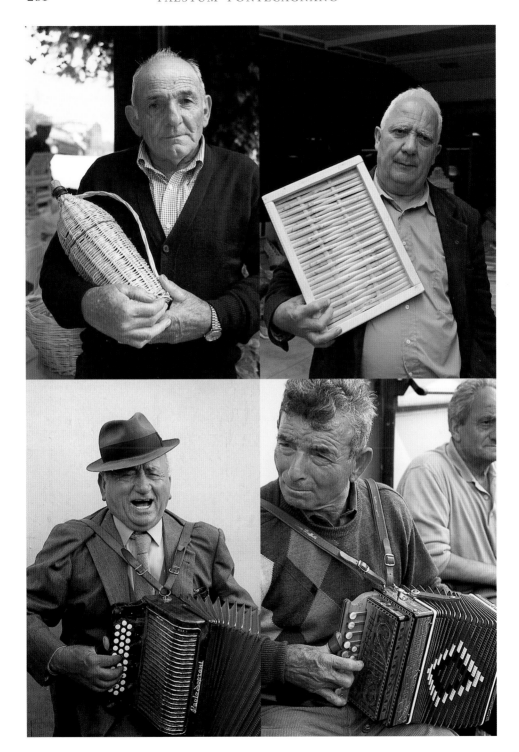

Vegetable Preserves, Agriturismo

Tempa di Lepre
Via Consortile
TEL 0828 722953
E-MAIL info@
antichisaporicilentani.it
INTERNET
www.agrimaida.it

MIVA Antichi Sapori Cilentani

This small vegetable-preserving company goes under various names including Vastola, Antichi Sapori Cilentani, Maida and MIVA. It specializes in hand-made, artisanal *sott'olii* (vegetables preserved in oil) and other vegetable- and fruit-based conserves. It has become known thanks, in part, to Alfonso Iaccarino (see p. 212-215) for whom its owners have developed a line of organic products.

At the heart of the operations – which include a simple but attractively done *agriturismo* with restaurant – are Giovanni Miglino and Francesco Vastola, or Mi-Va. 'We started eight years ago, just the two of us doing everything,' says Francesco as he shows me a room filled with local ladies peeling baby artichokes. 'We have built up from there. Now we are selling all over Europe, especially in the north, where people understand high-quality products.'

They use extra virgin olive oil from the Cilento and high-grade agricultural produce for their preserves. Artichokes are a speciality, given that Paestum is famous for its own variety, the Carciofo di Paestum IGP. MIVA bottles the artichokes under oil in various sizes, from walnut to egg. I like the lightly pickled orange pumpkin, *zucca*, cut into chunks and preserved under oil. It makes an easy *antipasto* to serve alongside *salumi* and cheeses. Other preserves combine carrot and lemon, apple and juniper.

Hotel

Via Laura, 13
TEL 0828 851333
FAX 0828 851596
INTERNET
www.hotelariston.com

Hotel Ariston

This large, modern-style hotel is very efficiently run, and has a rare commodity: a heated indoor swimming pool for the use of its guests, as part of its Centro Benessere where all sorts of beauty treatments are available. There is also an outdoor pool.

Pontecagnano

Mozzarella

Sant' Antonio
TEL 089 383268

Caseificio Taverna Penta

The Morese family have been breeding herds of buffalo since the 17th century. Their modern dairy is located inside a restored old country house. The mozzarella they produce is some of the best in this area, once an important Greek colony.

Panificio Barella's staff on the day of the festa

Roccadaspide

This hill town is built around an imposing 12th-century castle, some of which was destroyed during the earthquake of 1980. The town is surrounded by chestnut woods whose fruits are highly prized: the Marrone di Roccadaspide has IGP status. Chestnuts have been documented as being in Campania since the 12th century. The Roccadaspide chestnuts were grafted onto wild chestnuts at the end of the 19th century in order to obtain larger fruits with less 'veining' of the bitter inner skin. Most of the large crop of chestnuts is sold to the confectionery industry.

For information about Roccadaspide's woods and surroundings: Comunità Montana Calore Salernitano, Via Cesina Rocca; TEL 0828 941132.

Antonietta Scovotto at the festa

Panificio Barrella (Via XX Settembre, 54; TEL 0828 941053) Lucio and Giovanni Barrella run this bakery in the town centre. The bakery is located down a *vicolo* off the main street, in a cellar carved out of the *tufo* hill.

Every year, Antonietta Scovotto, a local doctor, organizes a wonderful *festa* for the elderly people of the area, *Anzianinsieme*. This is the moment for them to show off their artistry and become protagonists once again. The arts of basketmaking and woodcarving are at risk of being lost for ever, yet they deserve to be saved as much as any other endangered species. For information: TEL 333 3742740.

The bay of Salerno

Salerno

AZIENDA SOGGIORNO E
TURISMO SALERNO
Via Roma, 258
TEL 089 224744
089 231432
FAX 089 252576
INTERNET
www.crmpa.it/EPT
www.aziendaturismo.sa.it
www.salernocity.it

The city of Salerno is built into a natural amphitheatre of hills that faces out, past its port, to the sea. Cut through the modern sprawl that surrounds it and you find a medieval centre, complete with Romanesque Duomo. From the 9th to the 13th centuries, Salerno was home to Europe's oldest Scuola Medica, or School of Medicine, a university where men – and women, a radical idea for the times – studied medicine, philosophy, theology and law. The School also played an important role in the lemon's success by spreading the medicinal use of this yellow citrus fruit, whose culture and research came from the Arab world. (Perhaps it is thanks to this ancient notion of healthy diet that fast food has not taken root in Salerno – the city's McDonald's quickly closed down for lack of takers.) Salerno hosts an annual summer Festa della Pizza (not considered fast food as it contains high quality ingredients). For information about the *festa*: TEL 089 725890; FAX 0896306490; E-MAIL info@festadellapizza.it.

The beautiful Giardino della Minerva (in Via Tasso) high in the *centro storico* overlooks the sea and is worth a visit.

SALERNO: A GASTRONOMIC GUIDE

Salerno is an active city, with busy shopping streets, as well as a well-preserved medieval part of the town around the Duomo. One of the most attractive streets is Via dei Mercanti – the merchants' street – and it's well worth walking through to admire the *palazzi* and the current shops.

Here are some of Salerno's most useful food and wine addresses.

Pasticceria Pantaleone (Via dei Mercanti, 75–77; TEL 089 227825) is a fabulous pastry shop known for its classic Campanian specialties: *delizie al limone* – the creamy lemon 'dome' – *babà*, layered *sfogliatelle* and a fresh ricotta tart. Just down the street, Testa (Via dei Mercanti, 104–106; TEL 089 241192) sells wines. If you're looking for fresh pasta to cook at home, or good pasta that is cooked and ready to eat, Il Tortellino, Laboratorio di Pasta Fresca, is in the *piazza* near the Town Hall (Piazza del Municipio, 32; TEL 081 488300): Giuseppina Lionessa makes delicious Neapolitan *lasagne*, fried potato and rice *crochette* and *arancini*, as well as stuffed vegetables to take away. Enoteca Baccanalia (Via Roma, 272; TEL 089 224608) is a shop for fine wines. Via Roma (parallel with the seafront) leads east into Corso Garibaldi, where Casa Bianca (Corso Garibaldi, 144–146; TEL 089 225442) is a 'white' house based on dairy products rather than politics. You'll find carefully selected Campanian cheeses, including fresh-daily buffalo mozzarella, plus aged cheeses like the Caciocavallo Podolico, assorted *salumi* and some cooked foods that are ready to eat – great for picnics by the sea.

If it's fresh-roasted coffee you're after, Torrefazione San Pietro (Corso Garibaldi, 231; TEL 089 232125) has everything one needs for the perfect home-brewed *caffè*. Manzoni Dolce e Salato (Corso Garibaldi, 244; TEL 089 233782) specializes in miniature pastries (*mignon*) and take-away foods. When you're on the waterfront, stop in for a great *gelato* at Gelateria Bar Nettuno (Via Lungomare Trieste, 136; TEL 089 228375). It's open from 7 a.m. to 2 a.m., and has lots of tempting flavours, including *nocciatella*, a chocolate–hazelnut blend. If you fancy a lemon ice while strolling along the seaside promenade, the Chiosco (kiosk) in the garden of the Villa Comunale near Teatro Verdi is where the Salernitani go: you can't miss it when you come off the boats.

Alimentari Enrico Marchetti (Via Arechi, 25; TEL 089 231441). If you're looking for speciality foods from the area, this grocery shop has everything from fresh fruits and vegetables

to cheeses and pasta. Biscottificio Manzoni (Via De Granito, 11; TEL 089 227465) makes biscuits, breads and fresh brioches that are favourites with the Salernitani. Laboratorio di Pasticceria Sabatino Sirica (Via Marconi, 135, Parco Pia; TEL 081 2551672) has been going for over fifty years, and is known for its *babà* and airy *sfogliatelle*. I like the streets around Via Piave, with its morning street market. For anyone looking for organic foods and produce, O Sole Bio is in Via Diaz in that same neighbourhood.

Along the seafront towards Paestum, Enoteca Manzo (Via Lungomare Colombo, 42–44; TEL 089 752520) has a good selection of Campanian and other wines.

Consorzio Sapori...Sapori (Via Santoro, 10; TEL 089 2580311) is run by the Salerno branch of Coldiretti – a nationwide co-operative of growers.

If you're organizing a wedding or large dinner, why not hold it in one of the beautiful villas along the coast from Salerno? Emidio Trotta runs Campania's most elegant banqueting service: www.intavola.com. Or try GP Group Catering, TEL 081 5872811.

Restaurant

Piazza Alfano I, 4–6
TEL/FAX 089 238818
CLOSED Sun eve; Mon
PRICE €€€€

Al Cenacolo

This has long been the most attractive restaurant in Salerno, and its position – across the medieval street from the Romanesque Duomo – couldn't be more central. Gina and Pietro Rispoli have been here for over ten years, and their dining rooms are quietly elegant, decorated with hand-painted Vietri ceramics and some of the cellar's 950 wines – indeed this is one of the best-stocked cellars in Campania.

The food is knowingly based on local country dishes, as in the *torta salata* of seasonal vegetables or a rustic *ma non troppo* soup of *scarola*, potato and *baccalà*. Some dishes are more adventurous without losing sight of their roots: the classic layering of the *parmigiana* is here applied to fresh anchovies that are stuffed with cheese, fried, then butterflied in a sauce of ripe tomatoes. As one often finds in seaside towns surrounded by hills, some dishes combine the peasant and fisherman cultures: *linguine* are served on a purée of chickpeas and topped with small clams and shrimp; main courses include both seafood and meat. For dessert, I was taken by the *spuma* – literally, froth – of local hazelnuts, which was creamy and satisfying. Attentive service completes this perfect setting for a lovely meal in town.

Opposite: Melanzana flower and fruit – one of Campania's most popular vegetables

Restaurant

Corso Garibaldi, 29
TEL 089 233738
CLOSED Sun eve
CARDS All
PRICE €€€

Simposium

You could be forgiven for not being drawn to this restaurant from the outside: it's on the ground floor of an unassuming modern apartment building near the station, on the main road that runs parallel to the sea. The interior is modern and unassuming too, but the food is certainly worth the visit. The Matassino family come from the hills above Salerno, and have brought real home cooking down to the town with them. Signora Matassino makes fabulous pasta: I go just for her *ravioli con le pettole* – a pasta pillow with a cloud-light buffalo ricotta filling, and wide borders of pasta (*pettole* means 'extra bit of fabric' in dialect). They are served with a little fresh sauce made of crushed cherry tomatoes. The Matassinos like to use other mountain ingredients like fresh mushrooms and the aromatic black truffles the woods are full of (if you know where to look). Simposium has also gained a following for its use of unusual meats to complement the more standard choices of lamb, beef and pork: ostrich meat (*struzzo*) and game (*caccia-gione*). This is also a fine place to taste some of the best local cheeses – like a well-aged Caciocavallo Podolico – to go with a good bottle of wine chosen from the shelf. Desserts are typically Campanian: sweet and satisfying. Prices are fair, as is the service – the family is friendly and warm – and that's what counts.

OTHER PLACES TO EAT IN SALERNO

Antica Pizzeria del Vicolo della Neve (Vicolo della Neve, 24; TEL 089 225705; OPEN for dinner only; CLOSED Weds; PRICE €€) is a classic Salerno address: the trattoria, whose name refers to the snow-store that was once here for keeping fish chilled, has been a fixture in the city for 150 years, with its modest but flavourful *piatti tipici* – like *baccalà* with potatoes, or rustic *pasta e fagioli* – and delicious pizzas still made in a wood-burning oven. Vinissimo (Vicolo della Neve, 14; TEL 089 250925; CLOSED Tues; Aug) is a recent wine bar in the same narrow street, where the choice of wines is much better than at the pizzeria, so you can stop in for a glass after dinner.

Ristorante O'vulijo (Via Molo Manfredi, 2; TEL 089 256924), usefully positioned between the port (Molo Manfredi) and Teatro Verdi, with easy parking nearby, is a comfortable restaurant in a little triangular *piazza*, with a few tables outside in summer. It offers both fresh seafood and local pasta and meat dishes.

If it's pizza you're in the mood for, try La Brace (Lungomare Trieste, 11; TEL 089 225159, 089 231733; CLOSED Tues). It too

The boardwalk gardens of Salerno's seafront

is near the port, and has a pretty garden and wood-burning oven for making more than twelve types of pizza. *Alla brace* means 'over wood embers' and you can also have fresh fish here, grilled or simply cooked, to go with a good selection of wines.

San Cipriano Picentino

Wine, Agriturismo

Via Montevetrano, Nido
TEL 089 882285
E-MAIL
montevetrano@tin.it
INTERNET
www.montevetrano.com

Montevetrano

Montevetrano is many things: a medieval castle on a hill in the Picentini mountains north-east of Salerno, flanked by an estate of twenty-six hectares of woods, olive groves and vineyards. A villa: large, rambling, crumbling in parts, with the feel of a South American hacienda given by exotic large-leafed plants and equatorial – or Pompeian – colours. Its high walls contain an inside-outside world of courtyards, porticos and stairways into which it's always a pleasure to retreat. Montevetrano is also a woman, Silvia Imparato, until ten years ago a successful por-traitist and photographer of street life. She is an artist turned businesswoman, who moved from capturing reality in images to capturing the essence of this place in a bottle. And so, Montevetrano is a wine.

Silvia Imparato

Montevetrano wine

'I have always loved these mountains, this land and the people who work it, and this house,' says Silvia as she shows me the modern vinification cellars that have been built beyond the villa. It's early summer and she is dressed in spare, stylish linens of ochre and rust. 'I didn't set out to make wine. I had a challenging career in Rome and was invited to join a small group of amateur but very serious wine tasters there. We met once a week for ten years, tasting some of the world's greatest wines. I kept thinking about my family's house in the country, where the wine made by the *contadini* was better used as vinegar than for drinking.' One of the occasional members of the group, Renzo Cotarella, is an œnologist, and encouraged Silvia to improve her wine. 'I grafted Cabernet and Aglianico onto plants of Barbera and Uva di Troia,' she says. 'Not because I don't believe in the indigenous varieties, but because I was passionate about Bordeaux. I wanted to see if in an area like ours, with no history of fine wine-making, I could do something interesting.'

The results were encouraging, and within a couple of years she met Renzo Cotarella's brother, Riccardo – now considered one of Italy's star œnologists. He was amazed at the potential expressed in Silvia's wine. 'I explained that my ambition was to make a great, world-class wine here,' she says. 'I couldn't see the point of changing my life for less.' In 1991 he agreed to work with her – at that time there were no new big wines being made in Campania – and by 1995 she had the first three vintages in bottles. 'Unbeknownst to Cotarella I sent them to Robert Parker Jr., the influential American wine critic. He was very impressed, calling the wine the "Sassicaia of the south" – that triggered the collectors. I still wasn't sure we could make a wine like this for the market – as opposed to just for a circle of friends,' she confides, 'but I decided to try.'

The rest is history: Montevetrano became – and still is – a cult wine, and a beacon for southern Italian wines. It has won every possible prize, not just once, but consistently, and showed that even areas with no tradition could produce characterful, territorial wines to compare with the world's best. It is made as a team effort, by Silvia, her cellarman Mimì and assistant Patrizia, with Cotarella as consultant, and the vineyard workers. Montevetrano is currently made from six hectares of vineyards, of Cabernet Sauvignon(60%), Merlot (30%) and Aglianico (10%) of the Taurasi variety. It is a silky, mellow wine, complex, elegant and intriguing – just like the woman who makes it.

Silvia Imparato's sister, Anna, runs a lovely *agriturismo* with her daughter, Carmen, La Vecchia Quercia (Montevetrano; TEL/FAX 089 882528; E-MAIL lavecchia_quercia@tin.it), located in the villa adjacent to Silvia's at Montevetrano. Anna is also a wonderful cook, so guests are treated to delicious breakfasts, and dinner on request.

Sieti

Bed and Breakfast
Palazzo Pennasilico

Via Le Piazze, 27
TEL/FAX 089 881822
E-MAIL
info@palazzopennasilico.it
INTERNET
www.palazzopennasilico.it

If you're in the vicinity of Salerno to visit the archaeological zones, Paestum, and the surrounding nature reserve, and would rather stay in a private *palazzo* in a charming and well-maintained country village than in an impersonal hotel, then Palazzo Pennasilico will be right for you. Sieti is in the hills of the Monti Picentini national park, to the east of Salerno. The historic 16th-century *palazzo*, with its romantic courtyard and imposing central staircase, has attractive rooms – each quite different from the rest – and a personable, lively host, Luigi Pennasilico, who makes staying there all the more enjoyable.

Chapter 7

South from Paestum

A new Riviera: the unsung natural beauties of the Cilento and Vallo di Diano

FOR TOURIST
INFORMATION:
www.aziendaturismo.sa.it
OR SEE P. 275

The Cilento is one of my favourite areas of Campania, and anyone who loves the unspoiled Mediterranean countryside, with fig and olive groves, stone villages and a truly beautiful coastline will feel the same way. It's hardly surprising that UNESCO has designated the large Parco Nazionale del Cilento e Vallo di Diano a World Heritage Site. It is to be hoped that the laws governing building within it will be respected and it will remain as unspoiled as possible for future generations.

The Greeks settled along the Cilento coast – an important part of Magna Grecia – as the ruins of the city of Velia and the other remaining sites testify. After them came the Romans, Saracens, Aragonese... the multitude of conquering forces whose cultural vestiges characterize so much of the south of Italy. The Salt Road passed through the Cilento, carrying the riches of this precious commodity.

During the era of the Grand Tour, this wild area of bandits and rough terrain was braved by writers such as Craufurd Tait Ramage in search of archaeological and architectural remains. More recently, Professor Ancel Keys found inspiration here – and evidence to back his theories regarding the healthiness of the Mediterranean Diet.

Archaeological sites are visitable (usually open from 9.00 a.m. to one hour before sundown); antique finds are on view in the Antiquarium at Palinuro, and at Castellabate; the Charterhouse of Padula is one of Europe's most important – until the last century it was surrounded by mulberry trees, for the production of silk for the Bourbon silk-works at San Leucio (see pp. 80-81). For nature lovers, there are trekking routes and guides to the

Opposite: Antonio Longo sun-drying white Cilento figs

coast's caves and cliffs; the WWF has a wildlife reserve in the Grotte del Bussento (visits by prior appointment), and the spectacular grottoes of Pertosa are the largest in southern Italy. For those who just want a seaside holiday in a country setting, the coast from Agropoli to Sapri offers clean beaches and a wide choice of places to stay and to eat. As with everything to do with Campania, the most seductive thing about the area is its people: warm, hospitable – *'solare'*.

Wild fennel

Wild and exhilarating perfumes will arise as soon as the clouds disperse. As volatile oils, they start from the ground; afterwards, when the sun has warmed the withered plants, each one begins to breathe out its characteristic odour. It is rather hard to analyse this fragrant, multi-herbal emanation: I suspect that the dried fennel stalks are the Leitmotif in the symphony. The cistus bushes, whose frail purple and white roses would enchant a Japanese artist, give forth a pungent aroma when the sun beats upon them; other spots are dominated by the honey-sweet savour of scorched thistles, of the wild juniper which, nowadays, can be seen to full perfection only on the inaccessible crags of Montalto, or the common fig.
Norman Douglas Siren Land

EATING AND DRINKING
The Cilento is still a rural – and, in many cases, poor – area, and its *cucina* reflects this. If on the coast the *pescatori* of Pisciotta still fish anchovies in the manner of the ancient Greeks, the domestic cooking in the hill towns is based primarily on local *legumi*, hand-made pastas and vegetables. There are many small *trattorie* and restaurants – sometimes too touristy, alas – but at their best they offer the simple, flavourful dishes of land and sea that characterize this country food.

Extra virgin olive oil is an important part now of the country economy: the Cilento DOP was one of the first three to be granted in Campania. The Cilento is also known for its delicate white figs (see pp. 290-91). As for wines, Cilento DOC and Paestum IGT appellations have given recognition to a culture that has existed here for centuries, if not millennia, though not on a very large scale. Several young producers have recently brought about a qualitative revolution in the Cilento, making wines that have gained approval on the national and international stages.

The area is also rich in cheeses, from the Caciocavallo Podolico named for the indigenous breed of cow that is best able to cope with the south's heat, lack of water and scarce but flavourful pastures; to the sheep's-milk *pecorini*; to the compact *cacioricotta di capra*, of goat's milk; to the *mozzarella nella mortella* (see p. 286). Roberto Rubino's ANFOSC has studied these cheeses and published two books in Italian about them and the Cilento pastures they depend on (see Bibliography).

Il Parco

Palazzo Mainenti
Vallo della Lucania
TEL 0974 719911
E-MAIL info@pncvd.it
INTERNET www.pncvd.it
ALSO Comunità Montana
Vallo di Diano
Viale Certosa 1
Padula
TEL 0975 577111

The Parco Nazionale del Cilento e Vallo di Diano extends over an area of 180,000 hectares within the province of Salerno. It includes mountains and plains, kilometres of coastline and dozens of villages, archaeological and historical monuments. It is the centre of many agricultural, wildlife and other nature projects. One that particularly interests me is the experimental reforestation programme that is being tried after the all-too-frequent summer forest fires – many of which are set by local arsonists. In this project, helicopters are used to sow millions of seeds of indigenous *macchia mediterranea* plants that have been mixed with natural *agar agar* jelly (a seaweed extract) which glues them to the ground and provides a bit of moisture for the first phase of germination. This cycle takes several years to grow well, but repopulates the environment with the correct sorts of native species of flowers and bushes for the fauna to appreciate, and for the slowing of erosion.

Podolico cow grazing freely by the road

Ricigliano •

Potenza •

• Contursi Terme

• Battipaglia

Caggiano •

Pertosa •

Paestum •

Trentinara •

• Sala Consilina

Teggiano •

• Felitto

Padula •

Ogliastro Cilento •

Valle Dell'Angelo •

Agropoli •

• Cicerale

Torchiara •

• Prignano Cilento

• Stio

Laureana Cilento •

• Rutino

Buonabitacolo •

Montesano

S. Marco •

• S. Maria di Castellabate

• Gioi

sulla Marcellana

Castellabate •

• Cannalonga

S. Mauro Cilento •

Vallo della Lucania • • Novi Velia

• Rofrano

Casal Velino •

• Acquavella

Grotte del Bussento

Acciaroli •

Caselle in Pittari •

Pioppi •

Velia

Futani •

Torre Orsaia •

• Morigerati

Ascea •

• Massicelle

Lagonegro •

San Mauro la Bruca •

Roccagloriosa •

• Torraca

Marina di Pisciotta • • Pisciotta

Celle di Bulgheria •

Policastro •

Sapri •

Villammare •

S. Giovanni a Piro •

• Scario

Palinuro •

• Camerota

Maratea •

Marina di Camerota •

Acciaroli

Agriturismo

TEL 0974 904172
FAX 0974 904036

Le Serre

Paola Visone's large pink house has a terrace overlooking the sea, six rooms, and a perfectly peaceful position between beach and hills: just right for a quiet holiday in the Cilento.

ALSO AT ACCIAROLI: Dom Florigi (Via Porto; TEL 339 4434335) is a great shop featuring local wines and oils.

Acquavella

Cheese

Via Fontana Medina
TEL 0974 906116

L'Arenaro

Mariacarmela Di Feo makes wonderful cheeses from her goats' milk. 'My parents had always made some cheese here but in 1995 I took over from them, and increased the herd to seventy goats,' she says. Mariacarmela makes *cacioricotta*, a goat's cheese that is found a lot throughout the south of Italy. 'In summer it's so hot here that fresh milk doesn't keep well, so the *contadini* developed this system which involves scalding the milk and then cooling it to 43°C before adding the rennet.' The result is a compact round cheese with a pleasant goat tang and just the right balance of salt. It comes *fresco* and *stagionato*, fresh and aged.

Agropoli

Agropoli is a busy seaside town with an active port – a good place to buy fish directly from the fishermen as they come in.

Restaurant, Hotel

Via Madonna del
Carmine, 31
TEL 0974 843036
(hotel 0974 843044)
FAX 0974 843234
E-MAIL
info@hotelristorante
ilceppo.com
CLOSED Mon; Nov
CARDS All
PRICE €€€–€€€€

Ristorante Hotel Il Ceppo

One-and-a-half kilometres from the centre of Agropoli, on the road to Vallo, is this long-standing restaurant, with the little hotel across the street. Inside, there are two main dining rooms: one in the luminous terrace by the entrance, the other up a few steps in the cosier nucleus near the kitchen.

The accent at Il Ceppo is on the fresh and varied seafood the coast can offer. There are always lots of *antipasti* to choose from (or have a succession of them, as the chef suggests), including baby shrimp topped with breadcrumbs and grilled on aromatic lemon leaves, deep-fried *zucchine* sticks with *calamari*, or *scungilli* – sea-snails. Pastas too are dressed with the local catch, or with the vegetables that are always so flavourful in the south. For *secondi*, fish are simply baked, grilled or stewed with tomatoes or potatoes – red mullet (*triglia*), *ombrina*, or small sea bass. If you prefer, have meat, or a good pizza (at night), and one of the many desserts to follow. The Laureana family are charming and attentive, and also provide an ample wine list to complement their native cuisine.

Wine Shop

Via A De Gasperi, 67
TEL 0974 827317
380 7132134
E-MAIL
quintessenza@cilento.it
INTERNET
www.laltrabottiglia.it

Enoteca L'Altra Bottiglia

Vito del Verme is an enthusiastic young man, a huge fan of wine, who sold everything he had to open this speciality shop. 'I started in 1992,' he says, 'and in the past three or four years there's been a big boom in demand for the wines of the Cilento and Campania. I'm very pleased because it means that our area and its products are finally being discovered and appreciated for their real value.' His little shop is packed full of wines, many of them from local producers who do everything themselves, from planting the vines to selling the bottles. 'When I sell a good bottle, it makes me sad,' he laughs. 'It's as if a good friend were going away.'

Wine, Agriturismo

Via Fontana Saracena, 9
Contrada Moio
TEL 0974 821719,
368 7747889
E-MAIL
info@vinimarino.com
INTERNET
www.vinimarino.com

Marino

Raffaele Marino makes Cilento Rosso and Bianco DOC wines exclusively from his own grapes on a large, attractive farm that benefits from being in the best of both worlds: Agropoli is at the beginning of the Cilento hills by the sea, yet just a stone's throw from the plains of Paestum and the straight, easy road to Salerno. The Marinos were the first to bottle their wines under the Cilento DOC that was established in 1992 as they had been making wine in the area since the 1970s. Visit the attractive tasting room, or stay at the farm in the family's *agriturismo*, surrounded by the vineyards and olive groves that are the heart of their production.

Just down the road from Marino is another of the original Cilento wine producers, Botti (Contrada Moio, 3; TEL 0974 822195) who produces authentic style wines from the area's indigenous grape varieties, including an Aglianico aged in oak. Ristorante La Veranda (Via Piave, 38; TEL 0974 822272; CLOSED Mon) offers a mix of sea- and land-foods, in a rustic, family run environment. A nice selection, too, of wines, oils and cheeses.

Ascea

Agriturismo, Olive Oil
Agriturismo Le Favate

Terradura Elea
Contrada Favate
TEL 0974 977310
FAX 0974 977949
OPEN
All year for half-board
E-MAIL e.licusati@favate.it
INTERNET www.favate.it
CARDS All

Elvira Licusati makes wonderful oil, Olea, and has created a beautiful *agriturismo* in the exceptional large stone villa from 1600 that is the focal point of this big farm, surrounded by impressive old olive trees overlooking the sea. There are also oil and flour mills, and a private chapel. The estate produces its own fruits and vegetables, as well as jams, *limoncello* and some wine, products that are on sale in the farm shop. The restaurant is only open to its guests, and serves the traditional dishes of *la cucina povera* that form the basis of the area's best food. A lovely place to stay.

Caggiano

Cheese
Pasquale Lo Russo

Santo Stasio
TEL 0975 393539

Pasquale makes cheese from a herd of sheep (plus a few goats) that are free to eat in the high pastures of Serra San Giacomo all year. He makes a *pecorino* from the mixed milks, as well as *ricotta* and *cacioricotta*.

ALSO:

Four sisters and a brother run the welcoming Ristorante Pizzeria Cocò (Via Principe di Napoli; TEL 0975 393008). Maria Rosaria is a fine cook: one of her specialities is the substantial *pasticcio caggianese*, a thick pie filled with eggs, several cheeses, ham and sausage. Filling but delicious. La Tana del Lupo (Contrada Fontana; TEL 0975 393768), the 'wolf's den', is in the mountains and serves very local, rustic dishes, including some that are medieval in origin.

Camerota, Marina di Camerota

Restaurant, Wine Bar
La Cantina del Marchese

Via del Marchese, 15
Marina di Camerota
TEL 0974 932570
INTERNET www.
lacantinadelmarchese.it
CLOSED Nov and Jan
OPEN All week
CARDS All   PRICE €€

This rustic-style but *simpatica osteria* is a classic: wooden tables with butcher's-paper mats, wooden beams and barrels, terra-cotta plates with a large kitchen at the back filled with local women cooking up a storm. This is a perfectly informal place for a tasty meal of local *salumi*, cheeses, soups and pastas, with traditional meats for those who still have room.

Street in Camerota

ALSO:

Antica Trattoria Valentone (Piazza San Domenico; TEL 0974 932004) is the oldest trattoria in Marina di Camerota, in a small *piazzetta* of the *centro storico*, with a nice leafy terrace to eat out on in summer. It serves the simple, flavourful dishes of the area: seasonal vegetables with capers and olives or *peperoncino*; pastas in soups or with vegetables; the classic *parmigiana di melanzane*, or stewed or grilled meats for *secondi*.

La Casa Rossa (Lentiscosa; TEL 0974 936282). This B&B with land down near the sea is located in a family-run farm making its own oil and growing pulses and vegetables.

Cannalonga

In September, Cannalonga hosts a fair that has medieval origins; here the special food is *la capra bollita* – stewed goat.

Restaurant

Agri-Locanda La Diga

Maddaloni, 9
TEL 0974 3272
CLOSED Tues
PRICE €–€€

Raffaele Tangredi's family trattoria is open all year; it has become a favourite with local workers and tourists alike. I admire the pasta Raffaele's mother makes by hand: her *fusilli* are not twisted, but rolled flat, about six inches long, and are made from two types of flour – of soft and hard wheats. They are not at all gummy or heavy, and are best served with a hearty sauce of tomato and cheese. The menu changes daily, depending on what's in season. I love southern Italy's bitter greens, so I was happy with a dish of broccoli leaves and sprouts with fiery *peperoncino*, but there are simple meats too.

Red hot peperoncini, drying in the shade

Casal Velino

Speciality Foods Shop

La Dispensa di Teodora

Via Lista, 5
Marina di Casal Velino
TEL 329 3175487,
333 2231817

A shop of all the local specialities that include the fragrant olive oils from the Cilento hills in which even *caprini* cheeses can be stored. There are also preserved vegetables such as tender little artichoke hearts and herbed sun-dried tomatoes. Those with a sweet tooth will also find pastries, and the honey that is made from the *corbezzolo* (the 'strawberry tree') whose intensely scented white flowers produce the bitter honey that goes so well with cheeses. (The *corbezzolo* is one of the rare trees that flowers as it bears fruit – the lemon is another.)

A sprig of corbezzolo

Caselle in Pittari

Restaurant

Zi' Filomena

Viale Roma, 11
TEL 0974 988024
CLOSED Mon except in
summer; Nov
CARDS All
PRICE €€

This is an authentic family-run restaurant, with the charming women of the family – Grazia with Giuseppina and Angelina – carrying on the tradition of hearty, *saporiti* dishes that are so characteristic of this part of Campania. The restaurant has recently restructured the larger dining room on the main floor, while retaining the cosier room downstairs next to the kitchen. If you order the house *antipasti*, you may not have room for anything else: they're an infinite succession of delicious dishes of cheeses, *salumi* and vegetables in baked, sautéed and preserved forms… then the pastas, hand-made with hearty sauces of meat or tomatoes, or in thick satisfying soups with beans or potatoes or chickpeas. Local meats are simply grilled, to save room for desserts: home-baked cakes and pastries, like the *caunzuncieddi* filled with chocolate and ricotta.

Castellabate

Wine

Luigi Maffini

Cenito San Marco
TEL 0974 966345
338 3495193
E-MAIL
maffini@costacilento.it

Luigi Maffini, along with Bruno De Conciliis (see p. 299), has become the symbol of the younger generation's approach to modern winemaking in the very particular, age-old area that is the Cilento. 'A little wine has always been made in certain parts of the Cilento,' he explains as we look out from his terrace over his flat Fiano vineyards to the sea, a stone's throw away. 'In the 17th century, the Bourbons made wines here for the courts of Napoli and Spain. But overall, it's an area without much wine

Luigi Maffini opens a bottle at San Marco

history – and that's a shame, because it has all the right ingredients for becoming an important wine-producing zone. The problem is that nowadays it's almost impossible for young people to get started here: only olive oil is being encouraged by the EU or the Region, whereas the territory is better suited to vines than olive trees.' In order to set up a new winery, both land and planting rights have to be bought – but the planting rights are strictly controlled within each region, and are practically unobtainable. On top of that are the costs of building a cellar. 'The total comes to a prohibitive amount,' he continues. 'I think the Region should give financial aid to launch this territory for winemaking, because otherwise it will die out with the few of us who are currently doing it here, and that would be a pity.' Maffini is determined to expand, however hard it is, and has invested in 25 hectares of land between Giungano and Ogliastro that he will gradually plant to vines if and when he can buy the rights.

Certainly this generation of winemakers – Maffini is in his late thirties, De Conciliis is a few years older – have proved that high-level wines can be made in the hot, dry conditions of this hilly area. Maffini works with the experienced Campanian winemaker, Luigi Moio. 'We use both of our heads to make these wines,' he says, as we taste one of his new wines, Pietraincatenata, which means 'chained stone'. This is of Fiano grapes that are fermented and aged in barriques, giving balanced mineral and floral notes, and all the structure and character of a sun-kissed southern wine. 'I do several harvests of my Fiano,' he explains, 'to give more complexity of acidity and sugars; I even leave some grapes on the vines for a late-harvest picking.' The other new addition to Maffini's Fiano wines (the original wine, Kratos, is one of southern Italy's most characterful and territorial whites) is an unusual *passito*, called 'Passito'. 'Here the method is to pick the Fiano, and then to place it in the sun for about six to eight weeks in airy crates, so that it will develop botrytis.' These semi-dried raisins are then pressed and vinified in wood. The result is a complex, intruiging dessert wine.

Maffini's list also includes two fine reds: the warm, drinkable Kleos, of 50% Aglianico with Sangiovese and Piedirosso, and the super-Campanian Cenito, of 65% Aglianico and Piedirosso. In fruity concentration and territorial personality it's been compared to a New World wine – quite an achievement from such an old-world land.

Agriturismo, Restaurant

Agriturismo Giacaranda

Cenito San Marco
TEL 0974 966130
FAX 0974 966800
E-MAIL
giaca@costacilento.it
INTERNET
www.giacaranda.it
OPEN
All year; restaurant by
prior booking only

Also at Cenito, this *agriturismo* is one of Campania's loveliest. It has a well-tended botanical garden around it, with organic vegetable patches and fruit and olive trees. This is a cultured, personalized environment, with particular attention paid to the details that make the difference. As for the restaurant, the chef worked under Alain Ducasse before coming to create dishes that are both old and new: the traditional Campanian combinations of fish, vegetables and cheeses are here given a modern lightness that makes them all the more flavourful.

Nearby, at Punta Tresino, Mario and Ida Corrado, at the lovely Azienda Agricola San Giovanni (TEL 089 224896), are working nicely with Fiano for both the Fiano Paestum IGT and Tresinus wines, of Fiano fermented and aged in steel.

Celle di Bulgheria

Native Fruits

Arcella Coop

Via Cassolino, 20/b, and
Via Canonica De Luca, 242
Poderia
TEL 0974 987661
E-MAIL arcellacoop@
arcellacoop.com
INTERNET
www.arcellacoop.com

This is a project that I find particularly interesting: the Arcella co-operative is working on saving the bio-diversity of the Cilento by finding, cataloguing, and re-planting fruit trees – in particular, apples, pears and stone fruits – of varieties that are in danger of dying out. So far, they have tracked down over 380 different trees; the planting programme is part of a five-year plan begun in 2002, so it's early days to see the final results, but the sight (and perfume) of over one hundred of the fruits as they were exhibited at the Slow Food convention at Napoli in 2003 was a heart-warming beginning.

Cicerale

Restaurant, Agriturismo, Chickpeas

Viscigline Val Corbella
TEL 0974 834511
335 1410567
E-MAIL
agricorbella@hotmail.com
INTERNET WWW.
agriturismoinitalia.com
OPEN (by reservation only)
every day for lunch and
dinner in July and Aug;
weekends for lunch
during rest of year

Agriturismo Corbella

Visiting Giovanna Voria's restaurant at her *agriturismo*, Corbella, is an unforgettable experience. Just getting there is a trip, as you drive curved roads (clearly signposted) through woods and fields, past tiny stone villages and tangled *macchia mediterranea* to what feels like uncharted country. Down across the final bridge, along a well-tended dirt track for the last stretch, through some big gates, and you're there. A long stone barn has been converted into a personal, enchanting restaurant, filled with the collections and passions of this attractive, dynamic woman. 'I had to fight for all this,' she says as she arranges a basket of Indian-pink *corbezzolo* berries on a table. 'Everyone in and out of my family – including my husband – was against it, but I had such a strong dream of wanting to bring this piece of land, this unspoiled valley back to life that I refused to give up.' Giovanna spent most of her adult life working with her husband in his marble company at Agropoli; now that Corbella is a success, he too is enthusiastic about her accomplishment.

Pomegranate

Everywhere are arrangements of the natural, wild beauty that characterizes this terrain: sprigs of myrtle and olive frame piles of hot-coloured gourds and fruits, bowls of dried chickpeas are topped with their lanky growing stems. The tables are decorated with flowers and leaves.

'One of the things I wanted most here was to grow our native legumes – especially the small but intensely flavoured chickpeas that are woven into Cicerale's history,' she explains as we sit down to her lunch that includes these fine, thin-skinned *ceci*. Giovanna serves them in many ways – stewed and in soups and pastas – they are truly delicious. 'We're inside the Parco Nazionale del Cilento, and I believe we must all contribute to keeping its humble but rich culinary traditions alive.' She has found a local couple to tend the gardens when she is too busy cooking for her guests. In addition to her set meals using organic produce, which are perfect for a long leisurely lunch, Giovanna also has six comfortable rooms to let for people wanting peace and quiet in a rural, beautiful setting.

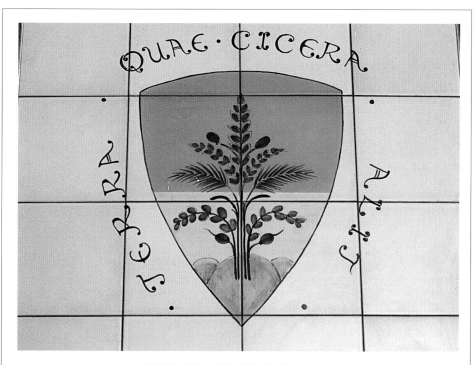

QUAE · CICERA

TERRA

ALIT

Cicerale's coat of arms

CICERALE AND ITS CECI

Giuseppe Mollo is an expert on the town of Cicerale's history, and on its connection to *ceci* – chickpeas. 'There are accounts of *ceci* at Cicerale as early as the 1700s – there are even period maps with *ceci* drawn on them – as the terrain here is well suited to them,' he says, 'but their origins are much much earlier. Indeed, our town's coat of arms is from the year 1000, and it too has chickpea stalks on it. This area was a cereal-producing zone in the 19th century, and we know that *legumi* of all types were used as currency for barter from the Middle Ages until quite recently.'

According to Mollo, the name Cicerale comes from *ceci*. 'Cicero talked of them, describing the area from Vallo to Paestum as *una terra di ceci* – though not specifically Cicerale.' The chickpeas all but disappeared after the 19th-century emigrations, when many people sold land to buy tickets to leave the area. Now the *comune* gives the seeds for free to forty or fifty people each year to encourage replanting. In the meantime, supplies of the precious peas are scarce, but worth seeking out for their fine, nutty flavour and tender skins.

LA MOZZARELLA NELLA MORTELLA

Mountain landscape in the Cilento

Large areas of the Cilento that have not been cultivated or built on are covered with thick native scrub – *la macchia mediterranea*. Of the many indigenous plants that make up this rich collection – including cistus, rosemary and *corbezzolo* – is the myrtle bush: *il mirto* or *la mortella*, as it is known locally. The myrtle has small, stiff and pointed leaves that don't easily wither or drop. These bright green, aromatic stems are favourites for wrapping small, home-made *mozzarelle* in the hilly regions of the Cilento and other parts of southern Italy. This mountain mozzarella, of raw cow's milk, is unlike buffalo mozzarella, being much more compact and drier. It is made domestically, on a small scale, formed into flat patties, and bundled into a handful of the *mortella* stems. Wrapped with string, it forms a good way to keep the cheese fresh for market. Eat this mozzarella alone as an *antipasto* to best savour its subtle fragrance.

La mozzarella nella mortella – or *muzzarella co' a murtedda*, as it is known in dialect – is one of Slow Food's protected foods in Campania, and a *Presidio* has been set up to safeguard its production cycle. For more information, call 0974 719911 or consult www.slowfood.com.

Hand-made mozzarellas arranged with myrtle branches, ready for serving

Felitto

This village is famous for its *fusilli*, water-and-flour pasta hand-rolled around thin wires or reeds like little corkscrews – it even hosts a *sagra* for them in August. During the rest of the year, the best place to taste them is in people's homes, but since that is not easy to organize – although most women, if asked, would be happy to host any food lover really interested in tasting them – you can eat them topped with hearty wild-boar sauce at Agriturismo Difesa del Principe (Via Difesa Principe; TEL 0828 944836) if you book ahead. Nearby, at Torre, Roberto Schiavo's farm produces good extra virgin olive oil (TEL 0828 945048).

Futani

Agriturismo, Restaurant

Castinatelli
TEL/FAX 0974 953207
OPEN Lunch and dinner
PRICE for meals €–€€

La Locanda del Sorvo
Pietro and Giovanna Fatigatti produce goat's cheeses, jams of *corbezzolo* and figs, and serve wonderful autumn soups of *fagioli* and chestnuts, *lagane* and chickpeas, *castrato di capretto* perfumed with *erbe aromatiche* from their herb garden, *tagliatelle* made from *castagne* flour and served with *porcini* they have gathered. They also have four rooms for their guests to stay in, so there's time to taste them all.

Gioi

The village of Gioi and its surrounds have become well known in recent years for a specific salt-cured pork product – *la soppressata* – that would seem to have been made here for at least one thousand years. Indeed, Slow Food thinks so much of it that they have created a *Presidio* to defend it.

'The fact that this is the only Campanian *salume* to have whole chunks of fat at its centre, surrounded by the chopped pork that we are used to seeing in other forms of *salame*,' says one of Slow Food's representatives, 'confirms the suggestion that this sort of "recipe" travelled with the shepherds of the *transumanza* as early as the Middle Ages, for examples of similarly worked *salumi* exist in the nearby region of Abruzzo.' During the twice-yearly transhumance, huge herds of livestock walked from the summer grazing pastures to the winter, often over vast distances, and a rich culture of preserved foods was developed to feed the nomadic group of people that accompanied them.

'In this small *soppressata*, only the finest cuts of pork are used

– chopped into small pieces – and seasoned with whole black peppercorns and, of course, salt,' adds the butcher. 'The larger pieces of pure white fat in the centre were included to keep the *soppressata* from drying out – but they are also very delicious.' At Gioi everyone, including the mayor Andrea Salati, treasures this gastronomic gem. When sliced, you can recognize it easily by its contour, like a figure of eight, with the white *lardo* at the centre. *La soppressata* is most often made in private homes after the winter butchering of the pig, but you can also find it at: Macelleria Ersilia Barbato (Via Garibaldi; TEL 0974 991292).

Laureana Cilento

Olive oil

Serra Marina

Contrada Archi
TEL 0974 824689
FAX 0974 825922

This *frantoio* makes prize-winning extra virgin olive oil from trees in this beautiful area, on the border between the plain of Paestum and the Cilento hills. It is run with all modern equipment, and the Malandrino's company makes several lines – working their own olives as well as those of their neighbours – from Ogliara, Rotondella, Leccino and Frantoio olives.

Marina di Camerota see Camerota

Montesano Sulla Marcellana

Agriturismo, Cheese

Il Poggio di Valle Lungo

Via Perillo, 22/A
TEL 0975 864003
OPEN All year; restaurant
by prior booking only

This small farm is situated in an absolutely unspoiled rural landscape that seems to have been frozen in time. Cows and sheep graze freely in small fields tended by old women wearing headscarves. The farm buildings, rooms and restaurant are up on a rise that overlooks this bucolic scene. The food is delicious – simple but authentic: I ate my first *parmigiana* here made not with *melanzane* but with the last of the winter's pumpkins, and a series of preserved vegetables from the farm's own kitchen garden. The family also produces cheeses, *caciocavallo* from the cows' milk, and delicate ricotta and *pecorino* from its sheep. The pigs are used for home-cured *prosciutti* and other *salumi*. The few rooms share the magnificent view.

Opposite: Angelo Vinci making baskets of broom, near Le Chiusulelle (p. 291)

Nearby, at Montesano Scalo, Giuseppe Manilia makes some of the Cilento's best cakes and pastries, including a rich *torta* of chocolate and *mandarini* that won a prize at Sapri.

Morigerati

Morigerati is within one of the World Wildlife Fund's protected oases, thanks to its famous grottoes. It is also becoming a Città Slow – a medieval town recognized for its quality foods.

During the first ten days of August, Museo in Festa is a colourful get-together of local artisans and *contadini* at which visitors can buy their products.

Agriturismo
Agriturismo Murikè

Oliveto
TEL 347 1767700
E-MAIL
eugenio.cio@tiscalinet.it
OPEN April–Oct

Eugenio Cioffi owns 24 hectares of land in an unspoiled valley near Morigerati. His project is to surround his new *agriturismo* – it sleeps 25 – with fig and other fruit orchards, and olive groves. The name of a nearby village, Sicilì, means 'land of figs' in Greek, and this has inspired Cioffi in his project: 'I'm planting ten hectares of native white figs,' he says, 'and when they are all in production that will make me one of the largest fig producers in the Cilento.' All of the cultivation is being done organically. The location of this farm is a big triangle of land that goes right down to the Bussento river, 'whose ultra-clean waters will nourish everything that grows here'.

In the centre of Morigerati, Trattoria Pizzeria Rosella (Piazza Umberto, 1; TEL 0974 982091) specializes in good country soups and meats *alla brace* – grilled over wood embers. At La Forcuta (TEL 0974 982201) Rosa Vita makes delicious biscuits.

Novi Velia

This village, near Vallo della Lucania, holds an annual Sagra della Mozzarella nella Mortella in August. For information: Comune; TEL 0974 65031; FAX 0974 65078.

Ogliastro Cilento

White Cilento Figs
Azienda Agricola Santomiele

Via Garibaldi, 161
TEL 0974 833275
347 9614426
E-MAIL
santo@oneonline.it
INTERNET
www.santomiele.it

Antonio Longo is an ambitious young man with a mission: to maintain the production of the high-quality white Cilento figs that were once so popular in the area, and that now have DOP status. 'My grandfather had six hectares of fig and olive trees, but after his death they were uncared for until I started to work them again. Many people have stopped growing figs here,' he

A selection of Santomiele's hand-stuffed figs, including the fig 'capicollo' flavoured with spice and nuts

says, 'as they require a lot of work at harvest time, but I have gathered enough growers to supply my company.'

Longo started Santomiele six years ago, working with local women from his village. He sun-dries the figs on the roof of his house on large flat baskets (see p. 272), then works them in a variety of delicious ways for some really upscale sweetmeats.

'Our Cilento figs are unique: they are very sweet, and more tender and fine-seeded than the coarse Turkish, Greek or Calabrian figs you usually find in the market,' he explains. 'The best come from the *comuni* of Agropoli, Prignano, and Ogliastro.' He has gained a reputation not only for his attractive packaging, but especially for the high standards of his figs and fillings. If you stop into his deliciously perfumed *laboratorio*, you will find ladies stuffing the figs with cinnamon, almonds, lemon zest, walnuts, pistachios and chocolate: all irresistible.

Agriturismo, Restaurant
Agriturismo Le Chiusulelle

Contrada Chiusulelle
Eredita
TEL 0974 833211
338 8787529
E-MAIL info@
agriturismochiusulelle.it
OPEN
All year, but must be
booked ahead

Donatella Lanza and Antonio opened their simple but welcoming *agriturismo* a few years ago in four rooms at the top of a tall country house on a hillside commanding vast views down over the plain of Paestum. Donatella has an artistic eye, and has decorated the dining room with arrangements of dried plants and flowers, as well as baskets (some of which are on sale) made by her uncle of *ginestra* – broom – branches (p. 289). The couple have three young sons, so it's a good place to go with

Buffalo salame

children. The location is ideal for visits to the sea, Paestum or the Cilento.

Donatella also prepares good local dishes, with mixed *antipasti* that include her own preserved vegetables, traditional *salumi* and cheeses, or hot little red peppers with fillings of tuna and capers. After the pasta and main courses, you can also sample her fig creations, rolled and stuffed as the custom demands. All simple but very fresh and flavourful.

Buffalo Meat

Zona Industriale, Difesa
TEL 0974 844019
E-MAIL
info@consorzioalba.com
INTERNET
www.consorzioalba.com

Consorzio ALBA – Allevatori Bufalini Associati

This consortium is one of several groups in Campania now working with buffalo meat, using the many male calves that are born each year and that until recently were brutally discarded as they seemed not to be productive. Buffalo meat is much healthier than other meats, having only 130 calories per 100 grams (to beef's 280); 1.5 grams of fat (to beef's 19); and 35 mg of cholesterol (to beef's and chicken's 80). It is also high in iron.

Encouraged by these findings, and by the good flavour of the young animals' meat for eating fresh or in *salumi*, the consortium has been promoting a large range of buffalo meat products.

Olive oil

TEL 0974 844019
E-MAIL
gerardoantelmo@libero.it

Cilento Produce

Gerardo Antelmo is a food journalist and olive oil producer who has long been a champion of the Cilento's best artisan foods. His company olive mill Cilento Produce is situated in the

Industrial Zone below Ogliastro, and here he works the olives with the top-quality modern AlfaLaval equipment. His oils are on sale in many of the best Campanian food shops.

In Contrada Monaco, Nicola Marrocco runs an *agriturismo*, Monaco (TEL 0974 903042, 347 3661487; INTERNET www.agriturismo.provincia.salerno.it).

Padula

CERTOSA DI SAN LORENZO
Viale Certosa
TEL 0975 77484
INTERNET
www.comune.padula.sa.it
OPEN 9.00–19.30 daily

Padula is the site of one of Italy's most impressive religious monuments, La Certosa di San Lorenzo. This vast Carthusian monastery, or Charterhouse, is second in size only to Grenoble's, Europe's largest. (There are many other Carthusian monasteries in Italy, including at Napoli and on Capri.) The grandiose complex was built over four centuries, beginning in 1306 and ending with the re-designing in the Baroque style. The Carthusians were a very select, wealthy order: many of the monks came from rich families who helped maintain the communities. At Padula there were two types of monk: the lay brothers who kept contacts with the outside world, farmed and ran the day-to-day organization of the monastery, and the monks who lived within the inner part of the complex who took vows of silence and seclusion. These monks lived in separate cell-apartments, each with its own small garden. Here they meditated, prayed, sang, studied, gardened and did some artisanal work. They were segregated even when in the church, as they 'died' to the external world when they entered the community.

The courtyard within the Certosa di Padula

The last monks left La Certosa in 1864, and it was designated a national monument in 1882 (which didn't stop it being used as a prison camp during both World Wars); today the beautifully kept buildings are well worth visiting. Of the many architectural marvels within the Certosa, I was particularly struck by the beauty of an 18th-century cantilevered stone staircase inspired by the great architect Vanvitelli, by the attractive cells with their private gardens, and by the large, Moorish kitchens decorated with majolica tiles. The monks in their seclusion ate no meat, but lived on a diet of vegetables, eggs, bread and cheese served with a glass of wine. In or around 1534, the monks cooked a 1,000-egg *frittata* for Charles V. On August 10th each year the making of this huge omelette is re-enacted in the town in a custom-made giant frying-pan.

ALSO AT PADULA:
Villa Cosilinvm (Corso Garibaldi, Sant'Eligio; TEL 0975 778615; E-MAIL info@villacosilinvm; INTERNET www.villacosilinvm.it) is a recently completed, well-appointed four-star hotel with a restaurant, La Locanda di Ercole, open all year, featuring traditional pastas, game and the Primitivo wines that accompany them so well – after all, Padula was an important stopping place on the old Roman wine road between Lucania and Rome.

Palinuro

King's Hotel (TEL 0974 931324) Felice Merola runs this beautifully positioned hotel, with leafy gardens perched above a private beach and an expansive view of the unspoiled coastline. His brother has an *agriturismo* nearby, Isca delle Donne (TEL 0974 931826) where you can eat good local food in a very relaxed environment. After dinner, stroll down to the town: Bar Egidio sells its best *gelati*.

Pertosa

Via Santa Maria, 29
Pertosa
TEL 0975 397028
E-MAIL
comunedipertosa@tiscali.it
INTERNET
www.comune.pertosa.sa.it

Carciofo Bianco di Pertosa: Artichokes
I first tasted these exceptional artichokes from Pertosa, in the Valle del Basso Tanagro, thanks to Rosa Pepe, who has been instrumental in helping them get the Slow Food Presidium. Her research institute at Pontecagnano (Istituto Sperimentale per l'Orticultura, TEL 089 386211) held an artichoke convention, where more than sixty late-flowering varieties were presented from within Italy and the Mediterranean. They came in all

Pertosa artichokes

shades of purple and dark grey-green; the 'white' artichoke of Pertosa is in fact a pale, grassy green that is quite different from any of the other varieties on display. These artichokes are of a medium size, and very compact and weighty. When you cut into them, the flesh is pale green, sweet to the taste, with much less bitterness than is usual in Mediterranean artichokes. I found them delicious, both raw and cooked. One hundred years ago they were very popular and cultivated in large quantities in this area, but by the 1950s they had almost disappeared. Now more are being grown, and it is hoped that this variety will soon become better known for the real delicacy that it is. You can find them being grown in the *comuni* of Pertosa, Caggiano, Auletta, and Salvitelle.

Pertosa hosts an annual artichoke fair in May, and is also known for its grottoes, with their spectacular crystal formations (for information about the latter: Pro Loco; TEL 0975 23298; INTERNET www.grottedellangelo.sa.it).

Pisciotta and Marina di Pisciotta

Some fishermen had landed, and I proceeded with my friends to view the result of their night's labour… the fish consisted chiefly of anchovy and sardine, called by them alici and sarde. From October to the end of April these fish abound here. I was surprised to find a man, who had been watching their proceedings, step forwards and claim an item of the small sum they had received, as the tax imposed by government. I find that there is a regular guard of these tax-gatherers along the whole coast of Italy for collecting this paltry sum, and for preventing the people from carrying off the smallest quantity of salt water from the sea. Salt is a monopoly in the hands of the government, and produces a considerable revenue each year, which would be annihilated if the people were allowed to take salt water, and by mere exposure to the sun produce crystallised salt… when any infraction of the law is discovered, it is punishable by imprisonment and fine.

Craufurd Tait Ramage

FOR MORE INFORMATION:
Comune di Pisciotta
Via del Convento
TEL 0974 973875
FAX 0974 973035

This handsome hilltop village, with an unspoiled medieval nucleus and 16th-century castle, is famous in the area for the magnificent, centuries-old olive trees that surround it; down at sea level, its alter ego, Marina di Pisciotta – once a notorious smugglers' cove – is known for the delicious anchovies that are fished from its waters – in an unusual way.

In the centre of the village, tucked away in a narrow street, is a perfectly preserved olive-mill (*frantoio*) that dates from the

Marina di Pisciotta

end of the 19th century. Since electric power was not then available, the mill's heavy stone wheels were driven – or pulled – by a mule who was forced around and around in the tiny space. It's a fascinating piece of agricultural history, and those interested in visiting it can do so by contacting Pisciotta's Pro Loco at the *comune*. This mill also attests to the long-standing custom of producing oil in this area. The oil that can be made from its monumental trees – where the only system of gathering the olives was to wait until they were so ripe they dropped to the ground – is unlike the oils made by following today's precepts of hand-picking olives when they are barely ripe enough to change colour. Newly planted olive trees are being trained low with this in mind; meanwhile, the traditional harvest continues, as does the production of its oil, which is delicate, with a ripe-fruit flavour that pleases the Pisciottans, but that seems a bit flat or oxidized for those who prefer the decisive, fresh character of just-ripe olive oils.

In Italian, there are two words for anchovies: *acciughe* and *alici*. At Pisciotta, anchovies have for centuries been fished with a particular type of net, the *menaica*, that is believed to have been used by the ancient Greeks. (When using this system, the boats too are known as *menaica* or *menaide*.)

'This net, which is released into the sea like a vertical barrier though which the fish must swim, requires skill and patience,'

explains Pasquale Cammarano, one of the village's fishermen.
'Its hand-made weave is just the right size to trap big anchovies,
but it allows the smaller ones to escape.' The nets are put out at
night from April to October. The other unusual characteristic of
this net is that it traps the fish by their gills, and when it is carefully hauled in, the fish are picked off, one by one, leaving the
heads behind. 'This has the effect of enabling the fishes' blood
to wash away. And this in turn means that the flesh is much
sweeter in flavour than that of fish whose heads are left on.'

Once back on shore, the fishermen's wives are left to salt the
anchovies with Sicilian sea salt. The salted *alici* are packed into
terracotta urns with little wooden plugs at the bottom. A weight
is placed on top of them, and they are left to cure. The liquid
that forms within the urn, *la colatura* – half salt and half fish
juices – can be drained off after a few weeks and used as a
condiment. Just a few drops of this intensely marine-flavoured
concoction is enough to colour any dish. Slow Food has created
a *Presidio* to maintain the traditions of this rare product (for
more about *la colatura di alici*, see Cetara, pp. 182-83, the only
other fishing village that is famous for making it).

While the *colatura*'s intensity may not be to everyone's taste,
the delicacy of Pisciotta's *alici* is bound to please. The women
(and some men) in the villages are expert at creating delicious
dishes from the fish, alone or in combination with vegetables or
pasta. The best place to buy the salted *alici* is from the village
shops (at Marina di Pisciotta, Bar Fariello, TEL 0974 973752
stocks them), as they are produced in small quantities and hard
to find elsewhere.

The anchovies only thrive in very clean waters; fortunately,
Pisciotta's coast has been declared one of Italy's cleanest. In
cooking, you can use a little of the *colatura* instead of salt.
These associations have been formed to protect and promote the
town's anchovies: Associazione Aliciando per Alici (Via
Provinciale, 25; TEL 0974 973090, 340 3380231; E-MAIL
menaica@virgilio.it), who can arrange for you to accompany the
fishermen by day or night, from March to July; Associazione La
Menaica (Via Chiusa, 14, TEL 0974 973188; FAX 0974 973809;
E-MAIL marinadipisciotta@libero.it); and Piccola Società
Cooperativa Menaide (Via Scirocco, 2, Marina di Pisciotta;
TEL 339 5406060).

Restaurant

Via Passariello, 2
TEL 0974 973188.
OPEN Easter to end Oct

Ristorante Pizzeria Angiolina

This Marina di Pisciotta restaurant is one of the best places to
taste real Pisciotta cooking: marinated anchovies, *alici*, in a

gratin or *tortino*, wonderful combinations of vegetables – fava beans, artichokes, fennel, chard and potatoes – or the classic *parmigiana di melanzane* – all dressed with the local Pisciotta olive oil. The restaurant is right on the sea, with its own garden for eating outside – what could be more attractive?

Close by, up in the hills, Agriturismo Principe Vallescura (Via Marina Campagna, Vallescura; TEL 0974 973087, 348 7745309; INTERNET www.principedivallescura.com) is one of the best in the area. The large farm produces oil, fruits and vegetables, jams, and herbal liqueurs.

Hotel Marulivo (Via Castello; TEL 0974 973792; E-MAIL marulivo@tiscali.it) is situated in a 14th-century convent in the centre of Pisciotta, with panoramic sea views.

Policastro

Restaurant

Via Nazionale, 42
TEL 0974 984186
CLOSED Tues; holidays variable in autumn
CARDS All
PRICE €€€–€€€€

Ristorante Il Ghiottone

Maria Rina cooks wonderfully. Her spacious, luminous restaurant – with tables outside in warm weather – is on the main coastal road to Sapri. I feel an affinity with her cooking, for it has the instinctive rightness about it that women's eyes and hands often bring to their food. What could be prettier than a 'nest' of steamed shrimp on a salad of endive, orange, and *rucola*, dressed with a few drops of balsamic vinegar and scattered with ruby pomegranate seeds? Or more delicious than ravioli stuffed with *gamberi* and spring vegetables, in a sauce of baby clams?

'It's a mission to run a restaurant,' Maria says, as she brings steaming *taglierini* pasta to the table, topped with lobster, artichokes and candied lemon. 'I opened in 1978 and I've been here every day since then, whether there are customers or not.' Maria is flanked in the dining room by her charming daughter, Mara, whose natural grace is visibly appreciated by the loyal clientele. Wines are well-selected from throughout Italy, as the whites from the north are fine accompaniments to this varied, primarily seafood menu. Save room for desserts: Maria finds a balance here too between the freshness of ripe, seasonal fruits and the sensuality of pastry creams and cakes.

Maria Rina's pasta

Prigano Cilento

Wine

Contrada Querce, 1
TEL/FAX 0974 831090
E-MAIL
deconciliis@hotmail.it

De Conciliis

Bruno De Conciliis is one of the most interesting young wine-makers in Campania, not only for his wines, which are of a consistently high level, but also for his ideas: Bruno's question-ing mind, enthusiasm and ability to voyage in uncharted waters are contagious. A natural experimenter, his thoughts – and wines – travel so fast that if you don't see him for a year you feel out of date with his developments.

'The Cilento is an exciting place to be making wine because we have no œnological history here, so everything can be invented,' he says, as we sit in his tasting room, overlooking an expansive grey-green valley of olives and vineyards. 'We must run the risk that our wines may not be loved by everybody: the message of a territory that ends up in a bottle does not necessar-ily have to be that only perfection is good – flaws have charac-ter. That's what I want to communicate. We mustn't forget that wine should be pleasurable.'

De Conciliis wines

De Conciliis was born in Napoli, of parents who did not make wine, but raised chickens for eggs. 'My father bought land in the Cilento to be able to get rid of the chicken manure, so some of our land is incredibly mineral-rich,' he laughs. Bruno studied the dramatic arts at Bologna under Umberto Eco, and probably would not have returned to Campania if it had not been for the 1980 earthquake in Irpinia. 'It happened only thirty kilometres away, and when we heard about it we went mad. Through the work of reconstruction of the small farms and arti-sanal companies we did in the devastated zones, I discovered I had very strong ties to the region, and I've never wanted to leave again.' He pours me a glass of Naima, his ink-intense wine of Aglianico matured in wood that expresses itself as much through its complex tannins as its sun-ripe fruit.

'When I came back, I knew nothing about wine – in fact, I drank beer and Pinot Bianco. In the mid-nineties I told my father I wanted to give winemaking a try and, with my sister Paola and her husband, Giovanni Canu, we adapted a fridge to cool our first vats, and turned the cow stable into a cellar.'

Bruno's cellar now contains all the micro-vinification vats and different barrels that reveal the passions of a true winemaker. He also now collaborates with the oenologist Francesco Saverio Petrilli. 'At harvest time, we taste the grapes from each vine-yard, and based on each batch's personality and character, we decide how to vinify it,' he explains.

*Farmer's stone hut in
old olive grove*

CILENTO OLIVE OIL

The Cilento has long been an area favourable for the growing of olives, as the centuries-old olive trees on the coast
around Pisciotta testify. Modern olive producers insist,
however, that good extra virgin oil can be obtained only
from low trees that can be harvested by hand when man,
not nature, decides the olives are ready to be picked (as
opposed to when they are so ripe they drop from the trees).
As a result, new olive plantations are being kept low, and
picked and milled according to the new philosophy for producing superior oils.

   The Cilento DOP (Denominazione di Origine Protetta)
was granted in 1997, and controls the provenance, method
and quality of the extra virgin oil produced within the
Parco Nazionale. The principal olive varieties (cultivars)
allowed in this DOP are: Pisciottana, Rotondella, Frantoio,
Ogliarola, Salella, Leccino. The DOP decrees that all the
olives must be picked by 31 December, and must be pressed
or milled within 48 hours of being picked.

   The Cilento DOP oil's characteristics are:

*Olive nets are stored in
the trees after the season*

Colour: from green to straw yellow, more or less intense
Smell: medium to light fruitiness
Taste: fruity, with medium or light sensations of bitterness
     and piquancy
Maximum acidity per 100 grams of oil: 0.70 grams

Cilento olives at the end of the season are like ripe berries

Here is a list of some of the best producers in the area, including those who were featured at the Sirena d'Oro Prize 2004, held at Sorrento.

Frantoio D'Alessandro (Ascea; TEL 0974 977450)

L'Antica Spremitura (Caggiano; TEL 0975 393597)

Cilento Produce (Ogliastro Cilento; TEL 0974 833174) see p. 292

Emilio Conti (Vallo della Lucania; TEL 0974 75826) see p. 311

Corbellis (Vallo della Lucania; TEL 0974 4473)

De Conciliis (Prignano; TEL 0974 831090) see p. 299

De Vita (Vallo della Lucania; TEL 0974 72006)

Monacelli (Valle dell' Angelo); TEL 0974 942666) see pp. 310-11

Tiziana Nigro (Cicerale; TEL 0974 834023)

Aniello Notaroberto (Futani; TEL 0974 953472)

Cooperativa Nuovo Cilento (San Mauro Cilento; TEL 0974 903239) winner see p. 304

Olea, Le Favate (Ascea; TEL 0974 977153) see p. 279

Oleificio S.I.PR.IO (Buccino; TEL 0828 957434)

Alfonso Palladino (TEL 0974 904009)

Pappavoi (Ceraso; TEL 0974 953802)

Radano (Stella Cilento; TEL 0974 909003)

Sacchi La Pisciottana (Pisciotta; TEL 0974 976177)

Serra Marina (Laureana Cilento; TEL 0974 832573) see p. 288

Pietro Severini (Casal Velino; TEL 089 467065)

L'Ulivo (Lustra; TEL 0974 833306)

'I spent years tasting as many wines as I could, and little by little, I found that wines that were not completely perfect gave me the biggest emotions – they were *affascinanti* in their expressions of terroirs, grape varieties and the characters of their makers. It's our job as producers to reinterpret form, so we should be able to express this: you can understand someone's inner parts when you drink their wines.' We've moved on to his intensely territorial *spumante* wine of Fiano, called Antece.

'Wine is a means of giving pleasure,' he says, as he sees my reaction. 'It's a very sensual thing to think that somewhere, *il mio vino* is giving pleasure to the people who are drinking it.'

Ricigliano

Raffaele Beato is the director of ERSAC, the Campania Region's Agricultural Development Department. As one would expect, he is a great expert on the rural customs of the countryside, and gave me this wonderful description of the *'turniata' festa* at Ricigliano, a hill town high on the mountains of the border with Basilicata. This village is known for the special hams it produces, seasoned with salt and ground *peperoncino*, and hung to dry in barns within the chestnut woods – so as to 'absorb some of the trees' tannins', they say.

'Like so many other villages in the area,' says Beato, 'Ricigliano suffered dramatically from the 1980 earthquake, losing all but a few of its original houses and, what is worse, losing its identity in the process.'

However, once you are out in the woods, the countryside is as it was before, with huge oak trees still providing the pigs' favourite food. This village lives by raising pigs and sheep of the Laticauda breed. On June 15th, the day celebrating San Vito, the patron saint of the village, thousands of sheep mill around the little church built on the hilltop. The shepherds all gather together to meet, pray to the saint and – in a certain sense – offer up sacrifices. Here's what happens:

'The men and their herds start running at crazy speeds in circles around the church, whose doors are open. They run to the rhythm of the town band, more racket than music, running and praying wordlessly as the surrounding crowd claps its hands in growing excitement. If ever a sheep stops before the open church and ventures in to seek refuge from the sun… its fate is sealed, as tradition has it that whatever sheep enter the church belong to the priest, whose rôle it is to feed the poor.'

Rutino

Wine

Via San Cesareo, 18
TEL 0974 830050
338 3839224

Rotolo

Alfonso Rotolo is the youngest of three generations of small farmers making wine in the Cilento. 'It all started with my grandfather,' says the forty-year-old Alfonso. 'In his day, the white Fiano grape was called Santa Sofia, and was planted on the old training system, the *tendone* (a type of pergola) on a square grid.' At that time, people used mules instead of tractors, and workers with big feet were prized for their grape-crushing abilities. 'My father restructured everything in the 1970s, replanting in the Guyot system with the Cantina Sociale's help. Here again, the wine was sold *sfuso* – unbottled – and incredibly Sangiovese and Barbera were planted here.' (Presumably because that way the must could easily be sold to enrich the wines of Toscana and Piemonte?) 'Luckily my father kept some Aglianico, despite the Cantina's demands. When the Cantina stopped being able to pay its members, I pushed my father to make our own wines. That was in 1980, when I was seventeen.' Alfonso studied agrarian science, and soon was making decisions with his father. They took out all the non-Campanian grape varieties and planted more Aglianico and Fiano. Currently the Rotolos have seven hectares, divided between three areas, at heights of 350 to 500 metres. 'Some of our vineyards are quite steep, and the soil there is very very poor, so it takes six to seven years for the vines to begin giving of their best.'

Rotolo now makes six wines, including the whites Cilento Bianco, of Fiano worked in steel, and Valentina Paestum IGT, of Fiano from a vineyard at 500 metres. Part of the wine is fermented and spends four to six months in wood, when it is blended with Fiano that has seen only steel. The result is a well-structured, complex white that reflects its herbed and sea territory; it has a lot of extract and good ageing potential. Rotolo's best red is Cilento Aglianico Respiro: it spends eighteen months in new barriques and six months in the bottle before being sold. A pure, well-bodied, clean red with nice spiciness and lots of fruit. Like many other concentrated, intense reds, longer cellar ageing will only improve it. Alfonso recommends opening it several hours or a day before drinking it.

San Giovanni a Piro

Two authentic artisan wood and basket makers are to be found in and around this village: Francesco Petrillo (Discesa Fontana) makes wooden sculptures and objects, as well as baskets. Francesco Paladino (Piazza San Gaetano) makes traditional baskets, and basket-covered bottles.

San Mauro Cilento

Restaurant, Olive Oil

Cooperativa Nuovo Cilento

Ortale
TEL/FAX 0974 903243
E-MAIL
info@cilentoverde.com
INTERNET
www.cilentoverde.com
OPEN
Daily June–Oct;
Sat & Sun only Nov–June
CARDS All
PRICE €–€€

This enterprising co-operative has rightly become well known within Campania for its range of high-quality extra virgin olive oils – including some organic – as well as its attractive restaurant. 'We now have 230 members, each with small holdings of olive trees in this hilly area of the Cilento,' says Antonio Marzocco, one of the co-operative's directors. 'During the picking season, our mill is available to them to press their olives; they can choose to sell the oil under their own brand or give it to the co-operative.' The best oil goes into the prize-winning Terre dei Monaci line – the 2003 oil won in the Cilento DOP category at the Sirena d'Oro prize at Sorrento. The mill, of the modern, continuous cycle type, is situated under the restaurant, so it's easy to visit at any time of the year; if you go in the autumn, you can watch and taste the oil being made.

Upstairs, the large, luminous restaurant has lovely views of the countryside, and serves appropriately rustic (and organic) food. 'Our dishes are just the simple *cucina* of this *terra*,' says the jovial cook, Carmella Baglivi, who is a member of the co-operative. 'We offer the dishes we learned from our mothers and grandmothers, that are based on the fresh produce of these hills.' The repertoire includes mixed *antipasti*, of local mozzarella packed in stiff myrtle branches – *nella mortella*; *salumi*; crushed green olives; salted anchovies wrapped in bread dough and fried. To follow: thick, warming soups of legumes – peas, *cicerchie*, chickpeas, lentils and *fagioli* – cooked whole and served drizzled with the aromatic oil. Or hand-made pasta dishes sauced with wild field greens, vegetables or beans – even a baked potato offers a great way to savour the fruity oil. This is hearty, authentic country cooking, not to be missed.

A pretty 18th-century *agriturismo* in the country with sea views, decorated by the lady of the house, Casa Antica di Tonina Ferro (Casal Sottano; TEL 0974 903046, 089 756404; OPEN May–Oct) offers five rooms for guests who will be delighted with their hostess's cooking – she's a great expert.

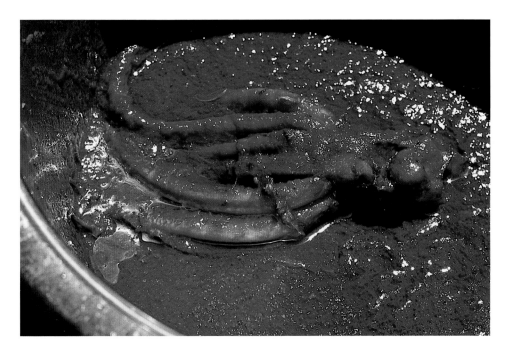

Octopus stewed in tomato

San Mauro La Bruca

Agriturismo
Agriturismo Prisco

Contrada Valle degli Elci
TEL 0974 974153
E-MAIL
info@mieledelcilento.com

A lovely, family-run organic farm specializing in honeys of various types, as well as organic olive oil. The stone house, with its tower for star-gazing, offers seven rooms and a restaurant for guests that focuses on traditional dishes.

Santa Maria di Castellabate

Hotel, Restaurant
Palazzo Belmonte

Santa Maria di
Castellabate
TEL 0974 960211
FAX 0974 961150
E-MAIL
belmonte@costacilento.it
INTERNET
www.palazzobelmonte.it

Palazzo Belmonte is unique: it reminds me more of a castle than a *palazzo* – this immense, perfectly preserved summer house by the sea belonging to the Principe Angelo Belmonte. Surrounded by a large private park, it has its own beach, yet is close by the lovely little port of Santa Maria di Castellabate. Inside the 18th-century *palazzo* are rooms decorated with antique furniture; at the bottom of the garden are suites with private entrances and sea-views.

The *Principe*, as he is called by visitors and staff alike, speaks the perfect English of a country gentleman. It has not always been an easy proposition to keep the *palazzo* going – indeed, the *principe* fought for decades to save the landmark house and its historic garden from unscrupulous developers. Happily, he succeeded, and it is a lovely place to stay. You can eat in the beach restaurant even if you are not a guest at the hotel.

ALSO:
La Taverna del Pescatore (Via Lamia; TEL 0974 968293; CLOSED Mon except in summer, holidays in winter; CARDS all; PRICE €€€) is the best place locally for seafood cookery.

Sapri

Bread

Via Mazzini, 88
TEL 0973 391639

Forneria Clotilde Zicca

This little bakery, with its traditional *forno a legna* – wood-burning oven – has become famous for a unique type of bread: *u pane ri pescatori*, 'the fishermen's bread'. 'These large rolls are made only here, along the coast of southern Campania,' explains Marco Congiusti, 'using our highly flavoured local ingredients: capers and crushed olives, *grano duro* and salted anchovies. Enriched with extra virgin olive oil, the bread makes a substantial meal – the kind needed by fishermen on their travels – as it stays moist and soft much longer than traditional types of bread.' The young man, a fourth-generation baker, has relaunched the family business with this and other delicious breads.

Restaurant

Corso Garibaldi
(prima traversa)
TEL 0973 603033
CLOSED Weds
PRICE €€

Ristorante Pizzeria Lucifero

Genesio Torre is an affable figure in his chef's whites, and his restaurant, on the main seafront road through Sapri, is a friendly place for an informal dinner of pizza or pasta or fish. Like the other restaurateurs of the area, Torre works with seafood that is locally caught, and the menu reflects this – there are also plenty of good wines to choose from.

Restaurant

Corso Umberto, 1
TEL 0973 603362
PRICE €€

Ristorante Pizzeria Da Sofia

Sofia Mendola is as modest as her food is good: an earthy, hard-working woman who has spent a lifetime in the kitchen and continues to offer the flavourful dishes of the cultures of the local *pescatori* and *contadini* – fishermen and peasants. With her husband, Salvatore, she runs a pleasant little trattoria just off the sea front in the town centre, where you can always get a great plate of pasta, fresh seasonal vegetables, or her specialities, including *baccalà*. On Thursdays, Sofia cooks the local traditional dishes that are now becoming so hard to find outside private homes.

Opposite: The bay of Sapri seen from the north

Coffee House, Wine Bar, Gelati

Enzo Crivella: La Chocolathera

Corso Italia, 54
TEL 0973 604305
333 9848418

Enzo Crivella is an indefatigable battler – for the dignity of his *territorio*, for the best artisan foods and their producers, for the right to bathe in an unpolluted sea... He's long been a key member of Slow Food and has helped put this southern Cilento community where it belongs: high on the list of Campania's most beautiful areas. 'We're a long way down the coast from Napoli,' he says, as we look out across the beautiful bay of Sapri to Basilicata and Calabria in the distance. 'If we don't stand up for ourselves, no one else will.'

In his elegant Chocolathera – which would be as comfortable in Paris or London as on the seafront of this tiny town – he's assembled more than a few of his favourite things: sixty types of tea, great coffee, chocolates from some of the finest artisans (including Paul de Bondt from Pisa, Italy's most talented *cioccolatiere*, as anyone who has read my Tuscan book will remember), cigars, top rums and *passiti*, wines by the glass or bottle, Baldino's cider (see pp. 419-21). To accompany the drinks are cakes and croissants, tarts and *tortini* hand-made for him by the ladies of Sapri, the home cooks who normally keep their best recipes close to their hearts.

There are a few tables, a comfortable banquette, an antique marble-top counter for displaying all these enticing treats.

In summer, Enzo and his sister, Mariella, also run a kiosk across the street for their delicious home-made *gelati*, with tables spread out around it in the park. At night you can sit out under the romantically lit trees and taste the ice-creams, all made from fresh fruits and good quality ingredients. My favourite is the soft, goat's-milk *gelato* sweetened with *miele di corbezzolo* – the bitter honey of the 'strawberry tree' that grows wild in the south's *macchia mediterranea*. The kiosk is open daily till late from April to October.

Pizza

Pizzeria Filippo's

Piazza Plebiscito
TEL 360 357295

'The secret of a great pizza is that the dough must rise for at least six hours, be shaped for three minutes, baked in a very hot oven for one to two minutes, and then brought to the table within two minutes more,' says Filippo, Sapri's best-loved *pizzaiolo*. In his small but wildly popular pizzeria, with its improbable tartan tablecloths, you'll find all the area's swells, watching as Filippo twirls and whirls his pizzas, and then eating them with delight. Join them.

Scario

TEL 0974 986 751
INTERNET
www.slow-dreams.com

Janie McFadyen (an American who has settled in the Cilento) and Lucia Pepice have created Slow Dreams, an agency that specializes in organizing romantic weddings in the area of Sapri and Maratea, in Basilicata.

Stio

FOR MORE INFORMATION:
Claudio D'Ambrosio
TEL 348 823 38 86
E-MAIL
info@dietacilentana.com
INTERNET
www.dietacilentana.com

Each summer, in mid-August, *Ciccimmaretati* or La Sagra dei Piatti Poveri is dedicated to the dishes of the Cilento's 'poorest' *cucina*. It's a colourful *festa*, with stands preparing and selling these wonderful local mountain foods, including: *ciccimmaretati* (a soup of pulses and grains that was traditionally made on the 1st of May to bring luck for the new season); *foglie e patane cù lu vicci* (beet greens and potatoes cooked with garlic, oil and *peperoncino*, accompanied by *il vicci*, a baked ring of bread dough pasta); *groano a lu furno* (baked wheat); *mulegname 'mbuttunate* (stuffed aubergines); *cavatielli* (hand-made pasta).

Teggiano

In mid-August (usually 12, 13 and 14) this town holds the fabulous medieval Sagra della Principessa Costanza (daughter of the Duke of Urbino). It is one of the region's best historic pageants, with foods to match.

Torchiara

Bed & Breakfast
Casa Albini

Via Vittorio Emanuele, 5
Fontana Vecchia di
Copersito Cilento
TEL/FAX 0974 831392
340 5548789
E-MAIL
casa.albini@virgilio.it
INTERNET
www.casaalbini.it

This lovely B&B, in a country *palazzo* of the 18th century with views of the valley and the sea – on a clear day you can see Capri – is part of the new association of historic houses in Campania that has brought together interesting properties for guests to stay in. This country house was built with its own chapel and olive press. It has four rooms available.

Gelati
Bar Di Matteo

OPEN 6:30 to midnight

Don't miss this simple bar's freshly made *gelati* and *granite* of fresh Mediterranean fruits: prickly pear, fig, mulberry, *sorba* – the little wild apples that grow here and there in the scrub – walnut, chestnut and almond… that are best savoured on the terrace overlooking the Copersito valley.

Torraca

Agriturismo, Restaurant, Olive Oil

San Martino
(just above Sapri)
TEL/FAX 0973 603331
OPEN Houses all year;
restaurant summer only

Tenuta San Martino

This lovely *agriturismo* is situated in a perfect spot: just a few kilometres from the beach, in the midst of fifteen hectares of natural country and olive groves, with views of the bay of Sapri and the sea. Guests can stay in seven apartments in little stone houses around the property that Fulvio Manzione has restored with care; the main house holds a small restaurant that is open from spring to fall, with a lovely terrace to eat on when it's warm. It's a great place for children, as the organic farm has sheep, horses, chickens and rabbits.

Pietro Bruno (Via Vittorio Veneto, 78; TEL 0973 398107) produces fine *cacioricotta* from his herd of magnificent black goats of the Capra Cilentana Nera breed.

Torre Orsaia at Giardinello

Honey

Via Santa Caterina, 3
Torre Orsaia
TEL 0974 985426
329 1925064

Rosa Lisanti Miele delle Colline Torresi

'I move some of my beehives around to follow the flowering seasons,' says the charming Rosa Lisanti, 'but I don't consider myself a completely "nomadic" beekeeper, as most of my hives are permanently placed.' Rosa has been making honey for twenty years, concentrating on the exceptional assortment of wild flowers that this uncontaminated part of the Cilento offers. 'The flowers here grow in very dry, hot conditions, and this makes the honeys richer in flavour and more nutritious than other honey,' she explains. Rosa is a convinced organic producer, and uses no chemical products on her bees or hives.

Cilento wild flowers

I love her honey: the Mille Fiori – thousand flowers – has exceptional intensity and complexity, with aromatic perfumes of dried figs, chestnut flowers, wild herbs and fruit trees. It's not too sweet, either. Other 'flavours' include *erica* (heather) and *corbezzolo* (the 'strawberry tree'). Rosa also sells pure propolis.

Valle dell'Angelo

Olive Oil

Valloni
TEL 0974 942666
347 9924525
E-MAIL
info@aziendamonacelli.it

Monacelli

Situated in the northern-central part of the Cilento, in the hills above the Calore river, this oil-producing farm is run by Giovanni and Silvio Pipolo. Giovanni is an oil expert, head of

the tasting panel of the OLEUM association. For the Biancolilla,
Frantoio and Rotondella olives grown on their fourteen hectares
of land, the Pipolo family prefer the Sinolea machines that
certainly have produced some of the best oils throughout Italy
that I have tasted. The Pipolos also produce a characterful
organic extra virgin oil, Nativo.

Vallo della Lucania

This is one of the most important towns in the Cilento; among
other events, it hosts a jazz festival in summer.

Olive Oil

Via Nazionale Massa, 11
Massa di Vallo della
Lucania
TEL 0974 75826
333 2267684
E-MAIL
oleificiocontiemilio
@tiscali.it

Oleificio Emilio Conti

Emilio Conti is one of Italy's true olive oil experts. Over the
years, I have visited many olive mills, but I've rarely met such a
well-informed (and generous with his knowledge) *frantoiano* as
Emilio. In oil-pressing season, his mill is alive with the comings
and goings of *api* – the three-wheeled 'bees' favoured by the
contadini – laden with their precious cargo of olives. They know
that Emilio will tailor each batch to their requirements, giving
advice as needed.

'Around here, people prefer delicate oils to the stronger, more
piccante oils of Toscana or Umbria,' he says as he sniffs and
tastes a sample from some newly pressed olives. 'But we like to
keep as many of the *profumi* as possible. When you pick the
olives nice and early, the oils stay very fluid.' He works the
olives at the low temperature of 24°C or less, and favours
modern Alfa-Laval machinery, with a mill that uses cutting discs
instead of the traditional stones. 'The stone mill makes the paste
very hot, and this can cause the olives to oxidize, which ruins
them,' he explains. 'The old-fashioned castle-press also over-
heats the oil. On the other hand, if you go any lower than 23°C,
the oil becomes *margarinoso* because the margarines that are in
the oil need to be melted so they remain but don't thicken.'

Conti works for himself, selling his selection of oils made
from his own and bought olives, and for others. After spending
a few hours watching him working and tasting the olives and
their oils, I could well understand why one of his clients regular-
ly drives 400 kilometres to 'have Emilio take care of' his oil.

If you're looking for a good wine shop at Vallo della Lucania
selling the best local wines, try Vineria Lo Spechio (Piazza
Valenzani, 57; TEL 0974 75636).

Freshly made ricotta is sold still warm

Velia

Cheese

Caseificio Chirico

Contrada Stampella
Ascea Marina
TEL 0974 971584
OPEN daily 8.00–14.00,
16.00–20.00
INTERNET
caseificiochirico@yahoo.it

Silvia Chirico, with her father Benedetto, makes and sells cheeses using the milk of their cows and buffalo. In their attractive stone shop (on the main road between Vallo Scalo and Ascea Marina or Castelvelino Scalo, near Velia) you'll find a great assortment: ricotta, mozzarella, *ricotta salata*, as well as smoked cheeses and the speciality of the area, *mozzarella nella mortella* – preserved in fresh aromatic myrtle stems. For more on this cheese, see p. 286. The shop also sells a selection of buffalo meat *salumi*, for the family belong to the Consorzio Alba (see p. 292).

Don't miss summer concerts and dance perfomances in the archaeological zones (Scavi di Velia, Novi Velia; TEL 0974 65031).

Villammare

Restaurant

Corso Italia, 77
TEL 338 5617963

Taverna Portosalvo

This tiny restaurant – just six tables indoors, with a few more outside in summer – is sandwiched into a slip of a street facing the sea. On the walls, photos of motorbikers alternate with portraits of Isadora Duncan. The atmosphere is very relaxed – just right for a sea-side dinner. You couldn't ask for a more fish-dominated menu: 'When there's bad weather and no local catch, I close,' declares owner Gerardo Menza.

The seafood he does have is displayed in a big refrigerated table, glisteningly fresh from the sea, to pick as you fancy. In October these local specialties include *antipasti* of *ciccinielli*, miniscule whitebait fried into little cushions of sea-essence. Baby octopus are good too, very tender stewed lightly with *pomodorini*, tomatoes that seem sugar-sweet. *Calamari* are served steaming hot, with chunks of potatoes perfumed by wild fennel seeds – *finocchietto* – that taste like anise or caraway. They go well with Bruno De Conciliis's white Donnaluna of Fiano grapes, made nearby at Prignano Cilento (see p. 299).

Pastas are delicious here too, with a small selection each day based on whatever the fishermen have brought in. Bream is stuffed into yellow-pasta *raviolini di dentice*, and sauced with late-harvest tomatoes; *pasta allo scoglio* is a savoury mix of mussels, shrimp and clams, served over *candele* – long durum wheat pasta made at Gragnano (see p. 189).

If you have room, have a grilled or poached fish with tomatoes – *all'acqua pazza*, or just move on to a refreshing lemon sorbet to round off the meal.

Alessandro Cocorullo runs an organic farm, Donna Giulia at Vibbonati, where he also makes extra virgin olive oil. He's now opening a hotel at Villammare: Hotel Le Piane (Santa Maria Le Piane; TEL 339 7448044, 348 9007128; INTERNET www.hotellepiane.it), 150 metres from the sea, immersed in a grove of olive trees. The restaurant will serve local food cooked with his organic produce.

Bottarga: home salted and pressed roe

Chapter 8

Avellino and Irpinia
Beyond the earthquakes to native grapes and mountain foods

FOR TOURIST INFORMATION:
Ente Provinciale per il
Turismo (EPT) Avellino
Via Due Principati, 32A,
83100 Avellino
TEL 0825 74731
E-MAIL
info@eptavellino.it
INTERNET
www.eptavellino.it

The province of Avellino – otherwise known as Irpinia – is, to me, one of Campania's most fascinating areas. Its natural beauty is dominated by the forested Apennine mountains and the lower rolling hills around its river valleys – indeed, it's always been known as *la verde Irpinia* – the green Irpinia. It's hard to remain indifferent to a huge region that, over the centuries, has been repeatedly devastated by earthquakes and that, time and again, has had to start over. In 1980, the massive earthquake whose epicentre was near Sant'Angelo dei Lombardi lasted for 'one interminable minute': its destructive power, to a rural zone where the houses were often built simply of stone, was absolute. *Il terremoto* was felt throughout Campania and beyond, but claimed 3,000 lives and left 45,000 people homeless in Irpinia. The Irpinian villages that fared the best tended to be medieval *borghi* built onto solid rock, where the earth did not open or shift as much. In some places, the tragedy was compounded when the reconstruction work didn't take into consideration that it would be better to rebuild half-destroyed houses rather than tear them down, so many village centres were lost. The result is all too visible: new houses, when they were finally built, sprung up every which way, with little or no concern for æsthetics. Villages were patched together without the detailing and personal touches that make for character and harmony. It is only when one visits the villages that were either less affected, or have been rebuilt more carefully (like Nusco), that one gets a feeling for how lovely Irpinia must once have been. If Irpinia knew something of a golden age in the 16th and 17th centuries, when illuminated thinkers like Carlo Gesualdo (see pp. 343-47) brought art and music to some of its *feudi*, this faded gradually over the next 200 years.

*Opposite: Street in
Nusco before Christmas*

Irpinian winter harvest

That's one aspect. The interesting thing is that this unsung rural hinterland, with its post-volcanic soils, sloping river valleys and forest-covered mountains, now turns out to be holding some of southern Italy's trump cards. From the œno-gastronomical point of view, Irpinia has few peers in modern Italy. Only two other provinces – Cuneo in Piemonte, and Siena in Toscana – can boast of producing three DOCG wines within its territory. If, until twenty years ago, Mastroberardino was the only quality winemaker's name most people could come up with in Irpinia – or Campania, for that matter – there are now dozens of producers who are busy rewriting the region's winemaking history. And they are doing it with native grape varieties that seem at their happiest here: Greco, Fiano, Coda di Volpe, Aglianico (various clones), Piedirosso Avellinese, Janese... The Irpinian wine revolution is only just beginning – fifteen to twenty years in winemaking terms is very little, and the potential is enormous.

As far as food is concerned, here too Irpinia is experiencing an active rebirth as young chefs open restaurants featuring authentic country cooking and its re-interpretations. They have their pick of excellent, flavourful ingredients: unusual olive oils, handmade cheeses, seasonal vegetables. Unlike their parents' generation, they are well informed about what's going on in the food world – theirs is an educated *cucina povera*. Most of all, they believe in the identity, flavours and character of the rural world they have grown up in. Within an hour's drive of where I have lived for the last eighteen months, in central Irpinia, I can think of at least twelve restaurants of this kind that I enjoy eating in, where the new goes hand-in-hand with the old. And yet the area is still practically unknown to foreign tourism. This is an exciting moment in Irpinia for those with the vision to imagine how it used to be, and to see what it's now becoming.

EATING AND DRINKING
Cheeses

Irpinia is rich in pastureland, so it's not surprising that it produces good to excellent cheeses from sheep and cows, though sadly many smaller holdings have abandoned the practice of keeping little herds for family use. Unfortunately the traditional *transumanza* – in which the shepherds moved their herds up to summer pastures and down to winter, sometimes over very long distances – has been largely abandoned, but is still carried out on a small scale in the province. The seasons still have their impact on country life, and the spring and early summer are times in which local cheeses are rich in complexity from the wide range of plants the free-grazing animals can choose from.

Of the *pecorini*, the Carmasciano is to be sought out – if you can find the genuine article. So little of it is made that unless you come to Irpinia it's unlikely you'll be tasting the real thing, no matter what your local cheese-seller says. (For more information, see Rocca San Felice, p. 374). Another particularly good sheep's milk cheese is the Pecorino Bagnolese, from Bagnoli (p. 335).

Cow's-milk cheeses include *caciocavallo*, *scamorza*, *ricotta fresca* and *ricotta salata*. *Caciocavallo* is at its best when made from the milk of the indigenous southern-Italian cow, the Podolico. Once used for working the fields as much as for its milk production, this breed is the classic example of a cow that gives small amounts of excellent milk – as opposed to industry's ideal of the cow that gives vast amounts of milk (which, by definition, must be of low quality). The pale-coloured Podolico cows are lean, as agile as goats, and able to stand high heat and drought better than any other breed. Roberto Rubino, (see p. 224) at his research institute in Potenza, ANFOSC (INTERNET www.anfosc.com) has studied these cows and their milk extensively, and has played a key role in relaunching their *caciocavallo* cheeses as some of the Italy's finest.

Caciocavallo is a large, stretched-curd (*pasta filata*) cheese, and is best when made from raw cow's milk. The unpasteurized milk is heated to 40°C; kid's rennet is added; the curds are broken up to pea-size. The whey is re-heated to 50°C, and added back into the curds to help draw out the cheese's fat. The whey is drained off again. After two hours, the amalgamated curds

Smoked provole

are sliced into strips and placed in a large vat. Boiling water is poured over them, and the cheese and water stirred vigorously with a wooden instrument called *la menatura* until the cheese begins to form long, elastic strands. The cheese is formed into balls weighing upwards of 2.5 kilos, which are tied off by a string and immersed in cold water overnight to help set the traditional pear shape. After being salted for about three days, they are hung up in pairs '*a cavallo*' – as if balanced over the withers of a horse. *Caciocavallo* can be aged for over two years, but is normally eaten after four to twelve months. The raw-milk Podolico cheeses obtained from animals out at pasture are often quite yellow inside, due to the high levels of beta-carotene and riboflavin in the grasses the cows prefer. The texture is compact, and can be dotted with small air-bubble 'eyes' that are usually the indication of the lack of pasteurization.

Ricotta is produced from the 're-cooked' whey (of any type of milk). As the whey reaches scalding point, small granules or *grumi*, of fat and proteins remaining in the whey clump together and float to the top of the pan. They are scooped out and pressed into small baskets or perforated plastic moulds. Ricotta made this way is by definition a low-fat product. It is best eaten very fresh; in the south of Italy it is also often salted, *la ricotta salata*, to be grated over pasta or other dishes.

Ricotta being made

Scamorza is like a small version of the *caciocavallo*. It is sold plain or smoked – *affumicata*.

Chestnuts

Montella chestnuts

Chestnuts (or, *ghiande di giove*, Jove's acorns) have been considered a precious resource in the hills around Montella for at least 2,500 years. The chestnut tree was prized for its wood and fruit – fresh, dried and ground. The flour is nutritious and keeps well – for years, if necessary; it was useful for sustaining besieged cities and for surviving cold winters when other foods were scarce. In the Irpinian mountains, the chestnut woods provided work for generations of people, and were an integral part of the medieval forest economy that included the harvesting of wild mushrooms, berries and oregano. In those days, the woods were tended 'just like gardens'. Today large areas of the woods are still kept free of undergrowth with twice-yearly bonfires between the trees for disposing of weeds and leaves. Unfortunately, many of the stone houses used to smoke the chestnuts were destroyed in the 1980 earthquake, so modern technology has taken over. However, it is still possible to find chestnut trees aged well over a hundred years. For more on the Castagna di Montella IGP, see pp. 360-61.

Hazelnuts and *Torrone*

Avellino's hazelnuts (*nocciole*) are some of Europe's oldest, as many ancient Latin texts – from Cato to Virgil and Pliny – can attest. In the Middle Ages, Campania's hazelnuts were among the most prized in Italy for their sweet, fresh-tasting pale flesh, and ability to take to toasting. They were exported all over the world: in the 17th century, special hazelnut-measuring offices were created. Hazelnuts are nutritious, and offer distinctive flavours in desserts and sweetmeats.

N'drite: hazelnuts threaded onto strings

Avellino produces more *nocciole* than any other province in Italy. Much of the area around the city of Avellino is planted to hazelnut groves. You'll spot them easily, neat rows of bushy plants about two to three metres high that have been pruned to keep them regular. In summer, before the hazelnuts are ripe enough to start dropping, the ground beneath the bushes is raked perfectly clean so that it's easier to gather the nuts when they fall. Once cracked open, the sweet fruits are usually toasted before being used by bakeries and confectionery producers. During autumn *feste* around Avellino, *n'drite*– hazelnuts strung on strings – are sold to the delight of all and sundry.

Torrone – or nougat – has become one of Avellino's favourite sweets – and one of its most important agricultural industries. Many artisan *torronifici* can still be found in the province, especially at Dentecane and Ospedaletto (see pp. 341 and 371). To make *torrone*, egg whites are beaten slowly with sugar syrup and/or honey in a double boiler for at least three hours, depending on how hard the *torrone* is to be. Toasted nuts and other flavourings are folded in later. The mixture is formed into slabs in wooden moulds, before being sliced like bread.

Fresh hazelnuts before being shelled

Olive Oil

Irpinia is an excellent oil-producing province. A number of growers are now using the modern, stainless-steel continuous-cycle machinery that guarantees cleaner, less oxidized oils, so the quality is improving.

Ravece is Irpinia's native olive variety. Its oil is a clear golden yellow with green highlights, its nose intense and complex with rich, well-expressed fruit and vegetal notes of green tomato and grass. On the palate it is restrained and harmonious with hints of white fruits, and green notes of mint and cardoon. In the finish it is long, balanced and decisive, with a characteristic bitter pepperiness that makes it go so well with foods – from raw vegetables to pastas, to thick rustic soups. As is always the case with fruity extra virgin olive oils, you don't need much to add a wonderful dimension to dishes.

Ravece olives at the end of the season

It is hoped that, by mid-2005, the new DOP will have been approved: Irpinia–Colline dell'Ufita.

Wines

The province of Avellino is rich in native grape varieties, and now has three prestigious DOCGs: Taurasi (which was granted the 'Garantita' status in 1993), Fiano di Avellino and Greco di Tufo (which both became DOCGs with the 2003 harvest).

Taurasi is made of Aglianico grapes (85–100%). Aglianico (or 'father of the vine') is thought to have been introduced by the Greeks; its long-ageing wine is one of Italy's great reds. Here is the late Luigi Veronelli's description of it: 'It excites me, with its ruby-red colour to which age has brought a bright amber ring, its warm perfume that is underscored by notes of morello cherries and violets and subtle hints of spices, its complete and authoritative flavour, its sustained nerve, and its full and elegant body.'

The white Fiano vine does best in the post-volcanic hills of Avellino. And it too is an ancient grape. Nicolas Belfrage, in his erudite and diverting book on Italian grape varieties and their wines, *Brunello to Zibibbo*, spends a paragraph on the various theories behind this grape's name. One thing is certain – Pliny, in *Naturalis Historia*, writes: 'the bees gave Fiano its name, because of their desire [for it]'. It was also appreciated in the 12th century, but by the end of the 19th century had all but fallen out of use. In 1945, Antonio Mastroberardino (see pp. 325-26) rescued it from heading towards what Belfrage elsewhere calls 'that great vineyard in the sky' by making a wine from the few remaining Fiano plants that were dotted around in his vineyards.

Greco is also an indigenous Campanian variety that is grown successfully in various parts of the region. It is probably another vine that was brought to Italy by the Greeks over 3,500 years ago, and was lauded by Virgil and Cato. Greco di Tufo is grown in eight *comuni* of Avellino province.

Wine labels from Avellino and Irpinia

BED AND BREAKFAST

A group of B&Bs in historic villas and farms has been assembled by the GAL Partenio Valle Caudina. They are divided between the provinces of Benevento and Avellino. The Avellino B&Bs are in the westernmost part of the province, north-west of Avellino (see p. 403 for the others). They include:

Il Ciliegio (Via Pirozzelle, Cervinara)
Situated in the centre of a village that is set in the Partenio hills, a regional park. There is a lovely garden in this architect-owned house.

Partenio (Via G. Di Grezia, Ospedaletto d'Alpinolo)
Along the road to the Sanctuary of Montevergine, this house has a panoramic view of the valley and Partenio hills. It is located in an important *piazza* in the town famous for its *torrone* – made too by the house's owners.

Da Emma (Via Partenio, 74, Pietrastornina)
This B&B is located in the medieval centre of the town that is now being restructured. It is next to the owner's family-run *trattoria*.

Nina (Via S. Caterina, San Martino Valle Caudina)
Two rooms in a beautiful villa surrounded by a large private park with swimming pool, near the town's *centro storico*. There is lovely countryside all around.

Brecce (Via Brecce, San Martino Valle Caudina)
This villa was once a hunting lodge for the noble Pignatelli della Leonessa family, who still run the farm that surrounds it, complete with vineyards. A perfect place for food lovers interested in how local foods are grown.

Rosa (Via Supierti, San Martino Valle Caudina)
An old stone farmhouse set in a small rural village.

For information, **GAL**: TEL 0824 841802
E-MAIL info@galpartenio.it or segreteria@galpartenio.it

OTHER PLACES TO STAY

The Province of Avellino has recently issued a detailed map of many of the agriturismi in Irpinia, as well as museums and sites to visit. More information from: Ufficio Agricoltura, Avellino; TEL 0825 790417; INTERNET www.agriturist.it, www.turismoverde.it; and see p. 329.

Sheep graze freely in Irpinia

BENEVENTO

Montecalvo Irpino

Ariano Irpino

Zungoli

Melito Irpino

Scampitella

Flumeri

Grottaminarda

Vallesaccarda

Lacedonia

San Martino

Venticano

Mirabella

Castel Baronia

Montefusco

Pietradefusi

Fontanarosa

Valle Caudina

S. Paolina

Carife

Bisaccia

Tufo

Torre le N.

Frigento

Altavilla I.

Montemiletto

Taurasi

Aquilonia

S. Angelo a Scala

Gesualdo

Luogosano

Summonte

Pratola S.

Lapio

Paternopoli

Rocca San Felice

Montefredane

Montefalcione

Villamaina

Guardia dei Lombardi

Ospedaletto d'A.

Manocalzati

Torella dei Lombardi

Mercogliano

Chiusano

Castelfranci

S. Angelo dei Lombardi

AVELLINO

Salza I.

Montemarano

Cairano

Calitri

Atripalda

Sorbo Serpico

Ponteromito

Monteforte I.

S. Stefano di

Nusco

Lioni

Forino

Serino

Sole

Volturara I.

Teora

S. Andrea di Conza

Montella

Solofra

Bagnoli Irpino

Caposele

Laceno

Montoro Inferiore

Laceno

Calabritto

Acerno

Vietri

Altavilla Irpina

Wine

Via Orni, 6
TEL 0825 991696
E-MAIL
petilia@interfree.it

Petilia

Roberto and Teresa Bruno started making wines in 1999, so it's still early days for this brother-and-sister team to show what they are capable of. However, the wines are already full of promise: white Fiano di Avellino has a nice floral nose, and a long finish, while the Greco di Tufo offers warm, mellow fruit and good body. Hard pruning in the vineyards is producing its effects.

Aquilonia

Mushrooms, Preserved Vegetables

Contrada Pesco di Rago
TEL 0827 83033

Gaspare De Vito

De Vito has recently started cultivating the mushrooms known here as *cardoncelli* (*Pleurotus eryngii*), which he sells fresh or preserved under extra virgin olive oil; other '*sott'olio*' products include the bitter wild asparagus that are found in the fields in late spring. During the season, he also is a good source of wild mushrooms and truffles.

Nearby, his friend and partner Gerardo Marzullo (Via Malepasso, 6; TEL 0827 83033) is bottling prize-winning honey, especially the *miele di fiori* that the bees produce from the large mixture of wild flowers of spring and summer: it's quite sweet, and nicely balanced.

Ariano Irpino

Restaurant

Viale dei Tigli, 7
TEL 0825 872571
CLOSED Tues; last 2
weeks of Sept
CARDS All
PRICE €€

La Pignata

Ariano is perched on the top of a high hill in north-eastern Irpinia; La Pignata is located on a steep street near the town centre. Guglielmo Ventre and his family run a classic-style trattoria in their large stone and wood dining room with a fireplace for grilling and baking, and a pizza oven – there's even a wild boar's head mounted on the wall. 'My mother's cooking inspired all this: I loved to cook, and the restaurant grew from that,' he says as he serves us a dish of winter mixed *antipasti* that includes lightly spiced beef jowl '*a soppressata*', *melanzane* fritters and Hirpus wild asparagus under oil (see p. 337). *Pancotto arianese* follows: day-old bread cooked with cabbage and chicory, oil and water, and covered with paper-thin slices of *lardo* – these are unusual, authentic dishes. 'We've always believed in keeping Ariano's *cucina contadina* alive,' continues

Ceramics of Bourbon design are still being made by the Russo family

Guglielmo. This large, jovial, generous man is a mainstay of his town's community, playing an active part not only in Ariano but in charity work in developing countries. I love his mountain *primi*: rustic soups of white Quarantini beans, chestnuts and *orecchiette*, and *paccheri* pasta dressed with broccoli, potatoes, *peperoncino* and anchovy sauce. The menu continues with local meats, cheeses and desserts – and of course wines. So go with a healthy appetite.

Coat of arms above Ariano villa gate

The Russo family are famous at Ariano for their majolica. Now that the father, Peppino Russo – a painter and ceramicist – has retired, his daughter Mariella (TEL 338 8638163) and son are carrying on the work in two shops on the same main street in the centre of the high town of Ariano (Via Mancini, beside the Comune). Not only do they each produce their own modern versions of the traditional Ariano style of pottery, which is quite handsome, but they also share the moulds of a group of 17th-century pieces whose originals are in the Ariano Ceramics Museum. I found these objects very intriguing: each has a dou-ble function or 'secret': the boot is also a hand-warmer, and was used by society women in church; the fish is a bottle; the large cup-vase is a trick for dividing water from wine... a lovely piece of history whose labours haven't been lost.

Cookies

Via Cardito
TEL 0825 891880

Antico Forno Sorelle Belardo

The twin Belardo sisters, minute and thirty-something, have created an elegant shop to display their home-baked cookies and other delicious sweetmeats.

This is a good oil area, with the native Ravece olive taking precedence. These producers are among those waiting for the Irpinia-Colline dell'Ufita DOP to be approved. You can buy oil directly from them:

Coprovoli (Via Vico Lapronia, 8; TEL 0825 824955; E-MAIL coprovoli@libero.it). Duchessa De Piano (Serra La Guardia – Stillo; TEL/FAX 0825 891567). Alfio Lo Conte (Via Brecceto; TEL 0825 876027).

Atripalda

Wine

Via Manfredi, 75/81
TEL 0825 614111
FAX 0825 614231
INTERNET www.mastro.it

Mastroberardino

If, twenty – or fifty – years ago, you had asked for the name of the most important Campanian winery, the answer would have been unanimous: Mastroberardino. This is one of *the* historic winemaking families, not only of Campania, but of Italy, and the repercussions of its ground-breaking work are only now beginning to be fully appreciated.

'Our family has been making wine since 1734 – in fact, I represent the tenth generation,' says Piero Mastroberardino who, with his elderly father Antonio, runs the winery from its headquarters in Atripalda. 'In 1890 we were already exporting our wine to the US, Brazil, Argentina and Canada. But there were also difficulties: we have survived wars and all sorts of natural catastrophes, including the phylloxera scourge of the 1930s, the 1944 Vesuvio eruption, and the earthquake of 1980.' The family villa was badly damaged in that earthquake and was ordered torn down, despite their willingness to restructure it.

In 1984 the Mastroberardinos made news again when Antonio and his brother, Walter, had a falling out that led to the property – vineyards, cellars and brand name – being split between the two. In that division, Antonio kept the cellars in Atripalda and the right to call his wines Mastroberardino, but relinquished the vineyards. Since then, other vineyards have been acquired and rented, resulting in two of the most imposing estates in Irpinia, if not Campania (see pp. 357-59).

Radici Taurasi is Campania's longest-standing great red wine

The Mastroberardinos are to be thanked for having been the first to believe in the autochthonous grape varieties that Campania is unusually rich in – and for having saved them. 'My father always insisted on the unique character of the native grapes – Aglianico, Greco, Fiano, Coda di Volpe, Falanghina, and Olivella,' says Piero, as we walk through antique cellars that survived the earthquake, now decorated with colourful modern murals. 'And this was after the Second World War, when everyone was introducing Trebbiano, Sangiovese, Barbera – even Chardonnay – in Campania. But he was an innovator and he held firm in his belief that these *vitigni* were what made Campania different from Toscana or other winemaking areas. After all, they have been here since the Greeks first brought them to Italy.'

Of course, history has proved him right: Campania's viti-cultural heritage of more than 100 varieties is a priceless resource that will only improve with time, as people worried (and bored) by the standardization of globalization look for original wines that express specific territories and cultures.

Today's Mastroberardino is a large, modernized winery, complete with a lovely shop for direct sales. Antonio and Piero Mastroberardino work in collaboration with their talented young winemaker, Vincenzo Mercurio, on a full portfolio of more than twenty wines – including those made on Vesuvio and at Pompei (see pp. 128-129). The Greco di Tufo appears in several versions, from the lovely, natural 'base' wine worked in steel, to Nova Serra, a more structured Greco fermented and aged in barriques – both with the characteristic vein of bitter-ness in the finale that makes them such good accompaniments to food. Fiano, too, is well represented – indeed, it has been thanks to Mastroberardino's long commitment to this grape that it has recently been recognized with the DOCG. The top Fiano di Avellino Radici is complex, with flowery notes of acacia and honey that merge well with the minerality of this post-volcanic terrain. Of the reds, I have a real affinity with the Taurasi Radici: in early 2004, I was knocked out by a vertical tasting of this great wine of the 2000, 1997 Riserva, 1991, 1980 Riserva and 1968 Riserva vintages. What impressed was the *freschezza*, the pure vivacity of the fruit that emerged from a grape that so often shows itself austere, if not aggressive. Here the tannins were elegant and ripe, especially in the 2000, the 1991, and the amazing 1968, a spectacularly young old wine that easily out-classed some of the more recent vintages – a true pioneer, just like its makers.

Restaurant

Via Pianodardine, 112
TEL 0825 626115
CLOSED Sun; Aug
CARDS All
PRICE €€€

Trattoria Valleverde – Zi' Pasqualina

This is one of the most popular trattorias in Irpinia – and the oldest: Zi' Pasqualina opened it in 1959, and for the next forty years cooked six days a week for the loyal clientele. 'This was a stopping place for many travellers,' explains her grandson Sabino Alvino who, with his parents, has taken over the running of the restaurant, though his now-frail grandmother looks in whenever she feels up to it. 'And they expected to find the classic dishes of the area: soups of *baccalà* cooked with potatoes and *accio* – our powerful celery; lots of vegetables, from *friarielli* to *melanzane*; home-cured *salumi* and raw-milk cheeses; succulent, simply grilled meats... all the foods of the mountains that surround Avellino.' Over the decades, little has changed here: the mood in the dining room, and in the large outdoor pergola-shaded terrace, is relaxed and homey. The rustic foods match the atmosphere – it's still a nice place to come back to.

Pastries and Savoury Baked Goods

Via Manfredi, 86/90
TEL 0825 611453

Dulcis in Furno

I'm hooked on the delicious foods that come out of Chiara Di Maio's ovens: the savoury tarts – like the plaited brioche (*treccia*) with soft peppers in it, or the *casatiello*, the Easter tart with eggs, cheeses, ham and black pepper – are meals in themselves. For breakfast, afternoon tea or desserts, there are cakes and pies of all descriptions, from deep chocolate *torte* to apple pies to ricotta and walnut tarts laced with *nocino*, the walnut liqueur. This enterprising young woman has based her output on style and quality, and the whole area is now addicted.

The bakery is across the street from Mastroberardino's headquarters, but there is also a small bar in central Avellino that sells the products (see p. 332). Cakes and other goods can be made to order.

If you find yourself in Atripalda looking for a colander or candlestick, table or tablecloth, plate or planter, fridge or folding chair, picnic box or tool chest... the Capaldo family's big store, Progress (Via Appia; TEL 0825 61521, 615268) has them all – and lots more. It's a native Irpinian Ikea.

Avellino

The city of Avellino is unusual in Irpinia for being located in a valley instead of up on a hill. The Longobards moved it from the site of its original Roman settlement (Veneria Abellinatium) and called it Abellinum. For centuries it held a strategic position as everyone going into Irpinia and across the Apennines to Puglia or Basilicata had to pass through this prosperous commercial city. From 1581 to 1806, under the rule of the Caracciolo, Avellino experienced a period of economic fortune and culture. During the *Risorgimento*, Avellino played an important role in forcing the Bourbon king Ferdinando I to recognize the constitution. When a train line linking Napoli with Puglia was re-routed through Benevento in 1913, Avellino lost its strategic power, and its cultural decline began. Avellino was badly bombed in 1943 and that, plus the 1980 earthquake, destroyed much of the city's historic centre: along with the buildings went some of its character and local colour. 'This is where the lovely market-place was, at the centre of the town's life each morning,' says Erminia Di Meo (see p. 375), as she points to a now-nondescript group of late 20th-century cement buildings – with no market is sight. 'All the *contadini* from the surrounding villages used to bring their produce here, as well as the "spontaneous" foods they foraged for in woods and fields. And there were wonderful bakeries around it where we children got our morning *merenda* while our mothers did the shopping.' Despite this, Avellino is now a lively provincial city, and the seat of most of the area's administrative and cultural activities.

Restaurant

Antica Trattoria Martella

Via Chiesa Conservatorio, 10
TEL 0825 31117
CLOSED Sun eve, Mon; Aug
CARDS All
PRICE €€€

I've always liked this friendly trattoria, strategically positioned in the heart of Avellino, in a narrow street that still conjures the idea of what the city must have been like before the earthquake. This is a favourite haunt of many of Avellino's bright young things – from wine producers to architects and shop-owners – who use its warm, vaulted rooms like an extended home, dropping in for a plate of pasta, a glass of wine, or an after-dinner card game.

For those of us who long for fresh vegetables to start a meal, Enrico Della Bruna's colourful *antipasto* table is a dream: he presents all the seasonal best: grilled *melanzane* with extra virgin oil and *peperoncino*, wilted chard, artichokes raw in salads, roasted or used to stuff *frittata* or tarts, *parmigiana* of *melanzane* or other vegetables, roasted pumpkin, peppers every which

Opposite: Carmasciano pecorino; the authentic cheeses are hard to come by

way... Help yourself to them, along with small bite-size *mozzarella bocconcini*, or hand-cured ham or *salame*. You can taste the aromatic black truffles from Bagnoli (see p. 333) when they're in season, as toppings for pasta or on their own in a 'salad' – an intriguing, acquired taste some people find overwhelming when served alone but the locals adore. This is also a good place for comforting peasant soups, of beans or winter greens, or pastas home-made with just water and flour, as is the custom of this part of the country. *Secondi* include steak cooked with herbs, meatballs in tomato sauce, sautéed and stewed rabbit, or slices of grilled smoked cheese, *provola affumicata* – classic dishes of *la cucina povera*. Helpful service, a fine wine list and great desserts complete this ever-popular restaurant.

Restaurant

La Maschera – Locanda d'Autore

Rampa San Modestino, 1
TEL 0825 37603
CLOSED Sun eve, Mon
CARDS All
PRICE €€€

Each time I go back to La Maschera something new has been done to make it even better: an overgrown courtyard is refurbished and becomes a romantic summer dining area; a walled-in space is opened and turned into part of the wine cellar; an outdoor grotto is now an ageing room for cheeses... plus there is the recently renovated kitchen, and the smoking room for after-dinner cigars that is like a personal *salotto* for Luigi Oliviero – La Maschera's talented *padrone*. As it is, the setting is unusual: the restaurant occupies the high vaulted rooms beneath one of Avellino's biggest 18th-century churches, onto which Oliviero has superimposed a layer of modernism – lamps, artworks and table settings – so there's plenty of atmosphere and architectural detailing to make it interesting.

The food, too, has recently found a clearer voice. The chef, Lino Scarallo's emphasis is on the authentic flavours of local dishes, with a new twist: the traditional *baccalà in casseruola* here becomes a martini-glassful of warm, soft *baccalà* mousse (very pure in taste, not over-salt) topped with an emulsion of *piénnolo* tomatoes, with accents of capers and olive. A simple soup of delicate white Tondini beans – half whole, half puréed – is complemented by just-wilted *scarola* with a touch of fruity olive oil, and crunchy toasts of bread from De Nardo's *pane di Picarelli* (see opposite). A *passata* of the rustic legume, *cicerchie*, is here lifted to bisque status by four firm *gamberi*, floral olive oil and a squeeze of lime. I love the '*carbonara d'élite*', organic spaghetti from Baronia with soft fava beans, subtle leeks and crisped *pancetta* that is balanced and satisfying. Main courses are more land-based than sea, though fresh fish is available at times. Save room for the cheese course, as Oliviero has selected and ages local Caciocavallo Podolico, *pecorino* from Filiano in Lucania, and goat *caciotta*. Desserts go from the *divertente* de-structured *pastiera* to classic deep chocolate-filled pastry cups. La Maschera is also a fine place to taste the pick of the local wines: Luigi Oliviero has assembled a knowledgeable collection, and doesn't over-charge for them.

The restaurant is 100 metres from the Duomo, under the church of San Francesco Saverio, better known as Santa Rita.

At Valle, in a north-western area of the city, the young chef Francesco Spagnuolo has recently opened his own little restaurant, Il Patriota (Via De Napoli, 71; TEL 0825 33991; CLOSED Sun eve and Wed). Francesco trained for some years with Antonio Pisaniello (see p. 367) and left to start this relaxed, family-run dining room serving local dishes revisited – in the style of his *maestro*.

Pizza

Via Cannaviello, 79
TEL 0825 21579

Pizzeria De Pascale

The best kind of street food – pizza to go – baked in large pans that just seem to keep coming, topped with thinly sliced potatoes and rosemary, raw *rucola*, fresh artichokes, cherry tomatoes and mozzarella... the list is endless. There are also variations on the theme, closed into savoury tarts or made in individual *pizzette*. A large friendly woman serves while the diminutive *pizzaiolo* pops in every few minutes from the back room with a new trayful. Perfect for a snack or dinner to take away.

Bread

Via Scrofeta, 11
TEL 0825 22457

Panificio De Nardo

You'll need a car to find this bakery as it's on an external road around Avellino, but it's worth getting there as the sourdough bread is made in an oven that burns on hazelnut shells – a perfect way to use the waste from the hundreds of acres of hazelnut groves that surround Avellino. The delicious yeasty wheaty bread – or *pezzo lungo* as the large loaf is called – lasts for a week. In the meantime, feast on a doughnut: these *bomboloni* are best plain (*vuoto*) but if you like Nutella, they also come filled with that hazelnut-chocolate confection.

ALSO AT AVELLINO
If you're hungry but don't want to cook, Il Salumiere (Via Terminio, 4) is not a sausage shop but a *gastronomia* selling savoury tarts, home-made *pasta al forno* and *lasagne*, hand-formed pastas, and many other delicious ready-cooked dishes to

take out or take home. In the same street, Granese di Montella is a tiny shop selling cheeses from the nearby town, as well as home-made pizzas and pasta to cook at home from Immediata Pasta (see p. 362). For those with a hankering for hot (*piccante*) food, the Avellino chapter of the Academia del Peperoncino is run by Adriana Bilotta (TEL 339 3122555) and organizes '*forte*' dinners.

For a great mid-morning snack or for dessert, Dulcis in Furno has a coffee bar in Avellino (Corso Europa, 2D; TEL 0825 783370) that sells slices of this small bakery's excellent cakes, or whole pies and cakes to take away (see p. 327). Pasticceria Enoteca De Pascale (Via De Concilii, 24/B; TEL 0825 781654; INTERNET www.depascale.it) was one of the historic pastry shop–bars in Avellino. Sadly the old building was destroyed in 1980, but the *babàs* are still classics here. Aliberti (Via Serafino Soldi; CLOSED Tues) is one of the few *pasticcerie* still baking some of the pastries that were traditional to Avellino: *la bombarda* is a baroque creation – as red as a cardinal's hat – soaked in Alchermès and enriched with ricotta, chocolate and nuts. On the same nostalgic note, Bar Tiffany (Via Mancini; CLOSED Mon) makes *mattonelle* – like an ice-cream sandwich – and *baci*, chocolate-covered *gelati* that may now be a bit outmoded but are still very appealing. Fitag – Torrone Garofalo, a century-old *torrone* manufacturer from Dentecane (see p. 341), has an outlet in Avellino: Corso Europa, 16; TEL 0825 780430.

Wine

Via M. del Gaizo, 12–14
TEL 0825 74951

Evoè Wine Bar
Sommelier Luigi Landolfo has two spaces: a stylish modern shop for buying wine, and the Vineria that is open at the weekends and holds special events, theme evenings, and wine tastings.

Wine

Via Filande, 6
TEL 0825 627252
FAX 0825 627224
E-MAIL
info@vinimarianna.it
INTERNET
www.vinimarianna.it

Dedicato a Marianna
Ciriaco Coscia is a rather dapper man, who has created an attractive cellar and tasting room for his wines. He's been fascinated by native grape varieties since his first vintage, in 1995, and has made an interesting single-variety wine from the red Sciascinoso – the grape that does so well on Vesuvio's volcanic soils with Piedirosso in Lacryma Christi – but that is also quite widespread in Irpinia as a blending grape. This wine, classified as an Irpinia IGT, provides a rare opportunity to taste it alone: it's vinified in steel and produces a light, drinkable, *amabile* wine. The estate also makes wines of pure Piedirosso, Aglianico (Taurasi), Falanghina, Fiano, Coda di Volpe, and Greco di Tufo.

Bagnoli Irpino

PRO LOCO AND COMUNE
Via Roma, 19 (Comune)
Via Garibaldi, 39 (Pro Loco)
TEL 0827 62003
INTERNET
www.bagnoli-laceno.it

CHESTNUTS, MUSHROOMS AND BLACK TRUFFLES

The lovely hill village of Bagnoli Irpino, with its medieval nucleus and imposing churches in varying stages of reconstruction, is surrounded by the mountains and woods of the Monti Picentini, and overlooks the long valley of the river Calore. Above it is the winter ski resort of Laceno, one of southern Italy's best known. Situated at 650 metres, Bagnoli's main income until recently derived from the wild foods of the *sottobosco*: mushrooms of many types, chestnuts and, most particularly, truffles. Several types of truffle are found, but the black winter truffle that is common to the area – *Tuber mesentericum Vitt.* – has been given the town's name: *il tartufo nero di Bagnoli*. The Comunità Montana Terminio-Cervialto is currently helping to place this high-quality truffle alongside its more famous northern counterparts. 'For years we have been told that only Alba and Toscana or Umbria were capable of producing great truffles,' says Nicola Di Iorio, the president of the Comunità Montana. 'But this was just propaganda to boost prices and sales of those northern products. The truth is that our hills are full of very aromatic *tartufi* that many truffle-workers from the north take from here and label as northern to make more money and supply demands.'

Prize-winning truffles from Bagnoli

Each year the town hosts a *sagra* on the last weekend of October that celebrates both the chestnut harvest and the beginning of the truffle season. Bagnoli's streets are lined with booths selling all manner of cakes, biscuits and breads of chestnut – don't miss the great *gelato di castagne* from Bar Roma in Piazza Di Capua – as well as hearty pasta and *polenta* dishes cooked by the local women. The town brass band creates a Fellini-esque mood, and adds to the fun.

Chestnut desserts at Bagnoli's bars

You can also buy whole truffles – the biggest are considered real treasures and are auctioned – or sample some of the sauces and oils flavoured with the heady tuber. These truffles grow underground around the root systems of the beech (*faggio*), black pine (*pino nero*) and hornbeam (*càrpino*) trees and are found by specially trained dogs. An average annual harvest for the area is of 15,000 kilos. The species was identified in the mid-19th century and is the source of ongoing study at the local universities. In 1924, a huge truffle weighing 800 grams was sent to the King of Italy, Vittorio Emanuele III who was, understandably, thrilled. The Bagnoli truffles must be allowed to air for a few hours after being taken out of the ground, and are at their best shaved thinly over hot pasta, cheese, meat or other simple dishes, when the aromas and flavour are (pleasantly) dominant.

HOW TO STORE TRUFFLES
When you buy whole truffles, they will usually already have been scrubbed carefully under running water to remove any peat or dirt. There are several ways to store them:

They can be kept for a few days in a jar filled with rice, which absorbs some of the moisture (and flavour). Or, wrapped individually in paper towels and placed in a closed jar, they will keep for two to three weeks in the refrigerator. Another system is to seal them into plastic bags and freeze them at −20°C; they will keep for several months with a loss of only about 10% of their perfumes. Some chefs add salt to this plastic bag, to help maintain all the scent. Truffles can also be kept in oil or butter, for use in recipes.

Bagnoli is also known for its cheeses, of which the Pecorino Bagnolese is currently being considered for DOP or IGP status. Indeed the Pecora Bagnolese is an indigenous variety of sheep – with characteristic black faces and white bodies – that is now also being saved.

Baskets on sale at Bagnoli's festa

Ricotta salata three ways: smoked, plain, and flecked with peperoncino

Also at Bagnoli Irpino

At Lenzi Tartufi (Via Buozzi, 31; TEL 0827 62124, 338 8126677; INTERNET www.lenzitartufi.com) a large range of little jars contains pastes, creams and oils flavoured with truffles from near and far. Ninnoli Lavorazione Artigianale (Piazza L. Di Capua, 7; TEL 347 6845479) is run by the elderly gentleman who makes the smooth wooden carriers that are reminiscent of Shaker boxes with handles (shaped like baskets but without the weave) that have always been used in the woods around Bagnoli for bringing in the chestnuts.

For the traditional cheeses from Bagnoli, of sheep's and/or cow's milk, visit Carmine Nigro (Contrada Rosole; TEL 339 6148347, 339 5048227). From his herd of sheep which are pastured in the area, Nigro produces a choice of cheeses, from the sweet, light fresh ricotta to its aged and salted cousin (great for grating over pasta), to the *primo sale*, to cheeses that have been aged for longer. He also has a stand at the twice-weekly market at Avellino by the Partenio Stadium. Grazia Buccino (Via Carpine, 26; TEL 0827 62349, 347 8705712) makes what she describes as 'the typical cheeses of Laceno', the high plain and lake above Bagnoli, such as *ricotta salata* and *pecorini*.

Just outside Bagnoli, at Caliendo, Cappetta Castagne (TEL 0827 602003, 0827 62147; INTERNET www.geos.it/castagne_cappetta) still works the chestnuts artisanally, selling them fresh, dried, ground into flour or as softened, ready-to-eat *castagne del prete*.

At Laceno there are several unassuming trattorias serving rustic local dishes, including Lo Spiedo (Via Serroncelli, 25; TEL 0827 68073).

Bisaccia

Restaurant

Via Mancini, 195
TEL 0827 89278
CLOSED Mon
CARDS No
PRICE €€

Grillo d'Oro

This trattoria has been going since 1872, offering the simple foods and dishes of *la cucina contadina*. It's the place to try rustic soups made with sun-dried vegetables like *zucchine* and *zucca*, hand-made pastas, and game in season. Sadly, 'Louis' Arminio, whose presence defined il Grillo d'Oro for so many years, is no longer with us but his children are carrying on in his place, in order not to let the peasant culture whose flavours are celebrated here die out.

Nearby is a family-run dairy producing raw-milk, pulled-curd cows' milk cheeses: Giuseppantonio Arminio (Via Cavallerizza, 41; TEL 0827 89504).

Calitri: pigs are still
precious commodities

Bonito

Olive Oil

Terra di Bonito

Viale della Vittoria, 187
TEL 0825 422292

Irpinia is becoming known for its indigenous olive variety,
Ravece, with an oil that shows enormous potential as it is
flavourful without being aggressive, and goes well with fish and
vegetable dishes – sea and land. This small estate has 600 trees,
and is in the process of being certified as organic.

Calitri

This part of Alta Irpinia doesn't appear on most tourist itiner-
aries, but it is quite beautiful. This is the real *interno*, near the
inland borders with Basilicata and Puglia. Here too, the 1980
earthquake had its way, and much of the town is still in an
unfinished state of reconstruction – despite the large sums of
money that were sent for this purpose over twenty years ago.
Those who chose – or had no choice but to – remain have strug-
gled to rebuild their villages and their lives here. I find the town
of Calitri fascinating, built as it is high on a steep hillside, with
streets running parallel one above the other among the houses,
many of which are quite imposing. They look out over the start
of the soft rolling hills of Basilicata and Puglia that are planted
to grain crops in quite a different type of landscape.

For a simple, home-cooked meal at Calitri, try Ristorante Il
Sambuco (Contrada Palude di Pittoli; TEL 0827 38480).

CONSORZIO CERAMICA E
TERRACOTTA DI CALITRI
Contrada Carcatondo
TEL 339 2616889
E-MAIL giovannipolestra
@tiscali.net

Calitri has always been an important centre for ceramics: an attractive museum has been set up in the ruins of the castle, and a number of ceramics workshops remain active: MAC – Maioliche Artistiche Calitrane (Via Campo Sportivo, 40; TEL 0827 30171) is one of the oldest. Others include: Ceramica Antica Calitri (Contrada Marana; TEL 0827 38959), Rosa Cestone (Corso Matteotti; TEL 339 3031250), Grafio (Via Ferrovia; TEL 335 1024523), La Tartaruga (Via Canio Zabatta; TEL 339 5454967), La Giara (SS 399, km 13; TEL 339 2616889), and Teresa De Luca (Contrada Forestella, Rapone [over the border in Potenza]; TEL 0976 96430).

Caposele

Fig trees beneath the hill town of Cairano

This is known as the 'water town': the natural springs that surround Caposele (which means 'head of the Sele river') provide water for the whole of the south of Italy. The grottoes can be visited by contacting the Società Acquedotto Pugliese.

On a gastronomic note, this is also an area known for its pork products, especially *la soppressata*, the premium *salame* that is made from choice lean cuts of pork. Marco Guarino's farm (TEL 0827 58013) both raises the pigs and butchers them, producing a range of excellent *salumi*. If you are interested in *dolci tipici*, Forno Gerardino Vitale (TEL 0827 58488) produces its own version of *amaretti* from local hazelnuts. Raffaele Merola (TEL 0827 58093) grows organic produce: figs, chickpeas, beans and lentils.

Carife

Olive Oil, Organic

Hirpus

Viale A. Moro, 7
and Via Modena, 57
TEL/FAX 0827 95626
TEL 328 3824902
E-MAIL
m.minieri@agora.it

Michele Minieri is the first person I've met who descibes himself as a Samnite – a descendant of the powerful tribe that once ruled this entire area. He has a way of seeing beyond current-day trends to the heart of the matter – and to its historical origins. That's why it's not surprising that he should have named his company Hirpus. 'Hirpus was the name for the sacred wolf worshipped by the Irpinians (a colony of pre-Christian Oscans who fled the Etruscans and settled in Irpinia),' he says. 'After studying philosophy, I travelled a lot but, for me, nowhere else matched up to my native *terra* – I had to come back!' he laughs. 'I also had an intuition about our native oil, made from the Ravece olives that only grow in Irpinia.' This large-fruited indigenous variety was practically unknown and little valued until recently, yet it makes some of Campania's most wonderful, characterful extra virgin olive oils. 'They best express this part of Irpinia, the valley of the Ufita river,' he continues. Another variety, Ogliarola, is '*bello*, perfect for salad – generous,' he says, as he opens his arms wide to show just how much. 'Ravece is more problematic, but more *affascinante*.' Minieri uses the nearby Santoro *frantoio* to stone-grind the olives.

Minieri also produces small quantities of delicious vegetables 'under oil' using organic produce and his best extra virgins. He is an expert on organic olive-growing and oil, and is happy to share his knowledge with others. He's also an activist for the ecological and structural safeguarding of the area – a modern-day Samnite.

Castel Baronia

Bread

Via Valle, 3
TEL 0827 92111

Marisa Di Nita

Marisa's *forno a legna* has been making wholesome breads for over a decade. This area has long been famous for its high-quality grain production, and the Di Nita family selects the best for its slow-rising, natural-yeast breads baked in their traditional wood-burning oven. They last a week and freeze well, so stock up.

Castelfranci

Wine

Contrada Braudiano
TEL 0827 72392
INTERNET
www.collidicastelfranci.com

Colli di Castelfranci

Castelfranci is situated on the Calore river, in an area of Irpinia that is beginning to be recognized as one of the most interesting for winemaking (see also Montemarano). This *azienda* has been formed very recently, but takes advantage of some very old Aglianico vines that belong to the family. White grapes are bought in, and have produced promising results in the fresh, fruity Fianos called Paladino and Pendino, as well as in a Greco di Tufo, Grotte.

Wine

Contrada Valle, 19
TEL 0827 72252

Opposite: Michele Minieri with Ravece olives late in the season

Perillo

He's been called a *garagiste*: Michele Perillo has only been making wine for a few years, but he's found a good vein – his barrique-aged Taurasi has an imposing, modern style that produces good concentration and fruit without losing the liveliness and

distinctive tannic definition that characterizes the best Taurasi. His very limited first vintage was 1999; in 2003, there will be about 10,000 bottles, as Perillo – with his fine consultant Carmine Valentino – only works the grapes from his own four hectares of vineyards. Lots of promise for the future.

Chiusano di San Domenico

Olive Oil

Via Carducci, 15
TEL 0825 985095
E-MAIL azdemarco@tin.it
INTERNET
www.oliodemarco.it

De Marco

The De Marco family have long been known for their olive mill, situated in the gentle hills above Avellino before the landscape changes to the more rugged, mountainous zones of the Irpinian *interno*. Recently the young Luigi De Marco has added a certified organic, or *biologico*, oil to the *fruttato* and *delicato* oils they make from Ravece, Ogliarola and Frantoio olives.

Dentecane (part of Pietradefusi)

In recent years, Dentecane has become one with Pietradefusi, but they were once separate villages. The name Dentecane – or dog's tooth – is associated in Irpinia with *torrone*: the honey-and-nut nougat is produced in myriad ways here and is an ever-popular presence on winter tables and over the Christmas holidays.

Torronificio Vincenzo Di Iorio (Via Roma, 156; TEL 0825 962097) is a family business that has been making more than fifteen types of *torrone* since the 18th century using the well-flavoured honeys of Alta Irpinia (chestnut, borage, acacia) and Avellino's home-grown hazelnuts, the Nocciola Tonda di Avellino. The Garofalo family started their *torronificio*, Fitag-Torrone Garofalo (Via Roma 112–114; TEL 0825 962039), in 1896, working up from the classic *torroni* in white, chocolate, almond and hazelnut-studded varieties to a list that now includes other types of biscuits and sweetmeats too. They also have an outlet in Avellino: Corso Europa, 16; TEL 0825 780430. For three generations the Nardone family (Via Roma 151; TEL 0825 962028) has produced *torrone* in all its forms, from soft to crunchy, almond to hazelnut, coffee to chocolate. Their specialities include hard, chocolate-covered *pannardelli*, and *pannardone* – chocolate-covered nougat stuffed with liqueur-soaked cake.

Opposite: Irpinia's white hazelnuts are sweet and much sought after by confectioners

Flumeri

Olive Oil, Agriturismo

Via Scampata
Serra dei Lupi
TEL 0825 443319
E-MAIL petrilli@3df.it
INTERNET www.petrilli.it

Petrilli

Ciriaco Petrilli's organic farm specializes in making olive oil from its 9,000 olive trees. Flumeri is one of the 'Cities of Oil – Città dell'Olio' (INTERNET www.cittadellolio.it): this is an area where the delicate Ravece olives grow, and Petrilli works them with the excellent Sinolea equipment that extracts the oil without stressing the fruit. To complement this seasonal work, Petrilli and his wife run a lovely *agriturismo* on the farm – with restaurant – and are also producing essential oils from herbs (lavender, chamomile, sage and thyme).

Fontanarosa

This village is known for its stone carving: Irpinia has a long tradition of decorating the façades of its buildings – especially its doors and windows – with this stone work. It also holds a spectacular annual harvest festival in mid-August, the Festa dell' Obelisco di Paglia, when a high straw obelisk is carried through the village on a float. For information: TEL 0825 475003.

Forino

Wine

Via Contrada Rapone, 1
Celzi
TEL 0825 761649
INTERNET
www.fratelliurciuolo.it

Urciuolo

Two young brothers have in recent years taken over the running of this *azienda* – with four hectares of their own and fifteen rented – from their father, a producer of vineyard poles. Working with their highly talented œnologist, Carmine Valentino, they are making crisp, fruity wines from Fiano and Greco, and well-rounded reds from Aglianico.

Frigento

Bread, Pizzeria

Via Pagliara
TEL 0825 440448
CLOSED Mon afternoon

Delizie del Grano

Gianni Pascucci and Luisa Competiello make a range of wonderful breads: of *polenta* flour; *farro* flour; enriched with olives; laced with walnuts and honey... the list is impressive. There are such good pizzas to go that you probably won't make it out of the store without buying another slice; as well as crunchy *freselle* and ring-like *taralli* – a cross between a pretzel and a

Gianni Pascucci's pizzette make great snacks

cracker. The young couple are also making unusual rustic desserts of *cicerchie* flour, eggs and cinnamon, and fragrant *panettone* at Christmas – a lovely little shop.

Gesualdo

The town of Gesualdo is dominated by a compelling, tragic personal story: to see its castle as it is today – half still in ruins after the earthquake, half restored to give an idea of its former beauty – it's hard to believe that it once housed the creative genius of a tormented prince. Carlo Gesualdo, prince of Venosa, (1566–1613) was born into an important Neapolitan family – Carlo's uncle, Carlo Borromeo, was canonized as San Carlo Borromeo – with extensive feudal holdings in Irpinia (including Taurasi and Calitri). The story goes that Carlo Gesualdo was a deeply religious man, and very much in love with his beautiful young wife, Maria d'Avalos. When, after only four years of marriage, he discovered her in bed with another man, the rules of chivalry obliged him to have them both killed. This act changed his life – he was tortured by remorse until his death. He withdrew to the castle at Gesualdo to mourn her, and to protect himself from possible revenge by the two families.

Carlo Gesualdo was enlightened and multi-cultured – a true Renaissance man. He transformed feudal Gesualdo, creating an

innovative system of underground waterways for drinking and irrigation, and building its many churches. He started a printing press, created a theatre within the castle walls, and immersed himself in his greatest passion – music.

Carlo Gesualdo's madrigals for five and six voices, with their innovative, complex harmonies, have been seen as forerunners of the polyphonic music of the 20th century – 300 years ahead of their time. Indeed, it is thanks to the interest of Igor Stravinsky in the 1950s that the cult of Gesualdo – subscribed to by musicians and artists of all kinds – has continued to grow. In 1960 Stravinsky composed *Monumentum pro Gesualdo* based on three of Gesualdo's madrigals, to which George Balanchine set a ballet; in 1995 Werner Herzog made a prize-winning documentary about the composer–prince, and two years later Bernardo Bertolucci began work on a film script of the story. Each summer Gesualdo hosts concerts of music new and old, performed by first-class musicians from around the world.

Via Campo San Leonardo
c/o Circolo PRC
'G Di Vittorio'
OPEN Sat 15.00–17.00,
Sun 11.00–13.00

For more information and guides, contact P.A.R.T. At other times, phone Emilio Savino 338 2553175 or Carmine Cogliano 328 9454826: they are voluntary guides, and extremely knowl-edgeable about the town and its culture.

Restaurant, Agriturismo

Via Freda, 4
TEL 0825 401435
CLOSED Weds

La Pergola Ristorante

Franca De Filippis and Antonio Ferrante have created one of my favourite country restaurants in Campania just a kilometre below the castle of Gesualdo. Franca, who trained as an architect, is the cook, while Antonio runs *la sala*; together they have transformed what was a Circolo ARCI into a large dining room with a shady terrace for summer, with rooms for guests and a swimming pool. A perfect place in which to celebrate the *cucina povera* of Irpinia. 'I always loved the simplicity of the dishes my mother and grandmother cooked,' says Franca. 'They may sometimes seem elementary for their lack of complicated technique, but to me they express the true *sapori* of this territory.' I agree. Franca's soup of Gesualdo celery – *accio*, as it is known in dialect – is unforgettable for its purity of flavour, and she emphasizes this by serving it without trimmings or garnishes – a courageous move in today's clutter-crazy food world. In another winter speciality, pork shank – *stinco di maiale* – is served, trotters and all, with a mixture of wild greens. 'We call these "found" field herbs *sciatìzza*,' she says, 'and they include borage, *scarola* and many other bitter greens

Opposite: Gesualdo and its castle

Esterina Iannuzzi in her vegetable patch

to balance the sweetness of the pork. It speaks of this land in this season – and to think that many people didn't believe Irpinia had a *cucina* of its own.' *Paparotta* is 'polenta of the south' from the 17th century, made without maize but with hard, durum-wheat flour flavoured with onions and pounded red peppers dried on strings – *paparuci sicch' 'nzertati*. I love this warming, red-stained mush, unlike anything else I've eaten. 'A hundred years ago the peasants in Irpinia were still under feudal rule, and they were starving – there was nothing to eat,' says Antonio as he serves a local Taurasi red to accompany the next dish. 'But still they were imaginative with the little they had.' The final *secondo* in Franca's sequence is a triumph: *cosciotto d'agnello cotto nel fieno di Maggio* – leg of lamb baked in May hay. It arrives on a large platter, a heap of steaming, aromatic hay. Buried inside is the tender, slow-cooked lamb, flavoured with the spring flowers of *sulla* and *lupinella*. Now, whenever I see pastures full of wild flowers in May just before they are cut, I think of the inimitable fragrance of that dish.

Salumi, Meat

Macelleria Mario Carrabs

Via Campo San Leonardo
TEL 0825 401624
E-MAIL
mario.carrabs@tiscali.it
INTERNET
www.carlogesualdo.com

Mario Carrabs is a Central-Casting butcher: large of build, red-faced, friendly, and with an expansive personality. I'm grateful to him for having been the first to introduce me to Gesualdo and its culture – gastronomic and otherwise. Indeed, he has long been a promoter of this interesting town and its local foods. In his centrally located butcher's shop, with the help of the lovely Virginia, he sells fresh meats and the *insaccati* he produces – cured pork products: *guanciale, pancetta, pancetta piccante, coppa, capicollo, soppressata, salsicce secche...* a fine list of delicious *salumi*.

Carrabs belongs to a co-operative, Prodotti Campani di Carne, that was founded several years ago to work on the traceability of meats. 'With the worries that have grown in recent years about the safety of food, it's extremely important to know exactly where one's meat comes from,' he says, as he shows me the print-out from his computer detailing the path – from the animal's birth to its butchering – of a side of beef in his cold-store. 'This code number allows me to know everyting – from what the animal ate to who its mother was.' Carrabs is also one of the few butchers in Campania who believes in hanging his meat (*frollatura* in Italian) to increase tenderness – indeed, Italian meat is often very tough as hanging is not often practised as part of the culture. Currently he hangs the meat for about ten days before selling it.

Carrabs butcher shop sign

The shop, which I think of as an homage to Dario Cecchini, the exceptional, extrovert Tuscan butcher at Panzano in Chianti, is like a cosy sitting room – with a sofa and food and wine books – that puts food in its rightful context: a good excuse to be sociable, a way to share knowledge and hospitality.

ALSO AT GESUALDO

Nicola Bianco (Contrada Pettoriello; TEL 339 1362432) grows vegetables in the fields beneath the Castello di Gesualdo. Celery – *il sedano di Gesualdo* – is a speciality here: crisp, bright green and vibrantly flavoured, it is the quintessence of that all-too-often uninspiring vegetable. Pastificio Nonna Lisa (Piazza Vittorio Veneto; TEL 0825 401601) is an artisan pasta-maker producing hand-made pastas from durum wheat and water, including *fusilli, cecatielli, orecchiette* and *pasta alla chitarra*. If you order ahead, they will also make stuffed pastas. Esterina Iannuzzi (Contrada Mariaturo; TEL 0825 403067) grows and sells a range of vegetables and fruits, and also 'courtyard' animals such as rabbits and chickens.

Grottaminarda

Christmas wouldn't be the same without torrone

This is one of Irpinia's top *torrone* towns, with many producers competing to make the best-tasting nougats. I love the elderly Sisina Cataruozzolo's plain nougat with almonds (Via Piave, off Corso Vittorio Emanuele; TEL 0825 441005): it's the real thing, hand-made and exceptional. Franco Cataruozzolo: Azienda Spanbocconi (Via Minichiello 19; TEL 0825 446742, 0825 445527; E-MAIL francocataruozzolo@libero.it) is a relative of Sisina's: he specializes not only in the classic Irpinian nougats, using local honey and hazelnuts, with or without chocolate, but also in fig-filled biscuits and the signature 'spanboccone': liqueur-soaked cake and *torrone* covered in chocolate. Mottola (Via Carpignano,19: TEL 0825 441281) is another small producer whose soft nougat is delicious.

Pastries, Gelati, Tea Room

Pasticceria Ciotola

Via Valle
TEL 0825 441917
CLOSED Tues

Ciro Ciotola is a Neapolitan who moved to Irpinia twenty years ago, bringing with him the big city's rich pastry-making traditions to marry with the Irpinian. His range now includes cakes, *torte, babà* and pastries as well as fresh fruit *gelati* and a variety of *biscotti*. Upstairs, an elegant tea room offers savoury foods to accompany the sweet, especially at *aperitivo* time.

Guardia dei Lombardi

Honey

Via Coste
TEL 0827 41187

Apicoltura Salvatore Rossi
This organic farm makes wonderful honey, and has a shop at
the beginning of the village, on the right if you are coming from
Sant'Angelo.

Cheese and Pastries

Via Sasso, 71
TEL 0827 41313

Rosaria Celetti
Rosaria's farm produces the unlikely combination of cheeses
and pastries: Rosaria makes the cheeses, and her daughters,
Elisa and Lucia Siconolfi, started baking and have set up a small
business. They make all sorts of pastries, including pastry
pillows filled with local chestnut paste, and a delectable little
cake that looks like a snowball, of their mother's ricotta mixed
with lemon juice and sugar, and rolled in coconut – like a
coconut cheesecake without the crust.

Laceno see Bagnoli

Lapio

Wine

Via Arianiello, 47
TEL 0825 982184

Clelia Romano – Colli Di Lapio
I've always admired the Fiano di Avellino made by Clelia
Romano with the help of her children and the œnologist,
Angelo Pizzi. It has a clear, fresh, floral style, with the
recognizable bitter notes of hazelnut that characterize this
grape at its best. 'Fiano originally seems to have come from
Liguria, and arrived in Campania here at Lapio where it found
a natural habitat,' she says, as we tour the new cellar the family
is completing. It's well-organized, as clean as a kitchen, with a
red-brick wall of ageing bottles that gives warmth to the space.
'Like many other growers in these parts, my grandfather sold
his grapes to Mastroberardino. But eventually he rebelled and,
in 1994, the family bottled its first own-label wine.'

The vineyards are some of the best for Fiano, situated high
enough – between 450 and 600 metres – to give the grapes
elegant perfumes. Until recently Clelia was known just for the
Fiano but recently she has launched into a new venture with a
promising Taurasi, Vigna Andrea (of which 4,000 bottles are
currently being made), and a younger Aglianico. 'We're

Traditional vineyard near Sant'Angelo dei Lombardi

completing our range,' she explains. 'By only making a single wine we felt we were missing something.'

Lioni

Lioni was completely destroyed by the 1980 earthquake, so it's hard to talk about traditions here, but the town has created a new story for itself: in the last twenty years it's become the place that the area's young people hang out at the weekends, with a great choice of *localini*, *birrerie* and pubs selling good *panini* – stuffed with *salsiccia* or grilled *scamorza* cheese – and well-selected wines and beers to go with them. There are many, but Bar Birreria Alfonsina (Largo Stazione; TEL 0827 46157) is one of the favourites.

Bread

Piazza della Vittoria
TEL 0827 46250

Panificio San Rocco
This bakery, located within the Parco Regionale, makes good breads, though its oven is, alas, no longer wood-burning.

Luogosano

Wine

Via Carazita, 1
TEL 0827 73564
FAX 0827 78114
E-MAIL
ponte@tenuta-ponte.com
INTERNET
www.tenuta-ponte.com

Tenuta Ponte

This winery is owned by five partners from three families, and its 35 hectares of vineyards are located within the Taurasi DOCG territory. In the past couple of years, the estate (with winemaker Carmine Valentino) has started making wines with a well-defined character, from the fragrant Coda di Volpe to the Merlot-based Cossano, to the traditional style, lively Taurasi that is aged in large barrels that allow the wine's fruit and elegance to express themselves unimpeded.

Manocalzati

D'Antiche Terre–Vega (Contrada Lo Piano, SS 7 Bis; TEL 0825 675689; INTERNET www.danticheterre.it) Located a few minutes' drive up the Ofantina from Atripalda, this estate has 40 hectares of vineyards planted to the local whites – Fiano, Greco and Coda di Volpe – and to Aglianico, for the production of an elegant Taurasi. Panificio Santoro (Via Variante Est; TEL 0825 624776) I love country bread baked in wood-burning ovens: this bakery does it well, and also produces stuffed *panzerotti*, and pizzas.

Melito Irpino

Restaurant

Corso Italia, 8
TEL 0825 472010
CLOSED Weds;
part of Sept
CARDS All
PRICE €€–€€€

Antica Trattoria Di Pietro

No gastronomic tour of Irpinia would be complete without a visit to this lively family trattoria. Crescenzo Di Pietro, with his parents and wife, were the first to feature and treasure the authentic country recipes from Irpinia – decades before the recent wave of interest in them. The ingredients, too have been selected with care: the tastiest *salumi*, cheeses, wines and other artisan products are the mainstay of this seasonally varied menu.

One of their classic dishes that I've never seen anywhere else is *cicatielli con pomodoro e pulieio* – hand-made pasta with a sauce of tomatoes and local wild mint. I also loved the Di Pietro's *minestra maritata*, the meal-in-one soup of field greens (*scarola*, *cicoria*, cabbage and *bietole*) enriched with different cuts of pork and served with yellow *polenta*. Desserts, too are delicious, so save room – if you can.

Mercogliano

FOR TOURIST
INFORMATION
Via Loreto
TEL 0825 787173
0825 787191

More than one million pilgrims visit the high Sanctuary of Montevergine each year, a clear indicator of how important this religious shrine is – particularly for the Neapolitans. Founded in the 12th century by Saint Guglielmo of Vercelli, Montevergine was a favourite of the kings of Sicily. The road up to the Basilica and monastery offers breathtaking views of the country-side around and above Avellino and, on a clear day, you can see as far as Napoli and its gulf. Closer to Avellino, at Mercogliano, are what were the monks' winter quarters and infirmary, in the handsome Palazzo di Loreto, begun in 1734 after the earth-quake of 1730 destroyed the previous buildings. Here the monks supplemented their incomes by making liqueurs using the wild herbs from the woods and fields. Until recently it housed a true pharmacy, whose beautiful wood-panelled rooms still exist, lined with original majolica vases made by Giustiniani at Cerreto Sannita (see p. 411). Loreto also contains a very impor-tant library, with rare parchment manuscripts and over 200,000 books including forty codices from the 12th to the 14th centuries. The large inner courtyard with its baroque gardens hosts concerts on summer evenings in July.

The courtyard of Palazzo di Loreto where the sum-mer concerts are held

Some liqueurs – the most famous of which is Anthemis – and local honeys are still sold from the small shop.

The Palazzo di Loreto is open only by appointment.

Torrone

Contrada Campo Marino
TEL 0825 691194
0825 691821

DG3 Dolciaria

Despite its less-than-romantic name, DG3 makes fine artisan *torrone* – or nougat – just above Mercogliano. The workshop is behind the roomy shop, and can be visited by appointment: it uses old confectioners' machinery to turn egg whites, sugar syrup, honey and nuts into delicious *torroni* in all sorts of flavours – including *caffè* and *limoncello* – and textures, from jaw-breaking hard to crisp to soft (Americans' favourites, I'm told). I love the classic *torrone* that uses honey instead of sugar, studded with the deliciously sweet toasted hazelnuts that are grown in neat rows all around the city. Almond *croccante* – or brittle – is also on offer, with or without a chocolate covering. *Torrone* is popular not only during the winter holidays, but also in summer, when it's too hot for chocolate. The shop, which is perfect for presents, also sells assorted biscuits, including *la pazienza* and *rococo* – a ring of dough with toasted almonds embedded into it like jewels.

Restaurant

Via San Francesco, 17
Capocastello
TEL 0825 788776
INTERNET
www.isanti.too.it
CLOSED Sun eve, Mon;
holidays variable
CARDS All
PRICE €€€

I Santi

There's a pleasant – if steep – walk to reach this little *osteria*, as it's set high above the Municipio of Mercogliano, in the part of the old town called Capocastello. You can park in the *piazza* in front of the Municipio. Walk through the arch to your left (with the town hall facing you), and up the hill, bearing right at the first fork. In five minutes you'll reach I Santi: two rooms that have been carved out of the pale rock, with natural wood beams still showing. This is a former cellar that was once used to store sheep, and snow for cooling foods in summer.

The menu here changes daily, or as the seasons command. Federico Grieco gets his inspiration from whatever is available at the market or in the vegetable gardens of the local *contadini*. It had just rained when I last ate there, and there were fresh mushrooms to be had, sautéed and served simply on a bed of wild *rucola*. *Antipasti* are almost a meal in themselves, alternating flavourful local *salumi* with vegetables and cheeses – and accompanied by real sourdough brown bread. I liked my *primo*: *gnocchetti* with *guanciale*, wild herbs and mushrooms, but there were others to choose from, like short durum-wheat pasta dressed with *zucchine* flowers and cheese. *Secondi* include a rustic *cinghiale* cooked with Aglianico wine, and pork shanks. Desserts, too, have a home-made feel – this is an imaginative cuisine based more on expression than technique, and the mood is young and informal. Local wines go best with these Irpinian flavours, but there are offerings from all over Italy for those wanting to venture further afield.

Mirabella Eclano

Wine

Quintodecimo

Contrada San Leonardo
TEL 0825 449321
E-MAIL
ladimarzio@yahoo.com
INTERNET
www.quintodecimo.it

In the 7th century AD, Æclanum was one of the major Roman settlements in this area (the archaeological dig can now be visited), and Quintum Decimum was the measured distance between Æclanum and today's Benevento. Luigi Moio, the Campanian œnologist who has contributed so much to the research on Aglianico, and Laura Di Marzio, his partner, have chosen Quintodecimo as the name for their new winery, on a gentle hill just beyond the modern town. 'We wanted to live surrounded by vineyards,' he says as we tour the recently completed new cellar under the house. Once the house is finished, the couple want to create a Bed & Wine, with several rooms for guests. 'These four hectares of vineyards have been planted in the last few years – all to Aglianico,' he continues, as we walk down through neat, symmetrical rows of young vines. The idea is to make two wines, a younger IGT called Vigna Cerzito, and a DOCG Taurasi, Quintodecimo. 'We've been vinifying the fruit for the last three years, but the first official vintage is the 2004.'

Luigi Moio comes from a historic winemaking family (see pp. 75-76), and makes wine for some of Campania's most important estates (see Index), but he's particularly happy to have some Aglianico of his own to work with. Indeed, there are already new barriques in the cellar, as if to hurry the grapes along. Moio spent several years studying œnology in France, so he's well used to working the small wood barrels. 'I've got the idea of the final wine in my head,' he says, 'and I can't wait to taste it.' Neither can I.

Filiberto's Restaurant (Via Nazionale, 87, Passo di Mirabella; TEL 0825 449199; CLOSED Mon) is an unusual mix of simple Irpinian cooking, pizzas and some American dishes, as the owner spent a lot of time in the States. Mario Imbriano (Piano Pantano, 39, Via Nazionale; TEL 0825 449560) is an authentic old-fashioned stone-grinding olive mill, working Leccino, Ogliarola and Ravece olives.

Montecalvo Irpino

Organic Produce

Valli, 23
TEL 0825 818646
333 6028370

Cooperativa Valli Montecalvo

Vincenzo Lo Conte runs a co-operative of organic growers producing cherry tomatoes, cherries, garlic, peppers and some *melanzane* in the sloping fields of the area. Most are sold wholesale, but private customers can also buy here.

Montefalcione

Honey

Via Carrani, 19
TEL 0825 973742

Apicoltura Antonio De Vito

De Vito produces honeys from acacia, chestnut and eucalyptus, orange blossom, thyme and borage, and also specializes in selling single-variety honeys from various parts of the south.

Monteforte Irpino

Restaurant

Via Campi, 3
TEL 0825 753101
CLOSED Tues; July
CARDS All
PRICE €€–€€€

O' Pagliarone

Entering this large, busy trattoria is like stepping back in time, into a country restaurant as they used to be, with hams, cheeses and peppers hanging from the rafters, and colourful displays of *antipasti* and desserts for customers to help themselves from. Central to the activities is a long open grill for cooking meats – from T-bones to lamb chops and pork steaks. Beyond the main *sala* is a series of smaller rooms, each decked out with paintings, commemorative photos and plaques. It's what the Italians call *caratteristico*. The whole revolves around the owner, 'Don' Antonio Di Somma, a friendly, extrovert personality who has spent his life in the business and looks as if he could tell a story or two. After the *antipasti*, there are always lots of options for *primi*, from sausage-stuffed pasta shells to gnocchi with cheeses, asparagus and ham. Then go for the grill, and a choice of dessert – like the classic *babà* or a fruit *crostata*. (If you are coming from Napoli, leave the *autostrada* at Baiano, head back towards Napoli, and then follow signs to the restaurant.)

Montefredane

Wine

Contrada Vadiaperti, 17
TEL/FAX 0825 607418

Pietracupa

Sabino Loffredo is one of the most interesting – and talented – of the up-and-coming young winemakers in Irpinia. In 1997, after studying in the north and abroad, and seeing the world by working on an ocean liner, he returned home to join his father in making wine. With the œnologist Carmine Valentino 'as a point of reference', they produce circa 35,000 bottles per year, and have become known for their whites, especially Greco and Fiano.

'Since 2003, Irpinia has been experiencing a big boom in its winemaking,' the engaging 33-year-old begins. 'It's an exciting time: we're *meridionali* – southern Italians – and we like to take risks, that's our nature. Lots of things are changing very fast: in my generation, we've broken through the barrier that stopped our parents exchanging ideas or sharing experiences. Now we're more united and often taste wines together or compare notes on winemaking techniques.'

Pietracupa is located very near Avellino, on a hill whose vineyards face south yet are subjected to the high day-to-night temperature changes that assure good *profumi* to the wines.

'Luckily, among many producers now there's a return to the terroir and to our indigenous grapes,' he continues. 'But others are paying for earlier mistakes, of planting varieties that aren't ours, or forcing wines into fashionable stereotyped modes imposed from outside. The barriques, for example, that coloured so many wines: they seemed to guarantee success, but in reality they were just a flash in the pan. I prefer to leave our whites unclouded by wood. I like to work our grapes naturally, almost intuitively, and dedicate more energy to the work in the vineyard. Each grape variety has its own voice. What's encouraging is that in our area, vinicultural technique has improved enormously in the last ten years, so the wines are no longer coming in flawed by oxidization or poor winemaking.'

Of the native white varieties, which does he prefer? 'I must admit that I am more intrigued by Fiano: it may be harder to pair with food, but it's more aromatic to both nose and mouth, and goes best with simple dishes that will not overpower it. Greco, on the other hand, is more flexible, and goes easily with food as it's crisper.'

The Loffredos make two versions of each of these whites: they undergo identical winemaking, but depend on different selections in the vineyard. As for the red, Sabino has recently started experimenting more with Aglianico, what he calls *la bestia nera* – the black beast – for its complexity both in the vineyard and cellar.

'To me, if Mastroberardino represents the past of Irpinian wines, Feudi di San Gregorio stands for the present... but the future is in the hands of the new generation, the small, independent producers who are free to express their individual

personalities through their wines.' It seems the furure is already here: Sabino's wines are truly exciting – among my Campanian favourites.

Contrada Vadiaperti
TEL 0825 607270
info@vadiaperti.it
www.vadiaperti.it

Vadiaperti

Another of the 'new generation', Raffaele Troisi is carrying on what his pioneering father, Antonio, began before his untimely death: working the local grapes Fiano, Greco and Coda di Volpe.

Via Toppole, 16
TEL 0825 30777
FAX 0825 22920
antoine.gaita1@tin.it

Villa Diamante

Antoine Gaita and his wife, Maria Renna Diamante, work the Fiano grapes of their three hectares of organic vineyards to make one praised wine, Fiano di Avellino Vigna della Congregazione. It is worked in wood and expresses a French style in its almost smoky energy.

Honey

Via San Marciano, 7
TEL 339 3223793

Zeffiro

This honey maker has a hundred hives, and works the different flower seasons, from acacia to chestnut.

Montefusco

From 700 to 1600, Montefusco was the capital of the Principato d'Ultra, a powerful southern Italian state; it also played an important role under the Kingdom of the Two Sicilies – today many cultural and historical monuments remain as evidence of this noble past.

Restaurant

Piazza Castello
TEL 0825 964716

Castello Borbonico

High up in the main *piazza* of Montefusco, this trattoria-pizzeria occupies a large room under the castle. It's a popular place for winemakers, workers and visitors who like to eat in big, vivacious spaces where the food is local and unpretentious, the service friendly and fast, and there's always plenty to look at. A good place to try the fresh vegetables of the fields and pastures, as well as simply grilled meats – or pizzas.

Wine, Olive Oil

Via Serra
TEL 0825 968215
E-MAIL
info@terradora.com

Terredora

In 1994, the Italian wine world was shocked to learn that the Mastroberardino brothers, pioneers of Campanian winemaking from one of southern Italy's most famous wine dynasties, were

The olive harvest at Terredora

splitting up. A deep rupture had taken place within the family, and the result was the creation of two wineries where once there had been just one. In the division, Antonio and his son Piero took the family name and the historic cellars in Atripalda, while Walter and his sons Paolo and Lucio kept the 120 hectares of vineyards but were barred from using the name Mastroberardino in their publications or on their labels. Their new company name became Terredora Di Paolo – Dora Di Paolo being Signora Mastroberardino's maiden name.

'It was a generational divide,' explains Paolo Mastroberardino, as we spend part of a morning driving around what are now the estate's 150 hectares of vineyards. 'My cousin and I had different visions for the future of the winery, and in the end these were irreconcilable. Lucio and I were brought up to be winemakers, and when our father and uncle separated, we were able to pursue our work of transforming the grapes as naturally as possible, with the help of our sister Daniela in the office.' A large, functional cellar was built just outside Montefusco, with all the latest technology to facilitate the extraction of the grapes' aromas. 'The notion of terroir is very important to us,' he continues, as he points out a wide vineyard on the steep slopes of the Calore valley. It is bounded on two sides by woods, and surrounded by a row of olive trees, as the company also makes fine extra virgin olive oil.

'We have focused on producing wines from the best local grape varieties, bringing out the characteristics that this specific terrain can give them,' he says. In this unspoiled part of Irpinia, with its historic hill towns, the vineyards are given over to Aglianico for Taurasi, with whites Fiano, Greco and the unusual Falanghina d'Irpinia, for which Terredora is the only producer in the province of Avellino. 'Falanghina d'Irpinia is very close to the Falanghina from the Campi Flegrei, with small bunches of delicate, fine fruit that make an elegant, *evanescente* wine. Whereas the Beneventano variety is much bigger and coarser – more like Trebbiano Toscano – and its wines have less *profumi*.'

I'm particularly fond of the estate's whites: the clean, clear, Loggia della Serra Greco di Tufo has a pure voice, with real balance in the mouth – the kind of wine you don't easily tire of. Not being a big fan of barrique-aged whites, I prefer the simpler of the two Fianos: Terre di Dora is worked entirely in steel, and has a sapidity – almost a salinity – that keeps it fresh and lively, with characteristic notes of honey and hazelnut. Of the bigger whites, CampoRe is a late-harvest Fiano fermented in wood, so it has more body; it is one of the best of its type. The winery's reds are also well made, from the powerful Taurasi cru,

CampoRe to its 'younger brother', Taurasi Fatica Contadina: this is a range that offers consistent reliability at affordable prices – a winning combination.

Wine

Via Serra di Montefusco
TEL 0825 963972
E-MAIL
info@colliirpini.com

Colli Irpini – Montesole

This very large cellar – over a million bottles per year – buys in grapes from all around this excellent wine-producing area and works them in its modern cellars. Its ample catalogue of wines is very reasonably priced.

Montella

FOR MORE INFORMATION:
Comunità Montana
Terminio-Cervialto
Via Don Minzoni, 2
TEL 0827 69377
FAX 0827 609411
www.cmterminiocervialto.it

This village is situated at the edge of the mountains, overlooking the valley of the Calore river. It is known for its chestnuts – they have IGP status – and its cow's milk cheeses: *caciocavallo*, *fior di latte* and ricotta. It's also a wonderful place for aromatic chestnut-flour breads. These wood-covered mountains are part of the Regional Park of the Monti Picentini.

Bread

Strada Provinciale San
Francesco, Follone
TEL 0827 601414
329 0073993

Spaccio Agricolo Follone

I love the dark, dense, smoky-sweet chestnut bread baked in heavy round loaves by this bakery in a wood-burning oven. It lasts for days. They also make a corn-yellow *pane di mais*, using *polenta* flour, and a series of large, flat savoury tarts filled simply with seasonal vegetables: *bietole*, or artichokes with a light vinegar astringency. The shop also sells bottled chestnut pastes, preserved vegetables, and flours of chestnut and other grains.

Cheese

Via Carbonara, 21
TEL 0827 61415
FAX 0827 601658

Gerardo Moscariello – Caseificio Artigianale

Located in a quiet residential street in the centre of Montella, this small family run dairy produces fine *caciocavallo* of *pasta filata*, and milky *fior di latte* from local cows' milk.

Cheese

Via Largo dell'Ospizio, 12
TEL 0827 61015
INTERNET
www.caseificiogranese.com

Caseificio Granese

This small cheese-maker's motto is 'timeless goodness' – the family has been making mozzarella, Caciocavallo Irpino, and *il burrino* (butter in a shell of *scamorza*) since 1895, but his specialities are the excellent ricotta and *ricotta salata*. Granese has recently also opened a shop in Avellino too (see pp. 331-32).

MONTELLA'S CHESTNUTS:
CASTAGNA DI MONTELLA IGP

Chestnuts, which were originally from Asia Minor, have been known in this area since the 4th century BC. During the Longobard era, in the 6th century AD, the chestnuts were so highly prized that a law was created to protect their cultivation. Montella's chestnut trees survived a form of cancer in the 1950s and are still now the main source of income for the town and its surrounding area. Today, Montella provides 60 per cent of the province of Avellino's production, with 7–8,000 tonnes. Montella's chestnuts were the first Italian fruit to receive the DOC which was replaced, nine years later, by the IGP. Currently 150 companies in the Montella area are licensed to work the chestnuts. The most prevalent variety in these hilly woods is the Palummina, whose fruit is said to resemble 'a little dove'. These chestnuts are of medium size and easy to peel. Traditionally they are prepared in an unusual way: the hulled but unpeeled chestnuts are dried – often over wood fires – then toasted or baked before being soaked for several days in water. These re-hydrated chestnuts keep for several months in a semi-soft state, can be peeled easily, and retain a lightly smoky flavour from the drying process. They are known as Castagne del Prete. The largest chestnuts are also used for *marrons glacés* and as ingredients for other sweetmeats. Dried chestnuts are ground for flour and used in pasta, bread and cakes.

Among the best companies working the chestnuts are:

De Sio – La Dolce Irpinia (Zona Industriale; TEL 0827 69033; E-MAIL dolceirpinia@interfree.it). This company makes *marrons glacés* and other chestnut- and hazelnut-related sweetmeats, working from local ingredients.

Salvatore Malerba (Via Verteglia, 104; TEL 0827 61420) One of the larger *aziende* working the chestnuts in all phases.

Cooperativa Castagne di Montella IGP (Contrada Sottomonticchio; tel 0827 61401). Lots of chestnut products, including in syrup and rum, dried and flour.

Castagne Perrotta (Contrada Baruso, Zona Industriale; TEL 0827 601588)

Montella's ancient chestnut woods are kept as neatly as gardens

Cheese

Strada Provinciale San
Francesco
TEL 0827 609740
FAX 0827 69222
E-MAIL
info@caseificiogambone.it

Caseificio Ezio Gambone

This large, efficiently run dairy produces cheeses of consistent quality, including aged DOP Caciocavallo. This is also a good place to visit if you're interested in seeing how these cheeses are made, as visits can be organized with advance notice.

Cheese

Via del Corso, 161
TEL 0827 69236

Caseificio Mario Gambone

Ezio's brother, Mario, makes plaited mozzarella – *la treccia*, *scamorza* and *caciocavallo*, from local farm milk he still does the rounds to collect.

Also at Montella

Pasta Fresca Immediata (Via del Corso, 18; TEL 0827 601484; CLOSED Mon; E-MAIL daidex@tiscalinet.it) As the name suggests, this is the shop for fresh pasta – ricotta-filled *ravioli*, and *le stese* (like *fettucine* but made without eggs) – immediately. Michele Zurlo (Via S. Capone; TEL 0827 61154, 347 1944466) has a *casalinghi* – a houseware and hardware store that sells everything from garden tools to jumbo saucepans for cooking the obligatory summer tomato sauce. A good place to pick up those hard-to-find Italian gadgets that our kitchens love to receive. Panificio Marano (Via Bonavitacola) is an old-fashioned bakery making good bread from wholewheat to maize, and is also a handy place for snacks like the healthy *pizza con le bietole* – filled with chard greens. Ai Boschi (Via Provinciale, 43; TEL 0827 69900) is a butcher's shop selling local meats. The owner, Aurelio Schiavone, has also recently opened a trattoria nearby (see p. 373). Lorenzo Patrone (Contrada Pezzalunga; TEL 0827 61024) is a good source for the aromatic local truffles.

Tomato presses come in all forms and sizes

Montemarano

Wine

Via Musanni, 19/B (on
SS 400 at Km 15.500)
Contrada Lampenne
TEL 0827 63424
FAX 0827 63722
INTERNET
selections.degrazia
@world.it

Salvatore Molettieri

Salvatore and his son Giovanni Molettieri make what is, to my mind, one of the most interesting of the Taurasis. Taurasi Vigna Cinque Querce has a unique character: it's an austere wine, almost moody, that gives a sense both of wines past and wines future. Yet it's a wine you don't get tired of, that becomes even more dignified as it ages. It is made from old vines of Aglianico, grown in a semi-mountainous part of Irpinia in family vineyards at 600 metres. A wine of the land, just as its maker is a man of the land: Salvatore's ruddy face is sun-burned and wind-wrinkled. He has worked as a farmer all his life, yet he only started bottling his wines in 1996, selling them *sfusi* before that. The Molettieri's cellar, too, is a functional, no-frills construction that is built over and out of the rock; their 11 hectares of vineyards fan away below it over the irregularly hilly terrain, surrounded in part by woods. It's a chilly – no, cold – part of the province: I live a few minutes from there, and it's not unusual for the first snows to arrive in early November just as the Aglianico is being picked. But we're also very far south, far enough for the sun to ripen the fruit as the cool evenings add to the elegance of its *profumi*.

'We have been working for a long time on our own selection of Aglianico, to use when we replant the vineyards,' explains Salvatore as we sit in his tiny office next to the cellar. 'The trick about working Aglianico is not to rush it but only bottle it when it's ready, and to maintain its fruit character while keeping its naturally abundant tannins in check: for that we can thank the help we get from our modern soft presses.' Other helpful suggestions have come from Marc de Grazia, with whom they have been working since 1996, and Attilio Pagli, the Tuscan winemaker. I'd like to add my own suggestion: not to move too far from the elegance of the 1998 and earlier vintages towards more concentration, or the *fascino* of the original Taurasi may get lost.

Montemiletto

Olive Oil

Oleificio Fina

Via Casale San Nicola, 27
TEL 0825 955977
335 5879676
FAX 0825 968498
E-MAIL
info@oleificiofina.com
INTERNET
www.oleificiofina.com

This large olive mill works both for itself and for what the Italians call *terzi* – or others. It's a family-run *frantoio* that in recent years has kept up with the times by dividing its machinery between the old style and the new.

'It all depends on what the client wants,' says Luigi Fina as he checks the contents of an *ape* full of olives that has been driven in by one of the local *contadini*. The back of the little van is full of black olives. 'You see, not all black olives are bad – these are fine as they are still green inside.' What Fina means is that his more 'enlightened' customers – Paolo Mastroberardino, for example, whose Terredora oil is milled here – know that high quality oil can only be obtained by olives picked early in the season (usually when they are only just beginning to change from green to black). Then the paste must be worked at 'low' temperatures (but not below 18°C or the olives won't even release their oils) in order to retain its fresh, green flavours. This 'modern' approach, however, has been slow in finding approval among some older growers who still equate quality with quantity: the more you heat the ground olive paste, the more oil it will release, but the quality will be lower. So Fina has found a way to compromise, by running separate 'lines' of oil production, thereby guaranteeing each producer the type of oil they are used to. Fina sells his own selection – worked at low temperatures – in bottles and cans from the *frantoio*.

Montoro Inferiore

Raffaele Ingino (TEL 0825 520758 www.raffael.it) A small company working the chestnuts in this area; they also sell them vacuum-packed.

Nusco

Stone carvings above the doors in Nusco

Nusco is perched on the top of a high hill at 914 metres, and overlooks 360 degrees of countryside. Roman artefacts have been found here, as well as the remains of the 7th-century *castello*. In 1254 Manfred of Swabia was offered protection in Nusco's castle, an event that Dante wrote of in the Divine Comedy. Sadly, the castle was sacked and destroyed in 1739. Nusco's fortunes were buoyed for almost a thousand years by being the seat of a bishopric. The baroque Palazzo Vescovile faces the cathedral; the arabesque stonework around its main door is a motif that is repeated on others of the village's noble *palazzi*. In the last forty years, Nusco's fortunes have been inextricably linked to those of its most important citizen, Ciriaco De Mita, the eminent elder statesman and ex-prime minister who was born in Nusco. He was in power in the years following the 1980 earthquake, and Nusco benefited from his commitment to rebuilding the village as it had been before (being built on rock, Nusco was anyway less badly affected than many other areas of Irpinia). Thanks to this policy, Nusco is unlike most other Irpinian villages, whose souls were lost when their buildings fell or were pulled down.

I must admit to having a special relationship with this small medieval hill town: I have been living in it since July 2003, and have grown accustomed to its ways. I came to spend a few months near my friend, chef Antonio Pisaniello, and have stayed on because living close to an exciting new restaurant is addictive.

In the meantime, the village has become used to me too: independent foreign women are not very common in this part of

Angelo and Rosa Pasquale outside their shop

southern Italy, but the village has welcomed *la giornalista*, as I'm known. I include below a synopsis of the shops I use the most, in case any of my readers decide to take up residence here too.

Rosa and Angelo Pasquale (Via Santa Croce, 7). With their children, Gianni, Raffaele, Francesco and Maria Teresa, the charming Pasquales sell the best of what's in season, fruits and vegetables from their own farm as well as from Irpinia and Salerno. Facing the large church, Pasticceria D'Urso (Via Santa Croce, 4) is the place if you want to sit at a table for a cup of tea and pastries, especially the jam-filled cookies. Sonia Di Paolo, at the newly revamped Edicola on the corner of Piazza Sant'Amato (at no. 3; TEL 0827 64030) sells daily papers and magazines, books (including cookbooks), as well as some art supplies. On the main street through the village, my local grocer's is run by the diminutive Signora Maria Cristina Maiurano and her son Claudio (Corso Umberto I, 15; TEL 0827 64964). They have all the fixings for sandwiches as well as the staples for those of us who live in the neighbourhood. On the same street, Liliana Lombardi's little shop, La Bottega dei Sapori (Corso Umberto I, 21) specializes in cow's milk cheeses made by the Meluzio family nearby: delicate ricotta, little *scamorzas* and large, pear-shaped *caciocavallo*, plus fresh mozzarellas. She also stocks a small selection of local honeys and truffle products. The charming Alfonso Conte and his wife Lina run two businesses in

town, across the street from each other: Blue Moon (Piazza Natale, 9; TEL 0827 64608) is a tobacconist's and stationery shop that has a fax and internet point and sells computers and related products; Borgo Antico (Piazza Natale, 3; TEL 0827 64967) is in the large pink house that runs along one side of the *piazza*. This bar–pizzeria is open daily from 8.00 to midnight (CLOSED Tues), and offers everything from coffee and drinks to hot meals in a relaxed environment. On the far side of the same *piazza*, Bar Prudente is a great place for home-made lemon *granita*, and sorbets of black mulberry (*gelso*) and *fragoline di bosco* in summer, when it also has tables outside. Or have a real, made-to-order *caffè shakerato*.

Signora Rosa Mottola (TEL 0827 64256) runs the flower shop where I go to get my lilies and balcony plants. The well-stocked hardware store of Michelina and Franco Natale (Via SS Giovanni e Paola; TEL 0827 64775) is on the road that cuts down to the Ofantina from Nusco, and sells all sorts of useful country tools and kitchen appliances that can be hard to find. Outside of the village, Luciano Colucci runs an ostrich farm, Irpinia Struzzo (Via Serra Nudo, 1; TEL 0827 607404; E-MAIL irpinia.struzzi@tiscali.it). On the other side of the hill, on the old road that descends from the Q8 petrol station to Ponteromito, at her *panificio*, Maria Michela Mongelluzzo (Contrada Mito; TEL 0827 67279) produces wonderful sour-dough bread from the wood-burning ovens under her house.

Nusco's market day is Sunday: in addition to the usual *bancarelle* selling everything from farm tools to underwear, a few local farmers come in to sell their freshly picked produce – usually by the cathedral, next to the man selling his hand-made baskets.

Restaurant

La Locanda di Bu

Vicolo dello Spagnuolo, 1
TEL/FAX 0827 64619
329 3848162
E-MAIL
info@lalocandadibu.com
INTERNET
www.lalocandadibu.com
CLOSED Sun eve; Mon;
2 weeks in Jan;
2 weeks in July
CARDS All
PRICE €€€–€€€€
B&B available

Opposite: The Sunday market at Nusco

For some people, becoming a chef isn't a choice, it's a calling. And it doesn't matter how much your father would like you to be a surveyor – if you just have to cook, you find a way to do it. That's the kind of chef Antonio Pisaniello is. Self-taught and determined.

'When I was a kid, I loved hanging around in my grandmother's kitchen, trying to figure out what she had cooked by the way the food smelled,' he says, as he polishes a stainless-steel counter before the lunch service begins. 'I couldn't wait to cook. When I was in my early teens, I heard a pizzeria was looking for a pizza maker – I figured it couldn't be that hard. The boss was doubtful. 'Aren't you too young to be a cook?' he asked.

Chef Antonio Pisaniello with his thin chestnut baguettes

Antonio's fried Montella ricotta is served with three sauces

I bluffed my way in – I had never made a pizza in my life. In one week I learned by watching the outgoing *pizzaiolo* – and that was the beginning.' A few years later he opened Irpinia's first 'pub' – in his parents' basement. 'In no time it became the hot place in Irpinia for young people. I was practically getting hate mail from their parents who accused me of keeping their kids up all night.' Soon the beers and cocktails were being accompanied by snacks, then fanciful *panini*, then a few hot *primi*. Antonio was finally cooking. His father, a building contractor who had moved the family from Irpinia to Sicily and back, eventually agreed to sponsor him in a bigger venture. After all, the pub had been a runaway success.

They opened Il Gastronomo at Ponteromito in 1996, on a through road into Irpinia that had once been famous for its *taverne*. 'It began as a pizzeria with a few dishes, but soon became a trattoria with a few pizzas,' he laughs. His mother, Annamaria, is a wonderful cook of hearty local dishes, and she contributed slow-cooked *ragù* and other rustic staples. His brothers, Massimo and Francesco (see pp. 372-73) gradually joined in too. Antonio was by now reading everything he could about cooking, and his technique improved. The pizzas were banished to weekend take-aways, and Il Gastronomo became known for its authentic ingredients and well-cooked country food.

A beautiful girl turned up looking for work, Jenny Auriemma from nearby Montella. 'In just two days, I was head over heels in love,' he says. They shared the same dream – to open a more elegant, smaller restaurant which would showcase Antonio's food. It took several more years and a split from the family but,

in January 2004, La Locanda di Bu was launched. '"Bu" is our first son, Umberto,' says Jenny, who is a sommelier when she isn't too busy with the new baby, Filippo. Working with a talented young Irpinian eco-architect, Federico Verderosa, the couple transformed a dingy little pizzeria on the ground floor of a house in the medieval centre of Nusco into one of southern Italy's most charming restaurants. Its clean-lined, modern style would fit right into a design capital.

'We used only natural materials like *calce* (lime) for the walls and oiled woods for the floors to avoid chemical residues,' she says. The kitchen appears through a picture window, so diners feel an instant connection to the *cucina*'s energy – something Antonio has in abundance. Selected wines line the *sala*'s back wall: Campania's best producers are ever-present while you eat.

Lorenzo and Vincenzo stocking up the restaurant

And the food? It too has grown another step. 'With a maximum of thirty diners, I'm finally free to invent as many dishes as I like,' Antonio says as he puts an artistic dash of green sauce onto a tear-shaped plate. The chef's *menu degustazione* is economical, considering the quality of the *materia prima*, with hand-made pastas, seasonal vegetables, local meats and cheeses.

I love Antonio's delicate deep-fried '*gnocco*' of mixed ricotta and *fior di latte* from Montella, with its diverse sauces of *zucchine*, tomato water and *colatura di alici* (see p. 182). A pure purée of white Quarantini beans is served with bitter field greens, tiny pork meatballs, and crisped fennel-flavoured *polenta*. *La maccheronara* is a triumph: flour-and-water noodles formed on a traditional ridged rolling pin are sauced with tart-sweet cherry tomatoes and *ricotta salata*. Native lamb is boned, then baked slowly in a low oven. The result is seductively tender meat sharpened by its grapey Aglianico sauce. As in all these recipes, he's captured the essence of the native Irpinian dishes, but has changed the form and, sometimes, the content. Desserts use Avellino's hazelnuts and Montella's chestnuts, with fresh summer-melon sorbets to clear the palate.

Antonio has always been a catalyst for local (and other) young people: the average age of his restaurant staff is in the low twenties, and he has given Vincenzo and Lorenzo, 'chef' Antonio, Ore and Daisuke a rare opportunity to learn and grow in this intimate, creative environment. They haven't been the only ones to benefit from his talent: Christoph Hille – the chef of the recently opened, highly successful 'A16' restaurant in San Francisco, spent four months working in the kitchen at Il Gastronomo, learning Antonio's Irpinian repertoire. Chef Rocco DiSpirito was impressed by him too, and featured Antonio in his second *Restaurant* television series, filmed in New York in 2003.

Agriturismo
Nonna Rosina

Contrada Marmore, 2
TEL 0827 607098
335 6271283
INTERNET
www.nonnarosina.com
OPEN all year by
appointment
CARDS None
PRICE €–€€

This country *agriturismo* – just four kilometres outside Nusco – has six rooms, and a *simpatico* restaurant for its guests (or others who book ahead) serving home-made traditional dishes; it is set in a restored barn, with summer tables outside under a pergola. The farm is organic, producing vegetables, fruit and wine, as well as breeding farmyard animals.

Ospedaletto d'Alpinolo

Restaurant
Osteria del Gallo e della Volpe

Piazza Umberto I, 12
TEL 0825 691225
OPEN for dinner only,
except Sun lunch
CLOSED Mon; 26–31
Dec; 1–15 July
CARDS All
PRICE €€–€€€

At the top of the steepish central street of this intact medieval *borgo*, with panoramic views over Avellino and its valley, is a *palazzo signorile* from 1750. Inside the high *porticato* is a spacious restaurant with cool modern art on warm Pompeian-red walls. In over seven years Antonio and Marisa Silvestri have established a convivial place for *appassionati* to eat and drink.

The wine list is seductive: an extensive declension of producers and vintages – including Caggiano's Macchia dei Goti in every edition from 1994–2000. The only flaw? It's hand-written (as is the often-changing menu), so harder to read and understand – especially for us foreigners. You can visit the handsome cellar down the street – it's the kind only a true wine-lover could create.

As for the food, it's based on good precepts: fresh ingredients, home-made pasta, and recipes both traditional and original. This can lead to unexpected but successful results: in spring, the classic *pastiera napoletana*, the sweet Easter cake, is served with the *aperitivo* – minus the sugar. The Silvestris are keen on cheeses and these play an important role in the dishes. The *cupola di patate* is a potato salad surrounded by a velvety Gorgonzola cream. *Pettole*, large flat squares of pasta rather like *lasagne*, are served with grated *provola* cheese and chunks of *alici* – anchovies – dressed liberally with good oil from Salerno. *Gnocchi* are delicious tossed with green fava beans and a cheesy sauce of Pecorino di Fossa and dried mint.

Secondi include fillet of pork with *Annurche*-apple sauce – a combination that reminded me of England – and veal braised tenderly in spiced Taurasi wine. For dessert, a delicate mousse of hazelnuts was a fine showcase for aromatic honey from Eboli.

Apples ripening on a basket

ALSO AT OSPEDALETTO
As with other *pasticcerie* in this village, the speciality of
Pasticceria La Fonte del Torrone (Piazza Mercato, 1; TEL 0825
691587, 0825 691215) is *torrone*, and in particular *pantorrone*:
chocolate-covered, they're soft in the centre thanks to a 'heart'
of *pan di spagna* cake soaked in liqueur. GM & F Oliviero (Via
Chiusa di Sotto, 5; TEL 0825 691336, 0825 691565) The
Castagne del Prete were developed in medieval times, and this
village, which is in the Parco Regionale del Partenio, is known
for making them well. These chestnuts are first dried then re-
moistened while still in their shells, so they remain soft and
easy to eat right from the bag. Oliviero also makes *torrone*
and *pantorrone*.

Paternopoli

The village of Paternopoli has a reputation for its olive oil: at
the beginning of the 20th century there were ten olive mills
working in and around it. Today several good producers are
committed to producing well-made extra virgin oils from the
local Ravece olive variety – as well as organic, or *biologico* oil.
They are also lobbying for the Colline dell'Ufita DOP to be
approved – as it surely will be soon.

Barbieri (Acquara, 16; TEL 0827 71978; E-MAIL info@
oliobarbieri.com www.oliobarbieri.com). Famiglietti (Via
Sottochiesa, 3; TEL 0827 71023; E-MAIL marcellofamigliett@
hotmail. com). Le Masciare (Contrada Barbassano; TEL 0825
784579, 348 6412799; E-MAIL info@lemasciare.com; INTERNET
www.lemasciare.com).

Manimurci: Carmine Aliasi (TEL 340 8202990) has recently
started a new winery at Paternopoli, producing all three of the
DOCG wines.

Pietradefusi see Dentecane

Ponteromito

Ponteromito was once known for the fabulous noble *palazzo*
of the Conte Del Sordo, who bred eels and trout on the
Calore river, and used hydro-electric power to give Irpinia early
electricity. The first *pastificio* of Irpinia, Simba, got its flour
from the Count's mills. All these buildings were destroyed either

Traditional vines at
Ponteromito

by Allied bombing or the 1980 earthquake.

Ponteromito also held important livestock markets, and was a stopping point on the road between Napoli or Avellino and Alta Irpinia: at that time it had three *taverne* – inns for travellers making the journey through the hills. After the Ofantina highway that by-passed Ponteromito was completed, this main road became a back road, and now the village is peaceful and known only to the local people who frequent it.

Restaurant

Il Gastronomo

Via Nazionale, 39/40
(Strada Statale 164, km
51,7)
TEL 0827 67009
INTERNET
www.ilgastronomo.it
CLOSED Sun eve; Wed;
15–31 July
CARDS All
PRICE €€

In recent years, this restaurant has become a reference point in the area for good food cooked using fine local ingredients. The young chef, Antonio Pisaniello, with the help of his family, ran Il Gastronomo for a number of years before he moved up to Nusco at the beginning of 2004 to open La Locanda di Bu (see p. 367-69). Now his brother, Massimo, who trained under Antonio as a *pizzaiolo*, has taken over the kitchen – and is cooking really well.

Pizzas are only being made at the weekends, while the main focus of the *cucina* is on the seasonal dishes of *la tradizione*, somewhat re-visited. The young men's mother, Annamaria Contino, still lends a hand and a critical palate – after all, she has been the inspiration for many of the dishes. Massimo's repertoire includes some of the dishes his brother created, but he's now developing a personal style, with an instinctive flair that bodes well for the future. Pastas are wonderful here, dressed with vegetables like pumpkin and *porcini* mushrooms, or ricotta, walnuts and black truffles that come from the nearby fields and woods. Montella, the closest town, is famous for its dairy products, from delicate cow's ricotta to the more charac-terful *pecorino* or *caciocavallo*, and these ingredients are always present in the menu.

For *secondi*, try a hearty plate of lamb stewed in Fiano wine – *agnello in cassuola*, or a steak topped with mushrooms or truf-fles. And save room for dessert: hot chocolate '*tortino*' or unusual chestnut-filled pastries. The restaurant staff – Francesco Pisaniello and his father Umberto, Assunta Prudente, with Carmela and Assunta in the kitchen – are always welcoming, so you'll enjoy your meal here.

ALSO AT PONTEROMITO

Aurelio Schiavone is a friendly local butcher with a *macelleria* at Montella who longed to run a restaurant: he has recently opened a small bar and simple trattoria selling home-cooked meats and local dishes, Il Novecento (Via Nazionale, 18; TEL 0827 69900, 347 7773307; CLOSED Mon).

Le Delizie Pasta Fresca (Contrada Scandoglio; TEL 0827 67152, 0825 67157) is an artisan company making all the tradi-tional Irpinian pastas: *fusilli, la maccheronara, orecchiette*, as well as some stuffed pastas. They are located on the narrow hill road that leads from Ponteromito's rail tracks up to Nusco.

Pratola Serra

Wine

Via Limaturo, 52
San Michele
TEL 0825 967038
0825 37247
E-MAIL
casadellorco@olibit.it

La Casa dell'Orco

This winery gets its name from a legend that has roots near the vineyards: the *orco* was an ogre, Cronopa, who was killed here by the shepherd Silpa as proof of his love for the beautiful Matulpa. Whether it's true or not, this is certainly an area that has links to cultures past, for vast prehistoric stones have been found here. The Musto family have a fairly large estate – 25 hectares of vineyards – and recently their wines have been improving steadily. The Greco di Tufo is a rich gold in colour, and has a fine bouquet of fruits – pears, citrus and pineapple – whose promise is fulfilled by being nicely balanced to the palate. The Fiano is lighter, but retains all the characteristics of its type: with delicate floral notes to the nose, a good crisp structure, and toasted hazelnuts to the aftertaste.

ALSO: Nobilis (San Michele; TEL/FAX 0825 956033; E-MAIL

info@nobiliswine.com) is unusual in having an American œnologist, Karl Hornberger, making its wines. The owner, Armando Petruziello, lived in the US for many years and has his sights set on the transatlantic market.

Rocca San Felice

It is no wonder that past travellers were curious to see the 'Lake' in the Ansanto Valley for themselves. La Mefite, as it is known locally, was famous in antiquity, described in detail by Virgil in the *Æneid* (Book VII), and by Dante in *La Divina Commedia*. This stinking, bubbling spring was thought by Virgil to be the entrance to Acheronte, and by others to be a goddess who was worshipped by almost all of the Italic peoples of southern Italy. To the Mefite's archaeological and mythological importance, we can add the gastronomic: the sulphurous fumes and waters that still define this valley and its surrounding area has become linked with a special *pecorino* cheese, Carmasciano. Sheep that graze and drink in the area produce milk that is richer in sulphur, and this is said to colour their cheeses with a faint, but perceptible flavour. Certainly the cheeses made locally are excellent... the goddess approves, apparently.

Rocca holds an annual medieval fair in the third week of August, with jugglers, fire-eaters and falconers, artisan *botteghe* of arts and crafts, including cheeses and baked goods.

Restaurant

La Ripa Ristorante Museo

Borgo Medievale
TEL 0827 215023
347 2389097
CLOSED
Mon & Tues; Jan
CARDS All
PRICE €€

This medieval *borgo* was sensitively rebuilt after the 1980 earthquake to retain an ancient feel: narrow, winding streets, a large central *piazza* dominated by a 200-year-old linden tree and, above them, La Rocca – the fortress with its 13th-century dungeon. Inside it is La Ripa, a 'restaurant and museum' occupying several floors of the stone building. Up here the views are panoramic and in summer there's a breezy terrace for eating outside; indoors, the luminous dining room also has huge views. The eating formula is flexible: several small menus offer combinations of *salumi* and cheeses, or moderately priced courses. Many dishes are cheese-based: La Ripa has a good selection, including raw-milk *pecorini* like Carmasciano from the nearby valley. Baked fresh ricotta topped with fragrant slices of Val d'Aosta *lardo* is unusual, and I love the hand-made *fusilli* (made rolled around a wire) cooked in milk flavoured with juniper and herbs – an antique recipe from the area. Gragnano pasta tubes are tossed into an elemental sauce of *baccalà*, *alici* and olives.

Local lamb and Podolico beef are grilled deliciously over wood embers. Downstairs, the *enoteca* serves cheese or *salumi* with wines by the glass or bottle. All in all, an informal, friendly place to hang out.

Salza Irpina

Wine

Cantine Di Meo

Contrada Coccovoni, 1
TEL 0825 981419
FAX 0825 986333
E-MAIL info@dimeo.it
INTERNET www.dimeo.it

Erminia and Roberto Di Meo

The Di Meo villa at Salza Irpina

Luckily for me, I've known the Di Meo family since the first time I came to Irpinia. They have been wonderful: hospitable and generous, not only in personal terms – how many times have I spent nights, eaten meals, and been 'rescued' by them – but also in their contagious enthusiasm for Irpinia. With Erminia I've visited sanctuaries, restaurants and ceramics producers; Generoso (who more than lives up to his name) has shared friends and information about obscure bakeries and ancient customs; Roberto never fails to be kind and attentive, and is a mine of information about the wine world. As for the aunts, suffice it to say that I've learned as much about Irpinian cooking (and *ospitalità*) from them as from everyone else put together. So this is just to say, thank you all.

The Di Meos have lived in Avellino and been landowners in Irpinia for many generations; their villas at Volturara and Montella were tragically destroyed in the 1980 earthquake. Since I have known them, they have been carefully restoring the beautiful country villa at Salza Irpina which is beside the winery's headquarters (and on their labels). It's in the process of becoming one of Irpinia's most attractive *agriturismi*. For many years, the siblings' widowed mother, Alessandrina, ran the estate with the help of her children. She was a strong, independent woman I feel fortunate to have known. Now Roberto is the family's œnologist, Erminia runs the business, and handles PR with their brother, Generoso. The Di Meos do everything in style: if they throw a party to launch a new wine – or their now highly collectable annual art calendars – they do it at the palace of Capodimonte, or in a grand Roman villa – quite a switch from the rusticity of daily life in Irpinia.

Their wines, too, have been improving steadily as Roberto comes into his own as a winemaker. It was with them that I learned about the differences between Coda di Volpe and Greco di Tufo, Falanghina and Fiano. The Di Meo wines are made in a natural style, reflecting the characters of their grapes and territories. Roberto waits until the Aglianico is ready before he releases the Taurasi – there's nothing forced about it. Erminia is

also well known for her unusual and delicious after-dinner *digestivi*, Schiaccianoci and Ratafia, infused in a base of Aglianico wine.

'Ratafia is not distilled but is made following an old family recipe of my grandmother Erminia's,' she says, as she pours the dark liquid into small glasses. 'In this part of Italy, ratafia was drunk when sealing a piece of business or to conclude a pact. The word *ratafia* is Arabic for "cherry bush", and mine uses cherry leaves as one of the twelve *erbe* that go into the mix.' The next stage is the adding of the sugar and 36° proof alcohol. It is then aged for two years in cherry-wood barriques. The result is a complex but clean liqueur that makes a perfect conclusion to an Irpinian – Aglianico-based – dinner.

San Martino Valle Caudina

Organic Farm, Honey

Mafariello
TEL 0824 841219

La Selva del Duca
'The Duke's Wood' is a lovely organic farm located on a plateau at 700 metres in the Partenio Mountain Park, surrounded by chestnut woods that are fed by pure natural springs and waterfalls. The duke, Giovanni Pignatella della Leonessa, is active in promoting this area and its culture: he has helped set up an organization of characterful Bed and Breakfasts in the area (see pp. 321 and 403). On the farm, he rears a breed of black pig that has been crossed with wild boar and produces very lean meat for the making of *salumi*. There are free-range chickens and sheep, whose milk is made into raw-milk *pecorino* cheese. Chestnuts are puréed, without added sugar, for use in desserts, and the intensely flavoured chestnut honey (that is so delicious on yoghurt) is sold. By appointment, or on Saturday mornings, visits can be arranged to the family's spectacular castle at San Martino Valle Caudina.

ALSO: Virginio Clemente (Via Torrettiello; TEL 0824 833239): if you happen to be passing in early summer, this farm produces fabulous cherries, of the Ciliegia Imperiale variety.

Sant'Andrea di Conza

Opposite: The Aglianico harvest at Cantine Di Meo

Sant'Andrea di Conza hosts an annual *peperoncino*-eating competition, in which the object is to down as many hot chilli peppers as possible in thirty minutes. The only respite: a glass of water and a piece of bread.

THE FRIARIELLI DEBATE

Friarielli mean different things to different people – every Campanian area has its own version. Here are three I have tracked down and tasted:

In Irpinia, *friarielli* are smallish grass-green peppers, sometimes veering to light orange. They are thin-skinned, sweetish (not *piccante*, though they sell fiery, long thin darker green ones to cook with the *friarielli* for those who like the kick) and about four to six inches long. They are strictly local. June is the moment for them, and if you walk around the village at 11 a.m. you can smell them being cooked through many open windows.

You cook them alone, uncut, whole (not even taking off the stems): just rinse and throw them all into a deep frying pan with a little hot olive oil. Over high heat they soon wither and cook down, but I think a bit of that browned pepper taste is part of the attraction. If they get too dry as they sauté, throw in a glassful of water. The lady in the fruit shop, Rosa, likes to add a bit of chopped tomato right at the end, when they are soft and almost ready to take off the stove, but most often they are served uncluttered by other ingredients – indeed, that is something I admire about real Italian cooking, that flavours come at you courageously, one at a time. Rosa was selling at least eight lots of them, each a little different in colour and shape from the others. I asked her for the most '*saporiti*' (she knows my tastes by now), and she chose some that must have been picked just hours before. One kilo cost one euro. She threw in a bunch of basil for free. *Friarielli* are usually served warm (like so many Italian vegetable dishes), with a bit of day-old bread from the wood-burning oven to mop up the juices. The stems remain hard, so you can pick them out easily, or eat the peppers holding on to these 'handles'.

Top: Green Nusco friarielli peppers
*Middle: Gesualdo butcher Mario Carrabs with a sprig of
their broccoli-top friarielli*
Bottom: Long, leafy Neapolitan friarielli grown near Pompei

Restaurant

L'Incanto

Below the Carabinieri
station
TEL 0827 35021
INTERNET
www.ristoincanto.it
CLOSED Mon; 2 weeks in
July; 2 weeks Oct-Nov
PRICE
Menu degustazione €€€
Pizza only at weekends

Sant'Andrea di Conza is at the easternmost edge of northern Campania – twenty metres more and you're in Basilicata. It's also close to the border with Puglia: the three regions come together here as the landscape opens out into the softly rolling fields that characterize Puglia east of the Apennines. The restaurant–pizzeria is located in the centre of the village, below the *Carabinieri* station, where the road widens out into a small *piazza* (I mention this because the chef, Pompeo Limongiello, says the road they are on has no name).

L'Incanto is perfect if you're exploring the area's hill towns or countryside. The young couple have created an attractive, nicely lit restaurant that has shifted up from selling pizzas and simple *osteria* dishes to a more carefully approached cuisine. Pompeo is self-taught: he studied architecture before becoming a cook. What he may lack in technique he makes up for in enthusiasm: the food is attractively presented, and there are delicious hot *foccacie* and untopped pizzas to accompany the excellent *salumi* and cheeses selected for him by his uncle, Antonio Vespucci, an expert on this area's artisanal foods.

This is a good place to sample crisp, dried *peperoni cruschi*, with their intense, bitterish finish; they're wonderful over locally made *cavatielli* pasta with oil-roasted breadcrumbs – the poor man's Parmesan. *Paccheri* from Vallesacarda are served with *baccalà* Pompeo has smoked for him by a cheese-maker at Montella, and tangy oil from Potenza, over the border in Basilicata. The couple get some of their vegetables by barter: exchanging pizza dough for home-grown produce. *Secondi* vary too, with game, thick fillets of *baccalà*, and other simply cooked meats. The wine list is limited, but will grow over time.

Garlic and hot peppers are key summer ingredients

It's not easy for the young restaurateurs of deepest Irpinia to convince their peers and neighbours to eat in places that seem 'fancier' than they are used to. 'When we started,' says Angela, 'our customers didn't know about stem wine glasses, and would pour their water into the *ballons* and drink wine from the tumblers. Luckily we had positive role models like Antonio Pisaniello (see p. 367), who had encountered and overcome the same kinds of resistance.' The Limongiellos are doing a fine job, and I wish them well.

Sant'Angelo a Scala

Wine

Via Santa Maria, 2
TEL 0825 900963
INTERNET
www.rennavini.com

Renna

Baldo Renna has been bottling his grapes since the early 1990s. He has chosen to collaborate with Maurizio De Simone, the young œnologist who not only appreciates Campania's indigenous grape varieties, but works them in a natural, '*tipico*' style – without following fashions or rushing to wow or woo critics. A good combination for an estate whose price-quality ratio is admirable.

Sant'Angelo dei Lombardi

This medieval village was a centre for the making of majolica until 1980, when it tragically became the epicentre of the earthquake; as a result, most of the town had to be rebuilt from scratch – including the Duomo, which was put back together, stone by stone – and its traditional crafts were sadly lost. Each November, Sant'Angelo hosts a lovely *sagra*, in which many craftsmen, food producers and musicians from neighbouring villages take part.

Bread and Pastries

Piazza F. Pelullo
TEL 0827 24701

Panificio Bottega delle Delizie

From their wood-burning oven, the Squarciafico family bakes good bread, but also wonderful fried rolls stuffed with field greens and sausage and other nourishing snacks. In autumn and winter, many traditional *dolci* are made using the local chestnuts.

You can't miss Bar Moderno – Pasticceria Gelateria (TEL 0827 24171); it's located at the entrance of the town, surrounded by orange, post-modern planters. This is the best place for a great *caffè*, accompanied by a home-baked pastry or cake – including *mostaccioli* and walnut cakes in winter – and delicious *gelati* in summer, when you can sit out on the ample terrace and admire the view of the valley below. Outside of the town, near the Santuario di Santa Felicità, Letizia D'Apolito (Contrada da Montanaldo; TEL 0827 45331, 340 477093 E-MAIL ldapolito@ tiscalinet) makes excellent Pecorino Carmasciano from her herd of sheep who graze in sulphur-rich fields that have been 'coloured' by the Mefite (see p. 374).

Santa Paolina

Wine

Santa Lucia, 206
TEL/FAX 0825 964350

Cantina dei Monaci

A small cellar, with just three hectares of vineyards and a couple who are passionate about winemaking: their efforts are paying off, as their elegant, pure Fiano di Avellino – from the Lapio area that is producing other great Fianos – has been very well received.

Santo Stefano del Sole

Restaurant

Via Casina
San Pietro all'Olio
TEL 0825 673664
CLOSED Sun eve & Mon;
2 weeks in Sep
CARDS All
PRICE €€

Taberna Vulgi

Giovanni Mariconda's trattoria offers rustic country cooking, so it's a pleasant place – with space outdoors in summer – to sample some of Irpinia's hearty dishes. The *antipasti* go from local *salumi* and cheeses to vegetables, including basil-stuffed *melanzane* with tomato sauce, or hot winter *sformati* of pumpkin or greens; *fiori di zucca* are filled with ricotta and *pancetta* before being deep-fried. *Primi* always include some thick soups – of pulses and vegetables – to accompany pastas dressed with olives, capers, tomatoes and aubergine (like a Sicilian dish), or the slow-cooked *genovese* of onions and meat. Suet, pork lard and extra virgin olive oil are the fats that traditionally enriched Irpinian ingredients foraged from fields and woods, and Taberna Vulgi's dishes still reflect this tendency. (Anyone watching their salt intake should tell the kitchen when they order, as dishes here are often highly salted.) Winter main courses always feature pork, farmyard animals, or *baccalà*, or there are local cheeses from the Antico Casaro nearby. Save room for desserts: they are well made. You'll find enough local wines to accompany these vigorous flavours, as well as the after-dinner liqueurs the Italians are so fond of.

Serino

This is the area for another important DOP-status chestnut: the Castagna di Serino.

Restaurant

SS Terminio, Carpino
TEL 0825 542970
CLOSED Mon
PRICE €€

O' Carpino Ristorante Pizzeria

This restaurant, high on the road above Serino, is run by three charming and modest brothers – Raffaele in the *sala*, and Massimo and Antonio in the kitchen. Their spare ochre dining room is sizeable, and very popular at weekends when whole families gather to enjoy the local recipes and friendly atmosphere. In winter, the fireplace offers a warming focal point. Go with a healthy appetite: portions are generous and there are lots of them.

The brothers' repertoire varies with the seasons, but after abundant mixed *antipasti*, I enjoyed a thick soup of *fagioli*, cabbage and carrot, and soft pasta *tortelli* stuffed with sweet ricotta and artichokes, with a potato sauce – pastas are a speciality here as the men's mother still makes a lot of them by hand. To follow, guinea fowl came with *porcini* mushrooms, and a delicate ricotta filling under the skin; it went well with a lively local Aglianico. Desserts too are home-made, so save room.

Wine, Olive Oil
Villa Raiano

Via S Pescatore, 19
TEL 0825 592826
0825 595781
FAX 0825 595771
E-MAIL
info@villaraiano.it
INTERNET
www.villaraiano.it

When, four years ago, this very imposing olive oil producing company decided to start making quality wines, they called in the local expert œnologist, Luigi Moio, to give them a hand. 'We are used to making large quantities of good oil – 25 million bottles per year,' says Sabino Basso, the family's agronomist, 'and I think to begin with we thought that winemaking would be similar – but we soon discovered how different the two worlds are.' The wine adventure began in 1996 with the purchase of ten hectares at Venticano for making Taurasi, with vines over thirty years old.

After he arrived as a consultant, Moio quickly took control, bringing in French barriques for the key wines – including Ripa

A cooper's van, selling barrels mainly to families making their own wine

Alta, of white Fiano grapes, and the Taurasi. 'We're surrounded here by some great wineries, so we had to make a strategic market decision too when launching our wines,' Basso continues. 'We opted for very carefully manicured labels and bottles, and a pricing scale that was higher than Mastroberardino and Feudi di San Gregorio – there was nowhere else to go.' The wines have an international appeal, despite being made entirely with autochthonous grape varieties, as they are solidly constructed with good concentration. Personally I prefer the more natural 'base' Fiano to the barrique-matured version, but I usually prefer less- or un-oaked whites. In either case, the wines can be bought and tasted at the little shop on the cellar's premises.

I enjoyed our conversation about olive oils, as it confirmed some of my suspicions vis-à-vis certain sectors of the American market. The Bassos make many oils, from selected organic extra virgins, through 'normal' extra virgin oil from Campania, Puglia and Calabria, to olive oil and pomace or *sansa*, which are best avoided. 'Whereas in Italy the public is fairly well educated about olive oils, there seems to be a real lack of information in the United States,' Basso says. 'For instance, many Americans seem to prefer mild-tasting olive oils because they falsely believe that there is more fat in the higher-flavoured oils.' Indeed, so-called 'light' oils have exactly the same amount of fat as the rest. 'They also don't seem to understand that 'pomace' is a by-product made (as are seed oils) by using chemical solvents to extract oily residues from the discarded mass that remains after the ground olives have been pressed or centrifuged – in other words, they need to learn that the best oil is, and always will be, pure extra virgin olive oil extruded from the olives by mechanical – not chemical – means.' And, I would add, always check the sell-by date and buy oil as fresh as you can find it – unlike wine it does not improve with age.

Restaurant
Antico Raiano

Piazza Ianelli, 35
TEL 0825 592807
CLOSED Sun evening;
Mon; end July–
beginning Aug
CARDS All
PRICE €€€

If you're in the mood for the earthy flavours of Irpinia's mountains cooked without too much fanfare in a nicely redone stone cellar–barn, Antica Raiano is the place. It's set in the centre of the tiny stone village, on the *piazza*, and offers friendly service from its young team. The owner, Marianna Mariconda, passed her passion for food and wine on to chef Gianfranco Longobardi and Roberto Pasquale in the dining room. Here you can taste *polenta*, wood mushrooms and wild boar, or chestnuts, black truffles and pork – or the warming soups and pastas that are at the heart of *contadina* cooking – with wines to match.

The Serino Hotel (Via Terminio, 119; TEL 0825 594901; FAX 0825 594166) is situated high on the hillside above Serino, and is one of the better-equipped hotels of the area. Its restaurant serves good, home-cooked country fare.

Sorbo Serpico

Wine, Restaurant

Cerza Grossa
TEL 0825 986611
FAX 0825 986230
E-MAIL feudi@feudi.it
INTERNET
www.feudi.com
Marennà:
TEL 0825 986666
FAX 0825 986667
CLOSED Sun eve; Mon;
Tues lunch; 8–28 Aug;
9–26 Jan
PRICE €€€€

Feudi di San Gregorio, Marennà

Feudi di San Gregorio occupies a unique position in the panorama of Campanian wineries: the estate has grown rapidly in size and reputation since it began in 1990, and it now has an output of 2.5 million bottles; its headquarters are a streamlined, *modernissima cantina* set in open countryside designed by cutting-edge Japanese (Hikaru Mori) and Italo-New York architects (Massimo and Lella Vignelli); its consultant winemaker is the highly regarded Riccardo Cotarella, whose collaboration has ensured success; it was able, right from the start, to assert its wines (and brand) on the international market, catapulting the image of Campanian wines from picturesque rusticity to sleek minimalism while guaranteeing consistently high performances in guide books and market places; and its new restaurant, Marennà, has quickly become one of the hottest (and coolest) eating-places in Campania. Quite a record.

To have achieved all this in just ten years has taken dynamism, creative thinking – and big investments. Feudi's origins are, however, surprisingly modest. The Ercolino brothers – Enzo, Mario and Luciano – with Enzo's wife, Mirella Capaldo, began the winery in 1986, under '*Legge 44*', a European Community sponsorship programme created to stimulate young entrepreneurs in Italy's underdeveloped south. The Ercolinos are sons of Irpinian *contadini*. Enzo took a degree at Salerno University, then went to Rome to work for IRI – a vast, semi-private institute for industrial reconstruction. 'If it hadn't been for the earthquake, I might never have come back to live in Irpinia. Cataclysmic events put everything else into perspective. This *terremoto* lasted one minute, but it changed my world: up until that moment I didn't know or care that I was from Irpinia – if anything, I dreamed about getting out of here. There seemed to be nothing to hold me,' Ercolino admits.

'With Feudi, our strength from the beginning was that we knew we weren't experts, so we looked for the best people to help us achieve the results we wanted.' The strategy worked: both whites – the fine Fianos, Campanaro and Pietracalda, and the Greco di Tufo Cutizzi – and reds – Serpico, and Taurasi

Enzo Ercolino

Feudi San Gregorio's
vineyards in winter

Chef Heinz Beck, of La
Pergola restaurant,
Rome, outside Marennà

Selve di Luoti, Aglianico wines of elegant concentration and complexity, and Pàtrimo, of twenty-year-old Merlot vines that were 'discovered by chance' in one of the local vineyards – have won top awards. With continuing improvements, the winery – now run by Enzo Ercolino (his brothers parted ways with him in 2004), his wife and her brother, the powerful financier, Pellegrino Capaldo – seems unstoppable.

The restaurant, Marennà (the word means to have a light meal or *merenda* in dialect), has been Enzo's personal hobby horse. 'I love to eat well,' he says, as we walk through the luminous dining room past the large, glassed-in kitchen that commands panoramic views of the valley vineyards. 'I wanted to combine the sophistication and technique of the world's top restaurants with the seasonal, traditional and country recipes of Irpinia and Napoli; not to lose the flavours of those slow-cooked tomato ragùs and onion *genovese*, yet create dishes that could fit well into this modern context.'

As is his wont, Ercolino called in the great chef, Heinz Beck,

Marennà's chef, Donato Episcopo

to assemble a brigade that could meet the challenge, under the leadership of the talented young Donato Episcopo, who trained with Beck at Rome's Hilton Pergola restaurant for several years. I enjoyed working on the Marennà project in its early months, when the new chefs were finding their way in Irpinia. It was a fascinating, exciting process to watch and taste as the dishes evolved and a house style gradually came into being. The restaurant is now in full swing and Episcopo and his team are getting the recognition they deserve: *bravissimi*!

The big new cellar is now fully operational, with its imposing 150-metre *barricaia* and formal gardens. Many projects are in the works, from cooking lessons and food tours to a farm for local animal breeds... so watch this space.

Summonte

Wine

CELLAR:
Marroni Summonte
TEL 0825 691446
OFFICE:
Via Pianodardine, 2
Avellino
TEL 0825 626555

Guido Marsella

One wine, but it's a great one: Guido Marsella's Fiano di Avellino has acquired quite a reputation for itself in the past few years. It's a characterful, complex wine with an almost salty intensity, and a citrusy zing to it that balances the toasted hazelnut richness of the ripe grapes; very long and with good depth – a wine to pair with seafood or medium-aged cheeses.

Taurasi

Taurasi

The medieval nucleus of Taurasi is situated on a hilltop overlooking the wide valley of the Calore river, whose sides are all planted to vines. The town was half-destroyed in the 1980 earthquake and is still in urgent need of rebuilding. If it were carefully restored, Taurasi would be as beautiful as any Tuscan hilltown, and could become one of Irpinia's most important œnological centres. After all, wine has been produced and sold from here for centuries, as the hundreds of small cellars carved out of the *tufo* stone under the houses attest. It's no coincidence that the south's first DOCG was given to the big red Aglianico wine named for this village. Recently, thanks to the excellence of Taurasi wines made by a handful of pioneer producers – including Mastroberardino, Struzziero, Terredora and, more recently, Caggiano and Feudi di San Gregorio – the area's image has been catapulted to international attention, and more and more wineries are opening with these high standards in mind.

Wine

Antica Hirpinia

Contrada Lenze, 10
TEL 0827 74730
E-MAIL
info@cantinahirpinia.it
INTERNET
www.anticahirpinia.it

The *cantine sociali* have played an important role in the history of Italy's wine world. Often, as is the case in Taurasi, these co-operatives enabled the *contadini* – and the local wines – to survive during times of crisis. In recent years, many of the individual grape-growers, who for years had sold their grapes to the *cantina sociale*, have decided to start making and bottling wines under their own labels, despite the costs of new cellars and equipment that this entails. On the one hand, this has meant that some of the best grapes are no longer given to the co-operative, but it has also provided an impetus for the large cellars to maintain or improve the quality of their production, and play a more active role in the image and market of their area's wines. Antica Hirpinia has over 150 members, who own a total of almost 200 hectares in this important winemaking zone – so the potential is enormous, as recent results are beginning to show.

Wine

Antonio Caggiano

Contrada Sala
TEL 0827 74043
3389820074
E-MAIL
info@cantinecaggiano.it

Taurasi corks

Antonio Caggiano's winery cellar is quite unlike any other I've seen. It reminds me of the Watts Towers in Los Angeles by the artist Simon Rodia, with its eclectic mix of architectural elements patch-worked together into a personalized whole. If Rodia's fantasy extends high into the air, Caggiano's is played

Antonio Caggiano with a town vine he planted in Taurasi

out underground – in a warren of tunnels, grottoes and ageing rooms built around antique portals and staircases, pillars and jambs, transoms and balustrades – where it flirts with the kitsch. 'After the 1980 earthquake,' explains Caggiano, 'I worked to clear the debris of the fallen houses, and whenever I found interesting carvings or details, I set them aside. After all, no one else wanted them, it was just "old stuff". Then, in 1990, I began creating my *cantina* around them.'

Housed in this idiosyncratic engineering feat are some of Campania's most celebrated wines. 'Before the Second World War, everyone in this town bottled wines of pure Aglianico,' he says. 'And it was good. When I decided to make mine, I went to France to taste the wines there, and I ran into Luigi Moio (see p. 353 and the index), who had been studying French œnology. He didn't know much about Aglianico at the time, but I persuaded him to help me do some research on our native grape.' Once back in Italy, Moio began studies into this difficult but rewarding *uvaggio*, and has since become a top expert on it – he describes himself as 'the man who tamed Aglianico'.

Working with Moio, Caggiano has replanted many of his twenty hectares. 'The old-fashioned planting grid was of 600 to 700 plants per hectare, with space between the rows for the oxen to pass with the ploughs and vegetables to be grown. From there we moved up to 4,000 vines per hectare, and now one of our experimental vineyards has as many as 12,000.' Antonio Caggiano, with his son Giuseppe, has done clonal selections of the best Aglianico vines, so new vineyards are producing high quality grapes. In the cellar, French oak barriques have replaced the large wooden *botti* of times past, and Caggiano's wines – especially his classic cru Macchia dei Goti Taurasi and the more modernist Salae Domini – have a firm imprint of spicy oak to temper the Aglianico's tough tannins. The whole range of Caggiano's wines, including the whites Béchar and Fiagre, are personalized and well constructed, giving ample expression to this important Irpinian producer.

Wine

Contrade di Taurasi – Cantine Lonardo

Via Municipio, 41
TEL 081 5442457
TEL/FAX 0827 74704
E-MAIL
lonardo@interfree.it

This recently formed estate is working with a talented young œnologist, Maurizio De Simone, who has a penchant for Campania and is part of Roberto Cipresso's winemaking group. Sandro Lonardo used to sell the grapes from his high (grown at 450 metres) thirty-year-old Aglianico vines to other producers but is now making his own wines. When I last tasted the Lonardo wines with De Simone, I was impressed by the

Taurasi's mineral yet elegant, pure, fruity style. I was also intrigued by the work De Simone is doing with an unusual white grape called Greco Muscio, or Musc'.

'I noticed that all the *contadini* had the same white grape growing on the pergolas in their courtyards,' he explains. 'This grape has a particular trait: at the end of the season, when the terrains around Taurasi are short of water, Greco Musc' skin grows faster than its pulp and becomes crinkly.' At first he thought the grapes were turning to raisins, but they weren't. 'I figured that with all that skin, a wine made from this grape – which is not really a Greco – would have a lot of personality.' Tasted from the vat, the first experiment had a delicate colour and something of the character of a Sauvignon. We'll have to see how it develops.

Teora

Agriturismo
Le Masserie di Corona

Contrada di Civita
Superiore
TEL 0827 51550

Teora is centrally placed if you are planning to explore the eastern side of Irpinia: the lake of Conza and Calitri are nearby, as are Nusco and Rocca San Felice. This farm has a pleasant *agriturismo* with good home cooking, and offers riding and other activities. It produces organic vegetables and its own sheep's cheeses from a large herd.

Torella dei Lombardi

Torella dei Lombardi was the birthplace of the great film-maker, Sergio Leone; each summer the beautiful Castello Candriano hosts a film festival here in his honour.

Olive Oil, Agriturismo
Bellofatto

Contrada Pianomarotta,
16
TEL/FAX 0827 49083
E-MAIL
info@bellofatto.it
INTERNET
www.bellofatto.it

Torella dei Lombardi is wedged between the valleys of the Calore and Frédane rivers, in a part of the Irpinian countryside that is well suited to olive trees, and that seems luckily to be out of reach of the *mosca*, the olive fly that so often causes problems in lower land near the sea. Giovanni Pio, Bellofatto's owner, is applying for organic status for his extra virgin oil, of Ravece with Frantoio, Nocellara and Leccino olives. He also runs an *agriturismo* from the farm, with rooms, and a restaurant for the guests serving local dishes of pasta, game, and vegetables, dressed, as one would expect, with his own *extra vergine*.

Torre Le Nocelle

Wine, Olive Oil

I Capitani

Via Bosco Faiano
TEL 0825 969182
INTERNET
www.icapitani.com

If you look across the Calore valley from Torre Le Nocelle, you can see the town of Taurasi: this is the heart of one of Campania's best winemaking areas. Ciriaco Cefalo's father's family bought this property at the end of the 19th century, when it was still part of the hunting reserve of the noble della Leonessa family (see p. 377). Since the 1998 vintage, there has been a concerted effort to modernize the cellar and improve the wines – and the results are beginning to show. 'We are working to maintain an authentic feel to these wines, for they are part of the history here,' says Cefalo as we visit the lovely big tasting and dining room beside the cellar, decorated with many antique objects of rural life. 'We are using our own native yeasts too, which means longer fermentations, but more character.' The Taurasi is allowed to age for several years in the cellar until the tannins have softened and the wine is ready to drink.

I Capitani makes a wonderfully fruity olive oil – Aurum Silvæ – mostly from the Ravece olives. It has real character, with the grass and green tomato leaf aromas that characterize this variety. 'We have installed our own mill here, that works by decantation instead of centrifuge, and without any water being added, so the oil is not stressed at all and remains very pure.'

The family also have two apartments for guests as *agriturismo*.

Tufo

The village of Tufo is a must for anyone interested in the effect geology can have on wine: drive around the lower part of the town, past the historic di Marzo cellars, and see how the houses are built up and onto the yellowish rock, and their cellars carved right out from underneath. *Tufo* (the stone) is unusual in that it is quite soft and easy to work when it is still compact but hardens as it comes into contact with the air. Tufo (the town) was, until recently, famous for its sulphur mines and this mineral quality is reflected in the wines of its surrounding region.

Vineyards near Tufo

Via Gaetano di Marzo, 17
TEL 0825 998022
FAX 0825 998383
E-MAIL
azienda.dimarzo@simail.it
INTERNET
www.cantinedimarzo.it

Wine

Di Marzo

The di Marzo family have been important in the history of Tufo since the 17th century, not only for their historic cellars, but for their sulphur mines that were key to the area's development in the 19th century. The family's imposing *palazzo* was remodelled in the 18th century, and is fascinating to visit: its deep tunnelled cellars have been dug out of the sulphurous tufa. There is an attractive shop and tasting area for the company's wines, of which the most important are, naturally enough, Greco di Tufo.

Fraz S Paolo, 14/A
TEL 0825 998194
E-MAIL info@
benitoferrara.it

Wine

Benito Ferrara

The Ferraras, Benito and Gabriella, have a small but functional *cantina* under their modest country house, *sotto casa*. And four hectares of vineyards, some of which they can see from the house, on a sunny hillside that falls away in a soft slope. Until recently Gabriella and Benito have concentrated on making two wines from the same grape, Greco di Tufo, though they are now branching out with a Fiano di Avellino (of selected bought grapes) and some Aglianico. But it is for their Grecos that they have become well known. Working with the fine Tuscan œnologist, Paolo Caciorgna, they have established a house style in which the Greco is free to express itself with all the complexity of ripe fruit, notes of hazelnut and honey, zest of citrus and minerals that characterize this ancient grape. 'We're the fourth generation of winemakers in this family,' says Gabriella, and lucky to have some very old vines that are still producing grapes of an intense character. But we have also planted new vineyards that are being grown in the modern style: 80 cms apart, and trained low, so the fruit matures 10 to 20 days earlier than it used to, and there is better balance between the sugars and the Greco's naturally high acidity.' Vigna Cicogna is their best cru: one hectare of east–west exposition vines that benefit the most from the veins of sulphur that lace this soil.

Vallesaccarda

Restaurant

Oasis – Sapori Antichi

Via Provinciale
Vallesaccarda
TEL 0827 97021
FAX 0827 97541
INTERNET www.
oasis-saporiantichi.it
CLOSED Thurs; 1–15 July
CARDS All
PRICE €€€–€€€€
A few rooms are
available

It's always a pleasure to go to Oasis, because you know before you get there that the food will be wonderful – comforting and authentic – and the atmosphere both formal and familiar. Indeed, family is a key word in this spacious, elegant restaurant: la Famiglia Fischetti is almost a tribe, with its cheery women in the kitchen, the young men serving in the *sala*, and the patriarch – if you can pin that word on such a charmingly unassuming gentleman – growing vegetables and tending his orchard fruits. The restaurant is a success because each of these characters fits so well into the whole.

As for the food, the subtitle says it all – *antichi sapori* are the original, ancient flavours of an ancient land. Ingredients that, like the people, have withstood the tests of nature: fragile, just-set ricotta in tiny rush baskets, assertive *prosciutto* aged for two years, bitter wild asparagus that grow up through pasture grasses, the pungent *baccalà* that has always brought the sea to the *interno*.

'We try not to change our ancestors' recipes too radically,' explains Puccio as he serves a *primo* of *paccheri* with artichokes and sausage. 'We like to work with few elements in each dish, but they have to be excellent: here the flattened pasta rings we call *gli schiaffettoni* are hand-made by my mother, not factory dried; the artichokes are grown nearby, at Pietrelcina; and the forceful *salsiccia pezzente* is assembled from the less noble parts of the pig – the neck, cheek and head – and dried above a fireplace.' Its slight smokiness adds rusticity to this deceptively simple taste combination.

Puccio is one of the three brothers, two sisters, their wives, husbands and *fidanzati* who, with their mother and father, run

Signor Fischetti in his orchard

Wild field greens (cicoria) at Oasis

the restaurant – a total of twenty-two when they are all at home. 'Ours is *una cucina di terra*,' says Carmine, as he presents a shallow bowl of *pancotto* with *cicoria*, *peperoni cruschi* and 'raw' Ravece olive oil. 'When there was nothing in the larder but stale bread, the *contadini* still were able to create an appetizing meal.' Leaves of field chicory are boiled, and their cooking water used to moisten the day-old bread; sun-dried peppers add a bitter accent, and the whole is brightened by the fruit-and-pepper warmth of the golden oil.

Save room for desserts: the women are famous for their cakes and *semifreddi* – of wild cherries (*visciole*) and hazelnuts – or buffalo-yoghurt mousses flavoured with olive oil. The service is friendly but not too relaxed, and the food is always well matched with the rich tapestry of wines that Irpinia (and beyond) now offers.

Restaurant

Minicuccio Hotel Ristorante

Via Santa Maria, 24–26
TEL 0827 97020
CLOSED
Mon; holidays variable
CARDS All
PRICE €€

Franco Pagliarulo, the owner of this restaurant and modest country hotel, deserves credit as one of the first promoters of real Irpinian *cucina*: in the 1970s he ran a one-room restaurant with his aunts, who cooked traditional dishes from their home repertoire for the customers and friends who came from afar to eat them. That was before the earthquake, when Vallesacarda suffered serious damage. Today, he and his family run a large, attractively appointed modern dining room with hotel rooms above. They still serve classic local foods: rustic vegetable soups of wild field greens (*minestra asciatizza*) or bean (*fagioli*), and many delicious hand-made pastas. For *secondi* there is kid (*capretto*), rabbit, *baccalà* or lamb... all the farmers' favourites. The Pagliarulos are warm and welcoming, so you'll enjoy this very fairly priced slice of country life – and you may even learn a few phrases of the local dialect.

Venticano

Olive Oil

FAM

Contrada Ilici, 5
TEL 0825 965829
FAX 0825 965969
E-MAIL
info@oliofam.com
INTERNET
www.oliofam.com

Flora, Antonio and Maria Tranfaglia: put their names together and you get FAM. The three put their ideas together and have come up with a large, specialized oil-producing company that for the last three years has obtained good results working the local olives from their own and rented olive groves. This is the area where the Ogliarola di Avellino trees are prevalent, producing consistent yields of high-quality olives. The Ogliarola is picked when black. The Tranfaglias blend it with the more common varieties, Leccino and Frantoio, preferring to bottle the Ravece – which is picked when it is wine-red or purple-black – by itself as a 'Riserva'.

Wine

Struzziero

Via Cadorna, 214
TEL 0825 965065
E-MAIL
struzziero@struzziero.it
INTERNET
www.struzziero.it

I have been very struck by Mario Struzziero's wines: they have an austerity, a complexity, an inner life that obliges the drinker to focus on them; even when they are less than perfectly execut-ed, they are compelling. These are wines that need plenty of time to open – years, when necessary – indeed the Taurasi has a life-span of 25 years, and definitely benefits from extra cellaring. In 2004, the Taurasi Campoceraso 1997 Riserva was still almost impenetrable, inscrutable: the more time you gave it, the more its territorial authenticity revealed itself – a wine to take seriously.

Villamaina

Honey

Apicoltura Caputo

Contrada Piano, 57
TEL 0825 442126

For those who have had enough of Nutella (or never liked it in the first place) Giuseppe Caputo has created a mixed cream of honey and hazelnuts that provides an interesting alternative. He and his father also produce a balanced *idromele* – an alcoholic drink of fermented honey – and sell single-variety honeys of chestnut (*castagne*), acacia and mixed blossoms – some of which they produce themselves. And also *pappa reale*, royal jelly.

Olive Oil
Oleificio Montuori

Contrada Toppoli
TEL 0825 442175

This oil mill is situated in the Valley of the Ansanto that Virgil describes in the *Æneid*. It is run by a young family who are trying to educate their buyers – their brochure explains a lot about oil and its making. They have been working their olives for the past three years, using the most up-to-date milling system that presses the olives without losing any of their fruity character. Of their two oils, Ravis is made of pure Ravece, while Domus is a mix of several varieties: Cacazzara, Olivella, Cretaiola, Nocellara, Ogliarola, Leccino and Frantoio – all picked early and pressed in their own mill.

Volturara

This town is famous for its *fagioli Quarantini*, small white beans with tender skins that are delicious cooked with local *scarola*, and Volturara potatoes. If you are there around Easter, look out for *taralli di Pasqua*, large sweet double-ring pastries with nuts and glacé icing that are made at this time of year by the bread bakeries.

In the period between the two World Wars, Volturara was also known for legendary brigand Nardiello, one of the most infamous in Italy's south (a film was even made about him). Volturara, in the Valle del Dragone, occupied a strategic position between 'low' and 'high' Irpinia, and his band of *briganti* made sure everyone who passed through there payed for the privilege.

Zungoli

Cheese
Cooperativa Agricola Molara

Via Toppo dell'Anno
TEL 0825 845281
FAX 0825 845096
E-MAIL
coopmolara@libero.it

This co-operative farm produces *caciocavallo* cheeses from the native Podolica breed of cows who pasture in the hills of Irpinia. This is one of the south's greatest cheeses. These pear-shaped forms are allowed to age naturally in grottoes dug out of the *tufo* in the historic village of Zungoli for two years or more. When they are ready to be eaten, the mould is washed off their smooth crusts. Inside the cheese is compact, with tiny natural holes. The cheese has a sharp yet mellow aroma, and a long, full flavour that reflects the tastes of the many grasses the cows are free to graze on.

Chapter 9

Benevento and Il Sannio

Vineyards and villages of the interior

FOR TOURIST
INFORMATION:
EPT Benevento
Via Nicola Sala, 31
TEL 0824 319911
0824 319931
INTERNET
www.eptbenevento.it

Also in Piazza Roma, 11
TEL 0824 319938

If modern Benevento is relatively unknown to foreigners, it has not always been so: the area (which is often referred to as *il Sannio*, for the mountain range that forms its northern part) is rich in history, and played an important part in the geopolitical development of Campania. Even the dinosaurs liked it here: the only dinosaur fossil to have been found in Italy is in the Sannio mountains, at Pietraroja, where the Apennines form the northern boundary between Campania and Molise. As all Italian schoolchildren learn, Benevento was founded by the Samnites, the only people able to slow the Roman expansion by their fierce resistance to colonization: at the battle of the Forche Caudine (Caudine Forks), in 321 BC, the Samnites defeated the Romans by trapping them in a narrow defile between Benevento and Capua. But in 295 BC the Romans got their revenge by defeating Pyrrhus, king of the northern Greek state of Epirus, who had come to the Samnites' aid, and from then on the Roman colonization proceeded uncontested. It was around that time that the Romans changed the town's name: from the innocuous archaic 'Maloenton' it had become 'Mauentum' and then 'Maleventum' in Latin – a name that seemed to augur badly; they boldly reversed the trend by renaming the city 'Beneventum.'

The Romans left many signs of their greatness at Benevento: the Roman theatre held 10,000 spectators, and is one of the largest still in existence; it was built by the emperor Hadrian in the 2nd century AD and enlarged by Caracalla. It is now used for concerts in summer. Another masterpiece of Roman monumental building in the city of Benevento is the high triumphal arch of Traiano, Porta Aurea, built in 114 AD by the Roman Senate to commemorate the emperor Traiano (Trajan) and his

Opposite: Annurca apples are laid out under netting to ripen

Benevento's Roman arch

opening of the Via Appia Traiana – the road that shortened the distance between Roma and Brindisi. This road turned Benevento into an obligatory stopping place on the journey to Puglia. The impressive arch features images from the emperor's life in bas-relief – scenes of peace on the side of the arch that faces the city, scenes of war looking out towards the countryside.

In the 8th century, under the Germanic Longobards who had battled with the Byzantines for supremacy in southern Italy, Benevento became a powerful duchy that extended over much of the south of Italy; at that time the city was prosperous, and known for the *scrittura beneventana* that filled a profusion of illuminated manuscripts. In 1266, in a major battle against the forces of Charles of Anjou, Frederic II's illegitimate son, Manfred, was defeated and killed at Benevento. His body lay unburied for a long time by the bridge on the river Calore; in *La Divina Commedia*, Dante wrote of Manfred oppressed '*sotto la guardia della grave mora*' – under the stones the soldiers had thrown on to him.

Things quietened down somewhat over the next centuries and, from the 16th century onwards, Benevento led a tame – and ever poorer – provincial life that was disturbed once more by the terrible earthquake of 1688, after which it was almost completely rebuilt by Pope Benedetto XIII. (After the demise of the last Longobard principality, Benevento was governed by the Papacy until the unification of Italy.) Another cyclone – this time, Napoleonic – saw it become a principality under the rule of Talleyrand. Tragically, in May 1943, during the Second World War, 65 per cent of the city was destroyed by Allied bombing.

On a more esoteric note, in the 1st century AD, Benevento was a centre of the cult of Isis which flourished as late as the 6th century. With the advent of the Longobards, the practice of magic and mystic rites was considered incompatible with Christianity, and was officially stamped out. Yet it seems that believers continued to conduct rites outside the city walls, near a walnut tree in the valley of the Sàbato river. This gave rise to endless stories of the witches of Benevento and their sabbaths. According to legend, St. Barbato put an end to these activities in the 7th century by cutting down the walnut tree. The witches live on in the name of the town's famous liqueur, Strega. And right up through the 14th century, young women 'confessed' to the courts of the Inquisition to having 'flown on the devil's saddle' to the walnut tree to celebrate the sabbath.

EATING AND DRINKING

The Beneventano, or southern, part of the area called the Sannio still reflects the urban and rural structures of the medieval feudal system that for so long dominated the area, and that, in addition to the devastation of earthquakes, gradually brought its peasant farmers to their knees – indeed, many chose to emigrate. If today there is a return to the land and some recently found prosperity, it is thanks to the growing of the grapes, olives and wheat that have long been cultivated here, and that are now being approached differently to give higher quality products. The bulk production of grapes used both to anonymously 'enrich' northern wines and to produce large quantities of undistinguished plonk is giving way, with the younger generations, to a reduction of production in both vineyards and olive groves, and to much higher quality fruits. Individual producers as well as co-operative cellars – *cantine sociali* – have realized that this is the only way to make both names and money for themselves. The province of Benevento, like the rest of Campania, is very rich in indigenous grape and olive varietals, so there is no shortage of *materia prima* to bring ever more success to this up-and-coming area.

In the meantime, there are many gastronomic specialties here, including excellent *torrone* – nougats made with local honey and nuts – orchard fruits, pork products, and local cheeses of all three types of milk – sheep, goat and cow. There is also Italy's only artisan cider-maker, who works with the native Annurca and Limoncella apples (see p. 419-20). Those interested in crafts will also find lovely traditional ceramics here, as well as handmade lace (*merletti*) and wrought iron – ferro *battuto*.

In the little villages built on rocky crags throughout the mountainous northern parts of the province, or situated around Mount Taburno in its centre, you'll find authentic, rustic home-cooking using the plants of the fields and woods, as well as chestnuts and other 'spontaneous' ingredients.

Torrone

Torrone

In this area *torrone* dates back to the Romans, who called it *cupedia*; it was sold by street vendors known as *cupetari*. (In Latin, the verb to toast nuts is *torreo*.) Benevento's *torrone*, made of honey, nuts and egg whites, was already well known under the Papal State, but gained fame in the 17th century thanks to popes and prelates, and under the Bourbons in the 18th century, when it became a must at Christmas – as it is now. It might never have attained such a high status were it not for the excellence of the local honey and hazelnuts: San Giovanni is an elongated form of the *nocciola*, the Tonda Rossa, is rounder, while the Bianca di Avellino is yet another variety… and there are many more. *Torrone* may be made hard or soft, white or chocolate-stained, in infinite flavours and combinations, but its basic ingredients remain the same. Both Torrone di Benevento and Torroncino Croccantino di San Marco dei Cavoti have applied for IGP status.

Mela Annurca, or Melannurca

This apple has been a native of Campania for so long that it is even depicted in the paintings of Ercolano, in the Casa dei Cervi. It is thought to have originated near Pozzuoli, as Pliny the Elder describes in his *Historia Naturalis*. In that area, the apple was called *Mala Orcula*, the apple of the underworld: the *Orco* referred to the *Inferi*, as Pozzuoli was believed by the ancients to be the gateway to Hades. This is confirmed by Gian Battista Della Porta who, in his *Suæ Villae Pomarium*, says these apples were known commonly as *Orcole*. From *Anorcola* and *Annorcola* the name developed to *Annurca* as we see it in the *Manuale di Arboticultura* of G. A. Pasquale in 1876, and to the *Mela Annurca* and *Melannurca* of today. These small, well-flavoured red apples are unusual in that they won't ripen evenly on the tree, but do best picked still partly green and brought to maturity on straw or wood shavings. To see them spread out in rows in autumn is a thrilling – and colourful – sight. They are cultivated successfully in many areas of Campania, in particular

Turning the apples is patient work

Painted tiles decorate an olive mill wall

in the Caudina-Telesina and Taburno valleys. The Melannurca gained IGP status in 2001. In the apple-growing areas of the province of Benevento, many *sagras* are held in its honour.

The Beneventano is home to many other native varieties of apple and pear, including the Limoncella (see p. 420).

Benevento's Olive Oils

This area has been planted to olives for centuries, but only recently has this oil been recognized for its excellent qualities. Indeed, the extra virgin olive oils of the Sannio Colline Beneventane and Sannio Caudino Telesino are currently awaiting DOP status. (It will be interesting to see how they perform in the next years at the Sirena d'Oro competition at Sorrento, where only DOP oils are up for judging.) In the Beneventano most oils are made with the indigenous, antique varieties, Ortice, Racioppella, Ortolana, Femminella and Sprina – as, for example, at San Lupo and San Lorenzo Maggiore, where the oil is green, low in acidity, and with a characteristic fruity aftertaste. Many of the best individual producers are mentioned throughout this chapter.

Benevento's Wines

If the province of Benevento is becoming increasingly well known, it is thanks to its wines. Campanian wines were sung by the poets and writers Pliny, Cato, Columella and Horace. In the area of Benevento, the *cantine sociali* of the 1950s – large co-

operatives that each pooled the resources of hundreds of tiny
farmers – protected the individual growers and stabilized prices,
but they also encouraged the production of quantity rather than
quality. In the last twenty years, that has changed dramatically,
as the area's numerous DOCs can attest. Luciano Pignataro, a
leading expert on Campania's wine and its producers, predicts a
positive future for Benevento's wines: 'I'm confident that if the
cantine sociali and private producers concentrate on the reduction and improvement of the grapes in the vineyards, and on
more care in the cellars, this area has the potential to become
one of the south's most important winemaking zones,' he says.

As is often the case, it is thanks to a handful of pioneers that
this change of attitude came about. In the 1980s, when the big
cellars were pushing for ever-higher yields, a few forward-thinking producers were instead committed to finding the kind of
quality that had long been attained in France and parts of
northern Italy. Mustilli, with his rediscovery of Falanghina;
Venditti, for his determination to qualify Castelvenere as a valid
sub-zone within the larger Solopaca denomination; Ocone and
Troisi for their work with Coda di Volpe, again in areas that
until then had little credibility as distinct winemaking zones.
'These and other producers have been proved right,' adds
Pignataro, 'and they opened the way to a new future for the
winemaking of Benevento.'

Falanghina grapes

Today, Benevento produces 50 per cent of Campania's grapes
– and 70 per cent of its DOC wines – while 35 wineries now
bottle over 60 types of wine, and more and more growers are
working to produce quality rather than quantity in their vineyards. The area has been granted two IGT denominations
(Beneventano and Dugenta) as well as five DOCs: Solopaca
DOC, a vast area of 5,000 hectares, was among the first to gain
DOC status in 1992, and its 'Classica' sub-zone was added in
2002; Taburno and Aglianico del Taburno DOC, grown on the
slopes of Monte Taburno, in 13 *comuni*, 880 hectares, was
decreed in 1986 and 1993; Sant'Agata de' Goti, from just 33
hectares around the town of Sant'Agata, in 1993; Guardiolo or
Guardia Sanframondi DOC was granted in 1993 in 4 *comuni* in
the area of Guardia and San Lupo; the extensive area of Sannio
DOC, in 1997.

Indigenous grapes grown include the white Falanghina,
Greco, Coda di Volpe, and Malvasia di Candia that in this area
is known as Cerreto, and reds Aglianico and Piedirosso; with
large amounts too of Sangiovese and Barbera, as well as other,
'international' varieties.

BED AND BREAKFAST IN STYLE

Bed and Breakfast at Bonea, below Mount Taburno

A group of Bed and Breakfasts in historic villas and farms has been assembled by the GAL Partenio Valle Caudina. They are divided between the provinces of Benevento and Avellino (see p. 321). The Benevento B&Bs include:

La Locanda dei Quattro Venti
Via Corte Calce, Airola.
In the countryside near the Taburno mountain; with a large garden.

B&B Rianna
Via Portisi, Airola.
In the historic centre of Airola that offers many artistic monuments, this house also has a garden.

Il Belvedere
Via Capo, Bonea.
A country house surrounded by olive groves and woods; the owners also run a bakery.

L'Arca di Noè
Via Vignale, 1, Bonea.
This Noah's Ark is in a house with beautiful views of the valley, and pets are permitted.

L'Antico Granaio
Via Roma, Bonea.
In a 17th-century villa in the town, with a lovely courtyard and tree-lined avenue.

La Locanda
Via Riello, 2, Pannarano.
A house in the country with a large garden, swimming pool and hospitable owners who cook very well.

For information, GAL Partenio Valle Caudina,
TEL 0824 841802
E-MAIL info@galpartenio.it or segreteria@galpartenio.it

Airola

Olive Oil

Via Pace, 20
TEL 0823 712963

Falzarano

Gianvincenzo Falzarano is undoubtedly pleased that his (and many other growers') extra virgin olive oils are being granted DOP status – Denominazione di Origine Protetta. In order to qualify, growers abide by regulations about the varieties of olive tree they plant – they must be local, as recognized by the *disciplinare*, about the way they are fertilized or treated for pests, and of course about the way the olives are picked, carried, and milled.

In this area, the principal varieties called for by the new DOP are Ortolana, Ortice and Racioppella. Falzarano has just under a thousand trees, and produces a fine, low-acidity oil that can be bought directly from his farm.

Baselice

Contrada Defenza
TEL 0824 968765

Cheese

Michele Di Lella's Azienda Agricola San Giovanni produces local cheeses from cows and sheep: cow's *caciocavallo* and *ricotta*, and sheep's *pecorino*.

Beltiglio di Ceppaloni see Ceppaloni

Benevento

This is one of my favourite Campanian cities: despite having been bombed in wars and shaken in earthquakes, it retains a personal character and has some very handsome churches, buildings and monuments. One of the most moving is the great modern artist Mimmo Paladino's permanent installation in the courtyard of the Convent of San Domenico, in the town's centre. This 'Ortus Conclusus' is an open-air museum, a magical sculpture garden that should not be missed.

Detail of the decorated door of a Benevento church

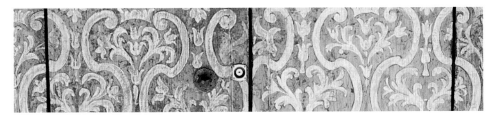

Hand-made salame

If you are interested in wines, Benevento has several good shops to choose from: the large Enoteca dei Vini del Sannio e della Campania (Piazza Guerrazzi, 4; TEL 0824 47845; closed Monday) operates on store hours and sells all the best wines from Benevento's DOCs, as well as a good selection from other Campanian provinces. Or try Enoteca Paradiso (Viale Mellusi, 90; TEL 0824 315565) for local wines, liqueurs and speciality foods. For fifty years, the lovely Euroliquori Orrera on Benevento's main street (Corso Garibaldi, 97–99; TEL 0824 25158; E-MAIL euroliquori@libero.it) has featured the top local products, including olive oils, liqueurs and of course, *torrone* – plus wines from Campania and beyond. Salumeria Bordi (Via Garibaldi 156; TEL 0824 21301) is a post-war, wood-lined shop specializing in the area's cured-pork products: *soppressata*, which here uses choice cuts from fillet and leg, and nicely peppered sausages. The Consorzio Agrario di Benevento (Via 25 Luglio, 12–14; TEL 0824 211133) has a shop near the station that sells a great selection of *prodotti tipici* – local artisan food products.

Arechi (Via III Settembre, 69; TEL/FAX 0824 326067; internet www.arechi-scarl.it) is a consortium of olive-growers and mills which has pooled its resources and produces three lines of very good oil from the Sannio area. Look for their top labels: Energia, of Ortice, Racioppella and Ortolana olives, and Arechi, of Ortice and Racioppella. Devi (Contrada Masseria Nuova; TEL 0824 21544; E-MAIL devi@netgen.it): with 15 hectares of vine-yards in the Sannio, the De Cicco family works the local grapes – Falanghina, Greco, Aglianico – and is gradually making a name for itself for its fresh, fruity wines.

Restaurant

Via Annunziata, 152
TEL 0824 29431
CLOSED Sun;
last 3 weeks of Aug
CARDS All
PRICE €€

Nunzia Osteria Tradizionale
When you're in the mood for a relaxed meal in the town centre, Nunzia is a colourful, knowledgeable cook of traditional cuisine. La Signora or her children will guide you through *antipasti* of local cheeses and *salumi* or individually prepared seasonal vegetables, hand-made pastas like *lo scarpariello* or *lagane* with chickpeas. I love the thick winter soup, *la minestra maritata*, of pork and field greens, that is practically a meal in itself. *Ammugliatielli* (rolled and stuffed lamb innards) are robust and flavourful, as is the *baccalà*, but there are also lighter options. Desserts come from local pastry shops, and go well with a glass of Strega; there is a decent list of local wines to see you through the rest of the meal.

Restaurant
Trattoria-Pizzeria Traiano

Via Manciotti, 48
TEL 0824 25013
CLOSED Tues, Aug
CARDS None
PRICE €

Located in a street leading to the Roman arch, Porta Aurea, this is an unassuming trattoria offering simple local dishes featuring pasta, vegetables and *baccalà* – as well as wood-oven pizzas.

Restaurant
Gino e Pina

Viale dell' Università
TEL 0824 24947
CLOSED Sun, mid-Aug
CARDS All
PRICE €€–€€€

This restaurant, on one of the centre's outer streets that leads to the Roman Theatre, is a good place for a wood-oven pizza, or you can choose from a large menu with lots of vegetables, buffalo *mozzarella*, soups and pastas, grilled meats, fish dishes, even game... plus the daily specials. You can sit in the garden in summer.

Restaurant
Enoteca La Corte di Bacco

Via Traiano, 65
OPEN 18.00–4.00am
CLOSED Mon

This is a lively wine bar that serves some food: *salumi* and cheeses, or a simple plate of pasta to accompany the wines, by the glass or bottle. It's worth a visit if only to see inside the beautiful baroque Palazzo Andreotti Leone – the wine bar is in what was once the *palazzo*'s theatre, and still retains a convincingly thespian air.

Liqueur
Strega Alberti

Piazza Vittoria Colonna, 8
TEL 0824 54292
0824 50328
INTERNET
www.strega.it

This is one of the most famous liqueurs, not only in Benevento but in all Italy. The inimitable saffron-yellow *liquore* with its red and gold Art-Nouveau label can be served as an *aperitivo* (over ice), a *digestivo*, or drizzled on to sponge cakes or ice cream. The Alberti family, now in its sixth generation, have been making Strega since 1860, and have come up with lots of delicious uses for their closely-guarded recipe – in chocolates, *torroni* and *croccantini*. In their shop facing the train station, you can treat yourself to one or all of these delicacies. Their range also includes other herbal liqueurs.

Strega

Strega means 'witch', and is a reference to Benevento's esoteric past. The recipe has Benedictine origins, and is a secret. We do know that it includes saffron, orange, and over seventy herbs and spices – some from the Far East, some local – including star anise, mint, lavender, juniper, cinnamon, Jamaican pepper... Only two people know the exact quantities – or so the legend goes. After being distilled slowly in steam-heated stills, the liqueur is aged for at least six months in oak barrels. Visits to the distillery are possible by previous appointment.

Strega has also become an important word on Italy's cultural

landscape, for the Alberti family have, since 1947, sponsored one of the country's most prestigious literary prizes.

Valisannio (Piazza IV Novembre, 1; TEL 0824 300410; E-MAIL valisannio@bn.camcom.it; INTERNET www.valisannio.com) is a special department of the Benevento Chamber of Commerce set up to aid small local businesses and artisans. It represents ceramicists, cheese, *salumi*, oil, honey, and other food producers, as well as *agriturismi*, hotels and restaurants.

If you are looking for somewhere to stay in or near Benevento, Hotel Villa Traiano (Viale dei Rettori, 9; TEL 0824 326241; INTERNET www.hotelvillatraiano.it) has recently opened and offers rooms in a 19th-century villa with a roof-garden view of the town centre. Agriturismo Le Camerelle and La Francesca are within a few kilometres of the town on the Benevento-Pietrelcina road (Contrada Camerelle; TEL 0824 311426, 0824 776134, 333 2699187; INTERNET www.lecamerelle.it, www.agri-turismolafrancesca.it).

Castelfranco in Miscano

This village, in the easternmost part of Campania on the border with Puglia, is known for its cheeses, especially those made with cow's milk. You'll find them at Caseificio Miscano (Contrada Seiarusso, 2; TEL 0824 960084).

Castelvenere

Wine, Oil

Antica Masseria Venditti

Via Sannitica, 122
TEL 0824 940306
FAX 0824 940301
E-MAIL
masseria@venditti.it
INTERNET
www.venditti.it

Nicola Venditti is completing his large new wine cellar just a few metres from the old one: near the centre of the village of Castelvenere, at his farm's headquarters. A few kilometres away is the *masseria* (farmhouse) from 1595 that gives the company its name. Venditti was an early champion of organic wines, and of the Castelvetere sub-zone that differentiates this territory from the larger Solopaca denomination.

'We're celebrating thirty years of making and labelling our own wines this year,' he says, as we tour the tall functional building. 'I have always believed that wine should be a pure expression of grapes, so I make wines without using wood barrels – in fact, we were still using an old-fashioned press until recently.' Venditti has been certified organic for ten years, and

Opposite: Sun-ripened tomatoes and fresh basil: the summer building blocks

was among the first to identify single vineyards for making his crus, working with the rare indigenous varieties from his neighbourhood: whites Grieco and Cerreto Falanghina, and reds 'Montepulciano' – which is not related to the Abruzzo type – and 'Barbetta'.

The Vendittis also produce fine extra virgin olive oil, as well as a little *mosto cotto* – boiled must – and *grappa*. They believe in spreading the culture of winemaking, and are currently planting an experimental, educational vineyard.

Two wineries that offer rooms and restaurants with home cooking: Feudo Santagatella-Foresta (Via Nazionale Sannitica, 31–33; TEL 0824 949335; E-MAIL eupengue@tin.it, safineis @katamail.it) This wine estate-farm has a full *agriturismo*, with wonderfully varied home-grown produce, oil, meats and cheeses that are served in its attractive dining room. Cellar visits, wine tastings and sales are also available for visitors. Fattoria Ciabrelli (Via Italia, 3; TEL 0824 940565; E-MAIL fattoria @ciabrelli.it www.ciabrelli.it) Ciabrelli is a well-known name in Benevento's wine history. Now the younger generation of the family is continuing to produce drinkable, reasonably priced wines that reflect their terroir, and there is a modest dining room for tasting local dishes.

Ceppaloni

Restaurant
La Rete

Contrada Masseriola, 11
Beltiglio di Ceppaloni
TEL 0824 46574
FAX 0824 384900
CLOSED Tues and Weds
CARDS All
PRICE €€€

La Rete sits on a hillside overlooking the high-medieval castle and attractive village of Ceppaloni, just nine kilometres from Benevento. Enzo Mignone opened it in 1978 as a fish restaurant but today he runs it with his son, Dionisio, as a friendly country trattoria, serving the home-made pastas, meats and cheeses of the *interno*. It's a lively place, with lots of space outdoors for summer dining and for kids to play (and a children's menu). Enzo is a wine lover, and you'll find good wines in all prices in his impressive 1,000-label cellar.

I enjoyed the food, with its emphasis on artisan *salumi* – local as well as Spanish and northern Italian – and rustic pasta sauces. Lasagne are filled with *ricotta*, basil and *pomodorini*, and *cicatielli* pasta is dressed with hearty wild boar sauce. 'Around here, there are boar in the woods and on the mountains. We're lucky to be near the cities while retaining a country life style,' says Enzo as he brings a platter of ham baked with chestnuts and rosemary. It's delicious. A large family at a nearby table was being served heaping trayfuls of *gnocchi* with truffles and cheese, and the perfume was irresistible. If you still have room, there are home-made desserts and cookies that go well with a glass of *passito*.

In the historic centre of Ceppaloni, La Buca dei Ladroni (Via Cortile, 18; TEL 0824 55401) is a small, informal restaurant.

Cerreto Sannita

Cerreto Sannita church

Cerreto Sannita was rebuilt after the earthquake of 1688 in the style of the day, the baroque, and luckily many of these buildings still remain, giving the handsome town an almost Spanish quality. There is a noteworthy Ceramics Museum here, with rare and interesting pieces from many epochs, as this is one of the towns that has actively maintained its artisan traditions. Indeed, there have been potters here since the Middle Ages when the *feudo* was controlled by the noble – and powerful – Sanframondi family. You may come across the name of Nicola Giustiniani, a great ceramicist in whose honour an association has been formed which also has a collection of historical pots and plates.

Ceramica Artistica Vecchia Cerreto (Corso Umberto, 74; TEL 0824 860017) is one of the present-day potteries – but there are several more here and at San Lorenzello (see p. 425).

Olive Oil

Olivicola Titerno

Via Lampione, 3/5
TEL 0824 861263
339 3983001
E-MAIL olivicola.
titerno@libero.it

This olive co-operative of some 60 members brings together many small olive growers in the area. They grow mainly the local Ortice, Racioppella and Ortolana varieties, which are pressed separately, by olive type, by Emilio Conti in the Cilento (see p. 311), an expert *frantoiano*. The Titerno oil won first prize at the Ercole Olivario competition at Spoleto. The oil can be bought through co-op members, or at San Lorenzello, in Via Napoli.

Restaurant

La Vecchia Quercia

Via Cerquelle
TEL 0824 861263
OPEN All year
CLOSED Tues
PRICE €

La Vecchia Quercia offers a little of everything: *ristorante*, pizzeria, bar, *residenza*, hotel… it is strategically placed on the hill road above the popular sanctuary of Madonna delle Grazie. At lunchtime in summer its large dining rooms are alive with visitors and pilgrims tucking into platefuls of pasta and meats *alla brace* that are cooked outdoors on large wood-burning grills. For those who don't want meat, try the smoked *provola* cheese grilled between lemon leaves… it's quite delicious.

Circello

This village is known for its traditional *salumi*: a good place to find them is at Sebastiano Di Maria's dairy (Contrada Casea Alta, 98; TEL 0824 935300; E-MAIL dimariamaria@tin.it).

Cusano Mutri

This extraordinary looking village is a mix of medieval, 17th- and 18th-century buildings constructed on many levels: particularly dramatic when seen against a backdrop of snowy mountains. It was the site of a peasant uprising in 1780 against the Spanish feudal landlords that had controlled it after the Sanframondi family. The woods here are full of *funghi* and chestnuts – there is even a *sagra* dedicated to the nuts in autumn. Cusano Mutri has long been a centre for wood crafts, especially of utensils.

Dugenta

Wine, Agriturismo, Restaurant

Torre Gaia

Via Bosco Cupo, 11
TEL 0824 978172
FAX 0824 978337
E-MAIL
tommasoriccardi
@torre-gaia.com
INTERNET
www.torre-gaia.net

A grand stately villa commanding sweeping views of the countryside, a vast estate with sixty-four hectares of vineyards, ballrooms big enough to hold conventions and weddings, a restaurant and fifteen nicely furnished rooms for guests... Torre Gaia's potential is immense. And since 2000, there has been a concerted effort on behalf of its new owners – a group of investors from Benevento – to renovate the buildings and improve the wines. Alberto Cerere is the resident œnologist, and the new philosophy, focusing on quality rather than quantity, is beginning to pay off. The wine list is long, with sixteen wines to choose from in categories from the big, barrel-aged Aia Vecchia Riserva, of Aglianico and Sangiovese, through a range of lighter reds and whites, to the Charmat-method Asprinio di Aversa and Malvasia. So watch this space.

Faicchio

This village, nestled into the hillside under the Monaco di Gioia mountain, has retained the ducal castle to which it belonged, with its four cylindrical towers. It is a good starting place for a drive through the unspoiled mountain woods.

Beer

Selva
TEL 0824 815402
335 5824264
INTERNET
www.saintjohnsbier.it

Saint John's Bier

Beer-making is very rare in these parts: after all, this is one of
Italy's prime wine zones. But that hasn't stopped two young
brothers, Gianni and Mario Di Lunardo, from deciding to make
a pure, old-fashioned artisan beer here. I discovered it by
chance, when I tasted a jelly from La Credenza that had been
made from the beer in the nearby province of Caserta (see p.
84-85). The brothers began in 2000, working with barley that is
cooked to 77°C. Hops are then infused in it, and yeast added.
After one week, the beer is put first into large tanks, and then
into wood. They use modern technology to control the fermentations, but the method is traditional. 'Beer is very nutritional,
for its mineral salts, folic acid, magnesium and potassium –
indeed, local mothers use it as a pick-me-up when breastfeed-
ing,' says Gianni. So here's to another enterprising group of
young people determined to re-vitalize the all-too-often abandoned countryside. Cheers.

Salumi

Via Provinciale
TEL 0824 863598
FAX 0824 819963
E-MAIL
info@tomasosalumi.it
INTERNET
www.tomasosalumi.it

Tomaso Salumi

Eugenio Tomaso is a country butcher: with his family he works
in the village of Faicchio, selling fresh and cured meats, especially from local pigs and Laticauda sheep, in the small Sisa supermarket. He has recently become particularly interested in
salumi, the salt-cured meats that are so popular throughout
Italy, especially in the *interno*, where the pig constitutes a precious natural resource. Eugenio has access to animals – in particular the *maialino nero casertano* – that are being raised completely freely in a large private estate nearby. 'Here the animals
are, to all intents and purposes, wild,' he says, as we drive up
the mountain in a Jeep to see them. A sow with a group of little
piglets catches a whiff of us and runs off into a bush for cover,
followed by her babies (see photo p. 422). 'They have huge
expanses of woods, pastures and *macchia mediterranea* to roam
free in, so their meat is particularly flavourful. The Casertano is
a fatty breed, but it's well balanced when the pigs get a lot of
exercise and are free to eat the foods they like.' Eugenio's
specialties are a fine, lean *culatello* – the most highly prized part
of the rump – that is best when aged for two years; he also
cures the *spalla*, shoulder, and makes a series of *insaccati* –
sausages that have been stuffed into a natural '*sacco*'. Of these,
the coarse-grain *salame Napoli* is dotted with large chunks of
fat; *finocchiona*, seasoned with wild fennel seeds, is eaten
quite fresh. Eugenio also uses local mountain thyme, *pimpinella*,

*Chef Raffaele D'Addio
from Puglianello, with
Eugenio Tomaso*

Opposite: Tomaso's home-made salumi

to flavour his *lardo* – the flat slabs of fat from the animal's stomach that are a delicacy sliced paper-thin onto hot toast. You can also taste the best of his production at Il Foro dei Baroni restaurant (see p. 424).

For delicious sheep's milk cheeses, Agriturismo Torrevecchia di Marafi (Via Marafi; TEL 0824 819063) is a lovely farm producing organic *pecorini* from the local Laticauda sheep. You can also eat here if you reserve ahead: Marilena cooks a repertoire of country dishes from the Sannio, including home-made pastas, *salumi* and traditional dishes such as herbed, braised lamb.

Foglianise

Each year, on August 16th, Foglianise hosts the Sagra del Grano, a lovely country fair at which giant sculptures made of wheat are mounted on to big floats for a parade. For information call 0824 878064 (*comune*).

Wine

Via Sala
TEL 0824 871338
FAX 0824 878893
E-MAIL
info@cantinadeltaburno.it
INTERNET
www.cantinadeltaburno.it

Cantina del Taburno

In the city of Benevento stands a large red-granite statue the locals call Bue Apis, as if it were a giant cow. Instead, it represents an ancient Egyptian divinity, Apis, and seems to have been linked to the temple that Domitian erected in the city to honour the goddess Isis, whose cult was closely followed here beginning in Roman times. Bue Apis's strength has also helped forge the image of an unusual Benevento winery, la Cantina del Taburno. 'Bue Apis represents the essence of Benevento's potential,' says Luigi Moio, the company's consulting œnologist, son of the historic winemaker Michele Moio (see pp. 75-76) and a wine producer in his own right (see p. 353). 'For it is a wine made only from one vineyard of Aglianico del Taburno whose vines are over a hundred years old. Indeed, thanks to these sandy soils, phylloxera didn't kill off all the vines here and we still have some that are 120 to 180 years old.' Aglianico is so late-ripening that it is usually picked in the first week of November, and Bue Apis is then aged in barriques to give it modern intensity and to round out its tannins and tobacco notes. A big, signature wine that is defined by its territory, and that in turn has defined this forward-thinking Cantina Sociale. It has won the coveted Tre Bicchieri award twice since it was first made, in 1999.

Moio teaches œnology at the university in Napoli, and joined the team at this semi-public winery in 1999, pooling his research on Aglianico and other Campanian grape varieties with

*Another of the Cantina's
award-winners*

the investments that the Cantina del Taburno had already made in its cellars and 600 hectares of vineyards belonging to 350 members. Working with Filippo Colandrea, the resident wine-maker, Moio banished the practice of selling bulk wines *sfuso*, and insisted on the reduction of yields in the vineyards to better express the unique character of the area's vines. 'At first I wasn't sure I wanted to take on such a big winery,' he says as we taste our way through the Cantina's impressive list in the large tasting room behind the shop. 'But I quickly got involved, and since then the results really have been encouraging. We are seen as pioneers in this province, and have one of the biggest cellars in Campania.' The shop also sells the Cantina's extra virgin olive oils, produced from selected olives from 8,000 growers in the area. No appointment is needed for the shop, but cellar visits must be booked in advance.

Guardia Sanframondi

Every seven years, in August, (the next time will be in 2010), the town of Guardia Sanframondi puts on a rather gruesome display of faith as men dressed in long white robes and hoods, '*i battenti*' (spookily reminiscent of the Ku Klux Klan), flail themselves with sharp chains in penitence to Our Lady of the Assumption. This is just one expression of the Samnite legacy that continues to weave mysticism, paganism and sainthood together in this part of Campania. After all, Padre Pio was born near here, at Pietrelcina, and 'received the stigmata in a pasture at Piana Romana'.

Olive Oil

Azienda Olivinicola di
Maria Pacelli
Via Municipio, 105
TEL 0824 864312
FAX 339 6822213
E-MAIL
terrestregate@libero.it
INTERNET
www.terrestregate.it

Terre Stregate

It is little wonder that Maria Pacelli has chosen Terre Stregate (bewitched lands) for her brand name – this area is full of sto-ries of sorcery. Whatever spell she uses to produce her extra vir-gin, it works – she makes great, prize-winning oil from about 2,000 trees, of the native Ortice, Racioppella and Ortolana vari-eties. Pacelli's Primo Fiore is an organic, well-balanced oil that has worked magic on its many fans.

Wine

Contrada Starze
TEL/FAX 0824 817705 E-
MAIL c.delucia@tin.it

De Lucia

Carlo De Lucia runs a fairly large privately owned *cantina* in the gentle hills of the Calore valley, where he works with the young Roman œnologist, Roberto Mazzer, who handles the winemaking for several estates in the Beneventano. Unlike many

Vineyards at the De Lucia winery

of his neighbouring cellars, which offer confusingly large portfolios of wines in every category and type, De Lucia has drastically cut back the number he makes to just two grape varieties, the Benevento classics, Falanghina and Aglianico. Whatever other grapes are grown are sold on. Indeed, he currently only bottles 10 per cent of his grape production.

'This way we can do a super-selection at harvest time to improve the wines,' the young man explains. 'This area of the Beneventano produces 50 per cent of all the grapes grown in Campania, but very little of it is top quality – in this area they bottle everything, even at one euro per bottle. So I want to aim for quality by replanting good clones of the grapes that do best here, in this dry terrain, even if it will take a few years to build up to the level I am looking for.' This is a courageous but also highly pragmatic philosophy, one that will surely stand him in good stead in the years to come. At the moment De Lucia is producing two wines from each grape type, all under the Sannio DOC. The Falanghinas are worked, one in steel, one in wood; the Aglianicos use barriques of first (Murellaia) and second (Aglianico Sannio) years. And the prices are very fair.

Wine, Olive Oil

Contrada Sapenzie, 20
TEL 0824 817004
FAX 0824 817914
E-MAIL
info@cortenormanna.it
INTERNET
www.cortenormanna.it

Corte Normanna

The Normans governed this area for over four hundred years, and the effect can still be felt in the orderly rule imposed on the hills, with their neat vineyards and olive groves. Alfredo and Gaetano Falluto's estate was formed in 1927; it now comprises eighteen hectares of vineyards and two of olive trees in the heart of the most productive part of the Sannio. In 1984 they took the decision – brave at that time – to come out of the local Cantina Sociale to which they had always sold their grapes, and to start working on more personalized wines. More recently, with œnologist Roberto Mazzer, they have been reducing yields in the vineyards and improving quality in the bottles. They have also been making a name for themselves with their oil, which is in the process of becoming completely organic.

Wine

Santa Lucia, 104–105
TEL 0824 864034
FAX 0824 864935
E-MAIL guardiense
@laguardiense.com,
info@janare.it
INTERNET
www.laguardiense.com
www.janare.it

La Guardiense and Janare

Two brands from one large co-operative *cantina* that, in 1960, took a stand and grouped its then thirty-three members together to get strength from numbers in the grape-selling market. Since then, as has become the pattern in an area eager to be known for its own territorial and personal value, La Guardiense has built up an imposing collection of 2,000 hectares from its over 1,000 grape-growers, as well as an efficient nucleus of vinification and ageing cellars complete with tasting rooms and offices. Recently they have also added a new higher-end line, Janare, to the good-value La Guardiense list of wines that almost all fall under the three local DOCs and the Beneventano IGT. With two œnologists – one for each of the lines – they are well-placed for further improvement.

Moiano

Apples

Via Giovanni XXIII
TEL 0823 712007

Carmine Oropallo

Carmine has a large apple farm in the Parco Regionale Taburno-Camposauro. It specializes in the cultivation of the Annurca apples that are picked while still reddish-green and set out for several weeks to ripen and turn red on straw.

Molinara

Apple Cider
Luca Baldino

Via Roma, 85
TEL 0824 994525
E-MAIL
lucabaldino@tiscalinet.it
INTERNET
www.baldino.it

'Molinara is practically the last village in Campania, historically and culturally,' says Luca Baldino as he points east past the valley he's in. 'Beyond this you're in Puglia: from here, even the dialects change and become more Pugliese.' We're in the Alto Sannio, high in the Tammaro river valley in a beautiful landscape of little fields, orchards and olive groves. 'This has always been a very poor Apennine zone, halfway between the two coasts. Recently, it's been recognized for its great oil, made from the Ortice and Frantoio varieties. One of the problems is that the farms are all small, with only about one hectare each of land, and the custom here is not to band them together to make bigger pieces, even within the same family. We are descendants of the Samnites, a strong but closed people. Hard-headed.' He laughs. Luca Baldino is young, handsome, and anything but closed.

The hard-headedness has probably helped: it's not obvious to set about making cider in a country that has practically no culture of fermenting apples. Yet, in just a short time, Baldino has placed his Sidro del Sannio in some of Italy's best restaurants as an alternative to the after-dinner *passi*to to accompany dessert.

Limoncella apples are always tiny

'I spent a lot of my childhood here with my grandfather,' he says as we walk down to his spic-and-span cellar, with the high-tech Piemontese winemaking equipment Baldino has adapted to apples. 'He was as ignorant as he was wise. Every year he made a little wine – the usual undrinkable stuff – and a little cider from the nine apple trees he eventually left me. Each one is a different kind: Mela San Giovanni, Santo Nicola, Limoncella, Scocca, Faccia Rossa... most are half-wild and close to extinction, but the principal variety is the Annurca. My grandfather's cider was so over-oxidized it went mouldy after a week, and you couldn't even use it for vinegar.'

The young Baldino studied economics in Roma, then went to Provence to learn French. 'I found studying boring. I wanted to be outdoors picking things. I moved up to Normandie – the homeland of cider. After a few weeks in the orchards I asked to be moved into the chateau's cellar: I was fascinated by the old barrels and stills. Up there, if you asked for water, they give you Calvados – 'Only frogs drink water.' was their motto.'

He stayed for three years, more interested in Calvados than the French ciders, for he found the apples there very low in both sugar and acidity.

'The Mela Annurca gives almost as much sugar as the Falanghina grape,' he explains. 'But it also has nice high acidity that keeps the cider crisp. Of course the French feel their ciders are the root of tradition, and therefore the best, but I prefer British cider to theirs.'

After trial and error, Baldino hit on a combination of Annurca and Limoncella apples – the latter are green and very small but nicely tart – for his cider. 'When I was in France I realized we had a great patrimony here in Campania with our apple varieties, but it's also true that we have not known how to make the most of it.' Currently his *sidro* is made of 60–70% Limoncella, and 30–40% Annurca. 'The secret is to use only ripe apples, and to keep every stage of the production very very clean so the juices are never given a chance to oxidize.' He favours the use of selected yeasts, and low-temperature fermentation at 12–14°C – with higher temperatures you lose the *profumi*. Working with a friend, Pierino Guarnieri, he has planted specialized orchards of Limoncella – 'practically a vineyard,' he says – and now has five hectares of apples to work with. Indeed, the analogy with wine-making is not far off – Baldino's cider has all the elegance, complexity and class of a fine dessert wine, with hints of *amarena* and a seductive almond flavour that comes from the pips. It goes best with creamy desserts, almond biscuits, or blue cheeses.

Baldino currently produces around 10,000 bottles of *sidro* (500 ml), 5,000 of distilled apple *acquae vitae*, and 2,000 bottles of vinegar.

Morcone

In this town near the border with Molise, the limestone houses look as if they have been piled on to the side of the hill. This is the heart of the semi-mountainous, unspoiled countryside of the Upper Sannio. So it's a fine place to get honeys culled from chestnut and other forest plants. Mastrofrancesco (Via Piana, 262; TEL 0824 957033) is a small co-operative that brings together the honey-gatherers. Nicola Ciarlo (Via Cuffiano 316; TEL 0824 951055) makes cheeses from the milk of the local sheep breed, the Laticauda. Giuseppe Solla (Via Piana 275; TEL 0824 956508) is a good place to get local *salumi* – *capocollo*, *soppressata* – made from pigs reared on the farm.

Opposite: Limoncella apples: tiny and tart

Paduli

Le Delizie del Sannio (Via Longo; TEL 0824 927117) sells all manner of local foods, including the crisp *taralli* that make such good travel snacks.

Pietraroja

At the last count, this tiny mountain village, situated at 818 metres in the Parco Regionale del Matese, had just 699 inhabitants. Yet it is famous for two distinct and unusual 'finds'. The first is 'Ciro', the only dinosaur fossil (from *Scipionyx Samniticus*) to have been found in Italy, in what is now the Parco Geopaleontologico.

The other is almost as rare, *il prosciutto di Petraroja*, and it too was in danger of facing extinction. Luckily it has recently been given a new lease of life as the Regione Campania has applied for DOP status for this ham. What's so special about it?

'Up here, each of our families always kept a pig,' explains Tonino, an elderly farmer I got talking to in the village. 'It gets cold up here in winter and the pigs give us meat and fat to keep us warm. We dry our *prosciutti* in the attics, with cold air and some of the smoke from the *caminetto*.' Wood-burning fireplaces are still the main source of heat in the little stone houses.

The *prosciutto di Pietraroja* is cured in salt for twenty days before being pressed between two wooden boards, and flavoured with black pepper and *peperoncino*. The special drying method is to hang the hams in attics under terracotta tiled roofs where there is a good passage of air as well as the smoke from the chimney. After this phase, the hams are aged in cellars. The *prosciutto* has very white fat and a delicious, slightly *piccante*, lightly smoked flavour – and it's free of all preservatives. It's so good that families from nearby villages bring their hams to be cured and aged at Pietraroja.

A black Casertana sow runs with her piglets

Ponte

Wine

Via del Monte, 56
La Madonnella
TEL 0824 874040
FAX 0824 874328
E-MAIL
admocone@tin.it
INTERNET WWW.
oconevini.it

Ocone

Domenico Ocone comes from one of the oldest winemaking families in the Benevento area: his grandfather began at the beginning of the 20th century. Like many other growers, the Ocones produced large quantities of wine grapes until the 1980s, when the wind changed, thanks to the models provided by Mastroberardino and by Mario D'Ambra on Ischia. These producers – encouraged by Luigi Veronelli – began to value their local, native grapes. Ocone saw the potential of Coda di Volpe, a grape that had until then been used to blend with Fiano and Greco, as it was thought to have too low acidity to be vinified alone. Earlier harvesting and careful winemaking has proved that it, too, has a place in Campania's grape galaxy. Today, the Ocones produce a nice range of organic wines, especially the Falanghina that does so well under Mount Taburno.

Also at Ponte: La Cantina dei Longobardi (Via D'Andrea; TEL 347 5973707; OPEN 20.00 till late; CLOSED Mon) This *vineria* in the town centre is run by two AIS sommeliers, Nicola Pica and Lorenzo Cerulo, who have selected 300 wines from the Sannio, Campania and the rest of Italy. They pair them with local foods for those who want a bite to eat – *salumi*, cheeses and a few hot dishes prepared each evening. A relaxed place to go for a good glass of wine. Ponte dei Fiori (Via Ripagallo, 45/A; TEL 0824 874506) is an artisan company that makes jams and other preserves using the local Mela Annurca, as well as the unusual Mostarda di Aglianico – a delicious wine-based accompaniment for cheese. On that same street, Pasticceria Millevoglie (Via Ripagallo; TEL 0824 874506) is famous for the local *panesillo*, a winter cake made from November to February, baked only in this area. Giovanni De Michele (Via Stazione; TEL 0824 874201) makes authentic local *salumi*. Nifo Sarrapocchiello (Via Piana; TEL 0824 876450; E-MAIL l.nifo@libero.it): Lorenzo Nifo Sarrapocchiello worked with Luigi Moio at the large Cantina del Taburno (p. 415) before deciding to bring it all back home to his family's farm. He now has twelve hectares, all certified organic, for cultivating olive trees and vines, and is beginning to make some interesting wines, especially with the native Falanghina grapes.

Pontelandolfo

Olive Oil
Rinaldi

Contrada Cerquelle, 3
TEL 0824 851072
E-MAIL
info@frantoiorinaldi.it
INTERNET
www.frantoiorinaldi.it

This olive mill has specialized in working the Beneventano's Ortice variety of olives from the surrounding hills for over a century. It has, of course, kept up with the times, and now uses modern continuous-cycle stainless steel machinery to produce a clean, characterful yet elegant oil that has become the darling of some of the region's best restaurants. If you can, visit the Rinaldis in November and December, when the buzz of *api* – the small vehicles still favoured by the local *contadini* – and the perfume of freshly pressed olives fills the *frantoio* with excitement.

If you're in the mood for a good, home-cooked meal in a *simpatica* trattoria, try La Pignata (Via Ferrara, 1; TEL 0824 851635; CLOSED Mon). A perfect place for a thick country soup or hand-made pasta.

Puglianello

Restaurant, Pizzeria, Wine and Beer Bar
Osteria Il Foro dei Baroni

Piazza Chiesa, 6
TEL 0824 946033
E-MAIL
info@ilforodeibaroni.com
INTERNET
www.ilforodeibaroni.com
CLOSED Mon, and for
lunch except Sat, Sun &
hols; Aug
PRICE Restaurant: €€€

It's always a pleasure to discover young chefs who want to take the plunge and open on their own in areas that are little known but that, once you get there, you are glad to have visited. Puglianello is such a village, surrounded by orchards and countryside, it's just a stone's throw from the Volturno river that is the dividing line here between the provinces of Caserta and Benevento. And Raffaele D'Addio is such a cook. With his brother, Mario, and their friend and partner, Pasquale Marzano, he has found an intelligent formula for his cooking abilities: one central kitchen serves both a relaxed *pizzeria*, with a pretty pergola-covered space outdoors for summertime, and the more ambitious Osteria where Raffaele is free to be creative with his cuisine. The brothers have also just opened a *birreria* for the young people of the area in large atmospheric rooms in the village castle, a few metres from the restaurant.

Osteria Il Foro dei Baroni

Pasquale is a friendly host and positive presence in the dining room, and has assembled the makings of a good wine cellar. He and Raffaele met when they were both training at Antonello Colonna's restaurant near Rome. He agreed to come to Puglianello with Raffaele, and to start out together. Raffaele cooks well. He's full of ideas and works imaginatively with the flavourful local ingredients. 'For me, a crucial learning experi-

ence was spending a few months in Roma working with the
team from Palazzo Sasso at Ravello (see pp. 210-11), where I
was helped in particular by Alberto Annaruma, the second
chef,' says Raffaele. 'He was really supportive when we opened
the Osteria.'

The D'Addios have their pick of mountain *salumi* and
cheeses, fresh local lamb and pork from Faicchio (see pp. 413-
414), and the wonderful range of vegetables and fruits this area
offers. 'I'm lucky that I've been able to set up relationships with
the *contadini* around here, to bring me their produce as well as
rabbit, guinea fowl and other 'courtyard' animals. In fact, our
winter menu is when we're at our most expressive, as the hearty
dishes of the Beneventano are perfect for using as a starting
point for a more modern, imaginative *cucina*.' I look forward to
going back.

San Lorenzello

Like the nearby town of Cerreto Sannita, San Lorenzello has a
long history of ceramics. There is a Museo della Ceramica here,
and you can still find many small potteries, with hand-painted
objects for the table and house that make lovely presents to take
home. These are two of the best ceramicists: Bottega Nicola
Giustiniani di Elvio Sagnella (Via San Donato, 10 and Via N.
Giustiniani, 11; tel 0824 861700); and La Cer.Ba di Guido
Barbieri (Via P. P. Fusco, 6; tel 0824 861337.)

Biscottificio Fratelli Ricciardi (Via Comunale Reggia, 17; TEL
0824 860331) makes dried sweet and savoury biscuits, such as
the small round *taralli* – with olive oil and various seeds – and
the smaller *tarallini*, that are boiled then baked like bagels; perfect accompaniments to a pre-dinner *aperitivo*. This town has a
tradition of *biscottifici*: other bakers include Barbieri (Via
Pasquale Sasso, 24; TEL 0824 860415) and Monterbano (Via
San Salvatore, 38; TEL 0824 860410).

*Ceramicist's worktable at
San Lorenzello*

San Lorenzo Maggiore

Olive Oil

Contrada Laureto, 2
TEL 0824 813689

Frantoio Uliveto
The hills in this area are perfectly suited to olive trees. Giovanni
Procaccini and Gelsomina Cicchiello cultivate the local varieties
– Ortice, Ortolana and Racioppella – and mill them using both
traditional and modern techniques.

San Lupo

Like its neighbouring village, San Lorenzo Maggiore, San Lupo is making a name for itself for its oil, and olive groves characterize the hills here. Olivicola San Lupo (Contrada Grotticelle, Zona Industriale; TEL 0824 811220; E-MAIL olivicola@tin.it) is an oil-making co-operative that was founded in 1970, and now works with a consultant from the University of Naples Department of Nutrition. The 239 members concentrate primarily on indigenous varieties of olives – Ortolana, Femminella, Racioppella and Ortice – and produce two very good, fruity extra virgin oils.

L'Oliveta (Contrada Campopiano; TEL 0824 811194) operates as an *agriturismo* as well as an oil producer, working with 5,000 olive trees. The farm offers four rooms for visitors, and sells its own produce.

San Marco dei Cavoti

Mention this village, with its tower, ancient gates and clock museum, to any Campanian and they immediately start talking of Christmas, for the *torroni* – or nougats – which have made it famous are always on the winter holiday's shopping list.

Torroni

Via Roma, 64
TEL 0824 984060
INTERNET
www.borrillo.com

Premiata Fabbrica di Torroni Cavaliere Innocenzo Borrillo
This historic sweetmeat-making family began in 1891, when Innocenzo Borrillo, who had worked in Napoli's best *pasticcerie*, decided to go solo. In his small workshop he created the first 'baci Borrillo', a product that has remained popular ever since: almond and hazelnut *croccante* topped with dark chocolate. Only the best quality nuts from the south of Italy are used, including hazelnuts (*nocciole*) from nearby Avellino, and almonds (*mandorle*) from Puglia. The old-fashioned shop in Via Roma is like a child's dream, filled with the scent of sugar, honey and nuts, and stacks of nougats, cookies and other nicely packaged delicacies. And today there is another Innocenzo Borrillo who is carrying on the family tradition.

Other makers and sellers of *torrone*, *croccantino* and their endless variations include: Anna Maria Borrillo (Via Martiri di Bologna, 18; TEL 0824 984939), La Provenzale (Via Garibaldi, 70; TEL 0824 984668), and Dolciaria Palumbo (Seconda traversa Garibaldi, 7; TEL 0824 984548).

San Nicola Manfredi

Restaurant

Via Iannassi
TEL 0824 778400
0824 778101
OPEN Always
CARDS All
PRICE €€€

Antica Trattoria Pascalucci

By everyone's accounts, Pascalucci is one of Benevento's favourite restaurants. (It's just eight kilometres from Benevento, on the road towards San Giorgio del Sannio.) I certainly enjoyed this classic trattoria, a roomy, lively, busy, nicely appointed dining room that has been offering fairly priced food for ninety years – the owner's grandfather started out by selling *panini* and *salumi*.

There is lots of good food to choose from: mixed *antipasti* include fine *salumi* – including local *prosciutto* and *capicollo* – *crostini*, cheeses, and preserved vegetables. There are hearty *fagioli con cotenne* – beans with pork rinds, or *polenta* with *salsiccia* in tomato sauce. *Lo scarpariello* is like *spaghetti alla chitarra* with cherry tomatoes, and cheese, or there is *la minestra maritata*: a winter soup of mixed wild field greens with big chunks of *cottene* and *prosciutto* in it. The *secondi* are simple but satisfying: grilled lamb or beef, stuffed chicken, game when it's in season – decisive country foods from the *interno* that marries perfectly with a good Aglianico from the Taburno. Desserts include sweet *cassata*, sorbet-filled fruits from Lancusi (see p. 245-46), and the unmissable Benevento treat: *torrone* from Borrillo (see opposite).

Sant'Agata de' Goti

FOR TOURIST
INFORMATION
Sant'Agata de' Goti Pro
Loco Tourist Association
Largo Torricella
TEL 338 923854
0823 717159

Sant'Agata de' Goti was built on the ruins of the ancient Samnite city, Saticula, and got its present name when a group of Goths, defeated at the battle of Vesuvio in 553 AD, retreated and set up a colony here. Over the next centuries it was taken by the Longobards; allied with the Byzantines; conquered by Ludovico II, and in the 10th century made a bishopric. It flourished during the middle ages, and was well maintained in the hands of the family of the Dukes of Maddaloni until the end of feudalism. The town is one of Campania's most interesting, with a medieval centre, Romanesque churches, and works of art of all kinds. Don't miss the Last Judgment in the Chiesa dell' Annunziata – one of the most important examples of late Gothic painting in Campania.

Wine, Agriturismo

Via Dei Fiori, 20
TEL 0823 717433
E-MAIL info@mustilli.com
INTERNET www.mustilli.com

Mustilli

Sant'Agata de' Goti looks, from the west side, as if it had been shaped by a palette-knife: its high external houses, running along the steep bank of the river Martorano, finish in one long spectacular wall. Inside, the town is no less fascinating. The medieval *borgo* is still intact, and beneath it is a warren of cellars that have been cut deeply into the yellow *tufo* the town has been built upon. A fitting location for a historic Campanian wine family, Mustilli.

Leonardo Mustilli, now in his mid-seventies, can take the credit for having re-launched one of Campania's most significant white grapes, Falanghina, a variety that expresses this volcanic terroir better than any other. 'La Falanghina is a generic term for a grape that appears in many guises in different parts of Campania,' he explains. 'Principally, there are two main clones, now known as the Beneventano and the Napoletano. Of the two, the Beneventano (which is also grown outside of the Sannio area) has higher acidity – indeed, until recently, Falanghina was used primarily to blend with other regions' wines needing a boost of 'freshness'. Myself, I prefer the Napoletano.' In the 1960s, when Campanian wines barely had any regional identity, the Mustillis took a chance and planted specialized vineyards of this Falanghina, along with the other indigenous varieties, Greco, Piedirosso and Aglianico.

Wall frescoes in the courtyard of the palazzo

With his daughters Anna Chiara and Paola, and œnologist Mauro Orsoni, Mustilli produces a very pure Falanghina worked

*Marilì Mustilli in her
agriturismo kitchen*

exclusively in steel. What does he think of working Falanghina
in wood? 'I think it's a violence to put Falanghina in wood,
because these wines are easily overwhelmed,' he says. 'Wood is
too brutal for such a delicate, feminine grape: we say 'La'
Falanghina, whereas almost all other varieties are masculine.'

As for the reds, the range goes from the fresh, drinkable
Conte Artus (of Aglianico and Piedirosso worked in steel),
through the 100% Piedirosso that displays this grape's pleasant
pepperiness, to several Aglianicos aged in wood and/or steel, to
a new project: Stella Maiuri, of pure Merlot.

Signora Mustilli, Marilì, runs a lovely *agriturismo* – if that's
the right word for rooms in a historic 18th-century palazzo
right in the town centre – where she cooks wonderfully for her
guests. The Mustillis have also recently opened a wine bar…
altogether, a winery not to be missed.

ALSO: stop in for a unique Mela Annurca *gelato* at Gelateria
Normanno (Via Roma, 65; TEL 0823 953042) It's right in the
centre of town, and one of Campania's best. Ristorante-Pizzeria
Piazza Duomo is, not surprisingly, in the cathedral square, and
serves local and seasonal dishes accompanied by good wines
(TEL 0823 717683; CLOSED Tues).

Solopaca

Wine

Via Bebiana, 38
TEL 0824 977792
FAX 0824 971316
E-MAIL
info@cantinasolopaca.it
INTERNET
www.cantinasolopaca.it

Cantina Sociale di Solopaca

This is one of Campania's historic Cantine Sociali, located in an
area of the province of Benevento that has been planted to vines
for centuries – if not millennia – and lauded by writers that
include Virgil and Horace. In addition to this undeniable historical presence, more recent times saw Solopaca receive Benevento
province's first DOC, in 1992 – an important landmark.
Times are changing: if, in the 1970s and '80s the large co-operatives played an important role in bringing strength to numbers
of small, individual grape-growers, today's market is looking for
quality at competitive prices with a clear territorial personality.
A challenge for cellars such as this, that now represent over 700
members, but one they are undoubtedly rising to.

Telese Terme

Telesia was a thriving town under the Romans; it gradually fell
into poverty over the next thousand years, and was given the

final *coup de grace* in 1349 by a devastating earthquake. Ironically, it was this earthquake that unleashed the waters rich in *idrogeno solforato* (hydrogen sulphide) and carbon dioxide around which the *terme*, or spas, were built in the late 19th century. The sulphur-rich waters from these springs were used as a remedy in the various cholera outbreaks in Naples, and are still popular today.

Grand Hotel Telese (Via Cerreto, 1; TEL 0824 940500), opened in 1876, is an ample villa-hotel in a large park. It hosted many Italian stars of film and music when people still believed in 'taking the waters' to feel virtuous. If you would rather drink wine, La Cantina del Sannio (Via Lagni; TEL 0824 941734) and Enoteca Goglia (Via Colombo, 69; TEL 0824 941556) are two good options. La Locanda della Pacchiana (Viale Minieri, 32; TEL 0824 976093) is a recent addition to the scene, a colourful restaurant with fifteen rooms for guests, serving local foods in an informal setting; open daily.

Torrecuso

Trattoria-Gelateria Sweet Garden (Via Collepiano; TEL 0824 874862) is a fine place for *gelati*, or simple pastas and pizzas. Agriturismo Masseria Frangiosa (Contrada Torrepalazzo; TEL 348 7940859, 347 4045157; FAX 0824 874557) This organic farm sells and serves its own fresh and preserved produce, as well as other organic goods from the area. The restaurant is open all year if you book ahead.

Wine

Contrada Fontanavecchia
TEL 0824 876275
E-MAIL orarillo@tin.it

Fontanavecchia - Orazio Rillo
The Taburno area, under the sway of the stately mountains, has led to the creation of a sub-zone and its wines, such as the Aglianico del Taburno DOC: this intransigent red grape likes the slopes of the mountain. Working with the specialized œnologist, Angelo Pizzi, Libero Rillo has taken over from his father, Orazio, in working the family vineyards here. In addition to cultivating the local Falanghina and Coda di Volpe, the family also produce a successful rosé wine, Aglianico del Taburno *rosato*, a traditional type for the area, that here is vinified exclusively in steel. The most imposing wine from the estate is Vigna Cataratte, a red worked in steel but aged in wood.

Wine

Contrada Rivolta
TEL 0824 872921
FAX 0824 884907
E-MAIL
pcotron@tin.it wine
INTERNET
www.fattorialarivolta.com

Fattoria La Rivolta

Here too, the terroir is making itself felt. This estate, begun by the grandfather of the current owner, Paolo Cotroneo, is yielding interesting results with native grapes – and they produce over 200,000 bottles per year. The Coda di Volpe is considered one of the best of its kind, with distinctive notes of yellow fruits and lightly spiced honey. Working with one of the experts in the field of Aglianico on the Taburno mountain, Angelo Pizzi, the reds too are beginning to show their potential, especially the Terra di Rivolta – a powerful wine that will only improve with extra cellaring.

And finally

Cheese

Contrada Fontana Cappella
San Giuliano del Sannio
Campobasso
TEL 0874 791103
INTERNET
www.aziendagricoladeni-
gris.com

De Nigris

This farm is technically four kilometres over the border into Molise, but that's still in the heart of the Sannio, and Francesco Fimiani makes such good cheeses that I hate to leave him out. The De Nigris buffalo cheeses are a great example of a modern, imaginative attitude to dairy farming: Fimiani's family has had the farm since 1805, and his grandparents reared sheep and goats there. When, in 1991, Fimiani decided to go back to his origins and take up farming himself, he started by making sheep's cheeses, but soon felt stifled by the idea that it had all been done before, that history was simply repeating itself. So he switched tacks and brought in buffalo instead of the sheep. 'This left me free, by a process of *alchimia*, to invent a whole new genre: set-curd buffalo cheeses – something that had never been done before in Italy,' he says. Using all the latest dairy technology, he has produced a fascinating – and delicious – set of cheeses, from the signature Il Moro – a firm, compact, raw-milk cheese that is curdled at low temperatures and aged for four months in the farm's underground cellars, to the characterful Caciocavallo, and the more delicate Bufagella that is aged for just fifty days. The De Nigris cheeses offer a unique tasting experience, combining the richness and almost sweet warmth of buffalo milk with the textures of traditional cow's milk cheeses – yet coming up with something quite new.

Glossary

ACCIAIO INOSSIDABILE stainless steel

ACCIUGA, ACCIUGHE (pl) anchovy

ACETO vinegar

ACQUAVITE brandy

AFFETTATI sliced cured meats, a common antipasto

AGNELLO lamb

AGRITURISMO holiday rentals on farms or in country houses

ALICE, ALICI (pl) anchovy

ALIMENTARI grocery store

ALLA BRACE cooked over wood embers

ALLEVAMENTO animal breeding; farm

ALLORO bay tree or leaf

AMARETTO macaroon made with bitter and sweet almonds

AMARO bitter; a herbal liqueur used as a *digestivo*

ANGUILLA eel

ANNATA year of vintage

ANTIPASTO hors d'oeuvre, the appetizer course of a meal

APERITIVO pre-dinner drink

APICOLTURA beekeeping

ARAGOSTA clawless spiny lobster

ARRABBIATA a spicy hot tomato-based pasta sauce (literally, 'angry')

ASTICE lobster

AZIENDA company, business

AZIENDA AGRICOLA farm, AZIENDA VINICOLA winery

BACCALÀ salt cod

BAR bar serving coffee, alcoholic beverages, and snacks

BARRIQUES small barrels, usually of French oak, popular in modern winemaking

BENVENUTO literally, 'welcome': the *amuse-bouche* offered by a restaurant before the meal commences

BIANCO white

BICCHIERE glass

BIOLOGICO, BIO organic

BORGO village, especially medieval

BOTTARGA (DI TONNO) dried roe (of tuna)

BOTTE, BOTTI (pl) large wooden barrels

BOTTIGLIA bottle

BRACE wood embers

BRANZINO sea bass; it may be wild or farmed *(di allevamento)*

BRIOCHE generic Italian name for breakfast pastry, including croissant

BRUSCHETTA grilled bread usually rubbed with garlic and drizzled with olive oil

BUDINO sweet or savoury 'pudding'

BUE beef or cow

BUFALA buffalo

CACIO cheese

CACIOCAVALLO cheese usually made in pairs, as might be hung over the withers of a horse *(cavallo)*

CAFFÈ coffee; order *un caffè*, and you will be served an *espresso*

CALAMARO squid

CANNOLO tube-shaped biscuit or pastry

CANTINA cellar, wine cellar or winery

CAPICOLLO, CAPOCOLLO pork *salume* made from the lean shoulder meat

CAPPERO, CAPPERI caper(s)

CAPPUCCINO espresso coffee with steamed milk

CAPRA goat, CAPRETTO kid, CAPRINO goat's cheese

Opposite: Ischia's Castello Aragonese is linked to the island by a causeway

CARCIOFO artichoke

CARDO cardoon, a vegetable in the thistle family

CARNE meat

CARPACCIO as commonly used, very thinly sliced raw meat or fish

CARTA DEI VINI wine list

CARTOCCIO a method of baking in paper or foil

CASA VINICOLA winery

CASARO cheesemaker

CASEIFICIO cheese factory

CASTAGNA chestnut

CAVATIELLI short pasta made of flour and water

CECE, CECI chickpea(s)

CEFALO grey mullet

CENTRO STORICO the historic centre of a town

CERVO venison

CHIODINI two types of small edible wild mushrooms *Armillariella mellea* or *Clitocybe tabescens*

CICERCHIA a pulse or legume that resembles a squashed chickpea

CICLO CONTINUO modern style of olive oil mill (literally, 'continuous cycle')

CINGHIALE wild boar

COMUNE the 'town hall' or adminis-trative centre of a municipality

CONIGLIO rabbit

CONSORZIO consortium of food or wine producers; it oversees production and sales

CONTADINO peasant, farmworker, small farmer, or tenant farmer

CONTORNO used on menus to signify side dishes

CORBEZZOLO the 'strawberry tree'

CROSTATA open-faced tart, especially fruit- or jam-filled

CROSTINO, CROSTONE canapés

CRU French term used in Italy to indicate a superior single vineyard and its wine

CUCINA kitchen, cooking

CUCINA POVERA simple, peasant cookery, literally, 'poor cooking'

CULTURA PROMISCUA the traditional style of interplanting crops with vines and olive and fruit trees

DAMIGIANA demijohn, large glass wine flask

DEGUSTAZIONE tasting (of wine or food)

DIGESTIVO digestive, liqueur to aid digestion

DOC Denominazione di Origine Controllata

DOCG Denominazione di Origine Controllata e Garantita

DOLCE, DOLCI sweet, desserts

DOP Denominazione di Origine Protetta

ENO- relating to wine

ENOLOGO œnologist, winemaker

ENOTECA wine bar, wine collection, wine shop

ERBE herbs, grasses, or wild leaves

ERBORISTERIA shop selling herbal products

ESPRESSO coffee (or *caffè*)

ETICHETTA label

ETTARO hectare; measure of land used in farming, equivalent to 2.47 acres

FAGIANO pheasant

FAGIOLINI string or green beans

FAGIOLO, FAGIOLI beans, fresh or dried, white or other colours

FARAONA guinea fowl

FARRO spelt wheat, *Tritticum dicoc-cum*

FATTORIA farm or estate

FAVA fava or broad bean

FESTA party, feast, holy day

FINOCCHIO fennel, FINOCCHIO SELVATICO wild fennel

FINOCCHIONA a sausage of coarsely ground pork scented with wild fennel seeds, usually eaten fresh

FIORE DI ZUCCA courgette/zucchini flower

FOCACCIA, FOCACCINA flat crusty yeast bread, often topped with salt, olive oil and other savoury toppings

FORMAGGIO cheese

FRAGOLINE wild strawberries

FRANTOIO olive oil mill

FRAZIONE a sub-zone of a *comune*, literally, fraction

FRESCO fresh, cool

FRIARIELLI Campanian name for several different green vegetables, depending on the area, from peppers to broccoli sprouts

FRITTATA Italian slow-cooked omelette, often eaten at room temperature as a snack or antipasto

FRITTO MISTO mixed fried food

FRIZZANTE lightly fizzy

FRUTTATO fruity, of wine

FRUTTI DI BOSCO wood fruits, especially berries

FRUTTI DI MARE seafood

FRUTTIVENDOLO fruit and vegetable seller or shop

FUNGO, FUNGHI mushrooms

GALLINELLA (or COCCIO) a Mediterranean fish of the gurnard family

GAMBERO shrimp, prawn

GELATERIA ice cream shop, GELATO ice cream

GELSO mulberry

GIOVANE young

GNOCCHI, GNOCCHETTI small dumplings, usually of potato and flour, eaten as a *primo*

GRAMOLATRICE a machine used to churn ground olive paste before the oil can be extracted

GRANITA crushed-ice drink

GRAPPA distilled spirit made from the grape residues after the wine-making process

GRAPPOLO grape bunch

GRIGLIATA MISTA mixed grill (of meats or fish, etc.)

GUANCIALE jowl, of pig or beef

HECTARE see *ettaro*, a measure of land used in farming, equivalent to 2.47 acres

IGP Indicazione Geografica Protetta

-INO suffix meaning little

INSACCATI sausages or salumi, literally, something inside a sack

INTEGRALE whole wheat (of bread or pasta)

INTERNO interior, L'INTERNO, the interior

INVAIATURA the changing of colour of grapes or olives

INVECCHIAMENTO ageing, of wine

INVECCHIATO aged, of cheese or wine

LAGANE flour and water noodles often eaten with chickpeas

LATTE milk

LEGNO wood

LEGUMI pulses, legumes

LEPRE hare

LIQUORE liqueur

LITRO litre (1.065 U.S. quarts)

LOMBO loin

MACCHIA MEDITERRANEA scrub, the stunted plants that grow wild around the Mediterranean basin

MACELLAIO butcher, MACELLERIA butcher's shop

MACINE stone wheels, especially for grinding olives

MAIALE pork

MANZO beef

MARE sea

MASSERIA farm (in south of Italy)

MEDITATION WINE a 'contemplative' wine that may be drunk by itself, without food *(vino da meditazione)*

MELA apple

MELANZANA aubergine, eggplant

MERENDA mid-morning or afternoon snack

MEZZADRÌA system of share-cropping common in Italy until after the Second World War

MIELE honey

MINESTRA soup or first course

MISTO mixed

MORBIDO mellow, about wine or texture

MOSTARDA sweet-and-hot fruit preserve (often from Cremona)

MUFFA mould

NOCCIOLA hazelnut, filbert

NOCE walnut

NOCILLO liqueur made from unripe walnuts in their shells

NORMALE the 'basic' DOC wine, as opposed to the *riserva*

OLIO oil

OLIVA olive

-ONE suffix meaning big

ORATA gilt-head bream

ORECCHIETTE small 'ear-like' bunches at the top of bunches of grapes; type of short pasta common in southern Italy

ORTICA, ORTICHE (pl) stinging nettles

OSTERIA inn, now commonly used for informal restaurants

OVOLO delicious orange-capped wild mushroom, *Amanita caesarea*

PACCHERI wide pasta rings that flatten when boiled

PADRONE landlord, owner

PANCETTA salt-cured pork belly, like bacon

PANETTIERE baker

PANNA COTTA baked cream pudding

PAPPARDELLE wide noodles, usually made with eggs

PARAGO, PAGELLO Mediterranean fish of the bream family

PARFAIT in Italian used for pâté-like savoury dishes as well as desserts

PARMIGIANA baked sliced vegetable and cheese dish, typically of *melanzane*

PASSATA, PASSATO purée, especially of tomato

PASSITO, PASSITI (pl) semi-dried grapes and the sweet wine made from them

PASTA FROLLA short pastry

PASTICCERIA MIGNON petits fours or bite-size pastries

PASTICCERIA pastry shop, pastry

PASTICCIERE pastry chef or baker

PASTIFICIO pasta-making factory or shop

PECORA sheep

PECORINO cheese made from sheep's milk

PEPERONCINO 'hot' chilli or chili pepper

PEPERONE sweet or bell pepper

PESCE fish

PESCE SPADA swordfish

PESCHERIA fismonger's shop

PEZZOGNA blue-spotted bream

PHYLLOXERA aphid that is lethal to grape-vines

PIATTO TIPICO, PIATTI TIPICI (pl) traditional, local dishes

PIAZZA place, square

PICCANTE hot, spicy

PICCOLA PASTICCERIA petit fours, bite-size pastries

PIEDE FRANCO or FRANCO DI PIEDE ungrafted (as in grapevines)

PINOLI pine nuts

PIZZAIOLO pizza maker

PODERE farm

POGGIO hill

POLENTA ground cornmeal and the dish made from it

POLIPO, POLPO octopus

POLLO chicken

POMODORINO cherry tomato

POMODORO tomato

PORCINO, PORCINI (pl) wild mushroom, *Boletus edulis*

POTATURA VERDE 'green' pruning, carried out during the plant's growing season

PRIMI first courses, usually pasta or soups

PRODOTTO product, produced

PRODUTTORE producer

PROFUMO bouquet, perfume, scent

PROSCIUTTO CRUDO salt-cured ham

PROSCIUTTO ham

PROVOLA, PROVOLONE round-shaped cow- or buffalo-milk cheese

QUINTALE quintal, equivalent to 100 kgs

RAGÙ (NAPOLETANO) tomato sauce, slow-cooked, sometimes with some meat in it

RAGÙ (BOLOGNESE) meat sauce

RETROGUSTO aftertaste

RICOTTA soft curd cheese made from 're-cooked' whey, usually of cow's, buffalo's or sheep's milk

RIMONTAGGIO the action of pumping the must over the 'cap' in winemaking

RIPIENO filling

RISERVA reserve, applies to DOC or DOCG wines

RISO rice

RISOTTO rice dish

RISTORANTE restaurant

ROMBO turbot or brill

ROSATO rosé wine

ROSSO red

ROVERE oak

RUCOLA rocket, arugula

SAGRA food festival

SALA dining room

SALAME, SALAMELLA salt-cured salami

SALE salt

SALSICCIA, SALSICCE sausages

SALUMI ready-to-eat salt-cured meats, usually of pork, including *prosciutto*

SALUMIERE maker of *salumi*

SALUMIFICIO factory producing *salumi*

SALVIA sage

SAPORE flavour

SAPORITO flavourful

SCAMPO, SCAMPI (pl) large shrimp or Dublin Bay prawn

SCAROLA escarole (or chicory)

SCOGLIO rocks (by the sea) or rocky coast

SCORFANO scorpion fish

SECCO dry

SECONDO second or main course, usually of meat or fish

SEMIFREDDO dessert frozen after it has been made

SEPPIA cuttlefish

SFUSO loose; refers to unbottled about wine or liquids

SOMMELIER wine waiter or expert; French word used in Italy

SOPPRESSATA a choice pork *salame* (in the north of Italy the same word means head cheese)

SOTT'ACETO, SOTT'ACETI (pl) preserved under vinegar, usually vegetables

SOTT'OLIO, SOTT'OLII (pl) preserved under oil

SPALLA shoulder

SPIGOLA sea bass (also called *branzino*)

SPREMUTA (DI ARANCIO) freshly squeezed (orange) juice

SPUMANTE sparkling (wine)

STAGIONATO aged, as in cheese or *salumi*

STOCCAFISSO stockfish

TABACCHERIA tobacconist's shop

TAGLIATELLE, TAGLIATELLINE, TAGLIOLINI noodles (usually made with eggs)

TAPPO cork, bottle top, SA DI TAPPO (of a wine) corked

TARTUFO DI MARE shellfish of the clam family

TARTUFO truffle, also an ice cream

TAVOLA CALDA informal eatery selling hot foods

TENUTA farm or estate

TERROIR French word that denotes an area in winemaking

TERZI (working for) literally, thirds, i.e. to work for others

TIMO thyme

TIPICO typical, traditional, authentic

TIRAMISÙ a coffee and mascarpone dessert, literally 'pick-me-up'

TONDO round, round in shape

TONNO tuna fish

TORTELLI a type of stuffed pasta

TOTANO long-bodied, 'flying' squid

TRATTORIA a family-run country restaurant

TRIGLIA red mullet

TUFO TUFA, a yellowish volcanic soil

UVA grape

UVAGGIO grape variety or type

UVETTA dried raisin

VASSOIO tray

VECCHIO old

VENDEMMIA harvest, or grape harvest

VERA real, original

VERDURA vegetable

VICOLO small street, usually in the historic centre of town

VIGNA, VIGNETO vineyard

VINO DA MEDITAZIONE a 'contemplative wine' drunk on its own, without food

VINO PASSITO usually sweet wine made from semi-dried grapes

VINO wine

VITE vine

VITICOLTORE grape grower

VITIGNO grape variety or type

ZABAGLIONE, ZABAIONE egg and sweet wine custard

ZAFFERANO saffron

ZAGARA lemon or orange blossom

ZONA ARTIGIANALE, INDUSTRIALE industrial or artisanal zones (of a town)

ZUCCA pumpkin or long large gourds or squash

ZUCCHINA, ZUCCHINE zucchini/ courgette(s)

ZUPPA INGLESE a kind of Italian trifle

ZUPPA soup

Bibliography

This is a personal selection for reading around and about Campanian foods and wines. It doesn't aim to be an exhaustive list, as the books describing travels to Naples are in the hundreds, but these are the ones that I have stumbled upon, and found entertaining and informative.

Note: the dates given in brackets after the title refer to the original date of publication where that differs from current editions.

Acton, Harold, *The Bourbons of Naples 1734-1825* (1957), London: Prion, 1998

Afeltra, Gaetano, *Spaghetti all'acqua di mare: sapori di un'infanzia meridionale*, Cava de' Tirreni: Avagliano Editore, 1996

Agriturismi e fattorie biologiche, Milano: Touring Club Italiano, 2003

Alberini, Massimo, *Storia della cucina italiana*, Casale Monferrato: Piemme, 1992

Alla riscoperta degli antichi sapori: le alici salate, Notes from a convention held in December, 1994, Pro Loco Cetara, Cava de' Tirreni: Guarino & Trezza, 1997

Apicio, Marco Gavio, *De re coquinaria*, Italian translation from the Latin, Milano: Viennepierre, 1998

Arcamone, Lello, *La cucina ischitana: ricette popolari*, Ischia: Imagaenaria, 2003

Aspromonte, Luigi, *Vocabolario Napoletano-Italiano*, Lidial Italia, 2002

A tavola non s'invecchia, Napoli: 2001

Atlante dei Prodotti Tipici della Provincia di Napoli, Amministrazione Provinciale di Napoli, 2003

Baedeker, Karl, *Southern Italy and Sicily, handbook for travellers*, London: George Allen and Unwin, 1930

Belfrage, Nicolas, *Brunello to Zibibbo: The Wines of Tuscany, Central and Southern Italy*, London: Faber and Faber, 2001

Bergsøe, Vilhelm, *Henrik Ibsen a Ischia* (1907), Trans, Maria Grazia Calabrese, Ischia: Imagaenaria, 2001

Boncompagni Ludovisi, Orietta, *Pizza Supremo Sfizio*, Roma: Rai-Eri/Agra Editrice, third edition, 2002

Buchner, Giorgio and Alfred Rittmann, *Origine e passato dell'isola d'Ischia* (1948), Ischia: Imagaenaria, 2000

Bugialli, Giuliano, *Foods of Naples*, Stewart Tabori and Chang, New York, 2003

Calandrelli, Matilde and Donato Nicastro, *Formaggio fai da te: istruzioni per produrre in casa un buon formaggio*, In series: 'La biblioteca di Caseus,' Series Editor, Roberto Rubino, Potenza: ANFOSC Ediservice, 2003

Campania: I luoghi del vino, Various authors, Napoli: Edizioni Pianeta Italia, 2003

Capalbo, Carla, *The Food and Wine Lover's Companion to Tuscany* (1998), San Francisco: Chronicle Books, 2nd Edition, 2002; London: Pallas Athene, 2000

Capalbo, Carla, *The Ultimate Italian Cookbook*, London: Anness, 1994

Carlo Gesualdo: Musicorum Princeps, Edited by Francesco Barra, Avellino: Elio Sellino Editore, 2001

Cavalcanti, Ippolito, Duca di Buonvicino, *Cucina teorico-pratica* (1847), Napoli: Tommaso Marotta Editore, 1986

Cenatiempo, Ciro, *Cunicoli e lapilli: Ischia, conigli e dintorni*, Ischia: Imagaenaria, 2003

Chaney, Lisa, *Elizabeth David*, London: Macmillan, 1998

Chiusano, Giuseppe, *Folklore Altirpino*, Cava de' Tirreni: Di Mauro Editore, 1975

Columella, Lucius Junius Moderatus, *De Re Rustica*, *(L'arte dell'agricultura e libro sugli alberi)*. Translated from the Latin. Torino: Einaudi, 1977

Corrado, Vincenzo, *Il Cuoco Galante*, 2nd edition, 1773. Reprinted Roma: Vivarelli e Gullà, 1972

D'Ajello, Roberto and Elio Palombi, *Proverbi e maccheroni: antologia di antichi detti napoletani sul mangiare e bere*, Napoli: Grimaldi & C, Editori, 2003

D'Ambra, Salvatore, *La vite e il vino nell'isola d'Ischia*, Milano: Grafis, 1974

D'Antonio, Massimo, *Campi Flegrei*, Naples Chamber of Commerce, Massa Editore, 2003

David, Elizabeth, *Italian Food* (1954), London: Penguin, 1985

Davidson, Alan, *Mediterranean Seafood*, London: Penguin, 1972

De Filippo, Isabella Quarantotti, *Si cucine cumme vogli'i'*…Milano: Guido Tommasi Editore, 2003

De Matteo, Giovanni, *Irpinia tra Borboni e Savoia*, Lioni: Altirpinia, 2004

Di Iorio, Tiziana, *Tra vino e mare, la tradizione e l'arte del vino nell'isola d'Ischia*, Ischia: Valentino editore, 2002

Dickens, Charles, *Pictures from Italy* (1846), London: Penguin Classics, 1998

Douglas, Norman, *Siren Land* (1911), London: Penguin, 1982

Douglas, Norman, *Venus in the Kitchen: Recipes for seduction* (1952), San Francisco: Halo Books, 1992

Dumas, Alexandre, *Il Corricolo* (1843), Napoli: Colonnese Editore, 2004

Etienne, Robert, *Pompeii, The Day a City Died* (1986), Trans. Caroline Palmer, London: Thames and Hudson, 1992

Ferdinando IV, Re delle Sicilie, *Origine della Popolazione di San Leucio* (1789), San Leucio: Edizioni Saletta dell'Uva, 2003, (Reprint)

Fiore, Antonio, ed. *Il critico maccheronico*, Napoli: 2002

Fiori, Giacomo, *Formaggi italiani*, EOS Editrice, 1999

Forgione, Giuseppe, *1860, Notizie del Regno: La fine dei Borboni nelle Cronache di Don Giuseppe Forgione, canonico di Gesualdo in Irpinia* (1860). Edited by Mario Bernabò Silorata and Antonio D'Errico. Cava dei Tirreni: Di Mauro Editore, 1993

Formaggi d'Italia, Bra: Slow Food Editore, 1999

Forman, Henry James, *Grecian Italy*, London: Jonathan Cape, 1927

Foti, Salvo, *Come bere bene*, Catania: Bonanno Editore, 2002

Francesconi, Jeanne Caròla, *La cucina napoletana* (1965), Roma: Newton Compton Editori, 1992

Fusco, Gian Carlo, *L'Italia al dente*, Palermo: Sellerio editore, 2002

Gleijeses, Vittorio, *A Napoli si mangia così*, Napoli: La Botteguccia, 1990

Goethe, Johann Wolfgang Von, *Italian Journey (1786-1788)*. Trans. W. H. Auden and Elizabeth Mayer. London: Collins, 1962, and Penguin Classics, 1970

Gosetti della Salda, Anna, *Le ricette regionali italiane* (1967), Milano: Solares, 1990

Harris, Valentina, *Southern Italian Cooking*, London: Pavilion, 1993

I formaggi del Cilento: Guida alla ricerca ed alla conoscenza dei tesori dei sistemi pastorali cilentani. Series Editor, Roberto Rubino. Potenza: ANFOSC Ediservice, 2001

Hazzard, Shirley, *Greene on Capri*, New York: Farrar, Straus & Giroux, 2000

Il Buon Paese, Bra: Slow Food Editore, 2000

Il Caciocavallo Podolico e la Manteca, un grande formaggio del Sud. Series Editor, Roberto Rubino. Potenza: ANFOSC, 2001

Il coniglio da fossa dell'isola d'Ischia. Pamphlet produced by Confraternita del coniglio dell'isola d'Ischia

Interventi di Ingegneria Naturalistica nel Parco Nazionale del Vesuvio, ed. Carlo Bifulco, San Sebastiano al Vesuvio: Ente Parco Nazionale del Vesuvio, 2001

Italy in Mind, an anthology edited by Alice Leccese Powers, New York: Vintage Books, 1997

Keates, Jonathan, *The Rough Guide History of Italy*, London: Rough Guides, 2003

Kurlansky, Mark, *Salt, a world history*, London: Jonathan Cape, 2002

La Risorsa Genetica della Vite in Campania, Napoli: Regione Campania, 2001

La Risorsa Genetica dell'Olivo in Campania, Napoli: Regione Campania, 2000

L'Allevamento caprino nel Parco Nazionale del Cilento e Vallo di Diano. Series Editor, Roberto Rubino. Potenza: ANFOSC, 2001

Lawrence, D. H. *D. H. Lawrence and Italy* (1932), London: Penguin, 1997

Leonardi, Il Maestro, *L'Apicio alla Moderna*. In six volumes, circa 1850

Lewis, Norman, *Naples '44*, London: Eland, 2002

L'Italia dei Presìdi, Bra: Slow Food Editore, 2002

Manzon, Domenico, *La Cucina Campana*, Roma: Newton & Compton, 2003

Millon, Marc and Kim, *The Wine Roads of Italy*, London: HarperCollins, 1991

Minori, Rheginna Minor: Storia, Arte, Cultura, Salerno: De Luca Editore, 2000

Marotta, Eugenio, *Guida all'Olio Extravergine della Campania*, Sarno: Edizioni dell'Ippogrifo, 2003

Napoli e la Campania, 'Guide d'Italia'. Touring Club Italiano, 2002

Nazzaro, Roberto and Salvatore Cozzolino, *Le Orchidee del Parco: Guida illustrata delle Orchidee del Parco Nazionale del Vesuvio*, San Sebastiano al Vesuvio: Ente Parco Nazionale del Vesuvio, 2002

Neville-Rolfe, E., *Naples in the Nineties*, London: Adam and Charles Black, 1897

Norway, Arthur H., *Naples Past and Present*, London: Methuen & Co, 1901

Oreggia, Marco, *L'Extravergine 2005 – Guida ai Migliori Oli del Mondo di Qualità Accertata*, Roma: Cucina & Vini Editrice, 2005

Orsini Natale, Maria, *Francesca e Nunziata*, Cava de' Tirreni: Avagliano editore, 1996

Orsini Natale, Maria, and Alfonso Iaccarino, *Don Alfonso 1890: Una Storia che sa di favola*, Cava de' Tirreni: Avagliano editore, 2003

Osterie d'Italia, Bra: Slow Food Editore, 2003

Pesce, Angelo, *Salerno 1943: Operation Avalanche*, Naples, S. Maria La Bruna, 2000

Peyrefitte, Roger, *South from Naples*, Trans. J. H. F. Mc Ewen,
    London: Thames and Hudson, 1954

Piancastelli, Manuela, *I grandi vini della Terra di Lavoro*, Napoli:
    Publitaff, 2000

Piancastelli, Manuela, *I migliori vini d'Italia: Campania*, Milano:
    Hobby & Work/Veronelli Editore, 2003

Piancastelli, Manuella, *Mario D'Ambra*. In the series 'I Semi, vite
    dei protagoniste delle culture materiali.' Bergamo: Veronelli edi-
    tore, 2002

Pignataro, Luciano, *Agriturismo da Paestum a Palinuro*, Sarno:
    Edizioni dell'Ippogrifo, 2002

Pignataro, Luciano, *Carta dei vini della Campania e della
    Basilicata*, Sarno: Edizioni dell'Ippogrifo, 2004

Pignataro, Luciano, *Guida completa ai vini della Campania*, Sarno:
    Edizioni dell'Ippogrifo, 2003

Pliny the Elder, *Natural History*, London: Penguin, 1991

Ramage, Craufurd Tait, *Ramage in South Italy*, edited by Edith
    Clay, (original title: *The Nooks and By-ways of Italy*, 1868),
    Chicago: Academy Chicago Publishers, 1987

Ristoranti d'Italia, Roma: Gambero Rosso editore, 2004

Root, Waverley, *The Food of Italy* (1971), New York: Vintage
    Books, 1992

Rotondo, Antonio, *Mangianapoli*, Foggia: 1985

Rotondo, Antonio, *Proverbi Italiani, ovvero La Filosofia di un
    Popolo*, Napoli: Franco Di Mauro, 1992

Santasilia di Torpino, Franco, *La cucina aristocratica napoletana*,
    Napoli: Sergio Civita Editore, 1988

Sapori del Cilento Antico: cucina tradizionale e dieta mediterranea,
    Gruppo di Azione Locale Alento, Salerno, 2001

Schwartz, Arthur, *Naples at Table*, New York: HarperCollins, 1998

Scienza, Attilio and Maurizio Boselli, *Vini e Vitigni della Campania:
    tremila anni di storia*, Napoli: Prismi, 2003

Serao, Matilde, *Il ventre di Napoli*, Napoli: Edizioni del Delfino,
    1973

Silvestri, Giuseppe, *La tonnara di Lacco Ameno e altri mestieri di
    pesca nell'isola d'Ischia*, Ischia: Imagaenaria, 2003

Simeti, Mary Taylor, *Sicilian Food*, London: Jill Norman/Century,
    1989

Sontag, Susan, *The Volcano Lover: A Romance*, New York: Farrar
    Straus Giroux, 1992

Steinbeck, John, Article on *Positano* in Harper's Bazaar, New York:
    May, 1953

Strong, Roy, *Feast: A History of Grand Eating*, London: Pimlico,
    2003

The List of DOC and DOCG Wines, Siena: Enoteca Italiana, 2002.

Train, M. T., *Gardens of Naples*, New York: Scala Books, 1995

Turismo gastronomico in Italia, Milano: Touring Club Italiano, 2000

Twain, Mark, *The Innocents Abroad* (1869), New York: Dover Publications, 2003 (reprint)

Veronelli, Luigi, *Alla ricerca dei cibi perduti*, Bergamo: Veronelli Editore, 2004

Vini d'Italia, Gambero Rosso/Slow Food Editore, 2001, 2002, 2003

Zamparelli, Virginia, *Ricette in mezzo al mare*, Ischia: Valentino editore, 1998

Index

Entries in **bold** refer to illustrations
The following major entries are highlighted:

Captions: Cover and above: Maria and Ricccardo Giordano, of Tramonti,
produce small quantities of raw-milk pecorino from their own herd
Half title: Ravece olives from Hirpus
Title page: A scintillating basket of Cilento *corbezzolo* berries,
the fruit of the 'strawberry tree'
Opposite dedication: Signora Rosa, my downstairs neighbour at Cetara,
shelling beans in the *vicolo*
Page 4: top to bottom: garlic and onions in the market;
Ischian villa; cleaning fish at Lo Scoglio; home-grown artichokes for sale
Page 5: sea-urchins by the port; hand-made cheeses and bread
Page 6: summer *zucche*

The Food and Wine Guide to Naples and Campania
Text, photographs and all maps except inside front cover © Carla Capalbo 2005
The moral right of the author has been asserted
All rights reserved. No part of this book may be reproduced in any form
without written permission from the publisher

The author and publisher have taken due care to ensure that all the information
in the book is correct at the time of going to press. They cannot be held responsible
for any errors or inaccuracies. Readers' comments and suggestions for further editions
will be welcomed. Please write to the author care of the publisher or email carla.capalbo@tin.it

The generous support of the Regione di Campania in producing this book is gratefully acknowledged

First published 2005 by Pallas Athene (Publishers) Ltd,
42 Spencer Rise, London NW5 1AP
If you would like further information about Pallas Athene publications,
please write to the address above, or visit our website:
www.pallasathene.co.uk

Editors: Alexander Fyjis-Walker and Simon Coury
Design: Harold Bartram
Text maps: Carla Capalbo and Isabelle Lousada
Author photograph: Sandra Lousada
Inside front cover map: Netmaps – www.digitalmaps.co.uk
Pre-press and printing by Graphic Studio, Verona

Printed in Italy

ISBN 1-873429-71-1